New Interpretations
in Naval History

New Interpretations in Naval History

⚓

Selected Papers from the
Eleventh Naval History Symposium

Held at the
United States Naval Academy,
21–23 October 1993

Edited by
Robert W. Love Jr.
and
Laurie Bogle
Brian VanDeMark
Maochun Yu

NAVAL INSTITUTE PRESS
Annapolis, Maryland

Naval Institute Press
291 Wood Road
Annapolis, MD 21402

© 2001 by U.S. Naval Institute
All rights reserved. No part of this book may be reproduced or utilized in any form or by any means, electronic or mechanical, including photocopying and recording, or by any information storage and retrieval system, without permission in writing from the publisher.

Library of Congress Cataloging-in-Publication Data

New interpretations in naval history : selected papers from the eleventh Naval History Symposium, held at the United States Naval Academy, 21–23 October 1993 / edited by Robert W. Love, Jr.
    p.   cm.
Includes bibliographical references.
ISBN 1-55750-493-8 (alk. paper)
    1. Naval history—Congresses. I. Love, Robert William, 1944– II. United States Naval Academy History Symposium (11th : 1993 : United States Naval Academy)

D27 .N49 2000
359'.009—dc21   00-049613

Printed in the United States of America on acid-free paper ∞

07 06 05 04 03 02 01 00 9 8 7 6 5 4 3 2
First printing

Contents

⚓

Preface	vii
The Antikythera Device Rob S. Rice	1
Manpower and the Athenian Navy in 362 B.C. Vincent J. Rosivach	12
Reconsidering the Battle of Actium William M. Murray	27

English Maritime Commerce in the
    Mediterranean during the Jacobean Period
        Lee W. Eysturlid
	47

New England in Anglo-French Naval
    Operations in the Caribbean, 1689–1763
        Christian Buchet
	60

British Naval Response to Unorthodox
    Warfare in the Eastern Caribbean, 1795–96
        H. J. K. Jenkins
	73

The United States Frigate *President*: The Victor or the Vanquished? W. M. P. Dunne	83
Constitution's Winning Captains Tyrone G. Martin	98
The Crescent Adrift: Problems of Ottoman Maritime Power Douglas S. Brookes	105
English and American Mariners in Chile's First Squadron, 1817–18 Carlos Lopez	119

"To Preserve and Not Destroy": The U.S. Navy
    and Fugitive Slaves in the Civil War, 1861–62
        Barbara Brooks Tomblin
	133

The Union Sailor–Confederate Deserter Alliance in Florida George Buker	151

Temptations for the Small Navy of a
    Great Power: The Case of Austria-Hungary
        Lothar Höbelt
	165

Luxury Fleet: The Austrian Navy and the Battle of Lissa, 1866 　　Geoffrey Wawro	176
Philo McGiffin and the Chinese Navy 　　Paul W. Bamford	188
Teddy's "Ollie" and the Teflon Admiral: William S. Sims vs. Robley D. Evans in Theodore Roosevelt's Navy 　　James R. Reckner	196
Tirpitz and the Origins of the German Torpedo Arm, 1877–1889 　　Patrick J. Kelly	219
Preparing for War: Admiral William H. Standley and the Struggle to Build Auxiliaries for the Navy 　　Thomas Wildenberg	250
The Struggle for Control of Air Power in the North Pacific, 1942 　　William S. Hanable	267
Strange Parallels in Stalin's and Hitler's Naval Programs 　　Jürgen Rohwer and Igor Amosov	281
Down but Not Out: German Attempts to Regain the Submarine Initiative, May 1943–February 1944 　　W. J. R. Gardener	302
Images of Naval Aviation in the Second World War 　　Michael Paris	321
Intelligence and Hunter-Killer Groups, 1943–1945 　　David Syrett	330
Non-air-breathing Diesel Submarine Engines 　　J. G. Hawley	339
Hostilities along the China Coast during the Korean War 　　Edward J. Marolda	351
The Single Air Manager Controversy of 1968 　　Jack Shulimson	364
The Design and Construction of Soviet Navy Submarines in the Cold War 　　Igor Spassky	386

Preface

⚓

The Eleventh Naval History Symposium met at the United States Naval Academy from 21 to 23 October 1993. This volume includes a selection of the more than fifty papers that were read, practical constraints precluding the publication of them all. The selection was made by the Symposium Committee, which found itself confronted with an embarrassment of riches. To choose from so many outstanding papers was a daunting task, and the resulting collection should be regarded as representative of the diversity of interests in naval history and the standards that characterize the Naval History Symposia.

The Eleventh Naval History Symposium followed the same format used since 1977, a two-day event organized along the lines of standard academic conferences with a call for papers, multiple sessions, and the broadest possible representation on the program from the international community of naval historians. The Eleventh Naval History Symposium especially profited from the end of the Cold War by featuring several scholars from the former Soviet Union and other states of the former Warsaw Pact.

This volume is dedicated to Mrs. Connie Grigor, the secretary of the History Department, whose relentless efficiency, good humor, and indefatigable spirit makes this and other symposia, and much of the other work of the department, appear to be so effortless. Associate Professor Nancy Ellenberger, the Chair of the History Department, provided encouragement, as did Academic Dean Robert Shapiro. Lieutenant Colonel Robert Sullivan, USMC, administered the conference with exceptional skill and determination. Midshipman First Class Troy Shoulders, USN, spent altogether too much of his valuable time handling innumerable details.

For the Eleventh Naval History Symposium, our featured banquet speaker was Donald Cameron Watt, Stevenson Professor of International History at the London School of Economics, who delivered a challenging, and often amusing, talk on the "History of Scottish Seapower." In addition, the Eleventh Naval History Symposium previewed the PBS/WETA television series *Sea Power:*

A Global Journey, and our thanks are due to Executive Producer Leo Eaton Sr. for this treat.

The Symposium Committee wishes to thank all those who contributed to the conference by chairing sessions, delivering papers, or commenting: Douglas Brinkley, Jerzy Przybylski, Mihail Zahariade, Illie Manole, Peter M. Swartz, Hal M. Friedman, Francis Duncan, Gary E. Weir, J. G. Hawley, Michael A. Dennis, Alex Roland, Eduardo Dargent, Lawrence H. Hall, Carlos Lopez, Patricia Falcone de Azcarate, Guillermo Montenegro, R. Chalmers Hood III, Claude Huan, Raphael-Leygues, Francois Flohic, Robert Paxton, Jacques Bally, J. David Brown, Clay Blair, Michael Gannon, Eric Rust, Merrill "Skip" Bartlett, Gary D. Solis, Jack Shulimson, David Dawson, Bernard Nalty, Charles Fairbanks, Jon Sumida, Nicholas Lambert, Ronald Spector, Norman Friedman, Stephen R. Wise, George Buker, Edward W. Sloan, Barbara Tomblin, Charles Chadborn, Thomas B. Buell, Lawrence Sondhaus, Lothar A. Höbelt, Patrick J. Kelly, Keith W. Bird, Christopher McKee, Gene Smith, David Curtis Skaggs, Frederick Drake, H. P. "Ned" Willmott, Kim Kirshner, John Prados, Richard von Doenhoff, Charles D. McKenna, John L. Anderson, Kevin J. Foster, Glenn Alderton, Ulane Bonnel, Max Guerout, Thomas Gilmer, Gordon Watts, Roger Dingman, Adam B. Siegel, Peter E. Clemens, Edward J. Marolda, Marc Gallicchio, James Bradford, Richard Buel Jr., Norman N. Rubin, Mark L. Hayes, Russell Weigley, John Major, James F. Tent, Bradley Smith, John Hattendorf, Christian Buchet, H. J. K. Jenkins, Jorge Ortiz Sotelo, Gerald Jordan, David Langley, Eric J. Grove, W. J. R. "Jock" Gardener, David Syrett, Carl Boyd, David Trask, William N. Still Jr., Hubert C. Johnson, William J. Williams, Timothy Saxon, John L. Guilmartin, Lee Eysturlid, Douglas Brookes, Anne Kroell, Jürgen Rohwer, Gerhard Weinberg, Igor Agormov, Erik Wihtol, William Braisted, James R. Reckner, Richard H. Collin, Harold Langley, William Fowler, Robert J. Schneller, Elmer L. Gaden, Hans Christian Bjerg, Spencer Tucker, John R. Hale, Robert Rice, William Murray, Lionel Casson, Shelly Wachsmann, Jack Cargill, David Rosenberg, Boris Rodionov, George Sviatov, Norman Polmar, Robin Higham, H. Labrousee, William Barr, Michael Vlahos, Leonard Bushkoff, Lawrence Suid, Michael Paris, William Honan, Vincent Ponko, Jorge Pinto Rodriguez, Paul W. Bamford, Anita Hilber, B. R. Burg, Jeffrey Barlow, Barton C. Hacker, Igor Spassky, Sean Maloney, Karl Lautenschlager, Sam John Tangredi, Ivan Musicant, Thomas Wildenberg, Joel Davidson,

William Hanable, Bernard C. Cole, A. J. Graham, Clark Reynolds, Vincent Rosivach, Thomas R. Martin, William Dudley, Tyrone G. Martin, Stephen W. Duffy, William M. P. Dunne, and the late Patrick J. Rollins.

—Robert W. Love Jr.

New Interpretations
in Naval History

The Antikythera Device

Rob S. Rice

⚓

Sometime around 80 B.C., a heavily laden merchant ship sank to the bottom of the sea off the Southern coast of Greece. After two millennia, materials salvaged from that vessel's cargo have led scholars to speculate about several aspects of seafaring in Greek and Roman antiquity. The objective of this treatment of the chain of events involved is to provide a useful survey of early and modern underwater archaeology and the mechanics of artifact preservation and interpretation as well as to offer conclusions drawn from the data presented here concerning ancient celestial navigation and the island of Rhodes. The united efforts of a wealthy Roman, a frightened Greek sponge diver, an English physicist, and an American naval historian have combined to allow some further inquiry into civilian and military seafaring in the first century before Christ.

Sailing further south past the island of Antikythera off the southernmost coast of Greece offers an alternative to, as a very ancient proverb says, "rounding Malea and forgetting home." Whether he sought to avoid the pirates or the storms clustered around the infamous cape, the skipper of what apparently was a good-sized Roman merchant vessel of around 300 tons made a wrong decision. His ship crashed into and sank off the island's coastal cliffs, and what was probably a wealthy Roman buyer eventually learned that his treasure ship's cargo had gone down in nearly two hundred feet of very cold, current-swept water.[1]

"Treasure ship" is a legitimate label. The *corbita* had held everything from original bronze life-size statues to marble reproductions of older works, jewelry, wine, other bronzes, and at least one immensely-complicated scientific instrument. It was the statues that frightened a Greek sponge diver named Elias Stadiatos nearly out of his wits in 1900, when his captain winched him back over the side, removed his helmet and breathing hose, and found him babbling about a "heap of dead naked women."[2]

Rumors from around that time show a resulting pattern of events all too familiar to the modern underwater archaeologist. The local divers had found the ship first. The villagers of Simi, near the site, speak of many small bronze statues sold in Alexandria soon after the wreck was found, and when later archaeologists surveyed her, the vessel was missing all her heavy lead anchor stocks. The ship was big enough to have had five anchors, was in water too deep to have used any of them, and divers needed lead weights to find their sponges and rare black coral, just as they needed money to support their families.[3]

Still, Captain Kondos of the sponge vessel in 1901 told the Greek government of Stadiatos's discovery and agreed to hire his ship and divers for the salvage. He pushed his equipment and his men to the limit, but he recovered one of the most amazing troves ever winched from the bottom of the sea. Statues, jewelry, transport jars, utensils, and tableware of all kinds came to the surface. "Huge boulders," obscuring the cargo and hauled up to the salvaging vessel with difficulty, turned out to be statues covered with marine growth, their marble eaten away by the chemical action of centuries of sea-water and animals. The divers suffered from all the hazards of their trade, including one fatally. When the winter storms came up, the divers and the Greek government were ready to quit. The bronze statues went into galleries, the jewelry into display cases, and a great deal of material went into museum storage, waiting for careful analysis to determine the significance of, among other things, clumps of marine growth and corrosion surrounding what looked like some kind of gearing. What wood was brought up resembled wet cardboard in more ways than one as it dried out and shriveled away.[4]

It would be unfair to call this proto-excavation "unscientific," for there were trained archaeologists from the Greek antiquities service waiting to process the material once Kondos's divers had brought it to the surface. A modern excavation would, for all that, hopefully progress a great deal differently, using techniques pioneered by Peter Throckmorton and George Bass over the course of research beginning in 1959. Archaeologists themselves would descend to investigate the wreck. The hoses and helmets that had hampered the sponge divers of 1901 would be replaced by self-contained apparatus designed to bleed off the carbon dioxide that had exhausted and dazed the original divers. Modern compressors would be filling air tanks and pumping air down to the wreck level, and that air rising up again inside a tube would lift silt and small items up to the surface for sifting and removal. Inside plastic bags, rising bubbles would lift statues and jars. A decompression chamber would stand ready in the event of nitrogen narcosis, with atmospheric pressure within carefully regulated to let the nitrogen built up by the compressed air breathed underwater leave the divers' arteries slowly enough to avoid damage. A grid over the wreck made of plastic plumbing pipe would direct drawings and photography for stratigraphic records of the objects discovered. Drawings and recorded measurements would possibly be combined with stereoscopic photography, the whole allowing graphic reconstruction of the original ship and its cargo.[5] There might be a diving bell with a telephone to talk to the surface or a midget submarine to help with the photography. An underwater metal detector would be useful and an "air probe" to jet into the sea bottom with compressed air to prod for things under the mud. Computers would store information topside and, potentially, underwater as well, since one of the things that suffers with exposure to water is a diver's short-term memory.

Funding, as well as the physical difficulties of such intricate underwater activity, can act to limit such exploitation of first-hand ancient material. The additional hazard of post-recovery destruction of recovered material is not always countered by techniques of modern artifact conservation. Shifting, during the descent of the original ship's hull to the bottom, had already inflicted extensive damage on her cargo before the first diver approached the wreckage. The ubiquitous Mediterranean teredo worm employed the intervening centuries to destroy the integrity of the hull and larger wooden artifacts, while marine bacteria left only the hollow cell walls of the remaining timber. Marine shellfish devoured the limestone of the statues, while the sea's own electrolytic bath wrought havoc on all metallic artifacts unprotected by bottom mud. Unauthorized "pot-hunting" before the official excavation undoubtedly also further damaged the available material left behind.[6]

The bronze gearing retrieved from the Antikythera wreck, with its own chemical and animal accretions, broke into several pieces soon after its return to the surface. The ship's wooden planks and what appears to have been a case for the mechanism shriveled soon after retrieval. The marble statues were eaten away and disfigured wherever they had been exposed to the sea. As usual in terrestrial archaeological sites around the Mediterranean, ceramic material in some form survived, except for the damage inflicted by the heavier cargo and defacement by marine growths. The chemical composition of the glassware retrieved in 1901 was fortunate. The Phoenician beads that George Bass recovered off Cape Gelidonya exploded into dust once they began to dry.[7]

Modern conservators would place everything but the pottery into a tank of fresh water until preliminary analysis was possible. Marine conservators are a rare combination of archaeologists and chemists, employed on occasion, and on occasion, in vain. The wood could be preserved, as was the Swedish 17th-century galleon *Vasa*, in polyethylene glycol, which fills the empty cell walls with a waxy material over a great deal of time. Metal artifacts receive their own immersion in chemical solutions with the goal of stabilizing each piece and hopefully removing accumulated corrosion, an expensive and not always successful procedure. Cleaning off what has lived and died on all materials submerged for any length of time can be difficult as well, particularly when the person so doing is uncertain of what lies under the accreted material and how much cleaning the object can withstand before disintegrating or losing desirable features.[8]

In the case of the Antikythera fragments, the four large pieces and a box of much smaller fragments were momentarily overshadowed by the other staggering results of the first directed retrieval of archaeological evidence from the sea. The original excavators had their hands full reassembling the bronze statues, sorting and identifying coins, and cataloguing all the items for museum storage at Athens. Eventually, other scholars found time to consider the fragments of original artifacts. The initial belief was that the bronze object was an astrolabe—a type of navigational instrument first attested in 625 A.D. Correctly, one Konstantin Rados, in the earliest debate, insisted that what was visible on the lump's surface was too complicated for such a device, intricate as, in fact, were some medieval examples. At the same time, other scholars argued that the Greek artisans who had fabricated the wreck's statues could not have built even an astrolabe.[9]

In 1951, a British physicist and historian of science named Derek de Solla Price went to the Athens Museum for his own analysis of the fragments taken from the Antikythera wreck. Price himself was familiar with construction of medieval astrolabes, and the complexity of the device and the astronomical inscriptions visible on the surface led him to eight years of informed study. In 1959 Price published his own conclusion that the fragments represented some form of intricate clockwork.[10] The idea was sufficiently unthinkable to the experts of the time for one professor to claim in responding that someone in the Middle Ages had dropped a machine of that era into the sea, coincidentally over the same current-swept spot off Antikythera's rocky coast.[11]

Price remained undiscouraged and maintained his conclusions. In 1971 Oak Ridge National Laboratory published an article on the use of high-energy gamma radiation to examine the interiors of metallic objects. Price soon secured the assistance of the Greek Atomic Energy Commission in shooting gamma rays into the clumps of corroded bronze. He was able to produce photographic plates that not only allowed him to reconstruct the device but also to ascertain its date of construction.[12]

The Antikythera mechanism was an arrangement of calibrated differential gears inscribed and configured to produce solar and lunar positions in synchronization with the calendar year. By rotating a shaft protruding from its now-disintegrated wooden case, its owner could read on its front and back dials the progressions of the lunar and synodic months over four-year cycles. He could predict the movement of heavenly bodies regardless of his local government's erratic calendar.[13] From the accumulated inscriptions and the position of the gears and year-ring, Price deduced that the device was linked closely to Geminus of Rhodes and had been built on that island off the southern coast of Asia Minor circa 87 B.C. Besides the inscriptions' near-identity to Geminus's surviving book, the presence of distinctive Rhodian amphorae among other items from the wreck supported Price's deduction and date once Virginia Grace had re-examined the pottery recovered in 1901.[14]

Price's straightforward and viable analysis came despite a host of ideas the device's discovery should have dispelled. He was too concerned with what was before his eyes to realize that prevailing beliefs among historians of the period would lead others to slight or ignore what physics and archaeology had combined to discover. Price correctly noted that Rhodes was a center for astronomical thought. He mentioned Poseidonius, Cicero's friend and teacher, who built a much more complicated astronomical computer than the one recovered.[15] He was unaware of the widespread belief that continues to maintain that Rhodes in the first century B.C. was little more than a fading ghost of past glory, crippled economically by the competition of the Roman free port of Delos after 166 B.C.

It is neither facile nor uninstructive to remark that the Antikythera mechanism dropped and sank—twice. The second submersion came after Price's publication of *Gears from the Greeks* in 1975. Since that time little attention has been paid to our most exciting relic of advanced ancient technology. It was in the course of research into the navy of Rhodes that the mechanism first came to this author's attention, and it was that research and knowledge of extant flaws in earlier scholarship that allowed this assessment of the significance of the device and Price's reconstruction.

Scholars before and after Price ignored and continue to ignore the length of Rhodes' enduring reputation among the ancients themselves as a center for intricate military and naval technology.[16] Rhodes had resisted the largest and most advanced weapons systems produced by the Macedonian warlord-inventor Demetrius. In 305 "the Besieger" sent a siege tower nine stories tall, pushed by two thousand men, against the Rhodians' walls. Rhodes was a center for the construction and use of antiquity's heaviest and most intricate catapults. The historian Diodorus of Sicily would record how Demetrius's *helepolis*, or city-taker, had to retreat from one of the most intense artillery barrages of antiquity, burning from several direct hits with incendiary bolts.[17] The tradition of advanced technology in Rhodes continues to appear for centuries in the surviving historical records of the Hellenistic Age. Mithridates V of Pontus fared no better than the Macedonian attacker in his own onslaught of 88 B.C., in which he encountered what F.E. Winter considers to be one of the most formidable protected catapult batteries in antiquity.[18] Polybius, Strabo, and Aristides in later years attest to the legendary speed and surpassing deadliness of the ships and weapons built behind the wall of Rhodes's *neorion*.[19] The pirates of the Mediterranean feared and fled before the war fleet of a single island, and the last of the Greek democracies successfully warded off even Roman domination until 43 B.C.[20] Years afterward, the finest ships in the Mediterranean world could still be found in her shipyards.

In the light of the ancient literary evidence and the physical existence of the Antikythera mechanism, it is necessary for scholars of the period to discard the idea that Rhodes and her economy were ruined by the Roman actions concerning Delos. An impoverished, decaying backwater could not have provided impetus for such a mechanism, much less have supported the minds that conceived it. Among other advances, the apparatus, found among Rhodian coins and amphora, contained a differential gearing system more complex to design than to build, and its presence among original bronzes, gold jewelry, and marble statues clearly attests to the buyer's recognition of its value.[21] The Roman Cicero reports that the general Marcellus prized an orrery, or analog planetarium, of Archimedes' more than any other booty from captured Syracuse.[22] The Rhodians could apparently build similar devices for export to such wealthy Roman buyers—including, possibly, Cicero, who knew Rhodes well and was governor of a neighboring province shortly after the ship was lost.[23]

Further research into the island's history reveals additional nourishment for the speculation that the Antikythera mechanism's existence prompts and should have prompted about Rhodes, ancient technology, and our study of the past in general. On Rhodes, Philo of Byzantium encountered and described the *polybolos*, a "machine gun" catapult that could fire again and again without a need to reload.[24] Philo left a detailed description of the gears that powered its chain drive and that placed bolt after bolt into its firing slot. Philo and scholars since have believed that the *polybolos* was useless because the Rhodians had convinced him that it was for close range only and could not traverse from side to side.[25] The perspective of a naval historian can provide a kind of warfare where a fixed weapon at close range could be useful—in an era when ships routinely rammed each other. Anyone could have wondered why the Rhodians built and refined something so complicated if they had no idea of using it. Again, they conceived and built the Antikythera device, and someone else had thought enough of it to send it overseas.

The proof the mechanism offers of Rhodes' enduring technological expertise poses a question the device also helps to answer: What could have led to the construction of such an expensive and intricate device? Certainly the mechanical expertise that built the *polybolos* indicates the physical ability to build the mechanism. But what inspired the intricate theories and substantial body of astronomical knowledge that lay behind the mechanism? Rhodes, even in its supposed "glory days," was chiefly famous for the abilities of its seafarers—and therein lies the answer.

Very little, indeed, is known about ancient celestial navigation, besides indisputable proof that it did, in fact, occur.[26] It is worth noting, however, that the man who invented trigonometry and first scientifically catalogued the stars' positions was Hipparchus of Rhodes; that in more than one ancient system of latitude and longitude the meridians crossed at Rhodes; and that a man Strabo rated second only to Aristotle—Poseidonius—found support for his travels and devices on the same island where Geminus did his writings and inspired or built the Antikythera mechanism.[27]

There is evidence for a clear tradition of scientific research on Rhodes, just as there is an anecdote preserved by the Roman architectural authority Vitruvius concerning two engineers' competition for a city stipend.[28] Geminus's surviving book shows him making a determined effort to bring the transmitted data of the Babylonian astronomers to the attention of his Greek readers in the first century B.C. In the preceding century, Hipparchus had laid the groundwork for Geminus's efforts to "popularize" Babylonian astronomy by working their surviving eclipse data into his own astronomical writings. Modern scholars of scientific history have yet to pay Hipparchus his due honor for his *failure* to construct a planetary system of his own, even as he catalogued the observable stars. Although he had used observed parallax to make an extremely close estimate of the moon's distance from the earth, Hipparchus had the scientific honesty to state that there was insufficient data in his time to understand the true arrangement of the solar system.[29] The refusal of others to admit this fact hobbled scientific thought until well after Galileo's death. Geminus's contemporary Poseidonius did much more than build complicated astronomical devices of his own. One of the journeys, celebrated and preserved by his friend and pupil Cicero, took him beyond Gibraltar to the Bay of Biscay, where he was the first to note the connection between the tides and the moon phases Hipparchus had measured. He also posited the novel theory that all the world's oceans formed a single body of water.[30]

Hipparchus, Geminus, Poseidonius—we must still search out details of what may well have been an analogue to our own and Britain's naval observatory, in competition and parallel with the state-funded research at Alexandria's museum. The Rhodians' immunity to the pirates of the Mediterranean continued long after their supposed post-Delian decline. The island could not feed itself, but the grain ships continued to arrive—possibly steering by starlight through the deep sea while the frustrated pirates hugged the coast. The Rhodian navy displayed in a long and distinguished operational history an almost uncanny ability to function and maintain unit cohesion at night. In 198 B.C. a Roman fleet eluded a Syrian squadron sent to intercept it by what seems to have been a difficult nocturnal cruise—shortly before two of its Rhodian escorts openly made a night voyage to locate an arriving Roman praetor.[31] In 88 B.C., directly before Price's date for the device's construction, the Rhodian admiral Damagoras set the world an unforgettable example of Rhodian courage and naval expertise. After eluding a Pontic blockade of the city's harbor, Damagoras led a force four times the size of his own on a day-long chase, pausing only before sunset to turn and sink two of the larger enemy vessels and disable two more. With the rest of the enemy fleet alert and positioned to intercept his return, Damagoras kept his command integrated and functional for an entire night on the high seas and returned safely to blockaded Rhodes in the morning.[32]

The discovery of the Antikythera mechanism has much to offer besides tantalizing hints concerning state-funded research and technological expertise on Rhodes. The very existence of such a complicated gear train should also prompt fundamental change in the way the ancient sources are read. We have found the tracks for the emperor Nero's revolving ceiling, and the Tower of the Winds still stands in Athens, its clock faces empty, but its functioning success materially and textually preserved.[33] When Cicero, Ovid,[34] Plutarch, and others speak of "celestial spheres" going back to the time of Archimedes, and describe their use, the Antikythera device's very existence should prompt us to something besides unthinking skepticism. Perhaps we should take a look at the device and *believe* a little more of what we have been told. Wooden ships *have* been set on fire with sunlight,[35] and John Morrison's efforts to reconstruct the trireme demonstrate that the full complexities of ancient ship construction continue to elude us. When all the implications of Price's discovery are understood and acted upon, it will then be possible to say that we have begun to understand the Antikythera technology.

Cicero mused:

> Suppose a traveller carried into Scythia or Britain the orrery recently constructed by our friend Poseidonius, which at each revolution reproduces the same motions of the sun, the moon, and the five planets that take place in the heavens every day and night, would any single native doubt that this orrery was the work of a rational being?[36]

With the evidence before our faces, do we continue to believe that Rhodes declined, the ancients were technologically inept, and that our sources can be easily discarded? Or do we accept the existence of ancient advanced technology, study its implications, and look for deeper meaning in what we have difficulty understanding? Much has been learned about ancient technology and ancient seafaring. With the right set of mind and purpose, it is clearly possible to learn a great deal more.

1. Peter Throckmorton, "The Road to Gelidonya," in *The Sea Remembers: Shipwrecks and Archaeology from Homer's Greece to the Rediscovery of the Titanic*, ed. Peter Throckmorton (New York: Smithmark Publishers, 1987), p. 20.
2. Throckmorton, pp. 14–16.
3. Throckmorton, p. 16.
4. Throckmorton, pp. 16–18.
5. Throckmorton, p. 29 illus.
6. Throckmorton, p. 16; Victoria Jenssen, "Archaeology and Conservation," in *The Sea Remembers: Shipwrecks and Archaeology from Homer's Greece to the Rediscovery of the Titanic*, ed. Peter Throckmorton (New York: Smithmark Publishers, 1987), pp. 102–104.
7. Jenssen, p. 102.
8. Jenssen, pp. 102–105.
9. Throckmorton, p. 18; Derek J. de Solla Price, *Gears from the Greeks: the Antikythera Mechanism: a Calendar Computer from ca. 80 B.C.* (New York: Science History Publications, 1975), p. 10.
10. Derek J. de Solla Price, "An Ancient Greek Computer," *Scientific American* 200 (6) (June 1959): 60–67, with some detailed reconstructions of the device's original appearance.
11. Price, p. 10.
12. Price, pp. 10–13, Throckmorton, pp. 18–20.
13. The *Oxford Classical Dictionary*, second edition, (*OCD2.*) s.v. "Calendar" only begins to describe pre-Julian chronological chaos between the competing regional states.
14. Price, pp. 8–9.
15. Price, pp. 56-59; Cic. *Nat de.* 2.34–35.
16. Dio Chrys. 31.104.
17. D.S. 20.96.3–97.3.
18. App. B.C. 4.66–7, Winter, p. 199–201.
19. Plb. 5.88.5, Str. 14.2.5 (653), Aristid. 25.4.
20. Str. 14.2.5 (653), Plb. 21.7.1–4.
21. Price, pp. 60–61.
22. Cic. *De re pub*, 1.14.21.
23. Cic. *ad Att.*, 5.12.1, *Brut.* 1; Plu. *Cic.* 36.
24. Philo. *Bel.* 73. For reconstructions of the device, cf. Vernard Foley and Werner Soedel, "Ancient Catapults," *Scientific American* 241 (April, 1979): 155–6;

J. G. Landels, *Engineering in the Ancient World* (Berkeley: University of California Press, 1978), pp. 123–27.

25. V. P. M. *Ptolemaic Alexandria*, 3 vols. (Oxford: Clarendon Press, 1972), 2.431.

26. Homer, *Od.* 5.233–40, Libanus, *Progymnasmata, Sententiae* 1.13.

27. Dicaearchus Fr. 33, Strabo Str. 2.1.1 (67), 5.7 (114), 2.5.19 (122–23), 2.5.39 (134).

28. Vitr. 10.46–48.

29. Pappus, Comm. in Alm. 4.11.66 f., ed. Rome, *Almagest*, 9.2, OCD2.

30. Str. 16.2.10.

31. Liv. 36.43.8; 37.14.3. App. *Syr.* 22, Johannes Hendrik Thiel, *Studies on the History of Roman Sea-power in Republican Times* (Amsterdam: Noord-hollandsche uitgevers mij., 1946), p. 301.

32. App. *Mith.* 25; *FGrH* 434 F 22.13–15.

33. V. Joseph Noble and Derek de Solla Price, "The Water Clock in the Tower of the Winds," *American Journal of Archaeology* 72 (1968): 744–755.

34. Ov. *Fast.* 6.263–283.

35. C. A. Kinkaid, *Successors of Alexander the Great* (Chicago: Ares Publishing Company, 1980) p. 143.

36. Cic. *De Nat. Deo.* 2.34–5 (87–88), Rackham's translation.

Manpower and the Athenian Navy in 362 B.C.

Vincent J. Rosivach

⚓

The summer of 362 B.C. was a troubled time for Athenian interests in the northern Aegean Sea. Because Athens relied heavily on grain imported from the Black Sea region to feed her urban populace, a major aim of Athenian foreign policy[1] was to ensure the safe passage of grain transports from the north, an aim which Athens pursued by maintaining friendly relations with the littoral states along the sea lanes and by backing up diplomacy with military force when necessary and when possible. In 362 a combination of hostile forces in the northern Aegean interrupted the passage of ships.[2] With less grain coming to the Peiraieus, Athens' port, and with prices rising on the grain that did get through, the Athenians finally acted. Even though it was already September, and thus late in the sailing season,[3] the Athenians voted to dispatch a squadron of warships to the north.[4] Significantly, the Athenians sent only naval forces;[5] whatever they expected to accomplish would be by naval means alone, by protecting the grain transports against hostile raiders, and by assaulting the enemy coasts with raiding parties drawn from the small contingents of marines carried on every Athenian warship. We do not know how many ships the Athenians voted to send out on this occasion, but something on the order of twenty triremes is probably not a bad guess; a dozen years later, in 349 B.C., Athens sent out forty ships to protect the grain transports against Philip of Macedon, but none of the enemies against whom the present expedition sailed were likely to have had navies as powerful as Philip's.[6]

Two points are worth making here. First, the ships which the Athenians sent north were not already on station elsewhere and simply reassigned to a new mission; rather, they were a new squadron put into service only at this time and specifically for this purpose.[7] And second, although the Athenians voted for this squadron in roughly mid-September, they nonetheless expected the ships to arrive in the north soon enough to convoy the grain transports at what was only the start of the voyage south to the Peiraieus, a voyage which the transports had to complete before the onset of winter storms and the end of the sailing season in early November. This was a rather impressive undertaking, as a bit of background will make clear.

First of all, these warships were triremes, large ramming vessels which used sail-power to cover long distances but turned to rowers, 170 per vessel, when extra power was needed for speed and maneuverability, especially in combat.[8] Generally speaking the trireme rowers were drawn primarily from Athens' poorer residents,[9] both citizen and non-citizen,[10] with additional recruits from other states. As to these last, there existed in the fourth-century eastern Mediterranean a floating pool of mercenary rowers, Athenians and others, ready to sell their services to whoever paid their price. Athens appears to have made considerable use of mercenary rowers earlier in the century,[11] but mercenaries were expensive, and by 362 Athens had turned to conscripting her own residents to meet at least some of her rowing needs.

If we think of a navy as ships and the men who man them, then in the mid-fourth century, the time of the events we are here discussing, Athens did not have a standing navy. What she did have was a large number of warships which she maintained at public expense, but under normal circumstances (i.e. in the absence of a major war) only a fraction of these were at sea at any one time. Thus, for the two years for which we have this kind of information, of the 410 warships on the naval list of 330/329 B.C., only sixty-two were at sea at the time the list was prepared, and of the 417 ships on the naval list of 325/324 B.C., only thirty-nine were at sea.[12] Moreover, few of these ships were at sea year round. Some were engaged in routine patrols in the adjacent waters of the Aegean, guarding against the endemic piracy which preyed both on cargo transports and on the exposed coasts of Athens and her dependencies.[13] Others were launched in response to the dangers and opportunities which presented themselves and returned home when their missions were completed—indeed, one has the impression that most ships were kept in a sufficient state of readiness and that they could be easily made ready for sea duty when needed. Winter storms, however, were a real challenge for triremes, which were very fragile, and there was comparably little naval warfare during the winter months.

Whenever possible ships returned to their home port before the seas became impassable and were drydocked for maintenance and repair during the winter months. Similarly, it seems likely that most—and perhaps all—of the ships on routine duty closer to home were also hauled from the water and drydocked for the winter.[14]

Further, as far as we can tell, the sailors who manned these ships were engaged only for the length of time their ships were actually in service. Thus, while the government had at its disposal a large number of ships which could be easily launched as circumstances required, there was no corresponding standing force of sailors at the government's command immediately available to man these ships. Rather, each time a ship was put into service, a new crew was recruited from the "civilian" population (to use an anachronistic term); sailors remained with their ship as long as it was in service; and they left their ship and returned to "civilian" life when their ship returned home and was hauled from the water, usually at the end of the sailing season. If a ship was put into service again the following year, the cycle was repeated with a fresh crew recruited from the "civilian" population.

There are several features of this system that call for further comment. First of all, there was a lack of continuity from year to year. There was no guarantee that the same men would come back from one year to another to row in the same crew; in fact, it seems likely that they would not. A situation where different men rowed with different shipmates on different ships in different years implies a high degree of interchangeability and suggests, in turn, that the teamwork and coordination required to row a trireme were more easily achieved than we might perhaps imagine.

Second, crews were paid, but only for the time they were on active service.[15] In the fourth century, military pay for both soldiers and sailors was in two categories, food allowances (*siteresion*) and wages (*misthos*).[16] The food allowance covered a soldier or sailor's personal expenses while he was on campaign so that, at least in this sense, his military service was not a drain on his domestic resources. Wages were payment above and beyond the food allowance, the "profit" to be made from military service. The distinction between food allowances and wages appears to have crystallized in the early fourth century among mercenaries who were attracted to the military by the promise of profit. When Athens hired mercenaries, she paid them both food allowances and wages, or rather she paid food allowances and promised wages, though she was often in no condition financially to keep those promises. Until well into the fourth century, Athens relied on volunteers to row her fleet, but, as we shall see, the uncertainty of Athenian finances made it difficult to find an adequate number of rowers, and she turned instead to conscription.[17]

Following what was now established practice, Athens paid her conscripts their food allowances, promised them additional wages, and rarely kept her promises. What is important for our purposes is, first, that since sailors were paid only while they were in service, they had to have other sources of livelihood to which they attended when they were not rowing; and, second, that the food allowance was meant to pay for the sailor's personal needs but not for the needs of any family he left behind; money paid as wages might do this, but wages were, in fact, rarely paid. This may not have been that great a problem for mercenaries, whose lives were often too unsettled for them to raise regular families,[18] but it potentially raised some very real difficulties for "civilians" drafted into the fleet.

Crews, it will be recalled, were recruited only when the decision was made to launch ships. However, the number of ships engaged in routine patrolling was probably much the same from year to year, and their total manpower requirements were thus relatively predictable, even if their crews were not recruited until the ships were actually launched. Such predictability may well have favored the growth of a pool of sailors from both Athens and elsewhere who returned year after year to row these vessels as part of their regular annual cycle of employment. On the other hand, the special expeditions sent out from time to time in response to emergencies, like the expedition of 362 B.C. with which we began this paper, had very different manpower requirements. There was no way of telling whether or not emergencies would occur, when they would occur, how many emergencies would occur in any given year, how many ships each emergency would require, or how long the ships would be away at sea—indeed, in the worst case ships and their crews might even be required to winter away from Athens. Because emergencies are totally unpredictable, the expeditions sent to deal with them depended on a more flexible pool of potential recruits, and—once Athens turned to conscription—one that was locally available: men who were continuously available to row if needed, but who could also find other employment if they were not needed, and so were not in any way dependent on rowing for even a part of their livelihood.

Needless to say, the size and the flexibility of this locally available pool of sailors were at least as much potential constraints on the number of ships Athens could put to sea in an emergency as was her ability to find the money to pay the crews' food allowances and salary. Further, the potential manpower demands of these emergency expeditions were quite large when compared with Athens' total adult male population. As mentioned earlier, each trireme required 170 rowers, plus an additional complement of helmsmen, lookouts, etc., plus a small squad of marines, for a total crew of roughly 200 per vessel. Thus, the twenty ships we guessed as the size of the expedition sent north in 362 B.C. would have required about 4,000 crewmen, of which 3,400 were rowers. Similarly, the forty ships sent against Philip of Macedon in 349 B.C. required about 8,000 crewmen, of which 6,800 were rowers. And the total of sixty-two ships listed as at sea on the naval list of 330/29 B.C. required at least 12,400 crewmen, including at least 10,540 rowers.[19] These figures should be compared with Athens' total free adult male population, citizen and metic, of approximately 31,000 in the mid- to late-fourth century. Without a doubt, some of the sixty-two ships at sea in 330/29 B.C. were ships on ordinary patrol, and, as we have seen, some of the sailors on ships of this category may have come from outside Athens. But to take only the example immediately at hand, the 3,400 rowers[20] which we estimate were required for the expedition of 362 B.C. were to be conscripted solely from the local Athenian population.[21] Thirty-four hundred rowers were approximately 11 percent of Athens' free adult male population of roughly 31,000.[22] We do not know how many Athenians normally earned their living from the sea (as crewmen on cargo ships, fishermen, and the like), but the evidence, mostly negative, suggests that while more people may have depended on the sea in Athens than in most other Greek states, the Athenian seafolk were nowhere numerous enough to man emergency expeditions by themselves,[23] and we must assume that large numbers of people who did not normally earn their livelihood from maritime trades also served when needed in these emergency expeditions.[24]

Even if we grant that some of the crewmen for these emergency expeditions may have been mercenaries from outside Athens, and even if we grant that some slaves may also have been recruited,[25] the fact remains that the manpower demands of the expedition of 362 B.C., and of similar emergency expeditions, should have drawn off men from Athens' "civilian" population in numbers sufficient to cause severe economic disruptions in the years when the expeditions were sent out.[26] Our ancient sources, however, make no mention of disruptions caused by the loss of large numbers of men to the fleet in an emergency, suggesting that such disruptions never occurred. More important, it is unlikely that the Athenians would have ever developed in the first place, either consciously or unconsciously, a system for manning their fleets which would regularly disrupt the civilian economy.

How then were the Athenians able to find the large numbers of rowers they needed in emergencies without either maintaining a large standing navy or disrupting their domestic economy by drawing large numbers of men out of the "civilian" population and into the navy? And conversely, since sailors were paid only for the time they were on active duty, how did all these conscripted sailors secure their livelihood in those times of the year when they were no longer at sea and in the employ of the state? The answer lies, I would suggest, in a feature of the ancient Athenian economy which was, in fact, typical of most pre-modern economies, that the basic unit of production was the household, not the individual. To explain, even into the fourth century, most Athenians were still farmers working their own land; and most of those who were not farmers were small-scale craftsmen or shop-owners in the urban agglomeration. Subsistence farming, in particular, was a family occupation, with everyone pitching in to do his or her share. And "family" was not just the nuclear family, for the farm household could also include different members of the extended family (children, grandparents, unmarried adult brothers and sisters) and even a whole range of live-in help, servants, and slaves.[27] In such households the absence of a member, for example to row in the fleet, meant that the others had to work harder to make up the lost labor of the missing member, but with the remaining members doing more, the overall productivity of the household would not suffer, at least not in the short run. The same would also be true, albeit to a lesser extent, of urban craftsmen, at least some of whom were assisted by relatives, including wives, and by apprentices, helpers, and the like, who functioned, in effect, as part of their employer's household.

The relevance of all this to how Athens manned her fleet is clear. Indeed, I would argue that the peculiar structure of the Athenian navy, with a large number of ships permanently ready to put to sea[28] but no standing force of sailors to man them, evolved in no small measure as a consequence of how the Athenian economy was structured, and, particularly, of how "civilian" work was structured within that economy. Ships had to be ready: there was no time to build them in an emergency. But in the small and compact Athenian state, crews could be assembled, as needed, on relatively short notice from the "civilian" population. The arrangement met the military needs of the state without the burden of year-round food allowances and wages for a permanent force (at a time when, I might add, food allowances, even without wages, were still the largest naval expense by far). And the arrangement also fit the interest of the crews, for whom naval service offered, at least potentially, an additional source of income for their households in the form of wages. Assuming a sufficiently large pool of potential rowers (i.e. a sufficiently large adult male population[29]), when the system functioned properly, it could depend exclusively on volunteers from the local population. To function properly, however, the system could not keep too many men away from their "civilian" occupations for so long that their households felt the strain of their lost labor input, and, in particular, it should not keep farmers from their fall sowing and/or their spring harvesting. Athens seems to have had no trouble recruiting volunteers in the fifth century when most of her sailors served for fairly short stints during the slack period of the agricultural year,[30] and Athens had the financial resources to pay sufficient wages to the smaller number of sailors in year-round service. But the lengthening of the fighting season and the increase in low-intensity year-round warfare, which the greater availability of mercenaries now made possible, placed additional demands on Athens' military, which she initially met by hiring mercenaries (including some of her own citizens persuaded by the promise of greater rewards to accept the greater disruptions which military service now entailed). To fund this new kind of warfare, Athens initiated the *eisphora*, an extraordinary special levy on her wealthiest citizens assessed on an ad hoc basis as the need arose to pay for this or that specific campaign. Because the *eisphora* was assessed only after a specific military campaign had already been decided upon, and because the cumbersome procedures involved in its implementation allowed much opportunity for delay and evasion, the required funds were rarely raised in time or paid in full.[31] With funds for the wages so uncertain, volunteers were hard to find, and the trireme captains, who were drawn from Athens' wealthier classes and who were responsible for recruiting the volunteer crews, had to offer bonuses from their own pockets to recruit full complements of rowers.[32] It was all quite inefficient, and the need for bonuses put a considerable burden on the trireme captains. In conscription the Athenians found a way both to secure an adequate number of rowers and to relieve the captains of the burden of paying for them, all without raising taxes.

With all this as background, let us return now to the expedition of 362 B.C. We know a good bit about this expedition from a speech ([Demosthenes] 50) delivered a few years later in an Athenian court by Apollodorus, a wealthy Athenian who served as one of the trireme captains. Trireme captains were supposed to serve for a maximum of one year, but when Apollodorus' year was up, his successor refused to take over the ship and the financial obligations that went with it, and Apollodorus himself continued as captain for another five months until the ship finally returned to Athens. While the object of Apollodorus' suit was to recover the monies he had spent during his successor's term, his speech also incidentally tells us something about the conditions of the ordinary sailors on his ship and on the other ships in the fleet.

Thus we learn that the basic crew were conscripts, not volunteers; indeed, it appears from Apollodorus' summary of the decree authorizing the expedition (6) that it did not establish procedures for the draft but rather activated procedures that were already in place, presumably established by prior legislation.[33] In other words, in 362 B.C. conscription was not a one-time response to a temporary lack of volunteers, but rather an institutionalized structure intended to deal with a permanent dearth. It is also of interest that the authorizing decree directed officials of Athens' local communities, the demes, to provide the sailors to man the ships (6). Calling upon deme officials to supply the sailors implies that the sailors were to be drawn from all across Athenian territory and not just from the coastal districts, confirming what we said earlier to the effect that rowers were drawn from the general population and not merely from the seafolk.[34]

The same decree also levied a special *eisphora* tax to finance the expedition (8). As we have seen, such special levies usually failed to raise all the money they were supposed to, and so it was in the present case. Apollodorus' crew received wages (misthos) for only two of the seventeen months they were away from Athens (10); they regularly received their food allowance, at least at the start of the expedition, but even this ran low from time to time (23), and by the end of the cruise, it disappeared completely (53). The wealthy Apollodorus helped out as best he could, borrowing funds to pay his crew their food allowances (23, 53) and giving other monies to individual sailors in need (25); but Apollodorus appears to have been the exception, and the other captains seem to have left their conscript rowers to make do with whatever they received from the state (cf. 35), secure in the knowledge that conscripts could not leave their ships until they were dismissed by the general (cf. 16). Apollodorus had also made matters worse for himself when, at the start of the expedition, he dismissed some of the weaker rowers which the draft had provided, and replaced them with mercenaries (7)[35] to improve the performance of his ship and make it the best in the fleet (cf. 7, 11, 15). To secure these mercenaries, Apollodorus had to advance their wages from his own resources (7); when they later failed to receive the regular wages promised them, they deserted and had to be replaced with other rowers whom Apollodorus also had to pay in advance (11–12).

When Apollodorus' ship returned briefly to Athens the unpaid mercenary rowers quit; the unpaid conscripts, who could be charged with desertion if they left the ship,[36] went on strike instead, as it were, refusing to put to sea[37] until they were at least paid something—at this point they had received only food allowances and no wages for eight months. Apollodorus was able to raise 3,000 *drakhmai*, which he distributed to his crew. Three thousand *drakhmai* works out to 15 *drakhmai* a man for two hundred crew-members, an amount which could support a family of four for less than twenty days,[38] but Apollodorus had to pay larger amounts to the mercenaries hired to replace those who had quit, and the conscripts probably received much less. Whatever the amount, however, it was enough to get them to put back to sea. Apollodorus' effort was so extraordinary that the Athenians voted a decree praising him for what he had done (11–13). As noted earlier, the other captains were not so generous with their crews.

In the incident I have just described, the conscripts refused to sail until they received some money "to make financial arrangements for their households" (11), and Apollodorus responded, giving them "something toward the financial arrangements of their households" (12), "since I was not unaware of the present need, how difficult it was for each" (ibid.). Not only had the conscripts been away for at least eight months,[39] but during that time Athens had suffered a poor grain harvest brought on by drought (cf. 61), which put even greater pressure on households already stressed by the need to make up the lost labor of their absent members. The amount of money Apollodorus gave each of his rowers was, as we have seen, really quite small, clearly not enough by itself to support a family for more than a few weeks, but enough to help them out when they already had another source for their livelihood.[40]

To pursue this point further, the fleet was away for a total of seventeen months, roughly from mid-September 362 B.C. to mid-February 360 B.C., during which time the draftees received wages (*misthos*) for only two months.[41] Apollodorus may have helped his rowers as best he could, but the other captains did not (15–16, 33), leaving their crews to make do solely with the small amount of food allowance and two months' wages which they got from the state. Clearly, the families of these other rowers were expected to survive with no income from the rowers for almost a year and half. They could do so, as we have seen, because the household, as an economic unit, could sustain the absence of one of its members without a significant loss in productivity as other members of the household worked more to make up for the lost labor of the absent member. The subsistence farm household, I would add, was particularly suited to absorb these pressures, since it did not depend on income for its survival but on labor inputs,[42] suggesting that farmers—or more precisely single members of extended farm households—could be most easily spared on short notice to man emergency naval expeditions. But seventeen months was a long time for any household to do extra work, and conditions had been made even worse by the poor harvest. The rowers' households could survive without them, but it would not have been easy.

In conclusion, we might reflect on how the rowers and their families came to find themselves in this state. Changed conditions of warfare in the fourth century made it difficult to find volunteers who were willing to serve for simple subsistence. Wages beyond subsistence might have enticed volunteers, but the *eisphora* system could not guarantee sufficient funds, and ships' captains found themselves paying bonuses instead to persuade volunteers to enlist. Athens might have reformed its taxing methods,[43] abandoning ad hoc *eisphora* levies and collecting the same funds on a fixed periodic basis, in order to build up a reserve sufficient to pay her sailors a decent wage for their extended services whenever the need arose.[44] For whatever reason, the Athenians chose instead to introduce conscription. With conscription at least the wealthy ships' captains were relieved of the financial burdens of recruiting, and the task of sustaining the faltering system fell instead upon the poor, who were drafted into the navy to serve whether they were paid or not.[45]

1. Cf. e.g. Demosthenes 18.301–2.

2. Troops in the pay of Alexander, master of the Thessalian city of Pherai in northern Greece, overran the island of Tenos in the Aegean and enslaved its inhabitants, practically on Athens' doorstep. Further to the north, Miltokythes had risen in revolt against Kotys, the king of Odrysai in Thrace (roughly modern Bulgaria); to gain Athens' support Miltokythes offered to restore the Gallipoli peninsula to Athenian control, a tempting offer at any time for the Athenians but particularly so at the moment, since they and Kotys, a former ally, were now on hostile terms. Still further to the north, Athens' ally Prokonnesos, an island in the Propontis, was under attack by the mainland city of Kyzikos, and its citizens had sent an embassy to Athens, pleading for help before the Kyzikenes destroyed them. And finally, because of a local shortage of foodstuffs, the Byzantians and the Kalkhedonians at the southern end of the Bosporos, as well as the Kyzikenes, were forcing passing grain ships bound for Athens to put into their harbors instead and off-load their cargoes. (This narrative is based on [Demosthenes] 50.4–6, our principal source for the events discussed in this paper.)

3. On the sailing season, see V. J. Rosivach, "Manning the Athenian Fleet, 433–426 B.C.," *American Journal of Ancient History* 10 (1985): 41–44.

4. The Greek says "to bring help to each place" (*boethein hekastakhoi*, [Demosthenes] 50.6), referring to the various areas mentioned in the previous narrative (cf. above, note 2).

5. In contrast to, for example, the expeditionary force of ships, infantry hoplites, and cavalry proposed by Demosthenes in his First Philippic (4.19–22).

6. The forty-ship expedition against Philip is described by Hesykhios of Miletus, FqH 390 F 1.28; cf. the forty ships sent against the Peloponnesians in 389 B.C. (Xen. *Hellenica,* 4.8.25–27). Note that in 351 B.C. Demosthenes (4.22) considered ten swift triremes sufficient to protect an Athenian naval expedition which was to avoid direct combat with Philip's forces.

7. The decree authorizing the squadron paraphrased in [Demosthenes] 50.6 contained a directive for the ship captains to put their ships in the water (literally, "to drag down" [*kathelkein*] the ships which were normally drydocked when not in service), as well as provisions for recruiting crews.

8. On the Athenian trireme, see, in general, J. S. Morrison and R. T. Williams, *Greek Oared Ships: 900–322 B.C.* (London 1968); J. S. Morrison and J. F. Coates, *The Athenian Trireme: The History and Reconstruction of an Ancient Greek Warship* (Cambridge 1976).

9. Especially men not subject to infantry service (which was limited to those who were able to provide their own armor). It is often assumed that men who were liable to infantry service never rowed in the fleet, but there is reason to believe that at least some did, especially at times when the demand for soldiers was low and that for sailors high. For such rowers, see Thucydides 3.16.1 and 3.18.3–4 and Rosivach (above, note 3) S4.

10. The non-citizens in question would be principally "metics" (metics were permanent—or at least long-term—Athenian residents, mostly manumitted slaves or their descendants, who did not have citizen status). Athens had no state-owned slaves to row in her fleet, but from time to time she appears to have used privately owned slaves as rowers; the condition of these rowers would not have been any different from the condition of free rowers, with the exception that money paid for the slaves' services as rowers would go to the slaves' owners, not to the slaves themselves. It is difficult to say how often and under what circumstances Athens used slaves in her fleet; on these questions, see, most recently, A. J. Graham, "Thucydides 7.13.2 and the Crews of Athenian Triremes," *Transactions and Proceedings of the American Philological Association* 122 (1992): 257–70. In any event, the evidence which we have suggests that even when slaves were used as rowers, they made up only a small part of the total complement of sailors.

11. I infer the wide use of mercenaries as rowers from the wage structures of the rowers (see below, pp. 4–5), and, more generally, from the pressures which led to the institution of a draft for rowers.

12. 330/29: *Inscriptiones Graecae* 22 1627.266–78; 325/4: IG 22 1629. 783–812.

13. On the problems posed by piracy, see H. A. Ormerod, *Piracy in the Ancient World* (Liverpool and London 1924): ll0–20; S. Isager and M. H. Hansen, *Aspects of Athenian Society in the Fourth Century* B.C. (Odense 1975): 55–57.

14. Even the "sacred triremes" used for messenger service, transporting ambassadors, and the like still had to be hauled from the water from time to time for maintenance.

15. And sometimes not even then, because of lack of funds, although they were supposed to be. Athens' continuing difficulties in finding funds to pay her sailors are well known; for the ancient evidence of these difficulties see, most conveniently, G. E. M. de Ste. Croix, *The Class Struggle in the Ancient Greek World* (Ithaca 1981): 607, note 37.

16. For the two terms, see F. W. Pritchett, *The Greek State at War: Part I* (Berkeley, Los Angeles and London 1971): 3–6; G. T. Griffith, *The Mercenaries of the Hellenistic World* (Cambridge 1935): 264–73.

17. It is not at all certain whether Athens met all or only some of her rowing needs through conscription. I suspect that only emergency expeditions were manned by conscripts, and routine patrols were still manned by volunteers.

18. Note, for example, in 362 B.C., mercenary rowers hired in Athens ([Demosthenes] 50.12) jumped ship in the Hellespont to become soldiers on the mainland or to row for Thasos and Maroneia (14); cf. 16: "trusting in their ability to row they went off to wherever they would receive the most money again."

19. *Inscriptiones Graecae* 22 1627.266–78. Ten of the ships listed as at sea were quadriremes; we do not know the size of the crew for these four-banked ships, but it was almost certainly larger than that of the three-banked triremes.

20. See below, note 22.

21. I confine the calculations here to rowers, since it would appear, from [Demosthenes] 50, 7 and 10, that the marines and non-rowing crewmen (helmsmen, etc.) were still volunteers, though one would reasonably assume that most of them were also drawn from the local Athenian population.

22. The size of Athens' population in the fourth century has been the subject of considerable debate. For convenience (and out of conviction), I have used the figures reported by Ktesikles (FaH 24 5 F1) for the census of 317, viz. 21,000 citizens and 10,000 metics; I further assume that by the first third of the fourth century Athens had recovered from the effects of the plague and the Peloponnesian War as far as she was going to—her population never again reached pre-war level—and that, absent similar demographic catastrophes, her population remained relatively constant through the remainder of the fourth century so that her population was roughly the same in 362 B.C. as it was in 317 B.C. (the same figures are accepted by A. H. M. Jones, *Athenian Democracy* [Oxford 1957]): 76, and E. Ruschenbusch, "Zum letzten Mal: die Burgerzahl Athens im 4. Jh. v. Chr.," *Zeitschrift fur Papyrus und Epiaraphik* 54 [1984]: 265). Even if we were to accept the higher figure of 31,000 citizens derived from Diododorus Siculus 18.18.5 and add in the 10,000 metics for a total adult male population of 41,000, an expedition of twenty ships (3,400 rowers) would still have drawn off about 8.3 percent of the free adult male population of Attika (the higher figure of 31,000 citizens is accepted by A. W. Gomme, *The Population of Athens in the Fifth and Fourth Centuries B.C.* [Oxford 1933]: 18). Since we really do not know that only members of the lowest class (thetes) rowed and that those eligible for infantry service (zeugitai) did not (see above, note 9), calculations of Athens' population (or segments thereof), based on the number of ships she put to sea in a given year, will never be convincing.

23. While familiarity with the sea was quite widespread in Athens, as we may judge from our texts, we actually do not hear that much about people specifically earning their livelihood from the sea. Again, if we may judge from the rare mentions of fishing in our texts, fishermen were among the poorest of the poor; while some fished from boats (cf. e.g. Xenophon, *Hellenica* 5.1.23), more typically they fished from shore or by wading in the shallows; for the motif of the poor fisherman, see V. J. Rosivach, "The advocati of the Poenulus and the Piscatores of the Rudens," *Maia* 35 [1983]: 83–93); it is hard to see how, for example, a shore-bound surf caster would be, a priori, any more qualified to row a trireme than a farmer would be. As to those on cargo vessels, in the two examples we have chosen, 362 B.C. and 349 B.C., many would already be up in the Hellespont waiting to be convoyed home by the emergency fleets, and so would not be available to serve in the ships sent to convoy them.

24. The implication of this argument is either that rowing skills were widespread in Athens' non-maritime population (or at least the poorer part thereof which was likely to serve in the fleet), or that these skills were relatively easily acquired, at least at the basic level. I have argued elsewhere that large numbers of rowers were drawn from Athens' farm population at the start of the Peloponnesian War (Rosivach [above, note 3], 53–55), and there is no reason to believe that the situation was much changed in the fourth century.

25. See above, note 10.

26. We can easily dismiss the alternative, I believe, that emergency expeditions were dispatched in most years and that a significant part of the adult male population was regularly engaged in rowing in these expeditions, since it would mean that large numbers of Athenians were unemployed in the years when comparatively few ships were sent out. For example, the total of thirty-nine ships sent out in 325/324 B.C. required approximately 4,100 fewer rowers than the sixty-two ships sent out in 330/329 B.C.; 4,100 would be approximately 13 percent of Athens' total adult male population of roughly 31,000, an impossibly large number to find regular employment without government assistance, something which was beyond Athens' ability (and perhaps imagination) to provide.

27. Farm households evolved over time as children grew up and left the paternal house, parents died, and a new generation was born; cf. the discussion of "Ancient Households and their Life Cycle" in T.W. Gallant, *Risk and Survival In Ancient Greece: Reconstructing the Rural Domestic Economy* (Stanford 1991): 11–33.

28. At least during the normal sailing season.

29. Note, though, that Athens' population never returned to the levels it had known at the start of the Peloponnesian War.

30. Rosivach (above, note 3): 44–56.

31. Cf. Demosthenes 22.44, which speaks of arrears of c.-5 percent still outstanding up to 25 years or more after assessment.

32. Cf. Demosthenes 21.154–55, where recruiting volunteer crews was an expense falling on the ships' captains that was eliminated when the state took over recruiting crews. Since it was never a question of the captain paying his crew's wages, the additional expense which a captain incurred in manning his ship with volunteers must have involved recruitment bonuses and the like; cf. Apollodorus' expenditures incurred in recruiting and retaining mercenary oarsmen.

33. Note, however, that the officials were to prepare fresh catalogues of those liable to compulsory service (katalogous Poieisthai...kai apoPherein nautas, 6). Thus, while there was a stand-by procedure for conscripting sailors, there was no pre-identified reserve standing by to serve; rather, those to be drafted would only be identified as the need arose. In particular, the language here tells, against the view of B. Jordan, *The Athenian Navy in the Classical Period* (Berkeley and Los Angeles, 1975): 226–27, that when appeals for volunteers failed, sailors were drafted from the *Zeugite* class, which normally supplied heavy-armed infantry, who then manned the ships according to their infantry organization.

34. Cf. p. 7 above and Rosivach (above, note 3).

35. The text here implies that he dismissed 'all' of the rowers produced by the draft, but that was not, in fact, the case, as we can see from 23, where he first mentions "the old sailors" who had "been paid little, only as much as I was able to borrow," finding employment as rowers is a rather far-fetched expedient to defend his view that *nautes* was a technical term for citizen/metic sailor, and not, as is generally assumed, the generic term for any sailor on the ship (Jordan [above, note 214, note 11]).

36. This is not specifically stated, but there must have been some legal pressure on the draftees to remain with the fleet, even when they were not paid (cf. 16); liability to the charge of lipotaxia (desertion) seems most likely.

37. The text says literally, "those of the sailors who remained did not wish to reembark," but Athenians triremes were so cramped that sailors stayed on board them only when they were actually at sea, so that "embarking" is synonymous with "putting to sea."

38. An average family of four needed somewhere in the order of 280 drakhmai to pay for living expenses for a year (Rosivach [above, note 3] 52, with note 60).

39. More accurately, they had received no wages (*misthos*) for eight months (12); they may have been away for even longer.

40. Specifically in the case of farmers, cash payments would enable their families to purchase imported grain to supplement their poor harvest.

41. Starting date, 4; length of service, and payment of *misthos* for two months. Note that farmers would have missed at least one spring harvest and one fall sowing.

42. Farmers grew their food; they didn't buy it.

43. Instead of merely tinkering with them, as she did through the *proeisphora*, instituted c. 369 B.C., in theory the *eisphora* tax was paid in advance in full by a small group of the richest of the rich, who then collected from the other members of their class the money they had advanced on their behalf.

44. Under the Athenian system, when *eisphorai* were imposed, they could be quite heavy, but they were not imposed that often, and the average over time was quite low. To illustrate: Demosthenes, during his ten years' minority (376–66) paid out 18 minae on his assessment of 15 talents, which works out at about 0.2 percent per annum. This is on capital, of course, but reckoning income was 10 percent of capital . . . , levies during this period, which was full of wars, represented only a 2 to 2 1/2 percent income tax (Jones [above, note 22] 29).

45. And on occasion the burden was displaced even further down the ladder, on metics and on *hoi khoris oikountes*, slaves who lived independently outside their master's household (Demosthenes 4.36–37); Demosthenes' insistence on the need for citizens to man the triremes (4.44) implies that they did not always do so.

Reconsidering the Battle of Actium

William M. Murray

⚓

The Battle of Actium ranks among history's most important sea battles because of the developments set in motion by its outcome. For example, it marks the birth of the Augustan Principate and has been recognized in succeeding years as the defining moment—the final victory if you will—in the rise of Augustus Caesar. It also marked the decisive reaffirmation of Rome's control over the Eastern Mediterranean and stands as the last great naval conflict of antiquity. In spite of these significant features, however, no one really knows for certain what happened on 2 September 31 B.C., the day the final struggle took place at Actium. Almost everything lacks certainty, from the battle strategy of the vanquished to the course and character of the battle itself. This is not because we lack ancient sources to tell us what happened. It is rather because the information they provide is not always convincing.

The two main battle narratives, written by Plutarch and Dio Cassius long after the event took place, are largely derived from sources favorable to the victors.[1] The other three (by Velleius Paterculus, Florus and Orosius) are pretty poor stuff. Although they provide a few details that may once have been in Livy's lost narrative, they lack the precision one needs to recreate a battle and are obviously grounded in partisan propaganda. Contemporary poetic references to the battle are few and are restricted to brief negative allusions to Cleopatra, vague movements of troops or ships, or grandiose battle scenes with divine portents and moralistic prophesy.[2] In general, all these accounts suffer from the inclusion of exaggerated rumor and hyperbole, and, for this reason, our view of the battle has not advanced significantly beyond the two reconstructions first proposed by J. Kromayer and W.W. Tarn during the course of the past hundred years.[3]

Why, then, do I feel a need to revisit this battle? Quite simply, new evidence, unavailable to previous scholars, suggests new clues

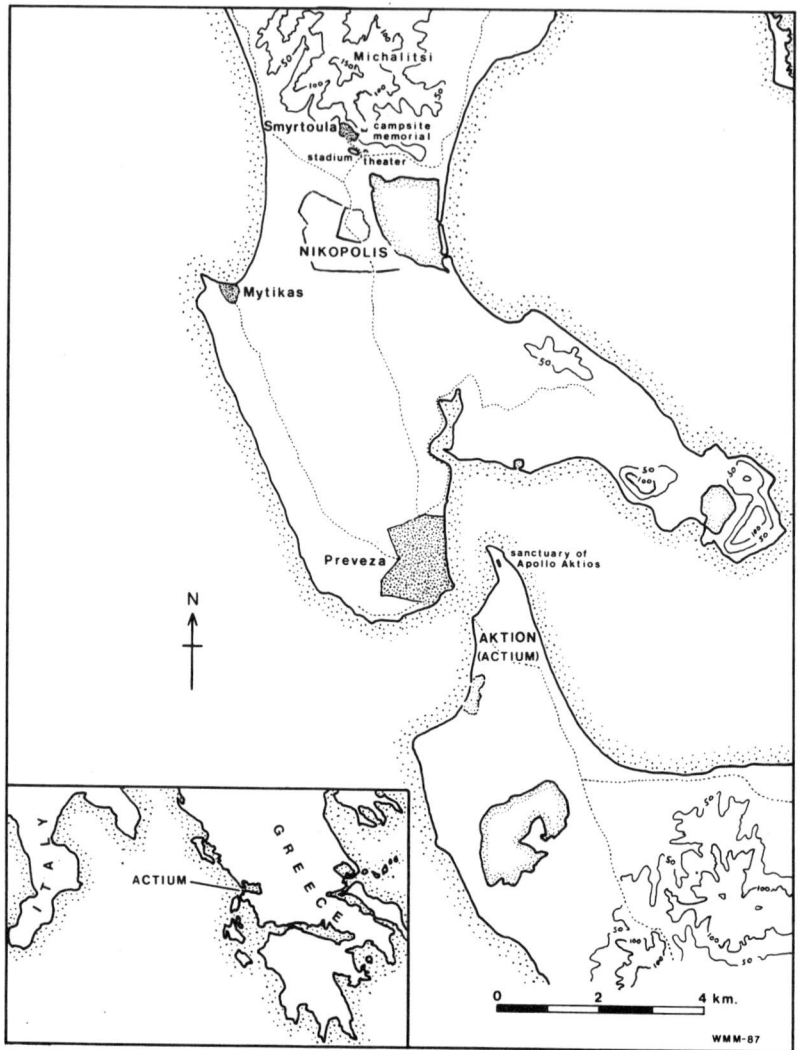

Figure 1.

about the battle and the ships that participated in it.[4] This evidence is preserved in the ruins of a war memorial built near Actium in the second year after the battle (see map, Figure 1. and reconstructed view, Figure 2.).[5] Octavian's engineers transformed the site of his hillside camp into a rectangular podium by means of a sturdy retaining wall. Into the southern face of this wall, they inserted 33–35

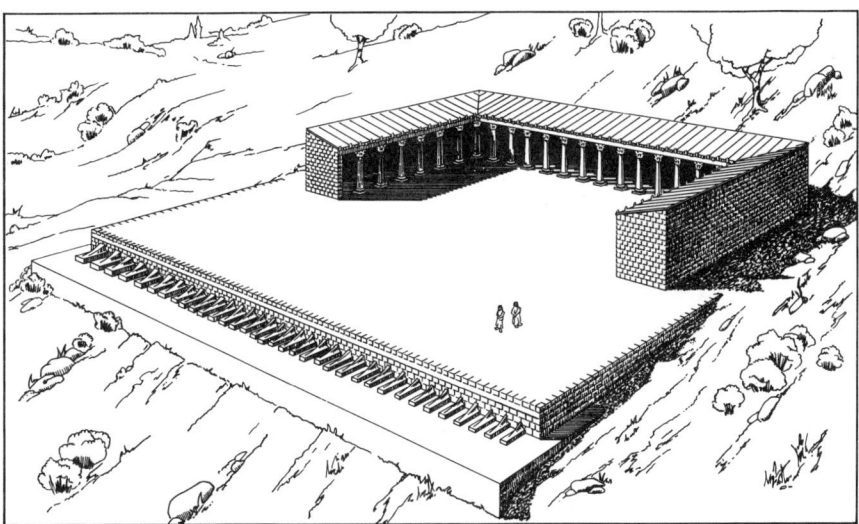

Figure 2.

bronze rams which gave a rostral front to the entire complex. Above the rams, along the face of the wall, they set a long dedicatory inscription and finished the complex with a Pi-shaped stoa on the podium where Octavian's tent had once stood. According to the inscription, Octavian consecrated both the site and the naval spoils to Neptune and Mars in thanks for his victory over Antony and Cleopatra in the Actian War.

Today, the rams are long gone, but one can still see 23 sockets, of at least four different gradations in size, preserved in the podium's southern retaining wall. I examined this wall in 1986 and found that as many as 35 rams were originally displayed here. I also found that the sockets' dimensions reflect the sizes of structural timbers (wales and ramming timbers) used to brace the bows of Antony's largest ships.[6] These ships were clearly built to deliver and to withstand ramming blows of terrific force.[7] This simple fact has important implications for our understanding of Antony's strategy, implications that in themselves demand a reconsideration of the battle. One other feature of this physical evidence also demands a reexamination of the battle. The number of rams (33–35), certainly a tithe or 1/10th dedication of the warship rams captured, implies that Antony suffered heavy casualties on September 2nd and tends to affirm two basic elements of the historical narratives: 1) that the battle involved fierce fighting, and 2) that many of Antony's ships were destroyed by fire.

I can best substantiate these conclusions by describing more fully some features of the monument and its sockets. Let us first consider the classes of the rams. It is likely that Octavian wished to present as impressive a display as possible when he constituted his tithe of warship rams. Therefore, it seems that he chose to display the largest examples from his collection of 330–350 rams.[8] If this supposition is correct, then the sockets preserve the dimensions from medium-sized *polyereis* such as "tens," "nines," "eights," "sevens," and perhaps "sixes." The relationship between the sockets and their bow dimensions became apparent when an authentic ram of similar design was recovered from Athlit Bay south of Haifa in 1980 with its bow timbers still in place (Figures 3 and 4). Although this weapon (weighing 465 kg.) is too small to fit into any of the preserved sockets (Figure 5.), its cross-sectional shape is identical to that of the sockets, and, as a result, the timbers preserved inside the ram correspond to the interiors of the Actian sockets and tell us how the lost Actian rams functioned as structural elements of their vessels.[9] The precise details have been recently explained by J.R. Steffy, who concludes from a study of the ram's timbers that the wales, ramming timber and bottom planks of the Athlit ship were designed to absorb the tremendous shocks generated by the ramming blow.[10]

We can now make the following three observations. First, the smallest weapons displayed at Octavian's campsite were much more massive than the example from Athlit, which probably comes from a "four."[11] Second, the massive timbers used in the Actian weapons reveal that these ships were built to deliver and sustain ramming blows of terrific force. Third, each Actian ram weighed much more than the 465 kg. of the Athlit weapon and must represent the most expensive piece of equipment on its warship.[12] This fact alone is ample proof of the rams' importance to their ships as tactical weapons.[13]

I mention the ramming capability of Antony's *polyereis* because this particular characteristic is largely absent from the historical descriptions of the battle.[14] Instead, we are told that Antony's ships were too heavy to be effective against Octavian's smaller, more agile vessels (Plut. *Ant.* 66.1; Dio 50.29.1–4; Velleius 2.84.1; Florus 2.21.5–7). This is only part of the story. Octavian knew well the ramming

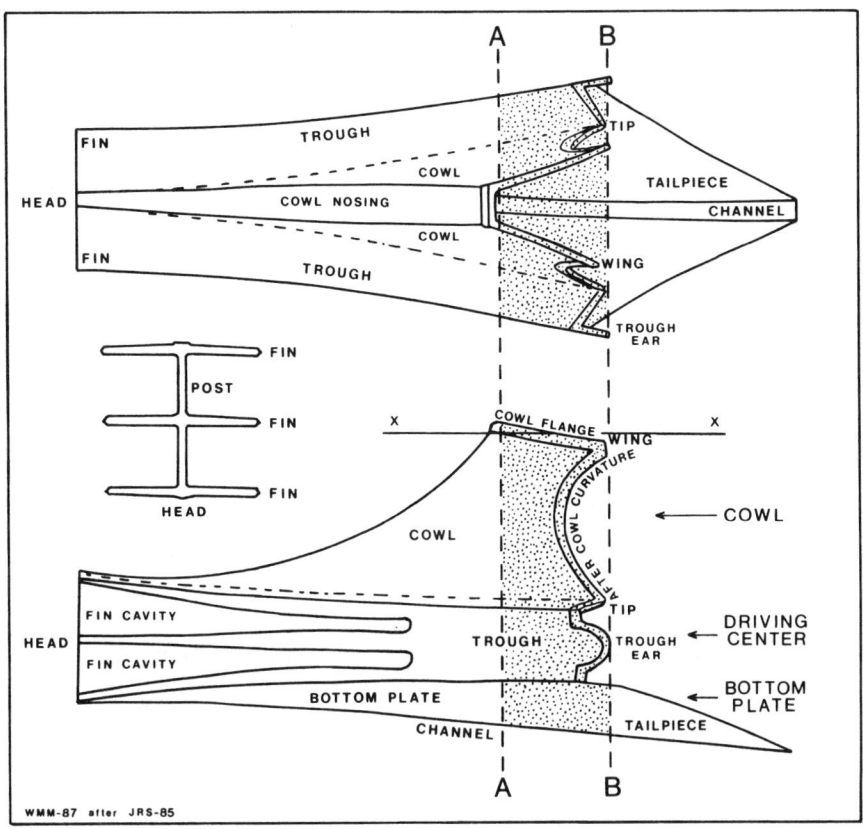

Figure 3.

potential of Antony's big ships because when the fighting began, he carefully avoided "dashing prow-to-prow against rough and hard bronze armor" (Plut. *Ant.* 66.1). In other words, he avoided the prow-to-prow charge that typically opened naval battles of this period.

A classic prow-to-prow charge involving medium-sized *polyereis* is described for us by Diodorus (20.51.1–3) at the Battle of Salamis (Cyprus) in 306 B.C.[15] Here, the two commanders (Ptolemy and Demetrius Poliorcetes) approached each other in a line-abreast formation. When the distance between the two fleets was about 600 meters (three stades), a prearranged signal (in this case, the hoisting of gilded shields) began the opening charge. Soon thereafter the trumpets blared another signal, the battle cry was raised and the

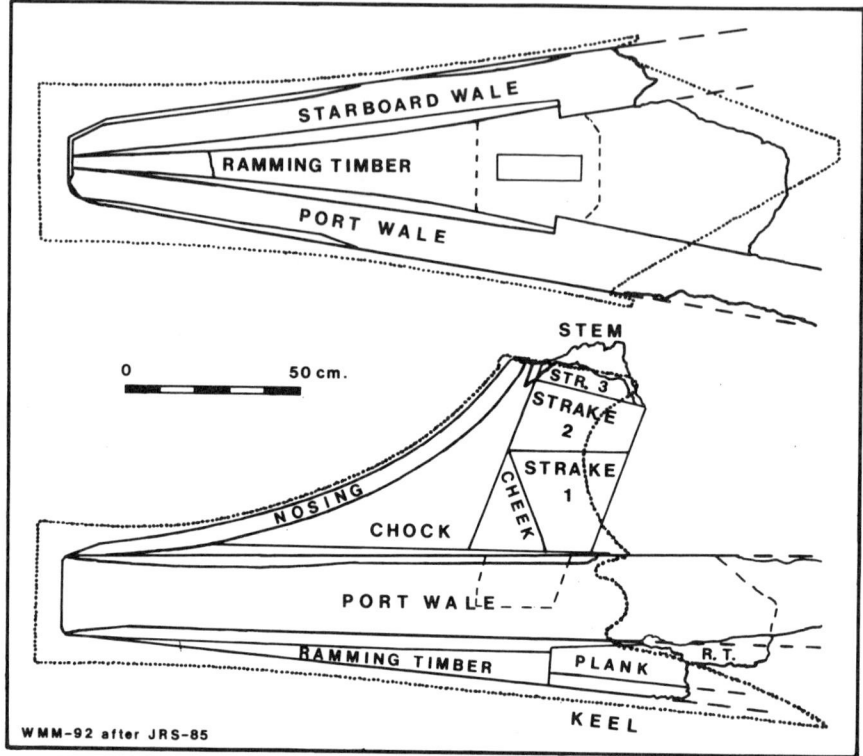

Figure 4.

oarcrews urged into a sprint. As each ship took aim at the prow of the vessel opposite them in the line, the archers and javelin throwers kept up a steady stream of fire, crouching down just before impact to hold on for dear life, and then resuming their fire at close range. If the initial prow strike was not enough to fatally damage or cripple one's opponent, and the battle lines were still intact, the vessels backed water and charged again.

Smaller vessels were clearly at a disadvantage when challenged by larger, more solidly built ones, and so they developed a maneuver to take advantage of their smaller size and greater maneuverability. At the last moment of the prow-to-prow charge, a few seconds before impact, the helmsman would execute a swerve past his enemy's flank in a maneuver called the *diekplous*. A skilled oarcrew would swing its oars parallel to its own hull as it passed by

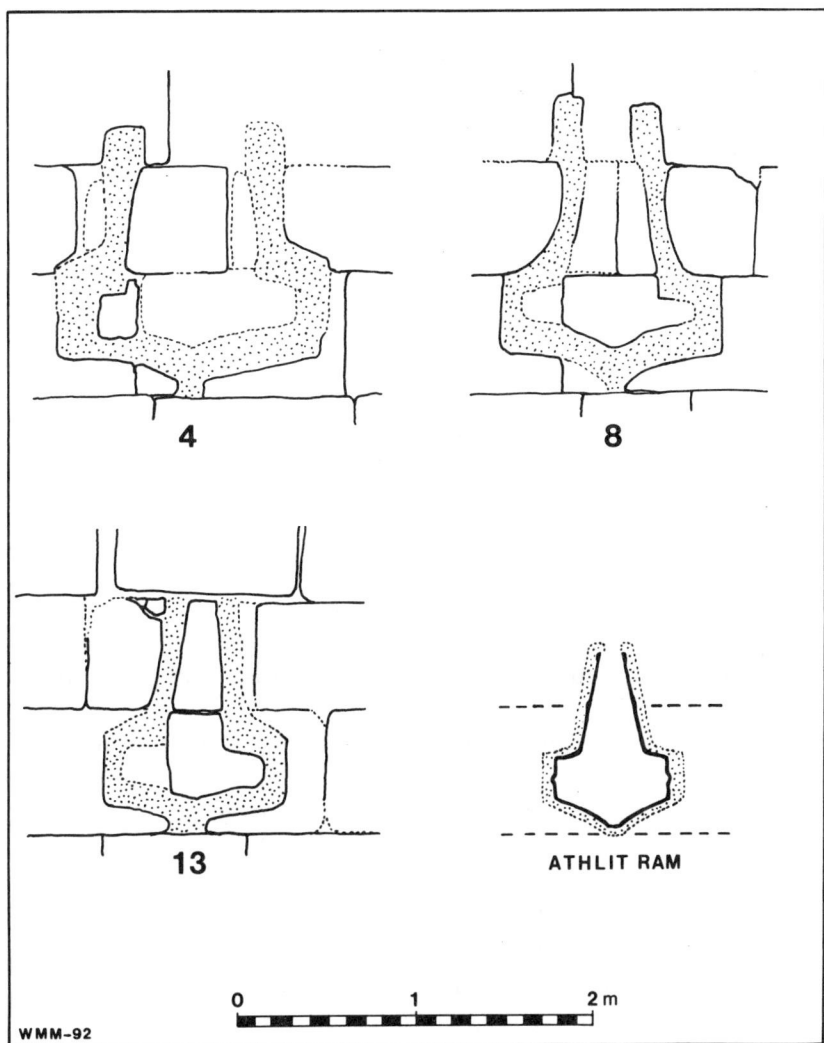

Figure 5.

the enemy vessel, shattering its extended oars. Once past the crippled vessel, they could turn about and destroy its two steering oars and thus put their victim out of action.[16] The disabled vessel could then be attacked from a safe distance with long range weapons, struck in the flank by ramming, or ignored until later when it might still be sunk or placed in tow as a captured vessel.[17] Predictably, the larger vessels preferred to crash into an opponent's prow and trust in their heavy design, while smaller vessels (like the "threes" and "fours" of the Rhodian navy) preferred to perfect the *diekplous* maneuver.

Presuming, therefore, that Antony understood how properly to use his "sevens," "eights," "nines," and "tens," it is surprising that he did not open the battle with a prow-to-prow charge. Why? The ancient answer, that Antony's ships were inherently ineffective because of their excessive weight, height, and mass, is not very convincing in light of the evidence from Octavian's Campsite Memorial. We can now appreciate Antony's ships as standard medium-sized *polyereis* which were designed for a specific kind of warfare. A more convincing answer lies in the poor condition of Antony's oarcrews, who had suffered severely during the course of the summer. Sickness (Dio 50.12.8, 15.3), hunger (50.14.4), and defeats had taken their toll, and, as a result, the men were utterly demoralized (50.15.3). So many men had died, deserted, or were otherwise unfit for service that Antony was forced to burn a large number of ships he could not fill with crews (Plut. *Ant.* 64.1; Dio 50.15.4).[18] It is not surprising, therefore, when we read in Plutarch that Antony's large ships were unable to gain momentum because they were undermanned (*Ant.* 65.5).

If we keep in mind the depressed and depleted nature of Antony's crews, we might begin to understand what Antony faced when he called a staff meeting at the end of August to decide what to do (Dio 50.14.4). According to Dio, Cleopatra suggested the plan that was finally adopted: to entrust the most important places to garrisons and to withdraw back to Egypt. It was a remarkable decision, and shows the bleak outlook of Antony's staff by the end of the summer. I see no reason to doubt Dio's account that Cleopatra supported this position and that she bolstered her arguments with reference to recent alarming portents (50.15.1–3). All armies are superstitious, particularly demoralized ones, and portents and omens are frequently effective in motivating the men to action.[19]

What follows next, however, is difficult to believe. Antony, according to Dio and Plutarch, hid the decision to withdraw from his men.[20] Dio makes this very clear when he presents Antony's prebattle speech (Dio 50.16–22), a composition that cannot be based on anything close to the original. In this speech, Antony makes no reference at all to the numerical superiority of the enemy, nor to the morale problems of his own men. What we get instead is hollow boasting and misleading generalizations that would have been apparent to everyone.

Antony implies, for example, that his men actually had an advantage over their adversary in numbers of ships (50.18.5), an absurd statement when we remember that he had just burned a portion of his fleet (50.15.4). The speaker also demonstrates a poor grasp of naval tactics when he maintains that no vessel could damage their ships owing to their thick timbers, high sides, and numerous archers and slingers (50.18.5–6). This might be true for a single "three" attacking a "ten," but most of Octavian's ships would have been "fives," which were capable of destroying larger classes, particularly when they fought in groups of two or more.[21] When he explains (50.18.5–6) that those foolish enough to approach their ships will be "sunk by the very number of our oars," I am not sure what his listeners were supposed to think. As a statement of fact, it is sheer fantasy, as any sailor in the fleet would have recognized.

What we should expect from a genuine speech delivered to a demoralized force before a crucial battle is a realistic appraisal of the problems to be faced plus the outlines of a plan that promised success. The speaker should acknowledge the superior numbers of the enemy and offer some strategy to counter this advantage. Examples should have been given to demonstrate how a force of inferior numbers but with superior classes could defeat its opponents.[22] If no acceptable examples could be found, then the speaker should have stressed the need for the oarcrews to keep a tight formation and to guard against letting the enemy outflank or sail through their formation to attack them from the rear. Above all, we should expect some reference to a brighter future if only the force could successfully remove itself from the gulf to some other location.

Neither this dubious speech nor the narratives of Dio and Plutarch convince me that Antony could, or would, have concealed a general plan to retreat from his men. His desperate act of burning undamaged ships would have signalled to everyone his intention to retreat. I am therefore unconvinced that he explained his order to take sails on board (Plut. *Ant* 64.2) by stressing their use in a vigorous pursuit of enemy fugitives. His commanders knew what was afoot. Three days after the battle, for example, Antony waited at Tainaron, in the southern Peloponnesus, for ships to join up with him (Plut. *Ant*. 67.4–5) before heading south toward Egypt. If Tainaron was designated the meeting place for those who managed to escape, does it not imply that a withdrawal was widely discussed and that this decision was communicated to the men and commanders of his ships?

Let us now turn to the nature of the battle itself. As I stated earlier, there are two basic views of the battle that have evolved over the past century (cf. n. 5). The standard version, first published by Kromayer in the 1890s, accepted the basic outline sketched by the surviving historical narratives. In the 1930s, W. W. Tarn led a movement to reject this standard view of the battle by questioning the reliability of the historical narratives upon which Kromayer based his arguments. He preferred to follow a hint in Horace's *Epode* 9 that most of Antony's fleet returned to harbor without offering battle, while Antony and Cleopatra managed to flee southward with about 100 ships. According to Tarn, there was never a great battle at Actium.[23]

If my interpretation of the evidence from Octavian's Campsite Memorial is correct, we should no longer doubt that a fierce battle was fought during the afternoon hours of 2 September 31 B.C. Let us begin with the fleet numbers. The available evidence implies that Antony manned approximately 230 ships out of his original fleet of 500 warships.[24] If the 33–35 sockets at Octavian's Campsite Memorial represent a tithe (as surely they must), then Octavian captured between 330 and 350 rams from Antony's fleet of 500 warships. I have argued elsewhere that Octavian must have counted rams taken from the enemy *in Greece* during the course of the summer-long war, and this would include those rams he managed to recover from the ships that Antony had burned before the battle.[25] After the battle's conclusion, therefore, some 150 ships remain unaccounted for.[26] When we subtract from this total the 60 ships that escaped with Cleopatra (Plut. *Ant.* 66.3), we are left with 90 warships for which we have no record.

What happened to these vessels? It is reasonable to assume that a few escaped from the gulf with Antony while others made their way to Egypt from duty stations around Greece. No totals are recorded for these vessels, so the number cannot have been large, perhaps less than a half-squadron of 30 ships (had the total approached a full squadron, some author would have mentioned them). If fewer than 90 ships returned to Egypt with Antony and Cleopatra, more than 60 have disappeared without a trace. Had these ships been abandoned, disabled, or burned on shore before, during, or after the events of September 2nd, Octavian would have eventually salvaged their rams and included their number in his tithe. These 60 vessels must have been completely destroyed in some way, and this implies to me their destruction by fire at sea.[27] This revelation is important because it renders Tarn's view of the battle impossible, and our much maligned sources regain some of their lost credibility, at least regarding the broad outlines of the struggle they describe, namely, the fierceness of the fight and the use of fire to destroy a part of Antony's fleet.

When we look at this in a slightly different manner, the conclusions are still the same. If a conservative estimate says that 60 warships were so destroyed that their rams were unavailable for salvage and that 90 escaped with Cleopatra and Antony, then Octavian managed to recover 80 rams from ships destroyed or captured during the course of the battle (60 + 90 + 80 = 230). This means that Octavian captured or destroyed a total of 140 vessels during the afternoon hours of September 2nd. When compared with known casualty figures from other major battles of the previous three centuries (see Table 1.), these totals are credible and affirm that Actium, like other battles of the period which resulted in a similar degree of destruction, must have involved a fierce fight and the use of fire, just as our sources tell us.

In my view, any plausible reconstruction of the battle must be based on two factors: 1) what we know about the use of medium-sized *polyereis*, and 2) what our sources tell us that is consistent with the reality of naval warfare when these classes were used. What follows is not a comprehensive reconstruction of the battle, but rather an attempt to focus on those elements of the battle most affected by these factors.[28] By now, we have seen that normal procedure called for a prow-to-prow charge to open the fighting. Such a charge began documented battles at Salamis, Chios, Side, Myonessus, and probably also Mylae and Naulochus.[29] We also know that a good way to attack a fleet with larger classes was to use the *diekplous* maneuver. For Antony's fleet, therefore, it was imperative that he adopt a plan to defend against this tactic.

What might he have done? Keep in mind that I am now offering an educated guess, based on what we know about the capabilities of Antony's ships and the use of these classes in recorded battles. We do not possess sufficient historical evidence to do more than this. Antony's only hope lay in his ability to cause

TABLE 1: Known Warship Casualty Figures Sustained by Defeated Forces in Naval Battles from 306–36 B.C.

Battle	Date	Casualties
Salamis (Cyprus).	306 B.C.	Losses = 85.7 percent of total fleet. Ptolemy lost 120 warships out of a total force of 140 (40 with crews by capture, 80 by ramming). Those destroyed by ramming were eventually towed, full of sea water, to Demetrius' camp before the city of Salamis.[30]
Mylae (Sicily).	260 B.C.	Losses = 33.8 percent of total fleet. The Carthaginians lost 44 warships out of a total of 130 (31 by capture, 13 by ramming).[31]
Ecnomus (Sicily).	256 B.C.	Losses = 26.9 percent of total fleet. The Carthaginians lost more than 94 warships out of a total force of 350 (64 by capture, more than 30 by ramming).[32]
Chios.	201 B.C.	Losses = 50.7 percent of total fleet. Philip V lost 103 warships out of a total force of 203 (10 by capture, 93 by ramming).[33]
Myonessus (Ionia).	190 B.C.	Losses = 47.2 percent of total fleet. Antiochus III lost 42 warships out of a total force of 89 (29 by ramming and by burning, 13 by capture).[34]
Mylae (Sicily).	36 B.C.	Losses = 19.4 percent of total fleet. Sextus Pompey lost 30 out of a total force of 155.[35]
Naulochus	36 B.C.	Losses = 61 percent of total fleet. Sextus Pompey lost 183 warships out of a total force of 300 (28 by ramming, 155 by capture and by burning).[36]
Actium	31 B.C.	Losses = 60.9 percent of total fleet. Antony lost c. 140 warships out of a total force of 230 (c. 80 by ramming and/or capture, c. 60 by fire?).

panic among one wing of the enemy's fleet, and then to encourage it to spread to the rest of the fleet. He might then concentrate his largest *polyereis* (his "sevens" to "tens") in one wing and hope to crush and scatter those who opposed him.[37] The victorious wing might then bear down on the undefeated ships of the enemy, cause them to break formation and flee, and thus allow his entire fleet to withdraw southward unopposed. Such a plan demanded that he place his strengthened wing on the north (right side) of his line, so that once it scattered the opposite wing of the enemy, it could proceed southward through the rest of the enemy's line and then retreat around Leukas to the south. His plan to protect against the *diekplous* maneuver (and a general encirclement as well) must have involved the positioning of Cleopatra's squadron of 60 warships in a second line to the rear.[38]

When the battle started, what did Antony do? First of all, there was no prow-to-prow charge. Why? Antony's ultimate goal was to get out of the Ambracian Gulf, and for this reason, he assumed a defensive posture with his ships bunched closely together. His battle plan, therefore, involved a wait-and-see strategy, hoping that his enemy would make the necessary mistakes allowing him to disperse a portion of their fleet and drive the rest away in fear. It was his only chance. There was another reason that no charge occurred. Octavian's commanders kept a distance of about a sea mile (eight stades) between themselves and the enemy (Plut. *Ant*. 65.4). If Antony ordered a sprint toward the enemy line, his depleted oar-crews would have been exhausted by the time the ships finally engaged.[39] Unable to attack with his right wing, Antony had no choice but to sit and wait, hoping that Octavian or one of his commanders would make a mistake. None was made. Finally, and very reluctantly, Antony began to extend his line out from the shore where his smaller, tighter formation of ships (cf. Dio 50.31.4–5) became more and more vulnerable to attacks from the side and rear. Plutarch writes (*Ant*. 65.4–5) that Caesar was delighted with this development, and that he ordered his right wing to back water and to draw Antony's line ever farther from the shore. Agrippa, whose greater experience at sea implies that he, not Octavian, directed the overall battle strategy, apparently did the same thing on the left wing (Plut. *Ant*. 66.3).

As Antony's line advanced into the expanding crescent shape assumed by Octavian's line, Antony's right became separated from his center (Plut. *Ant*. 66.3; Figure 6.). They really had no choice, since they feared being outflanked along the shore and yet were reluctant to increase the intervals between their ships for fear of *diekplous* attacks. At this point, Antony was forced to engage the enemy. When the ships of both sides finally came together, and no one scattered seaward, it became clear to those in the second line that no crushing

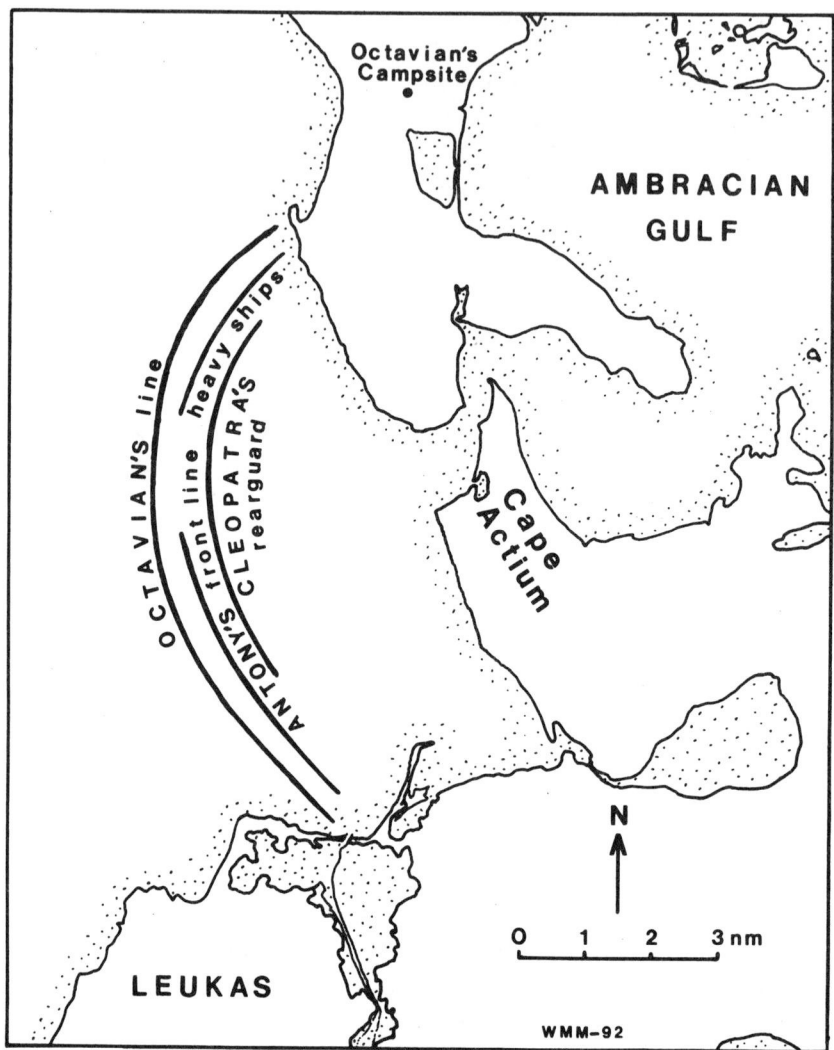

Figure 6.

victory would occur on Antony's right. Agrippa, in command of Octavian's own considerable force of *polyereis*, had successfully avoided a prow-to-prow contest with Antony's larger vessels.[40] The battle could now be decided by tactics more favorable to Agrippa's better conditioned fleet—deck fighting and gang attacks on individual ships.

Elsewhere, Octavian's commanders relied on their numerical superiority to attack their opponents in groups of two or three (Dio 50.32.6). In this way, they were able to avoid the prow strikes of a more equal contest and attack their enemies in the side.[41] Eventually, Octavian's numerical advantage began to take its toll, as more and more of Antony's ships were put out of action. At some point, when the possibility for dispersing the enemy had definitely passed, but when the fighting was still intense enough to limit pursuit, Cleopatra led her squadron through the gap that separated the right wing from the center and raised her sails. Whether we choose to censure or praise Cleopatra's action, we must admit that she personally commanded the largest portion of the ships that escaped. And if we admit that the primary objective was to retreat from the gulf with as many ships as possible, it is difficult to blame her for successfully leading an entire squadron to safety.[42]

Regardless of how we interpret her action, it precipitated a general flight on the part of Antony's fleet. Their plan to disperse the enemy had not been successful, and with the protective rear line moving seaward, it became the duty of each vessel to care for itself. The result was a general rout, except that Antony's ships were unable to flee from their pursuers. This is not because they did not try. Those who were able to disengage did so and threw their fighting towers into the water to lighten their ships (Dio 50.33.4 ff.). Antony himself transferred from his flagship (probably a "ten") to a "five" so as to make a speedier escape (Plut. *Ant.* 66.5). But the remainder of the fleet was not so fortunate, and they were abandoned to an enemy intent upon their destruction. At this stage, when Antony's vessels were more intent on flight than on defending themselves, it seems that many vessels succumbed to fire.[43] Almost the same thing had happened to Pompey's fleet at Naulochus (cf. Appian *BC* 5.121).

It is well known that during the chaos of a full flight, great numbers of casualties can be sustained by the defeated force. Judging from the "missing" 60–90 ships implied by the tithe at Octavian's memorial, the casualties must have been heavy. Plutarch maintains that Cleopatra fled before the battle was decided and that even after Antony's departure, the fleet fought on for a long time (*Ant.* 68.1). It might be closer to the truth to say that the killing went on for a long time, but not that the battle was in doubt. In this fact, we can probably find the reason behind the battle's troubled record in the historical accounts of the period. Although it is reasonable to expect that Octavian's fleet gave no quarter to their fleeing opponents, this fact became an embarrassment during the following weeks when Octavian wished to cement agreements of reconciliation with Antony's army and his allies (Dio 51.1.4–5; Plut. *Ant.* 68.3).

Thereafter, once the conflict with Antony and Cleopatra was over, Octavian's main concern was to heal the wounds of civil war, so he encouraged those who wrote about the battle to continue the line of propaganda that had led "all Italy" to support his cause. The conflict was therefore described in a general way that placed the blame for the war squarely on the shoulders of Cleopatra and Antony. The glorification of Romans killing Romans, no matter how critical for his cause at the time, was not to become part of the birth legend of the New Age. To provide an example, he wrote a personal account of the battle which stressed the role of his own Liburnians and minimized the role of Agrippa's *polyereis*.[44] The preserved narratives reflect the great influence and success of Octavian's version. For us, the results are frustrating and leave us to guess at important events that shaped the course of both the Roman World and Western History. Although we can never know for certain what happened at Actium on September 2nd, the new perspective explored by this paper allows us to further refine our understanding of the likely possibilities.

1. A similar version of this paper originally appeared as "Een nieuwe kijk op de Slag bij Actium," in a special edition of the Dutch Journal *Lampas*, edited by Fik Meijer [Vol. 26.3 (June/July 1993): 206–23]. I thank Prof. Meijer for the permission to reproduce the English text of the article here. Plutarch (*Ant.* 61–68) and Dio (50.11.1–51.1.5) provide our most complete record of the entire Actian War, from the first movement of troops to Greece, to the final battle on September 2nd.

2. Zonaras 10.29–30.

3. Vell. 2.84–85; Orosius 6.19.5–12.

4. See Hor. *Ep.* 9; *Carm.* 1.37; Prop. *Eleg.* 3.11 and 4.6; and Verg. *Aen.* 8.671–713.

5. Although Kromayer and Tarn drew the main lines of the debate, there were other scholars who joined in on one side or the other; for a partial review of this literature, see MURRAY 1989, 131–37. Throughout the notes, I refer frequently to my monograph for the sake of brevity. Readers interested in discussions of the secondary literature will find them here.

6. This evidence has also led to the formation of The Actium Project, a Hellenic-American research effort to survey the battle site and to recover evidence relevant to the Battle of Actium. The Project is co-directed by the author and by Dr. Elpida

Hadjidaki, Department of Marine Antiquities (Greek Ministry of Culture). Our first season of research took place during the summer of 1993, the results of which will be published in a separate preliminary report.

7. What is currently known of this monument is published in MURRAY 1989.

8. For the original number of rams and the evidence behind the details of the sockets, see MURRAY 1989, pp. 55–57, 34–55, and the article quoted below in note 9.

9. I have developed this theme more fully in a paper titled "Polyremes from the Battle of Actium. Some Construction Details," which will appear in *Tropis IV: Proceedings of the Fourth International Symposium on Ship Construction in Antiquity*, Athens, 28 August to 1 September 1991 (forthcoming).

10. See MURRAY 1989, 56 and 137–39, for the evidence relevant to the large number of ships captured by Octavian during the course of the Actian War.

11. "*Polyeres*" (plural: "*polyereis*") is a term borrowed from late antiquity to define vessels from classes larger than "threes." Since sizes substantially larger than "tens" are known (the largest was a "forty"), I feel justified in defining the classes from "six" to "ten" as being of "medium size." For the evidence behind the range of classes in Antony's fleet, see MURRAY 1989, 99–114.

12. STEFFY 1991, 6–39, especially 37–38.

13. See MURRAY 1989, 103–114. The casting of the Athlit ram weighs 456 kg. The weapon is 2.26 m. long, has a maximum height of 95 cm. and a maximum width of 76 cm.

14. The height of the Athlit ram's wales (at 24 cm.) is dwarfed by the Actian wales. The smallest examples (7, 12 and C) are still 10 cm. higher, while the largest example (5) is almost 40 cm. higher. This general impression is reinforced by the wale and ramming timber unit (the greatest distance from the ram's left to right side) which, in the smallest examples (13, 14, 15, A and D), are 25 cm. wider; in the largest examples (2 and 4), the unit is fully twice as wide as that in the Athlit ram. For the precise dimensions, see my forthcoming article in *Tropis IV* (cf. n. 9). The importance of the ram and its support structure was apparent to Appian, who recognized that a solid ramming blow on the ram of an enemy vessel was "most effective in shaking the marines on deck and in rendering the vessel inoperative" (*BC* 5.119).

15. The precise monetary value of these rams in 31 B.C. is difficult to judge, although it must have been considerable. We know, for example, that the value of the bronze in the Athlit ram was worth 560 days of work for a skilled Athenian laborer in 325/24 B.C.; see MURRAY 1989, p. 127, n. 16.

16. I should also mention that it is absent from the contemporary poetic traditions concerning the battle, except for Virgil's description of the scene (*Aen.* 8.689–95): "All rush together and the whole sea foams, torn by oar strokes and trident rams. . . ." You might think that the Cyclades were uprooted and floated on the sea, or that high mountains crashed together. . . ." It is difficult to know what to make of this description. If, in fact, it derives from a participant in the battle, the description fits best with the action at the north end of the battle line when the two fleets finally engaged; see below.

17. Two other examples can be seen at Side (Livy 37.24.2) and Myonessus in 190 B.C. (Livy 37.30.3–5).

18. For examples of these maneuvers, see Diod. 20.51.3, Polyb. 16.4.14, and Livy 37.24.2. If the oarcrew was not prepared, they could lose their own oars during the maneuver; cf. Polyb. 16.3.12–14.

19. See Polyb. 16.4.14–15 (attacks immediately after the *diekplous*), 16.6.12 (towing away previously disabled ships), and 16.6.13 (holing those ships that one could not tow away).

20. Out of the 500 warships that came with Antony to Greece, less than half (230 ships) were manned for the final battle. Although we are not told how many vessels burned, the number must have been large.

21. I am particularly reminded of the Athenians' reluctance to withdraw from the great harbor at Syracuse (in 413 B.C.) after an unexpected eclipse of the moon. The men's fears and the seers' advice forced the Athenian fleet to delay its departure, with disastrous results (Thuc. 7.50.4).

22. Plutarch (*Ant*. 63.5) wrote that Cleopatra was contemplating flight even before the battle and disposed her forces where they could best escape. Although this clearly implies that the others intended to fight for victory, Plutarch admits (*Ant*. 64.2) that Antony had no great hopes for victory because he ordered the sails to be put on board his ships.

23. For the composition of the two fleets at Actium, see MURRAY 1989, 143–51. Our record of battles involving medium-sized *polyereis* is not very complete but, nevertheless, demonstrates that smaller vessels could challenge larger vessels, and hope to survive. Two "fives" attacked and destroyed a "ten" at the battle of Chios in 201 B.C. (Polyb. 16.3.6). In this same battle, another "five" attacked a "seven," and still another, an "eight" (Polyb. 16.3.7), and although both "fives" were destroyed, they engaged the enemy willingly, fully intending to survive their attacks. A few years later, off Pamphylian Side in 190 B.C., a "four" sank a "seven" with a prow-to-prow strike. The sinking of the "seven" was clearly unexpected, but nevertheless occurred (Livy 37.24.3). In the same battle, another "four" attacked a flagship, which was also probably a "seven" (Livy 37.29.9).

24. For example, a reference to the Battle of Chios between Attalus and Philip V might have been made. In this battle Attalus successfully pitched 65 cataphracts ("decked ships" that were at least "fours"), nine trihemioliae, and three "threes" against Philip's 53 cataphracts and more than 150 open galleys (Polyb. 16.2).

25. The basic sequence of published articles is as follows: KROMAYER 1899, TARN 1931, KROMAYER 1933, TARN 1934, RICHARDSON 1937 (who supported Kromayer's position), and TARN 1938.

26. For references to the main arguments, see MURRAY 1989, 133–34. The numbers are those recorded by Florus (2.21.5) and Orosius (6.19.9, 11), which apparently go back to Livy's lost account of the battle. Accordingly, Antony manned about 170 vessels on the morning of the final battle; Cleopatra manned 60. This same tradition (Florus 2.21.5) records the numbers in Octavian's fleet at more than 400.

27. MURRAY 1989, 137–39.

28. For the purpose of this discussion, I will work from the larger number (i.e., a tithe of 35 rams) because it minimizes the number of ships for which we have no record.

29. See MURRAY 1989, 133–35, for those authors who record the use of fire before, during and at the end of the battle.

30. Although Dio (50.34–35) describes the fire in terms that are too sensational to be believed and falsely asserts that Octavian waited until this moment to call for fire from his camp, fire must have played a significant role in the final rout.

31. See MURRAY 1989, 134–35.

32. For the evidence, see MURRAY 1989, 143–51. For the totals given in this entry, see Diod. 20.49.2 (fleet size), and 20.52.6 (casualty totals). For the total number in the Carthaginian fleet, see Polyb. 1.23.3; he also preserves (1.23.10) the less exact "round" number of 50 as the total of ships that they lost to the Romans. The more exact figures derive from an inscription: *CIL* VI 31611 (= *ILS* 65). Polyb. 1.28.12, 14 (casualty totals); 1.25.9 (fleet size).

33. Philip's force consisted of 53 cataphracts (see n. 23), an unknown number of open galleys like trihemioliae, and 150 small open galleys called *lemboi* and *pristeis* (Polyb. 16.2.9). Of the 50 warships disabled by the Rhodians, 40 were *lemboi* (Polyb. 16.7.2). We must add to the totals, given by Polybius at the end of his account (16.7.1–3), one "eight" that was destroyed (16.3.2) and another that was captured (16.3.8–11) during the battle.

34. Livy 37.30.1–2 (fleet size); 37.30.7–8 (casualties totals).

35. Appian *BC* 5.118 (fleet size), 121 (casualties).

36. Appian *BC* 5.105 (fleet size), 108 (casualties).

37. Space limits other references to the extensive literature on this battle. A careful review of this literature, in light of my new approach, is certainly necessary, and I hope to produce such a study in the near future.

38. Salamis (Diod. 20.51.1–3); Chios (Polyb. 16.4.7); Side and Myonessus (Livy 37.24.2 and 30.3–5); Mylae and Naulochus (Appian *BC* 5.106, and 119).

39. Demetrius used this tactic at Salamis in 306 B.C. with great success (Diod. 20.50.3–4).

40. The options available to Antony were limited. One might defend against the *diekplous* by reducing the intervals between one's ships (something which he also seems to have done), but this left one vulnerable to encirclement (the *periplous*). The double-line formation was effectively used by Demetrius Poliorcetes at Salamis in 306 B.C. (Diod. 20.50.3). If the enemy managed to penetrate his front line of two "sevens" and 30 "fours," they became exposed to attacks from the second line, comprised of 10 "sixes" and 10 "fives." The other possible defense against the *diekplous* required more ships than Antony had at his disposal. This tactic was used in 201 B.C. at Chios when Philip V placed small open galleys in the gaps between his medium-sized *polyereis* (Polyb. 16.4.8). The maintenance of order was critically important for all three formations, and this required one's oarcrews to be well disciplined and in top physical condition.

41. The distance between the fleets at Salamis was three stades when the sprint commenced (see above). Sea battles were strenuous affairs and sick crews were at a decided disadvantage. In 190 B.C., sick Rhodian oarcrews had to pause to regain their strength during the battle of Side. Their weakened condition made them unable to overtake a fleeing enemy (Livy 37.24.5–10).

42. Octavian's fleet was not as "light" as the historical authors would have us believe. It seems that the largest units in his fleet were "sixes," and it is reasonable to assume that he possessed a considerable number of these. See MURRAY 1989, 143–51.

43. Plutarch (*Ant.* 66.1–2) mentions that Octavian's ships avoided prow attacks as well as flank attacks because they feared the strength of Antony's ships. This is surely an exaggeration, as Dio (50.32.6, and 8) makes clear.

44. This is essentially the argument put forth by KROMAYER 1899, 45–48, almost a century ago, and it has been followed by most commentators on the battle. Predictably, her action was described as an act of female deceit, cowardice and treachery by our surviving ancient sources.

English Maritime Commerce in the Mediterranean during the Jacobean Period

Lee W. Eysturlid

⚓

In late 1605 the Venetian ambassador to England sat waiting for a decision from the Lords in Council concerning several Englishmen accused of piracy in the Mediterranean. The ambassador, Nicolo Molin, an experienced and insightful man, penned a report home. In it he described how the English had turned a blind-eye to the piracies committed in the Mediterranean due to the lucrative return it provided both businessmen and government. He reflected Venetian doubts concerning English jurisprudence with regard to freedom of the seas in the Eastern Mediterranean by saying, ". . . everything is weighed in the scale of Material interest."[1]

Molin's correspondence embodied the essence, albeit simplified, of what was deemed to be the nature of Anglo-Turkish affairs in the Mediterranean during the Jacobean period (1603–25). In the latter half of Elizabeth's reign, relations between Protestant England and the Islamic Ottoman Empire expanded.[2] Scholarly research points to the Mediterranean grain crisis of the 1560s as providing England with her entry into modern trade relations with powers in that region.[3] Supplying the Italians and Ottomans with Northern European grain soon fueled further English economic interest. The only hindrance was the Spanish endeavor to maximize their military effort by exploiting their geographic location. They found it advantageous to try and seal the Mediterranean's natural bottleneck at Gibraltar in an attempt to curtail English penetration.[4]

The actual development of English and Ottoman relations, both commercially and economically, are best observed during the reign of James I. In a pragmatic sense Anglo-Ottoman relations had floundered despite years of royal support from Elizabeth I. With the coronation of James I in 1603, a new, but nonetheless vital, ambiguity came into being. Despite a stream of anti-Turkish rhetoric from no less a figure then his Majesty the King, trade with the eastern Mediterranean was on the increase. To better understand this dichotomy, several questions must be asked. What were the influences of trade, the Levant Company, piracy, commercial investment, the attitude of James, and the reactions of the Turks in the overall development of the situation? Was the importance of piracy, especially as it affected trade in the area, overemphasized? To facilitate the study a brief overview of events in later Elizabethan times is in order.

The formal entry of England and the Ottoman Empire into a stable economic and political relationship came with William Harborne's mission to the Sublime Porte[5] in 1580, representing private business interests and the Crown. In June of that year he succeeded in getting a favorable grant from the Sultan made up of twenty-two articles of trade which defined "English liberties on the subject." The articles were a success because they allowed the English official access to the Eastern Mediterranean market. The Venetian and French ambassadors, who jealously guarded their traditional economic rights in Istanbul, used their leverage against England at the court of the Grand Vizir (the primary minister to the sultan).[6] The only way to counter this negative influence was for the English to appoint an envoy to guard their interests. Since the Crown did not wish to pay for a formal ambassador, the financing had to come from another source. The problem led to the creation of a merchant monopoly, the Levant Company (sometimes called the Turkey Company), whose representative in Istanbul would also act as a representative of James I.[7] Once again English entrepreneurs had evolved a de facto role in foreign policy which combined mercantile and diplomatic activity.[8]

Harborne, having established the foundation for the venture, was the natural selection to represent the company. As ambassador, Harborne had two jobs, the first to protect English commercial investments and merchants, the second diplomatic. The English, unaware of actual Ottoman interest, hoped to lure the Turks into the fight with the "common foe," Spain. This was a recurring idea throughout the Jacobean period, hoping to pit the Catholics against the Muslims.[9] This use of unorthodox political maneuvering on the part of the English embassy caused numerous problems at the courts of Europe, whose rulers saw any attempt at an alliance with the Turks as traitorous to Christianity. English hopes for a military-diplomatic relationship were overly optimistic because the

Ottomans were over-extended in wars with the Persians and Habsburgs.[10] Since military assistance was not available, as demonstrated by the Ottoman failure to enter the fight in 1588, the English turned their attention to trade.[11]

Once the dominating need for grain subsided in the Mediterranean, the English looked to tie Turkey into their growing export market. At the time England was the newest of Europe's economically developing countries and was always looking for good markets. Ottoman domains represented an excellent potential market for textiles, which constituted 75–90 percent of all English exports.[12] In order to control this trade the merchants involved formed the previously mentioned Levant Company as a joint stock venture, with all buying and trading done as a unit. When the initial charter ended in 1592, the Company reorganized as an individual investment company, although it remained monopolistic in nature. This meant that members could finance their own voyages, but that rent on the monopoly had to be paid as a whole. The renewed charter lasted twelve years, ending around the time of Elizabeth's death in 1603.[13]

The death of Elizabeth in 1603 and the subsequent rise of James to the throne shortly thereafter represented the end of any direct royal interest in the development of diplomatic relations with the Turks.[14] The new king looked upon himself as one of the defenders of Christian Europe and did not feel the necessity to interact with the "infidels" on any level except commercial. In dealing with a delegation from the Levant Company just after his coronation, James stated that he saw no reason to maintain relations with the Turks and that the presence of an ambassador in Istanbul was unimportant.[15] Further proof of James's anti-Turkish feelings came with his statement that if the rest of the Christian monarchs of Europe would raise forces to fight the Ottomans, he would provide 6,000 troops upon request, although he declined the honor of acting first.[16]

What was the economic nature of the new market and how were the Ottomans perceived by the English? During the late 16th and early 17th centuries, the Ottoman Empire appeared to the English as a military behemoth which also held promise as a vast commercial emporium.[17] To merchants the Empire presented a fantastical world, with its collection of unseen Eastern goods and peoples. The stark absolutism of the Sultan also tended to shock Englishmen as well. Yet this did not prohibit them from exploiting a situation in which strategic affairs and tyranny had extinguished the so-called "spirit of enterprise," thereby offering a unique commercial opportunity.[18]

While the Turks were not as commercially naive as some authors have implied, they were handicapped by a narrow economic perspective. From 1566 to 1617 the Ottoman Empire was involved in almost constant warfare and suffered from poor leadership, corruption, numerous enemies, and overextension.[19] These factors, added to an anti-mercantilistic policy that combined favoring foreign merchants with high export taxes, only helped to weaken their existing infrastructure.[20] Worse still, the Turks viewed the English as inferior, making economic competition with them undesirable. This is not to say that certain Pashas (provincial Ottoman governors) were not clever enough to make use of tariffs and local laws to fleece numerous English merchants in the years to come.[21]

At this time the Levant Company also faced a crisis over the renewal of its charter. The main problem was that James frowned on any interaction, political or commercial, with the Turks. Secondary was that the merchants were adamant complainers about high impositions paid to the Crown and the cost of maintaining the ambassador in Istanbul.[22] Parliament was compelled to listen as the company aired its grievances against the home government. They adamantly fought the imposition of what they deemed to be exorbitant tariffs on commodities such as dried currants, which were prized by the English for their use in food and beverages. The debate ran for almost the entire year of 1604 and into 1605, with the powerful members of the Company trying to force the restitution of their rights on favorable grounds. At one point Parliament as a whole became incensed with the petitions, stating that they "showed the unreasonableness of the Turkey Company in petitioning the House of Commons."[23]

Many important economic factors were in the merchants' favor, and, in hindsight, restitution of the charter just seems to have been a matter of time. During the reign of James, the survival of the Company and its trade had become crucial to the development of English exports and power. The Company's political strength was based upon the many influential members who were either close to the court or seated in Parliament. The Governor of the Company, Sir Thomas Smythe, was a close friend of James and a strong business ally.[24] The Crown realized that the existence of strong merchant companies maintaining numerous ships at private cost increased the kingdom's naval resources. There was also economic incentive for His Majesty. As long as the Company continued to increase imports, the revenues derived from impositions would improve the finances of the king.[25] These considerations meant that the Company charter created in 1605 remained similar to the original with only minor exceptions.[26]

A single voyage into the Mediterranean, with possible stops at the Ottoman ports of Istanbul, Alessandretta, Alexandria, Tunis, or Algiers, held the prospect of a 300 percent profit. The potential of such outstanding returns, in spite of insurance costs, attracted numerous wealthy investors in England. The cost of building, outfitting, and victualing a vessel, combined with purchasing a cargo (referred to as lading), could easily be regained from a first voyage. Although the uncertainty of any voyage, due to piracy and weather, increased the risk, venture capital was always to be had and the period of James's reign saw a boom in the Levant trade. Ships captured by pirates were reported with cargos valued in excess of £80,000 or more, meaning even small commercial investors could make a sizable profit.[27] Sir Paul Pindar, a member of the Levant Company, eventually amassed a large enough fortune to become a primary lender to the king and the city of London.[28]

With the boom in trade beginning in 1605, the Levant Company experienced a rapid growth. The introduction of English broadcloth and kerseys, especially lighter fabric known as Spanish cloth, were extremely popular in the Ottoman Empire.[29] This material, less expensive than the Venetian and French product, allowed England to assume the dominant share of the textile market.[30] The commercial importance of a presence in the Mediterranean for the English was crucial at this time, as they were involved in a trade war with the Dutch. To the Crown the increase in exports was essential in the maintenance of royal finances, since impositions on the Company's imports were a steady source of revenue.[31] These two points, the progressive promotion of the English textile industry and the ability of the royal revenue collectors to tax imports, secured the trade's future.

The study of Anglo-Turkish piracy in the Mediterranean reveals a fusion of commercial and foreign policy interests embodied in the development of this special relationship. A long time tradition in the region, the Turks having been successful at it for centuries, piracy reached new heights in the early 1600s. The phenomenon of English piracy, and their mastery of it as a profession, stemmed from the naval war with Spain in the late 1580s. Unable to afford a fleet to combat the Spanish, Elizabeth had turned to officially commissioning privateers. Quite numerous by the end of the century, they operated extensively from the Caribbean to India, leading England to be called a "nation of pirates."[32] Piracy, especially for the English in this period, became inextricably tied to trade in the Mediterranean. As in all commercial ventures, the English showed great originality in their piratical efforts. The commissioned privateer was like an entrepreneur, with private citizens investing their capital in the ship, crew, and voyage, keeping a sense of mercantilistic patriotism about them.

The arrival of James saw a change from the Elizabethan acceptance of investment in privateering. Wishing to earn the title "Rex pacificus," James sought peace with England's enemies and to end the state promotion of privateering. Despite James's actions piracy continued in a similar fashion, but was no longer sanctioned by the government. From the beginning of James's reign, therefore, all investments in pirate ventures had to be done covertly.[33] An example of a typical sponsor was English nobleman Sir Robert Cecil, who took several separate options in English privateers starting in 1601.[34] Contrary to what had been accepted practice by many at the time, Cecil and many of his fellow investors were not members of the Levant Company. Piracy represented an outlet for the numerous individual investors who wished to trade in the area but were excluded due to the company's monopoly. By maintaining covert pirate operations, individuals were able to invest in profitable voyages of their own. Privateers offered the only opportunity for non-company investors, and it readily became a preferred investment alternative. The company soon became the leading voice in appealing for official government efforts to suppress piracy, continually petitioning the king for assistance. Levant Company investors realized that piracy was disruptive to trade, even if it was sponsored by fellow Englishmen.[35]

As the English privateers began operating in the Mediterranean, they quickly entered into a working relationship with Turkish pirates. The English had always been particularly capable seamen, and those that entered the Mediterranean were exemplary. The vessel of choice for the English was the berton, of medium tonnage, with three masts and a deep keel that gave it excellent handling in all types of weather. With a necessary crew of sixty men, it could hold twenty to thirty cannon and had a cargo capacity of 500 butts (term referring to a cask that could hold 63 gallons).[36] The combination of good seamanship and a technically superior vessel allowed the English merchants and pirates to sail even during bad winter weather.[37]

The result of the pirate menace meant that merchant vessels were forced to arm if they were to survive in the Mediterranean. The captains of these ships soon found that a well-armed vessel, once its trading had been accomplished, could easily engage in piracy before returning to England, thereby increasing the profit of the voyage. As merchant ships of all nations came under greater threat, they were forced to increase their armament. This increase in power strengthened the will to risk privateering.[38] By the end of the first decade of the seventeenth century, English bertons, particularly those of the Levant Company, were the only ones strong enough to operate freely in the Mediterranean. This advantage was the result of intense arming and superior seamanship, not to mention funding. Even the Venetians were reduced to carrying their cargo on English ships or to paying pirate warships to escort their merchantmen.

The first English pirates in the Mediterranean were merchantmen who capitalized on their strength to increase profits, but always maintained a commercial mission. To them piracy remained a secondary course of action. What followed very quickly, however, was the evolution of pirates who operated heavily armed and manned vessels with the intention to raid shipping. A great number of reports exist of ships traveling alone or in groups of up to twenty waiting along commercial routes to prey on passing merchant vessels.[39] Many of these ships had mixed crews of Englishmen and Turks, but were always captained by an Englishman. This mixture occurred mostly because it was the only way that English pirates operating out of ports like Algiers could recruit enough sailors. These pirate crews had long since abandoned their religious hostility towards each other for possible profit.[40] Once an Englishman had taken to working with non-Christians, he was said to have "gone Turk." Worse still, even as James attempted to outlaw piracy, the general lack of control in the Ottoman Empire allowed local Pashas, especially in Algiers and Tunis, to cooperate with and support their efforts.[41] Since many of the now outlawed English pirates sought to use Algiers as a base of operations, they also brought with them their technical and navigational skills. An example of one such individual was Captain Ward, who deserted the Royal Navy by seizing a ship from Portsmouth in 1613 and making his way to Algiers. An extremely successful pirate, he gained great notoriety for both his ruthlessness and wealth.[42]

The involvement of Englishmen in piracy necessarily produced two effects. First was the diplomatic problem of explaining to Venetian, French, Spanish, and Ottoman representatives that the government of "Rex pacificus" was not involved directly, and therefore not responsible. An example occurred on November 8, 1613, when the English ambassador was called before the Grand Vizir with demands that England make reparations for damage done to Turkish shipping. The Vizir said that the Sultan was "greatly exasperated against (sic) his nation for a long time on this account."[43] The second effect was the passing of technological improvements to the pirates, especially armaments and seamanship, thereby increasing their abilities. The result was a need for a naval campaign against the pirates. An English failure to move militarily would appear to Europe as self-incrimination. At the same time the lucrative trade to the eastern Mediterranean was too important to be interrupted. King James's ineffectual disclaimers smacked of duplicity to both European and Ottoman observers, who found his distinction between involvement and responsibility insultingly artificial.[44]

The proliferation of piracy aggravated the inconsistency of English policy toward the Turks. The government was constantly under pressure to do something about the dangers of commercial travel in the Mediterranean. As early as 1608 the Levant Company petitioned the king to act against this threat. Due to deficiencies in royal finances at that time, James was unwilling to take action.[45] By 1615 the Levant Company was demanding action, or the trade to the Ottoman Empire would be ruined. They proposed a fleet of six royal vessels with the Company covering operational costs. The so-called "war against the pirates" was hotly debated, but by 1617 had not progressed beyond the discussion stage.[46]

The only formal effort to suppress the pirates during James's reign was mounted in 1619, and mustered under the title the "Algiers Fleet," and listed twenty-five assorted vessels.[47] Sailing in 1620 the task force was readied for a six month voyage at the cost of £20,700. The fleet returned in 1621, having accomplished nothing but aggravating the pirates, who simply fled the areas patrolled.[48] The fleet only managed to seize a few vessels. One reported in November of 1620 was a large, well-armed berton with a crew of two hundred Turks and three English captains. In keeping with standard practice for Europeans sailing with Muslims at the time, the three Englishmen were immediately hung.[49]

Why were the Turks so keen on trade with the English, and what kept them interested after piracy had become epidemic? Why did the Ottoman government tolerate an ambassador whose monarch was openly hostile to the Sultan and supported state enemies? To understand the basis for Ottoman actions we must delve further into historically contemporary affairs.

The Ottoman Empire during the Jacobean period was beginning to suffer from the spiral of decline begun in the previous century. Some of the English observers present in Istanbul realized they were witnessing imperial decline and took time to record their impressions. In 1622 Ambassador Sir Thomas Roe wrote in shocked terms that the murder of Sultan Osman II had "poisoned the state."[50] At the same time, the Empire was also being forced to modernize its army, the key pillar of state, in order to compete with its Persian and European enemies. Throughout the early 1600s the Turks pushed to acquire more munitions and weapons to arm the increasing number of troops they were forced to maintain.[51] Therefore, in order to preserve the military might of the empire, the Turks were forced to turn to suppliers like the English.

The English answered this need as early as 1579 with the delivery of tin, which was necessary in the casting of bronze cannon. It was Harborne's promise in the trade negotiations to assure regular delivery of much needed casting metals that initially convinced the Ottomans to open up to the English.[52] Merchants followed by developing a thriving export in related items, such as iron, lead, copper, arquebuses, muskets, swordblades, brimstone, saltpeter, and gunpowder. In 1605 it was reported that the only good gunpowder in Turkey was imported from England and that munition merchants had established three arms shops in Istanbul.[53] Numerous examples of this trade exist. In 1607 the Sultan sent a cavass (embassy) to London to try and secure a deal guaranteeing a steady supply of powder and arms. After meeting with willing members of the Levant Company, he was scheduled to meet the king.[54] In 1609 the arrival of three munitions laden vessels at Istanbul was reported. The first was a ship carrying 6,000 sequins (standard unit of measure in the seventeenth century) of tallow, a necessary component in making cartridges, which was unloaded directly at the city's arsenal.

The next two ships carried tin, steel, and a number of arquebuses.[55] In 1611 the vessel carrying the new English ambassador also had a cargo of unmounted swordblades, English steel being highly prized by the Turks.[56]

This arms trade with the Ottomans, declared enemy of all Europe, caused particular problems. England was declared the arms supplier of Islam and some countries took direct action.[57] In 1607 the Grand Duke of Tuscany ordered the seizing of three English vessels at the Italian port of Leghorn. The reason that the Duke later gave ambassador Sir Henry Wotton was that they had been carrying ammunition bound for Turkey, and he was merely interdicting the flow.[58] Neither partner looked upon the other as friend but rather a necessary evil. England needed the wealth generated by the Levant trade, while Turkey relied on English munitions.[59]

By the time of his death in 1625, James's policy toward the Ottoman Empire was more sophisticated than it might appear on the surface. The great amount of rhetoric that he had directed against the "enemy of all Christendom" had not hindered English commercial interaction. The shift in trade southward, accentuated by the beginning of the Thirty Years War in 1618, placed greater emphasis on exports to the Mediterranean. Between 1609 and 1619 the export of cloth to the Levant increased from 46 percent to 79 percent of total English textile trade.[60]

The nature of trade in the Mediterranean also went a long way in furthering economic growth in England. Commercial activity between the English and the Turks satisfied the economic theory of the time that goods should be traded for goods of greater value or gold, but not to exchange gold for goods. This belief found strong advocacy in England, which protected its bullion reserves.[61] James also relied on the trade to collect revenue for his personal maintenance. To assist him in this, the exchequer determined that the regulation of duties was the king's prerogative, and that impositions could be placed on any import. In 1608 alone James collected £70,000 in duties from Levant Company imports.[62]

The policy of James I provides a distinct dichotomy between official policy and actual trade relations. By the end of his reign, James, the great Christian monarch, had allowed his country to become increasingly involved in trade with the Eastern Mediterranean. Despite his strong anti-Ottoman rhetoric, James's finances were tied into the revenues English trade from the Levant generated. He probably also realized that at the national level the growth of trade represented increased economic power for England. Monopolies, such as the Turkey Company, assured an outlet for English goods while it provided royal finances with an increasing opportunity for impositions. Although the trade into the Mediterranean meant problems with pirates and foreign policy, the economic significance outweighed the difficulties.

1. Calendar of State Papers, Venetian, 1603–07 (hereafter C.S.P.V.), p. 140.
2. Sir Thomas Shirley, *Discours of the Turk (1606–07)*; and E. Denison, ed., *The Camden Miscellany*, Vol. XVI., pp. 9–12.
3. W. E. Minchinton, ed., *The Growth of Overseas Trade in the Seventeenth and Eighteenth Centuries* (London, 1969), p. 7.
4. Geoffrey Parker, *The Military Revolution* (Cambridge, 1988), see chapter three.
5. The term Sublime Porte derived from the French literal translation for High Gate, meaning the Ottoman court and government.
6. Skilliter, *William Harborne and the Trade with Turkey* (Oxford, 1972), p. 53.
7. Alfred C. Wood, *A History of the Levant Company* (New York, 1964), p. 11.
8. The reason for Company involvement in most of the decisions made in the Mediterranean during this period was financial. They paid for the ambassador, furnished ships to fight pirates, and paid the government imposed impositions.
9. Michael Cook, ed., *A History of the Ottoman Empire to 1730* (Cambridge, 1976), p. 124.
10. Brandon H. Beck, *From the Rising of the Sun* (New York, 1987), p. 311.
11. Skilliter, *Harborne*, p. 178.
12. J. P. Cooper, ed., *The New Cambridge Modern History*, Vol. IV: *The Decline of Spain and the Thirty Years War, 1609–48/59* (Cambridge, 1970), p. 94; and Derek Hirst, *Authority and Conflict: England, 1603–58* (Cambridge, 1989), p. 6.
13. Wood, *A History of the Levant Company*, p. 22.
14. Skilliter, *Harborne*, p. 178.
15. C.S.P.V., 1603–07, p. 184.
16. C.S.P.V., 1603–07, p. 265, p. 362. James repeatedly made this statement for the benefit of anyone listening, in these cases the Venetian ambassador.
17. Shirley, *Discours of the Turks (1606–1607)*, p. 15.
18. Fynes Moryson, *An Itinerary, containing his ten years travell through the twelve dominions of Germany, Bohmerland, Switzerland, Netherland, Denmarke, Poland, Italy, Turkey, France, England, Scotland, Ireland* (London, 1617; reprint Glasgow, 1907). Moryson felt that The Ottoman's enthusiasm for near continual warfare had allowed the economy to become based on plunder and had ruined the economic spirit of the upper-classes.
19. Shirley, *Discours*, p. 5–8.
20. Cooper, ed., *Decline*, p. 61. All commerce within the Empire was handled by Greeks or Jews with the Turkish upper-classes remaining aloof from any such interactions.
21. Wood, *Levant*, p. 17.

22. Calendar of State Papers, Domestic, (hereafter Cal. S.P.D.), 1603–10, Vol. VIII, p. 218.

23. Cal. S.P.D., 1603–10, vol. 8, p. 311.

24. Robert Ashton, *The City and the Court, 1603–43* (Cambridge, 1979), p. 16.

25. Hirst, *Authority*, p. 4.

26. Ashton, *City and the Court*, p. 90.

27. C.S.P.V., 1603–07, p. 100, p. 163; and C.S.P.V. 1610–13, p. 312. Although this sum was probably an exaggeration, it represented a view of the wealth the Mediterranean trade could generate.

28. Wood, *Levant*, p. 42; and Shirley, *Discours*, p. 10.

29. Alberto Tenenti, *Piracy and the Decline of Venice*, p. 60.

30. Bernard Lewis, *The Muslim Discovery of Europe* (New York, 1982), p. 194. Lewis claims that the superior quality and price of English cloth received numerous mention by Muslim writers on the subject.

31. Cal. S.P.D., 1603–10, vol. 8, p. 51 and p. 168.

32. C.S.P.V., 1603–07, p. 312.

33. C.S.P.V., 1607–10, p. 43.

34. Kenneth R. Andrews, "Sir Robert Cecil and Mediterranean Plunder," *English Historical Review* 343 (87): p. 513.

35. C.S.P.V., 1603–1607, p. 42 and p. 89; C.S.P.V., 1607–10, p. 415; and Cal. S.P.D., 1603–1610, vol. 8, p. 487, vol. 10, p. 308.

36. Tenenti, *Piracy*, p. 64.

37. Cal. S.P.D., 1603–1610, vol. 8, p. 109; Cooper, ed., *Decline*, p. 232; and C.S.P.V., 1603–07, p. 109.

38. Kenneth R. Andrews, *Trade, Plunder, and Settlement* (Cambridge, 1984), p. 97.

39. Cal. S.P.D., 1611–18, vol. 9, p. 55.

40. C.S.P.V., 1603–07, p. 94, p. 163; C.S.P.V., 1607–1610, p. 470; and C.S.P.V., 1610–13, p. 100; C.S.P.V., 1619–21, p. 486.

41. Shirley, *Discours*, p. 8. According to Shirley: "Argier (Algiers) & Tunis obey him noe further then they please . . ." (This refers to the Sultan's inability to enforce his will on the Pashas).

42. C.S.P.V., 1603–1607, p. 94; and Logan P. Smith, *The Life and Times of Sir Henry Wotton*, Vol. I., p. 415.

43. C.S.P.V., 1613–15, p. 63.

44. Cal. S.P.D., 1603–10, vol. 8, pp. 41, 168 and 470.

45. *Ibid.*, p. 469.

46. C.S.P.V., 1615–17, p. 496 and 503; and Cal. S.P.D., vol. 9, p. 177 and 515.

47. Cal. S.P.D., 1619–23, Vol. 10, p. 11.

48. *Ibid.*, p. 185; C.S.P.V., 1619–21, p. 486; and C.S.P.V., 1621–23, p. 69.

49. C.S.P.V., 1619–21, p. 486.

50. S. Richardson, ed., *The Negotiations of Sir Thomas Roe in his Embassy to the Ottoman Porte from the Year 1621 to 1628 Inclusive* (London, 1748), p. 126.

51. J. V. Parry, ed., *War, Technology, and Society in the Middle East* (Oxford, 1975), p. 200. The aquisition of both arquebuses and muskets were particularly important for use against the modernized armies of the Austrian Habsburgs.

52. Stanford J. Shaw, *History of the Ottoman Empire and Modern Turkey* (Cambridge, 1977), Vol. I, p. 182.

53. Shirley, *Discours of the Turks (1606–7)*, p. 9.
54. C.S.P.V., 1607–10, p. 22.
55. *Ibid.*, p. 239 and p. 466.
56. C.S.P.V., 1610–13, p. 289.
57. Shirley, *Discours of the Turks (1606–7)*, p. 9. Shirley refers to the arms trade which, "bringeth mutche sclaunder to our nation & religion, whyche is powder & other munition for warre & shyppinge, broughte by the Englishe ingreate abundans thither, & by noe other nation els."
58. Logan P. Smith, *The Life and Times of Sir Henry Wotton*, Vol. I, p. 408; and Lewis, *The Muslim Discovery of Europe*, p. 193.
59. C.S.P.V., 1610–13, p. 330.
60. W. E. Minchinton, ed., *The Growth of Overseas Trade in the Seventeenth and Eighteenth Centuries*, p. 67.
61. Wood, *A History of the Levant Company*, p. 43; and Cal. S.P.D., Vol. 11, p. 432. In 1624 a paper was circulated titled, "A Discourse of Trade and Shipping in the Levant," that called for greater protection of trade and to make England a strong exporter.
62. Hirst, *Authority and Conflict, England 1603–58*, p. 109.

New England in Anglo-French Naval Operations in the Caribbean, 1689–1763

Christian Buchet

⚓

Although a great many studies have dealt with the Caribbean area, historians have neglected the military history of the region for a long time. The Caribbean was a site of many military and naval events in the warfare among European powers. Indeed, during the period considered in this essay—that is the four wars which took place between 1689 and 1763—Europeans sent no fewer than seventy-four military expeditions to this area.

During most of this period, England failed to seize the main Spanish and French settlements in America. Despite England's repeated attempts, the financial asphyxia of the French Navy and the shortage in the number of the Spanish Navy's ships, compared with the vast extent of the possessions Spain needed to protect, England did not manage, during thirty-eight years of hostilities spread over four wars, to get hold of the main sites forming the Franco-hispanic defence system of the Caribbean.

Suddenly, however, this state of affairs changed at the end of the Seven-Years War. In the space of four years, 1759 to 1762, Britain captured the key places: Guadalupe, Martinique, and Havana. My doctoral thesis at the Sorbonne[1] explored specific problems that the squadrons met in their "long term," or geo-strategic, expeditions. This approach led me to examine the characteristics of the warships, including their sanitary conditions and the associated problems of logistics.

In this short summary, it would require too much space to relate all the different results that I reached; however, I would like to avoid a simple narrative and to show in a more dynamic perspective, an analysis of the role performed by the New England colonies and the way in which their contribution explains the success the British finally achieved.

To do so, one must first see the difficulties with which all the British expeditions to the Caribbean had to contend. Then we can examine how England managed to surmount them in the light of the available technological system, utilizing the North American colonies as advanced bases.

From the very first naval expeditions to the West Indies, the admiralties in the different countries saw that the essential factor determining the success or the failure of any expedition was, without doubt, the uncertain health conditions in the region. One can not understand the importance of this issue for long distance expeditions without first considering the health problems resulting from the long Atlantic Ocean crossing to reach the West Indian islands.

Taking into account the fact that when a large fleet was sailing together, all the ships were obliged to regulate their speed to that of the slowest vessel; it required two to two and a half months to make the ocean crossing to the West Indies. Besides taking time, this long voyage affected the health of the men in a substantial manner. The direct effects of these crossings are reflected in the mortality rate of the squadrons reaching the Caribbean. In the individual ships, these ranged, in the case of one expedition, from 0.48 percent[2] to 17.2 percent[3] and, in another case, from 5.39 percent[4] to more than 32 percent.[5] There were also indirect effects. The length of the journeys, combined with the particularly unhealthy living conditions on board ships during these expeditions, diminished the men's resistance to endemic illnesses awaiting them in the tropics.

The principal cause of death seems to be scurvy, caused by the lack of vitamin C. The development of scurvy in the British fleets derived from the length of time that it took an expedition to reach its first base in the West Indies, where it could take on fresh supplies. In this respect, I concluded that there is a direct relationship between manifestations of scurvy and ocean crossings that took longer than seventy-five days. When seamen were on board ship for that amount of time without fresh supplies, they reached a state of immune weakness. At the same time, during those long voyages, they were exposed to "fevers," the so called "putrid" or typhoid fever and "malignant pestilential" fever, known today as typhus.

The conditions for typhus were exacerbated by several factors. During the first years of the War of the Spanish Succession,[6] for example, the British supplied their fleets with salted food that had been particularly poorly prepared. Poorly prepared food was not the only factor which explains the incubation of typhus and typhoid aboard the ships of the seventeenth and eighteenth centuries; others included the foul water, the permanent humidity on board, the *"vert-de-gris,"* the filthiness, and the vermin which infested the worn clothing of seamen. To these general conditions, one must add the great crowding of men on board ship for these expeditions. In most cases, these expeditions carried fighting troops both to serve in the planned expedition and to reinforce the garrisons in the islands. This double duty resulted in creating over-crowded conditions that favored contamination. If one is to believe contemporaries, the high death-rate which hit Hughes's expeditionary squadron on its arrival at Barbados in 1759 could not be explained by any other factor.[7]

English squadrons were, generally speaking, much more affected by mortality and sickness at the end of their ocean crossing than the French and Spanish expeditions.[8] Thus, these factors became a great burden on the offensive power of the British squadrons, and these factors must have played a part in protecting French and Spanish possessions in the Caribbean.

In an attempt to understand this phenomenon, we can point out the "press-gang" system. The English sailors who were rounded-up by the press-gangs were, we must remember, crammed on prison-ships for an average of two months before being assigned to a vessel. Hence, with seamen in a more weakened condition, there was a more rapid outbreak of scurvy in the British squadrons.

Another explanatory factor—which up to now does not seem to have been brought to light—probably lies in the different choice of routes taken by the French and the English squadrons. All the French expeditions to the Caribbean set out to cross the Atlantic at a point halfway between the Azores and Madeira, while nearly all the British expeditions set out on a more southerly course, in order to put in at Madeira.[9] In contrast to the French navy which gave wine to its crew, the Royal Navy took on board beer, at first. However, beer did not keep for more than three weeks at sea; hence, the English needed to stop at Madeira on the way to take on board wine.[10]

Owing to this detour and to the time spent at Madeira, the English spent comparatively more time on board ship than the French squadrons did on their voyages to the West Indies. In addition, the English had a less favorable position for sailing on the prevailing winds from English coasts. All these factors explain the longer duration for the British crossing[11] and its inauspicious consequences for the health of English seamen.

In the best circumstances, English seamen arrived in a debilitated state and, thus, were prone to the endemic illnesses which threatened them in the West Indies. Moreover, the main French and Spanish strategic bases were surrounded by marshes, the sort of land particularly unsuitable "for the good preservation of men." Often, English operations against these bases were carried out during the rainy season. The English squadrons normally set out for the Caribbean at the beginning of spring. The timing of the departure, it seems, was based on financial reasons, as well as on avoiding storms in the Channel. This, however, had its consequences in terms of the timing of the expedition's arrival. In the West Indies, the rainy season started in July. By departing in the Spring, the length of the crossing often prevented the English expeditions from accomplishing their mission before the rainy season. Hence, the English forces faced appalling health conditions, particularly when the campaigns dragged on. Death rates of more than 50 percent were not unusual. In 1695, for example, illnesses took away 61 percent of the expeditionary force that landed under Admiral Wilmot's command during a venture against Santo Domingo.[12]

In an attempt to limit the effect of epidemics and climate, the Admiralty decided, first, to release the squadrons systematically, sailing to relay stations so that the men could recover before as well as after the operations and, second, to carry out offensive operations in the shortest possible time. For example, Admiral Vernon considered that they should not exceed six weeks in length.[13]

However, in the event, these conditions proved for a long time to be irreconcilable. A succession of health disasters continued to strike the English fleet. In fact, the time that British forces spent at their Caribbean relay-stations, while delaying the start of the operations, often annulled the element of surprise that was necessary for effective operations to be carried out quickly. The presence of a squadron in the region was not an easy thing to hide, and the delay often gave time for some brigantine to give the alarm to the targeted spot.

Moreover—in another paradox—the French and Spanish islands, as well as the Spanish possessions of *"Terra Firma,"* saw a marked increase in their population over the years. As the years passed, it became necessary to increase considerably the number of the troops needed to seize a place and, above all, to keep it. Thus, it took much longer to arm the troops for an expedition, which again reduced the advantage of surprise. These factors added to the delays, forcing the British to arrive in the Caribbean at the rainy season and, thus, causing an increased death-rate.

This situation occurred as early as the War of the League of Augsburg. The fact that many expeditions took place during the unhealthy season was mainly due to the inability of the English to man the expeditions on an early schedule, as the required numbers had constantly to be increased. Often, they left European waters after more than a three-month delay.[14]

The increased number of fighting men, vital to the prompt success of operations, made the already poor sanitary conditions of the troops worse and added to the difficulties faced in manning the expeditions on time.

Beyond these factors, the employment of land forces in the naval expeditions often resulted in separate commands for the sea and for the land forces. This, too, often proved to be prejudicial to the speed and strategy of the campaigns. Although she continued to employ the same technological system, England eventually succeeded in surmounting the problems I have mentioned, and, in doing so, she won military victory in the latter part of the Seven Years War. She was able to do this for two reasons: first, England gradually formed a more geostrategical, overall view; second, she gave her navy a better structural organization.

England progressively developed inter-continental management for this type of overseas expedition. Indeed, it is because she had successfully experimented with the notion of relay-stations, along with the creation of advanced bases, that England succeeded in conquering the main French and Spanish strong-holds in the Caribbean. In fact, as far as their levying of troops and logistics support were concerned, the British had gradually made more and more recourse to their North American colonies.

This evolution began in 1740 with the more than 3600 men[15] who came from America to reinforce the troops under Admiral Vernon's command. The Duke of Newcastle had personally recommended that the Americans in the British army should be treated with all possible goodwill, hoping to encourage them to take part in future expeditions and even to settle on the land they hoped to conquer.[16] In the same way, an important part of the food supplies and equipment necessary for these expeditions came from the North American colonies. Recognizing this, Vernon did not hesitate to exempt the ships of these colonies from impressment, encouraging them to continue supplying these goods.[17]

Because of its proximity to the West Indies and the permanent relationship maintained with the Caribbean relay-stations, North America became a real advanced base during the Seven Years' War, indispensable to the success of a geo-strategic expedition. As the contributions from New England increased, in terms of men as well as in rations, many of the health problems were reduced.

The 14,000 soldiers from North America[18] were far less tired by their journey than the men coming from Europe. Moreover, by dispatching ships from various ports in North America and at the same time, it reduced the difficulties the Navy faced in England to supply men, equipment, and arms. For example, North American support allowed the expeditions commanded by Moore in 1759 and Rodney in 1761 to fulfill their mission before the start of the rainy season.

The fact that the food supplied came from New England also proved beneficial for the men's health. The proximity of the North American continent, joined to the more regular and, above all, more frequent timing of the convoys, allowed a diet of fresher food. In the Admiralty's opinion, the supply-boats from North America ran fewer risks of being attacked than the ones coming from England.[19]

The study of supplying naval forces sent to the West Indies is an interesting aspect. Nine chapters of my thesis is dedicated to that important question. An analysis of the Victualling Office's correspondence, in the ADM 110 series at the Public Records Office, shows, indeed, that by using North America, England could not only fulfill, but could supply even better the needs of the constantly increasing forces that she sent to this theatre of operations. Using this source of supply began merely in an empirical way, but resulted in becoming an established system of supply.

Up to time of the War of the Spanish Succession, when campaigns were strictly limited in length by the maximum quantity of rations that an expedition could carry, that is approximately eight months, the English Admiralty was wedded to a concept of food-supply that was not all geo-strategic in nature.[20] Admiral Wheeler, however, attempted to break down this narrow view. After he had been put in command of a squadron in 1693, he sent a long report to the Admiralty, advocating that the majority of rations be supplied by the North American colonies. Wheeler saw at least four advantages to this. First, it meant a better means to fulfill the needs of the squadron, since in less than two months, the ships coming from Boston or New York would have brought the required supplies. Second, it offered a lower cost-price, as the food was cheaper in New England than at home in England. Third, the duration of the expedition might be lengthened. And, fourth, the possibility of further developing the infrastructure of England's West Indian bases was enhanced. By reducing the considerable bulk of food supplies expeditions needed to carry, they would be able to take on board the necessary equipment for harbor installation.[21]

Attractive as these ideas were, Wheeler's propositions did not alter the prevailing opinion on logistics organization. The Admiral was therefore obliged to take on board all the necessary food supplies in England, thus limiting his campaign to a period of less than eight months.[22]

From the time of the War of the Spanish Succession, England was forced into keeping a permanent naval presence in the West Indies, not only to protect its growing commerce but also to intercept the fleets carrying the money which supplied its enemies with the means necessary to carry on the war. In order to economize as much as possible on the number of units, it was necessary to lengthen the periods of each campaign. Thus, the Victualling Office had to get out of its passive rut and to provide the uninterrupted supply that this decision implied.

In 1702, the Victualing Office established two stations in the West Indies: one in Jamaica and another in Barbados.[23] At first, it organized a liaison system to supply these two relay-stations from England, but this proved to be unsatisfactory. The difficulty in sending the goods on scheduled times and the fact that the salted provisions seem to have been of particularly poor quality, explain the serious problems in "bridging the gap." The poor preservation of food became all the more important in this context because of the length of time, generally six months, between the relay shifts.

In the War of 1739–48, the Victualing Office achieved much more positive results. The food supply was perfectly adequate in this war, despite the increased size in the naval force assigned to Jamaica. For most of the time, the number of men in the 1739–48 war was 7,000, but reached a peak of 20,000, and never went below 3,940. In contrast, during the War of the Spanish Succession, there had been a maximum of 4,000 and an average of 2,000 men. In the period

1739–48, there were only three actual cases of shortage.[24] At the end of 1744, the rations sent from England were so plentiful that the agents, Mr. Gray and Mr. Maynard, decided to sell part of them.[25]

The positive situation that developed came from the fact that the supply convoys were now regular and frequent, arriving every four months. This contrasted starkly with the irregularity of the convoys during the preceding war and the fact that they had taken about six months of food supply with them. The greater frequency in food supplies was not merely due to the increasing number of men, but mainly to the intention constantly shown by the commissioners of the Victualing Office to avoid losses resulting from the poor quality of food.[26] During the entire war, the Victualing Office gave the task of supplying food for the naval force attached to Barbados to a private supplier under contract.[27] Set up as early as September 1705,[28] the success of this system in Barbados appeared so obvious to the Victualing Office, both for its efficiency and its lower cost, that the Commissioners advised the Lords of the Admiralty, at the end of the war, to adopt the same system in Jamaica. The commissioners estimated the savings for the Crown at more than 14 percent.[29]

Consequently, during the entire Seven Years' War, the two naval stations in the Caribbean were supplied by private firms put out to tender.[30] The economic development of New England and the constant pressure that the commissioners of the Victualling Office put on the selected contractors through competition were the two determining factors in achieving a successful system. During the Seven Years' War, unlike the practice in the wars that had preceded it, the food sent to the Caribbean came from the North American colonies. Most of the contractors were important North American merchants. The result was advantageous. Less time was wasted on transport. Costs were lower. American goods were cheaper when compared to English ones. Freight costs were lower, and, additionally, it was easier to make more frequent delivery of consignments. During the Spanish War of Succession, supplies were delivered every six months. During the 1739–48 war, it was every four months, and, thereafter, every four to six weeks.[31]

Taking advantage of the competition between the various firms, the commissioners of the Victualling Office managed to establish conditions which were more and more advantageous for the Navy. These advantages included a clause forcing contractors to guarantee the good state of the food supplies, up to four months after their delivery.³² The result of this process meant that the more and more numerous fleets that sailed to the Caribbean were better supplied and at a cheaper cost.

There was a similar evolution in the logistics of naval equipment. From the Navy's incapacity of supplying a few units during the War of the League of Augsburg, the English succeeded in satisfactorily supplying powerful squadrons. During the first war in this period, the Navy Board did not think that it was necessary to watch closely the logistics of the units, because the squadrons were supposed to spend only a short time in a theater of operations. After serious shortages resulted, one would have been justified in thinking that the Navy Board would have installed a regular system of supplies for naval equipment, particularly after a permanent naval presence was established in the West Indies during the War of the Spanish Succession. Nothing of the sort. Despite the fact that the Victualling Office had started to organize a system for the West Indies, even though it was unevenly timed at this point, the Navy Board was content to send the necessary equipment, almost exclusively, with the squadrons.³³

This attitude reflected the Navy Board's persistently inaccurate appreciation of the needs of their naval forces in the Caribbean. The Navy Board did not realize that there was a need to over-supply because of the climatic conditions peculiar to that region.

During the entire War of the League of Augsburg, the Navy Board prosaically relied on merchant ships to supply equipment when the material brought by the squadrons was exhausted.³⁴ As the sailings of merchant ships were too irregular, this expedient proved to be no more successful during the following war.³⁵ The shortage of naval materials was even more acute during the War of the Spanish Succession. The longer duration in the periods of deployment for expeditions amplified the situation even more. Indeed, the shortage of materials was such that it often prevented many warships from accomplishing their assigned mission to protect merchant ships operating in the Caribbean. This, in itself, dissuaded ship owners from sending their vessels to the region. In that period, merchants calculated that nearly half the unescorted ships would be seized by the enemy.³⁶

To meet these difficulties at the beginning of the 1739–48 War, the Navy Board began to employ a convoy system to supply Jamaica and Barbados with naval equipment. The method they adopted was exactly the same one that the Victualling Office had used since the beginning of the War of the Spanish Succession. They used their own agents, who were on the spot and informed of the squadrons' needs. The Navy Board assembled the required materials at Deptford, hired the necessary ships to take them to the islands, and asked the Lords of the Admiralty for escort ships.[37] However, there was a short-fall in fulfilling the requirements of the squadrons, due to the lack of coordination between the Navy Board and the Lords of the Admiralty in the preparation of convoys[38] as well as in the frequently deplorable quality of the materials dispatched.[39] Thus, these factors often paralyzed the Navy's attempts to improve the accomplishment of their mission.[40]

In fact, it was only from the period of the Seven Years' War onwards that logistics were appropriately secured. This positive evolution seems to derive, on one hand, from the emphasis on the number of convoys[41] and their following a perfectly stipulated plan, clearly coordinated between the Lords of the Admiralty and the Commissioners of the Navy Board.[42] Simultaneously, the Navy Board also engaged a supplier from New England, called Hennicker, who was already in charge of providing North American masts for the English ships.[43] This, once again, pointed out the Admiralty's perspicacity during the Seven Years' War in dealing with ships' needs in the West Indies. To guarantee logistical supply, the Admiralty diversified its sources, both at home and in New England. Supplying material to West Indian bases from these two poles is the circumstance which provided a suitable supply to the squadron, despite the fact that risks were always at hand. Nothing better could exemplify the importance of North America's role regarding the consistent shipments to the Caribbean area than to note that from 1761, a substantial squadron's outfitting was made directly from that region.

The intercontinental management of these expeditions resulted also in modifying the organization of command. The freedom of action of the squadron commanders was limited by the Admiralty. Before 1759, the squadron commanders even had the possibility of choosing their objective. Moore, Rodney, and Pocock, in the expeditions they led respectively in 1759, 1761 and 1762, were given strict and detailed plans of campaign. At the same time, the duties and responsibilities incumbent on the army and the navy in joint campaigns were also clearly defined. The treatises of Thomas Molyneux, *Conjunct Expeditions*, (London, 1759), and of John Mac Intire, *A Military Treatise...*, (London, 1763), witness the developments in that direction.

Thus, the new centralized organization incorporated concepts of integrated command and reconciled the dual authority of both army and navy. The numerous disagreements between the expeditionary commanders, which had often had a disastrous effect on the issue of the earlier campaigns, now became the exception.

France had evicted the Dutch from the Caribbean in the 1670s because Holland did not have a base sufficiently equipped in men and armament.[44] In contrast to that earlier problem, England perfected a system of relay-stations and advanced bases, and, at the same time, greatly improved her naval administration, so that by the end of the Seven Years' War, she had been able to conquer the main strategic points of the Spanish and French defence system in the Caribbean.

A contrario, perhaps the increasing number of enlisted troops from the thirteen North American colonies and the heavy losses they suffered may, ironically, have helped promote the American desire for independence. Who knows?

1. University of Paris-Sorbonne, 1989; later published as Christian Buchet, *La Lutte pour l'espace caraibe et la façade atlantique de L'Amérique Centrale et du Sud entre 1672 et 1763*, (Paris: Librairie de L'Inde Editeur, 1991).
2. The French squadron was under Ducasse's command in 1702. (Archives Nationales, Colonies C9A6: Ducasse to the Minister, 17/08/1702; Archives Nationales, Marine G 1–37, 13).
3. The squadron was under Kerusoret's command in 1758. (Archives Nationales, Marine B4-81, f. 58: journal of navigation.)
4. The squadron was under Ogle's command in 1740. (D. G. Crewe, *British Naval Administration in the West Indies 1739–1748*, PhD thesis, University of Liverpool, 1978, p. 96).
5. The squadron was under Wilmot's command in 1695. (*Calendar of State Papers, Am. and W.I. (1693–1696)* 1983).
6. C.S.P., Domestic Series (2 June 1703–April 1704), p. 36 and 204.
7. T. Mante, *The History of the Late War in North America* —, (London: Strahan, 1772), p. 165.
8. Christian Buchet, "Santé et expéditions géo-stratégiques," Colloque International. *Marine et Technique au XIXe siècle*, (Paris: Service Historique de la Marine, 1987).
9. Study in process from the Public Record Office series ADM 50 to 54 and the French Archives Nationales series 4-jj.
10. Most of the consignment notes for these supplies to the different squadrons are preserved in the series ADM 110 at the Public Records Office, Kew.
11. It took the English squadrons an average of ten days more to reach the West Indies. Five to six days putting in at various ports to which must be added a navigational delay of 4 days compared with that of the French squadrons.

12. *C.S.P., Am. and W.I. (1693–1696)*, 1983; 1946; 2026; 2028.

13. Vernon to the Duke of Newcastle, 23 Jan. 1740, quoted by Herbert W. Richmond, *The Navy in the War of 1739–1748*, (Cambridge: Cambridge University Press, 1920), volume 1, p. 45.

14. This is what happened, for example, to the squadrons commanded by Wheeler, Wilmot, Ogle, Pocock, respectively in 1692, 1695, 1740 and 1762.

15. Public Record Office: C.O. 318, without folio: "Forces raised in North-America for the Cathcart's expedition (1739–1741)."

16. Brian Ranft, ed., *The Vernon Papers*, (London: Navy Records Society, 1958), doc. 176.

17. *The Vernon Papers*, p. 169.

18. P.R.O., CO 5/6 (1), fo. 530.: Summary report of troops sent from North America to the West Indies and P.R.O., ADM 1/307, fo. 318: Legge to Douglas, 02/06/1764.

19. P.R.O., ADM 110/19, pp. 46–48, 94, 496: The Victualling Office to the Admiralty.

20. See for example: *C.S.P., Am. and W.I. (1689–1692)* 968 and 1037; *C.S.P., Am. and W.I. (1693–1696)*, 167: The Victuallers of the Navy to W. Blathwayt, 04/03/1693.

21. *C.S.P., Domestic Series (Nov. 1691–Dec. 1692)*, pp. 346–352 and 447–448.

22. *C.S.P., Am. and W.I. (1693–1696)*, 167.

23. Charles Thomas was the Victualing Office's agent in Barbados. In Jamaica, it was successively: Ph. Rogers, A. Wilson helped by H. Gaine, S. Younghusband, J. Gyde, and M. Silvester. (P.R.O., ADM 110/2, p. 37; ADM 110/3, pp. 119 and 137; ADM 110/5, pp. 48 and 386.)

24. The first of these faults is pointed out by Vice-Admiral Davers in April 1745. He complains that an important quantity of the food supplies brought with him from England did not keep. P.R.O., ADM 1/233, fo. 652. A shortage of bread is noted by Davers in March 1746. P.R.O., ADM 1/233, fo. 745. The third and last shortage occurring during the period was pointed out by Dent in the spring of 1747. P.R.O., ADM 1/1697. The factors leading to these three specific shortages have been analyzed in my thesis.

25. P.R.O., ADM 110/14, p. 141: The Victualing Office to the Admiralty, 25/01/1745.

26. See for example: P.R.O., ADM 110/13, pp. 27, 72, 91, 387, 472; P.R.O., ADM 2/61, p. 55; ADM 2/62, p. 56.

27. Up to the years 1744–1745, this contractor was Henri Lascelles, an important merchant in London; (P.R.O., ADM 2/61, pp. 55 and 486). He was succeeded by Mason and Simpson, (ADM 110/13, pp. 138 and 473–474; ADM 110/14, p. 543), who renewed their contract on 8 February 1747 (ADM 2/70, pp. 290–291 and ADM 110/15, p. 130).

28. On 24 September 1705, Collins, an important North American trader, got the sole contract for supplying Her Majesty's ships in Barbados and the Windward Islands. The contract was to remain valid until 1740, at which date it was replaced by another concluded with Thomas Pindar, on the basis of fourteen pence for a man's daily ration. (P.R.O., ADM 110/3, p. 11; ADM 110/5, p. 155.)

29. P.R.O., ADM 110/15, pp. 216–217: The Victualling Office to the Admiralty, 08/01/1748.

30. In Jamaica, for thirteen years, from 1748 to 1761 (ADM 110/20, p. 207), following the contract signed on 29 June 1748 (ADM 110/18, p. 127.) and revised on 6 June 1755, Auguste Boyd was in charge of supplying the war ships (ADM 110/19, p. 93). From 1761 to the end of the war, he was succeeded by two important North American traders associated with this job, Nesbitt and Franks (ADM 110/20, p. 429). In Barbados and the Windward Islands, the suppliers in charge were successively: J. Biggin, from 13 August 1756 to 1 May 1758 (ADM 110/18, p. 493; ADM 110/19, p. 401); S. Fouchet, from 1 May 1758 to 1761 (ADM 110/20, pp. 92 and 411); and J. Biggin again from 1761 to the end of the war (ADM 110/20, pp. 411, 491 and 513).

31. P.R.O., ADM 110/19, pp. 41, 94 and 496.

32. P.R.O., ADM 110/15, p. 130: The Victualling Office to the Admiralty, 11/09/1747. See also, ADM 110/19, p. 401; ADM/20, pp. 92 and 104.

33. See for example, *C.S.P., Domestic Series (1702–1703)*, p. 545: Lord High Admiral to Benbow, 19/01/1703; *C.S.P., Am. and W.I. (2 Dec. 1702–1703)*, 737: Walker's Journal, p. 450.

34. *C.S.P., Am. and W.I. (1689–1692)*, 2110. *C.S.P., Am. and W.I. (1696–1697)*, 101 and 646. *C.S.P., Am. and W.I. (1697–1698)*, 427.

35. There were many reasons for this: the delaying of convoys, the embargoes when enemy squadrons were sailing off the British coasts, the climatic hazards such as those that for many months kept in British ports the ships destined for the Windward Islands; and lastly, the fear of the ship owners of having part of their crew pressed into service in the West Indies in order to complete the Complement of the kings ships. (*C.S.P., Am. and W.I. (1693–1696)*, 1807. *C.S.P., Am. and W.I. (1696–1697)*, 101, 1089, and 1318. *C.S.P., Am. and W.I. (1697–1698)*, 777. *C.S.P., Am. and W.I. (July 1711—June 1712)*, 267.)

36. *C.S.P., Am. and W.I. (1710–1711)*, 824: Hamilton to Dartmouth, 26/04/1710.

37. P.R.O., ADM 106/908: The Navy Board to the Deptford's officer, 17/08/1739.

38. Crewe, *British Naval Administration*

39. See for example: P.R.O.: ADM 1/232: Vernon to the Navy Board, 31/01/1740.

40. See for example: P.R.O.: ADM 1/1697: Dent to the Admiralty, 15/07/1747; ADM 1/232: Vernon to the Admiralty, 19/07/1747.

41. There were no less than 51 vessels specially chartered by the Navy Board to transport the supplies needed by the squadrons operating in the Caribbean Sea: 23 for Jamaica, 25 for Antigua, the last 3 being destined for Antigua as well as Jamaica. Facts established from the registers 2188, 2189, 2190, 2191, 2192, and 2194 of the ADM 106 series.

42. A new distribution of responsibilities between the Lords of the Admiralty and the Commissioners of the Navy Board concerning escort vessels proved to be most satisfactory (study in process).

43. P.R.O., ADM 106/2190, fo. 111.

44. See chapter II of Buchet, *La Lutte*.

British Naval Response to Unorthodox Warfare in the Eastern Caribbean, 1795-96

H. J. K. Jenkins

⚓

It is not surprising that the Caribbean of the late eighteenth century, with slavery as a major institution, became the scene of notable collision between French Revolutionary ideology and a number of established interests in the West Indies. The resulting conflict took various forms in various areas and years, but this paper is chiefly concerned with the question of Guadeloupe during the earlier part of Victor Hugues's time of power in that French island-colony. Earning himself the sobriquet of "the Colonial Robespierre," Hugues fashioned Guadeloupe into a novel entity which the British viewed as very daunting.[1]

With particular reference to operations of *circa* 1795, it can be fairly said that British naval forces found themselves waging warfare under perplexing and unfamiliar circumstances. Indeed, the sheer novelty of the Caribbean situation seemed to invalidate many longstanding assumptions regarding the West Indies, a part of the world which loomed large in the economic calculations of the Atlantic community in the late eighteenth century. Naval history has long since accepted that fleet actions and the like form only part of its province; with that in mind, it should be pointed out that the Royal Navy's response to Hugues involved an interesting example of seapower in conflict with an opponent whose great strength lay in the ideological sphere. Equally, it should be mentioned that the operations dealt with in this paper throw light on the complicated interaction between the interests of Britain, France, and the United States in the period. If the French were able to play an ideological card, the Americans had a commercial one of remarkable value in their hand. Thus, to some extent, this paper is a consideration of the interplay between naval, ideological, and commercial strengths.

Warfare was no stranger in the West Indies, and neither was irregularity of procedure, but the hostilities witnessed *circa* 1795 contained new features which caused great difficulties for the British naval presence. In the eastern Caribbean, including Guadeloupean waters, this meant in essence the Royal Navy's Leeward Islands Command. By the formal onset of the French Revolutionary Wars, indeed, the Leeward Islands Command had already experienced serious problems stemming from the impact of the new ideology. A paper by the present writer, dealing with the consequences of French colonial disorder in the eastern Caribbean from so early as 1790, was included in the Naval History Symposium held at Annapolis in 1987.[2] French colonial disorder continued into the opening part of the French Revolutionary Wars and contributed to the process whereby the British overran much of the theater, a process which included the capture of Guadeloupe itself in mid-1794.

Shortly thereafter, though, a relatively small expedition from France made its appearance. Among its personnel was Victor Hugues who, against the run of the play, proceeded to recapture Guadeloupe and establish a regime which swiftly turned it into what one senior French officer termed a "colonie guerrière," i.e. a warrior colony.[3] By the first days of 1795, Hugues had eliminated British control from Guadeloupe, and his plans then centered upon extending his ambit so as to embrace neighboring territories and waters. The resulting operations were generally viewed as being of a most unorthodox nature, involving both commerce raiding and efforts to capture, or at least destabilize, various islands. Within this context, Hugues's disregard for orthodox practice meant that the distinction between privateer and government vessel became blurred at times.[4]

Of Marseilles origin, he had served as a public prosecutor in the metropolitan country, and it seems likely that the exceedingly brisk (and, indeed, brusque) procedures of the revolutionary tribunals in Robespierre's day had shaped his attitude to administrative matters. Hugues has been convincingly accused of serious faults—including peculation on the grand scale, and even gratuitous barbarism (as in the sordid desecration of the grave of General Dundas)[5]—but he was nevertheless a man of great energy and resolution. It is noteworthy that the celebrated A.T. Mahan considered Hugues to have combined "the best and worst" of the French revolutionaries at the time of the Terror.[6]

The circumstances of the period, notably a British naval superiority in general, led to Hugues receiving very limited reinforcements and supplies from France. Moreover, the fall of Robespierre in mid-1794 produced a French Government which Hugues viewed with thinly disguised contempt. Factors of this sort helped to move Guadeloupe towards an increasingly independent posture.[7] However, if France supplied relatively little in material terms, it had placed in Hugues's hand a mighty political weapon, the Decree of 16 Pluviôse Year II, which absolutely abolished slavery in the French possessions.

This legislation, enacted in early 1794, proved a powerful means of subversion within the British-held colonies, driving the Leeward Islands Command to describe French emancipation as a "diabolical" process.[8] In effect, Hugues's political wooing of the slave-population throughout the eastern Caribbean meant that even small landing-parties from Guadeloupe could sometimes produce great upheaval in targeted islands. In consequence, a locally improvised transport system of strictly limited carrying power enabled Hugues to undertake very damaging operations. Propaganda-material, such as tricolor cockades and various handbills, played an important role, a fact clearly grasped by the British.[9] Hugues himself commented that such items could well produce very substantial results.[10]

It was not long before the Leeward Islands Command came under severe pressure. Early in 1795 a despatch from that source dealt disconsolately with what was termed "the wild and pernicious Doctrine of Liberty & Equality, which the French have so successfully established on Guardeloupe [sic]."[11] In the following September, Admiral Laforey wrote these words from the eastern Caribbean: "I have not a strength by any means adequate to the protection of commerce and the islands, the watching of the enemy's ports, the cruising to windward to prevent their supplies, and the complying with the exigencies of the army."[12]

For his part, Earl Spencer, as First Lord of the Admiralty, had already grasped the threat posed by Guadeloupe, particularly in so far as it involved subversion. In August 1795 he opined that, regardless of the number of vessels available, there was "not a sea officer in his senses" who would guarantee the effective protection of the British-held islands against the style of attack to which they were currently exposed.[13]

The correspondence of the Leeward Islands Command is informative regarding the nature of the warfare which was causing the

British so much difficulty. During 1795, London was notified on the subject of what was termed "Copper'd small craft from Guadaloupe [*sic*]." These were carrying personnel, arms and supplies to the various islands where Hugues had intervened. The vessels were evidently of unusual speed, and highly elusive. To supplement their activities, much of Hugues's short-haul work was entrusted to "perriagues and large canoes" which moved along the coasts under cover of darkness.[14] Such, in essence, was the system of transport which sustained the campaign against the British-held islands.

The results received considerable attention in the British press. In mid-1795, for instance, *The Gentleman's Magazine* stressed the daunting threat from the Guadeloupean "Republicans." A subsequent article made special reference to Hugues as the originator of upheaval on Dominica, while a Guadeloupean force sent to St. Vincent was dismissed as "another party of French desperadoes."[15] Within the Leeward Islands Command, light patrol-craft were seen as the immediate answer to Hugues's varied operations, and Admiral Laforey urged an increase in the number of "small armed Vessels for the service of this Command."[16] It was believed that orthodox naval strength, expressed in the form of powerful vessels, would not be sufficient. In the nature of things, such vessels would have to be relatively few in number, and they could not therefore counteract Hugues's numerous light craft in a really effective manner. Apart from other considerations, the ability of light craft to use all sorts of minor anchorages and out-of-the-way coves meant that efforts at blockade were unlikely to prove very successful. It was felt that the principle would have to be catch-as-catch-can, and that this implied naval craft which were numerous, though perhaps of very limited fighting-power in many cases. This sort of thinking may well have been fostered by the fact that the Leeward Islands Command had something of a tradition for employing "tenders"—small, locally acquired schooners and the like—which could be brought into service without too much expense or red-tape. It was perceived that a score or so of seamen and a few light carriage-guns could transform even a vessel of this type into a useful patroller.

At about this time, various British-held islands appear to have lost faith in the Royal Navy's ability to provide adequate protection against Guadeloupean landings. Such colonies brought into service small patrol-craft of their own. It was at Martinique that the development of *colonial* (rather than naval) patrol-craft received most attention. Under British occupation, Martinique was, at that time, administered by a peculiar arrangement that involved both British force of arms and a measure of French Royalist sentiment.[17] This excited Hugues's particular fury; thus, during 1795, Martinique's authorities felt obliged to bring into service several substantial armed vessels, some open gunboats, and a dozen or so armed canoes.[18]

Although this sort of assistance eased some of the problems facing the Leeward Islands Command, a pervasive air of confusion and uncertainty bedevilled the British naval presence, especially with regard to prisoners and various aspects of prize-procedure. Hugues's emancipation of the former slaves was accompanied by the imposition of military-style discipline; indeed, all Guadeloupeans, of whatever racial origin, were subject to strict requirements. Thus, racially mixed units played a key role in Guadeloupe's operations, but the British response was initially dismissive of the French legislation which underlay this development. The consequences were often serious for what were termed "Black Republicans."

For example, black crewmen on captured Guadeloupean vessels were commonly sold back into the horrors of slavery. A ruling by the British prize-court at Barbados, made during 1795, insisted that such Black personnel must be treated as prisoners of war, in line with French law.[19] However, this ruling produced a measure of confusion, dissent and recrimination within naval circles, helping to create an atmosphere far from conducive to smooth functioning. For various reasons, indeed, serious friction became evident as senior officers of the Leeward Islands Command contended with unfamiliar circumstances which appeared to threaten all established order in the West Indies. A particularly notable instance involved Admiral Laforey's bitter dispute with his subordinate, Admiral Thompson. This centered upon Thompson's alleged failure to provide proper protection for the British colony of St. Kitts.[20]

It should be pointed out that Hugues, at an early stage, included commerce raiding as a weapon in his armory. In that form of warfare, he was quick to incorporate an unusual degree of irregularity, even by the standards of the eighteenth-century Caribbean. Upheaval in France, great disorder in French colonial affairs, and Hugues's own fiery and grasping character, together, led to his exercising a remarkable level of control over an assortment of French naval vessels lying in Guadeloupe's ports—albeit for a limited period. For a while, claiming that the terms of his own appointment gave him all sorts of powers, Hugues was able to direct sizeable naval units so as to strike damaging blows, even against substantial convoys. The results were sometimes dramatic. John Hay has left an account of how, on one such occasion, hundreds of prisoners had to be given temporary accommodation in one of Guadeloupe's larger churches.[21]

However, commerce raiders of a much smaller sort proved more generally suited to Hugues's purposes; and, as already noticed, the irregular nature of his proceedings often blurred the distinction between privateers and vessels operated by Guadeloupe's authorities. Collusion with neutrals, commercial ramifications and disregard for administrative niceties led to some remarkable abuses *circa* 1795. The brig *Courier*, for instance, appears to have sailed from Guadeloupe carrying duplicate papers, flags, and even personnel—the idea being that, according to tactical circumstances, she could figure either as a French vessel or as a neutral Swedish one.[22]

Irregularities at sea were commonly mirrored in the proceedings of the prize-court which Hugues established at Guadeloupe. At an early stage, various American merchantmen were among those who felt the consequences. Although there was sometimes a measure of uncertainty in such cases, it is plain that idiosyncratic criteria were commonly applied by the court. As a result, a number of vigorous but unsuccessful representations were made by Americans present at Guadeloupe during 1795.[23]

For the British, there were problems of an even more serious kind. In one way and another, Guadeloupe's operations caused the Leeward Islands Command great difficulties. Late in 1795, Admiral Laforey wrote these words: "Victor Hugues keeps us in constant agitation."[24] However, improvised transport and all the measures associated with it had a limit to their value. Whereas France was unable to pour in heavy reinforcements, Britain was to prove perfectly capable of doing so. Response of this sort involved a large-scale expedition, incorporating both military and naval components, and reflecting a great deal of preliminary activity and debate within the British Government. Very valuable discussion of such political activity is included in Michael Duffy's *Soldiers, Sugar, and Seapower*. The employment of a massive expedition, intended to achieve what might be termed a "knock-out blow," was of course very different in nature from the "counter-measures on-the-spot" which could be undertaken by the ordinary forces of the Leeward Islands Command. For the purposes of this present paper, though, it is enough to note that, during the first half of 1796, fresh and powerful forces under Admiral Christian and General Abercromby produced sweeping changes in the eastern Caribbean.[25]

By mid-1796, indeed, Hugues had been forced to the conclusion that his schemes for extending control over neighboring islands had been effectively defeated. Reconciling himself to Guadeloupe as a more or less isolated stronghold, he changed the emphasis of his efforts, concentrating on a massive campaign of commerce raiding.[26] This alteration of policy, *circa* mid-1796, marked the end of the period central to this present paper. In reviewing that same period of upheaval in the eastern Caribbean, one is brought face to face with the extraordinary contribution of Victor Hugues. In British eyes, 1795 saw him emerge as a revolutionary bogey-man, molding Guadeloupe into an increasingly frightening entity which threatened all colonies within reach of its "Copper'd small craft."

One can also discern, during 1795, early signs of that clash between Guadeloupe and United States interests, which was to figure so prominently in the Franco-American Quasi-War. As a general comment, American commerce was a developing influence in the West Indies during the closing decade of the eighteenth century. But, although economically potent, American merchant shipping in the Caribbean was often temptingly vulnerable to attack, and this contributed to the remarkably irregular commerce raiding witnessed at that time. Matters were further complicated by inadequate information on the overall pattern of trade, a fact which sometimes led the French and British to reach curiously conflicting conclusions as to the real significance of American commercial activity in particular theaters.[27] On occasion, the results could be most unfortunate for merchant vessels of United States origin.

For the British, though, it was Hugues's operations against *islands* which caused great misgiving during 1795. Not all of the British perception was accurate with regard to developments in the eastern Caribbean, and throughout the West Indies; but it had, nevertheless, powerful influence on service attitudes. The image of slave-rebellion being systematically engineered by an official whose authority stemmed unequivocally from the French Government (after the fall of Robespierre, Hugues was confirmed in office by the new regime in Paris) meant that, in the minds of many British officers, a longstanding fear of revolt coalesced with the new disquiet regarding "Jacobinism" so as to create a context full of the most serious threat.

The Decree of 16 Pluviôse Year II was to prove a powerful weapon in Hugues's hand, enabling him to offer, in effect, immediate emancipation as a major inducement. In the British view, this tended to make all those of African origin or ancestry Hugues's actual or potential allies. The situation certainly enabled him to create and deploy very effective forces, more or less regardless of whatever help might arrive from the metropolitan country in terms of physical reinforcement. The *ideology* of Revolutionary France was enough, in combination with light seagoing transport, to produce very formidable results.

The British naval response showed an initial lack of comprehension regarding the French legislative process. It is plain, though, why so much emphasis was placed on the need to multiply light patrol-craft. Nevertheless, there is evidence that, among the various opinions held in the Royal Navy's highest echelons, there was a belief that no amount of patrol-craft could effectively counter the sort of attacks launched from Guadeloupe during 1795. The First Lord of the Admiralty was very clear when he wrote these words: "while the enemy are in possession of Guadeloupe, and continue to make the use they hitherto have done of that possession, there is no security for any of our Islands (hardly excepting even Barbadoes [sic] and Antigua)."[28] It is understandable, therefore, that considerations of this kind led eventually, after a great deal of debate and reappraisal, to the plan which underlay the despatch from Britain of very powerful forces, both naval and military, under Admiral Christian and General Abercromby—with, it should be noted, dominant British power at sea as the prerequisite.

The outcome regarding Guadeloupe was not, however, quite what had been envisaged in London. Hugues's incursive forces were certainly driven from such islands as St. Lucia, in effect the outposts of Guadeloupe, and as a result Hugues became convinced that he must abandon the style of warfare which he had been waging. But the demands of their preliminary operations left the British forces unable to launch a decisive attack against Guadeloupe itself. It therefore remained in Hugues's hands, and duly served as base for that intensive commerce raiding which formed the cardinal feature of his later years of power in that remarkable colony.

The change in Hugues's policy, *circa* mid-1796, continued until his political eclipse in late 1798; the results, although very serious for commerce, were generally perceived as having eased the overall threat to the British presence in the eastern Caribbean. However, this same change of policy during 1796 led to greatly increased pressure on American shipping in those waters. Thus, during the Quasi-War, considerable forces of the United States Navy were to make their way to that station, operating with mounting effect as time passed. In conclusion, it should be pointed out that, during the short-lived Peace of Amiens, Napoleonic measures restored the institution of slavery within the French colonies. After the resumption of Anglo-French hostilities in 1803, therefore, the image of Guadeloupe was very different from what it had been in the earlier period of conflict considered in this paper.

1. For discussion of early reaction to Hugues's regime, including the claim that he was "savage," see H. J. K. Jenkins, "Guadeloupe, savagery and emancipation: British comment of 1794–1796," *Revue française d'histoire d'outre-mer* 65 (1978): 325–331.

2. H. J. K. Jenkins, "British Naval Response to French Colonial Disorder in the Eastern Caribbean, 1790–93"—see official *Program* of Eighth Naval History Symposium, U.S. Naval Academy (1987): 5.

3. E. E. Boyer-Peyreleau, *Les Antilles françaises . . .* , (Paris 1823) 3:172.

4. For further discussion of such matters, see H. J. K. Jenkins, "Privateers, Picaroons, Pirates: West Indian Commerce Raiders, 1793–1801," *The Mariner's Mirror* 73 (1987): 181–186.

5. In its entry for Thomas Dundas, *Dictionary of National Biography* 16 (London, 1888), 196–197, outlines this desecration and the bombastic proclamation which accompanied it.

6. A. T. Mahan, *The Influence of Sea Power upon the French Revolution and Empire 1793–1812* (London 1893), 1:116.

7. A process which eventually found expression in what came close to an independent foreign policy: see H. J. K. Jenkins, "Controversial legislation at Guadeloupe regarding trade and piracy, 1797," *Revue française d'histoire d'outre-mer* 76 (1989): 97–106.

8. Public Record Office, London (hereafter P.R.O.), ADM 1/316, Letter 31 (second series).

9. See, for example, P.R.O. ADM 1/317, Letter 73. This correspondence of May 1795 emphasized the recent capture of a Guadeloupean schooner carrying "many large Packages of French National Cockades & Proclamations."

10. Archives Nationales, Paris, Colonies C7a 47, folio 31.

11. P.R.O. ADM 1/317, Letter 2.

12. J. K. Laughton (ed.), *Letters and Papers of Charles, Lord Barham . . .* , (Navy Records Society, 1907–11) 2:416–418.

13. J. S. Corbett (ed.), *Private Papers of George, second Earl Spencer . . .* , (Navy Records Society, 1913–24), 3:223–224.

14. P.R.O. ADM 1/317, Letters 34, 48, 94, and 96. Perriagues were two-masted boats, canoe-like in build.

15. *The Gentleman's Magazine*, May and October 1795 numbers: these contain a good deal of comment on Hugues and Guadeloupe, throwing an interesting light on British public opinion at the time.

16. P.R.O. ADM 1/317, Letter 94.

17. See H. J. K. Jenkins, "Martinique: The British Occupation, 1794–1802," *History Today* (November 1981): 35–39.

18. Victor Hugues's particular animosity towards occupied Martinique lasted throughout his time of power at Guadeloupe, 1794–98; for further discussion, see H. J. K. Jenkins, "Guadeloupe, Martinique and commerce raiding: two colonies in conflict, 1797–1798," *Revue française d'histoire d'outre-mer* 78 (1991): 465–475.

19. H. J. K. Jenkins, "Slavery and French Privateering in the 1790s," *The Mariner's Mirror* 72 (1986): 359–360.

20. Laforey assembled an interesting file on this matter for his own personal use which is now preserved at Berkshire Record Office, England: Preston Papers, D/EP1 0 3/1.

21. J. Hay, *A Narrative of the Insurrection in the Island of Grenada . . . 1795*, (London 1823), 119.

22. H. J. K. Jenkins, "The Case of the *Courier*, 1794–98," *The Mariner's Mirror* 76 (1990): 69–73.

23. See Hay, *A Narrative . . .* , 99–100, regarding an interesting example.

24. P.R.O. ADM 1/317, Letter 199.

25. The sheer weight of these forces indicated the reversal of much that Hugues had achieved. H. de Poyen's account of this matter in *Les guerres des Antilles de 1793 à 1815*, (Paris 1896), 128–146, remains of interest. For a recent and very informative treatment of large-scale British expeditions to the Caribbean in this period, see Michael Duffy, *Soldiers, Sugar, and Seapower: the British Expeditions to the West Indies and the War against Revolutionary France*, (Oxford 1987).

26. For further discussion, see H. J. K. Jenkins, "The Heyday of French Privateering from Guadeloupe, 1796–98," *The Mariner's Mirror* 64 (1978): 245–250.

27. See, for instance, H. J. K. Jenkins, "Franco-British disagreement regarding American commerce in the eastern Caribbean, 1793–1798," *Revue française d'histoire d'outre-mer* 73 (1986): 257–265.

28. *Spencer Papers* (as note 13) 3:223–224.

The United States Frigate *President*: The Victor or the Vanquished?

W. M. P. Dunne

⚓

Conventional 19th and 20th century American historiography informs us that Commodore Stephen Decatur engaged and defeated the British frigate *Endymion* before surrendering the American frigate *President* to a superior enemy force during January 1815.[1] The question of who defeated whom is the subject of this paper.

Events leading to this encounter began as early as the inglorious first of June in 1813, when the Royal Navy's Captain Robert Dudley Oliver inadvertently trapped Decatur, who had erred in his assessment of enemy power, in the Thames River at New London.[2] Following a winter of frustration, the commodore received orders in the spring to proceed to New York City and assume command of *President* and a squadron intended for a commerce-raiding cruise in the Indian Ocean. Government vacillation, local recruiting difficulties, scarce military provisions, and an ever-solidifying British blockade substantially delayed Decatur's departure. And then his legendary luck, which had contributed so handsomely to the fame and fortune he had garnered during a seventeen-year naval career, deserted him.

The misadventures that led to Decatur's downfall began once he left the watering place at Staten Island on 14 January 1815.[3] His 44-gun ship belonged to the largest class of American frigates. She carried between six and seven month's stores and, as a result, drew over twenty-two feet of water, a factor that neither the harbor pilot, Mr. Mings, nor the gunboat commanders who would guide *President* to her new anchorage sufficiently appreciated.

Decatur got under way at 9 A.M. The ship, gingerly clawing her way ahead of a vicious westerly gale, dropped down to the lower bay, where she anchored at noon. A brig carrying additional stores waited there to accompany her to the Far East. Turbulent gusts of wind, accompanied by often blinding snow, had driven the enemy's blockading squadron out to sea, thus opening the door for Decatur's escape attempt.[4] At about 4 P.M., he again weighed *President*'s anchor and stood toward the bar, where three gunboats waited to escort her through its treacherous channels.[5] Oddly, the pilot, instead of boarding the frigate, rode in the lead gunboat.

Decatur intended to move just inside the Hook and anchor there for the flood tide. John Templer Shubrick, *President*'s second lieutenant, recalled that "when they came near the first gunboat, the ship was rounded to, and the anchor let go."[6] Third Lieutenant John Gallagher placed the time "at about half after six, or near seven o'clock," making it after dark in January.[7]

As she came head to wind with her bow to the westward, *President* slid to a halt. The crew backed her sails and released her starboard anchor; but, as she began to gather sternway, disaster struck. Before her anchor cable came taut, the huge frigate crashed rudder first into the bar. She instantly swung broadside to the westerly gales with her bow pointed in a northerly direction toward Gravesend in Brooklyn and her entire starboard underbody hammering the bar. In addition to the constant battering, Decatur soon discovered that his ship had suffered several broken rudder braces. The damages sustained demanded a return to port, but the wind whistling down through the Narrows presented an insurmountable impasse. He could not sail his square-rigger within 70 degrees of the eye of the gale, much less straight into its teeth. Moreover, with high tide approaching, any delay would leave *President* high, dry, and defenseless, within easy range of the blockading squadron's cannon when the British ships beat back onto station off Sandy Hook. Decatur either had to drive her the rest of the way over the mile-wide sandbar or abandon ship.

First Lieutenant Fitz Henry Babbit and Sailing Master James Rogers immediately went to work to save the ship. Initially, they tried to sail her to safety by cutting the anchor cable and hoisting the fore and mizen topsails to force her onto a southerly heading. While Rogers supervised these measures, Babbit had the ship's boats launched to assist the gunboats in hauling her around. *President* responded by swinging to leeward and crashing along the bar for about a half-mile before grinding to a halt. Although she slightly deepened her water, her back-breaking thumping continued.[8]

Sizing up her predicament, Babbit set the larboard anchor and furled the sails. He had the royal yards struck down on deck to lighten the ship aloft. He then had the ship's main battery of guns shifted forward to bring her back onto an even keel. All that remained then was a frustrating wait for high tide. During the interval *President* continued to thrash against the bottom. The fact that the violence of the shocks decreased as the tide rose offered little solace to the stricken ship's sailors, who, but moments ago, had been looking forward to several months of highly remunerative hell-raising in distant enemy waters.

At about half past eight, with the tide now high, Decatur got the frigate under sail again, and signalled the storeship to follow suit. With the boats towing ahead in an increasing north-northwest gale, for a tortuous half-hour he drove his damaged command toward the seaward side of the bar. She bottomed several times during that passage, further injuring her fabric.[9] Shubrick later testified that "the ship was on the bar certainly not less than one hour and a half, and a great part of that time striking very heavily. The boats, as soon as the ship got clear of the bar, were run up, the anchors were stowed, and the ship, at about ten P.M. made sail and steered east by north."[10] Decatur reported to Secretary of the Navy Benjamin W. Crowninshield: "It being now high water, it became necessary to force her over the bar before the tide fell . . . we succeeded by 10 o'clock, when we shaped our course along the shore of Long-Island for fifty miles, and then steered southeast by east."[11]

The damage *President* sustained seriously affected her sailing qualities. During one, or several, of the times she had slammed into the bar, her false keel had been knocked askew. The broken ends protruded from either side of her bottom. These elongated pieces acted like drogues, drastically reducing the frigate's possible hull speed. To add to American woes, the senior British blockading officer, Captain John Hayes, anticipated Decatur's gambit. Sailing in *Majestic*,[12] with three crack frigates: the 24-pounder *Endymion*, Henry Hope; the speedy, ex-French *Pomone*,[13] John Richard Lumley; and the two-year old *Tenedos*,[14] Hyde Parker—all veterans of the American blockade—Hayes guessed that Decatur would sally forth using the storm for cover. He later reported to his own superior: "Although the Squadron was blown off again in a severe Snow Storm; on Saturday the wind and weather became favorable for the Enemy, and I had no doubt but he would attempt his escape that night."[15]

To Decatur's dismay, he had no sooner entered the ocean when the gale began to subside. The moderating weather conditions compounded the sailing disadvantage brought on by *President*'s damaged keel—the lighter the winds, the more detrimental its effect on the ship's speed. Reacting quickly to the changing conditions, he had Babbit and Rogers change over from the ship's heavy canvas to her light suit of cotton duck.[16] As soon as they finished this evolution, despite the freezing temperatures, the topmen steadily dampened the sails with buckets of icy seawater to make them draw better.

For the ship's crew it was a tense and sleepless period, especially after three o'clock the next morning, when Decatur turned away from Fire Island's friendly shore and headed out to sea. About five A.M. his lookouts spotted two ships ahead. Presuming them to be enemies, the commodore had *President* hauled up to the northeast. She passed two or three miles to the windward of them, and Decatur briefly believed he had remained unseen in the stormy darkness. But Hayes's lookouts spotted him. The British commodore had literally read Decatur's mind. He described his premonition:

> In preference to closing the Land to the Southward, stood away to the Northward and Eastward, till the Squadron reached the supposed track of the Enemy; and what is a little singular, at the very instant of arriving at that point, an hour before daylight, Sandy Hook bearing WNW, 15 Leagues, we were made happy by the sight of a Ship and a Brig standing to the Southward and Eastward, and not more than two miles on *Majestic*'s Weather Bow.[17]

Signalling *Pomone* to follow, Hayes let all the reefs out of *Majestic*'s topsails and hauled up to pursue *President* and her companion.[18] He signalled for a general chase thirty minutes later. *Endymion* and *Pomone* responded by making all sail and bearing up toward the Americans.[19] *Tenedos*, patrolling below the horizon, did not receive his message.

Decatur saw the largest enemy ship fire a rocket and burn a blue light. He guessed that they indicated *President*'s presence to other, distant enemies. In fact, when *Tenedos* reappeared, Hayes mistook her for a stranger. His 6:15 A.M. signals sent *Pomone* to investigate. Lumley responded to Hayes's order to abandon the chase with reluctance and later complained publicly of the disadvantage it put upon him:

> Another ship was seen hull down to leeward, and the commodore imagining her to also be an enemy, detached *Pomone* in chase; we immediately bore right up before the wind, and in three quarters of an hour ascertain-

ing her to be *Tenedos*, again hauled up to the east, being by this circumstance thrown seven or eight miles astern of the original chace.[20]

The gravity of Decatur's dilemma registered when dawn dimly illuminated the wintry seascape: "Four ships were discovered in chase, one on each quarter, and two astern; the leading ship of the enemy a Razee, about three miles distant."[21] The razee was Hayes's ponderous but powerful 58-gun *Majestic,* and he greeted the Americans by firing three shots toward them at 6:30 in the morning.[22]

By 8 A.M. *President* had gradually dropped *Majestic* astern. But the swift *Endymion* steadfastly cut into the American's lead, even as the dying winds lengthened out the chase. Two hours later, the American lookouts spotted a strange man of war lying across their course. This induced Decatur to alter his heading from northeast to the southeast, until he discovered she was only a gun-brig, the *Dispatch*,[23] which passed to windward and joined Hayes's squadron. With five enemy warships now fanning out astern, and his frigate seriously damaged, Decatur gave up all hope of continuing to the Indian Ocean. He ordered Babbit and Rogers to lighten the ship. They cut away the anchors, ditched the boats over the side, threw away spare spars and cables, started the water casks, and dumped their salt provisions and some shot overboard.

By noon the players in this developing sea drama lay about sixty miles south of Montauk Point. Decatur noted that "the wind became light and baffling; we had increased our distance from the razee, but the next ship astern, which was also a large ship, had gained, and continued to gain, upon us considerably."[24] With but fitful breezes coming over their starboard quarters, the antagonists generally steered east by north. Within a half-hour *Endymion* came close enough to fire several shots at *President*, which she returned. This exchange continued in a desultory fashion with bow and stern chasers until mid-afternoon, when, with the closing range, the fire on both sides increased within limitations set by the rambunctious sea state.[25] Without the benefit of a strong wind driving their sails, and thus stabilizing both hulls, the mountainous swells sent them into monotonously repetitive, gut-wrenching rolls.

In the meantime, *Tenedos* and *Pomone* literally boiled along in their charge to catch up to the battle. They swept by *Majestic* at 1 P.M. and gained steadily on *President*, until they too began to run out of wind.[26]

At 2:39 P.M., a lucky shot from one of the American stern chasers destroyed *Endymion*'s barge, a loss Captain Henry Hope could ill afford. It reduced his boat inventory to a partially repaired cutter, the launch and gig. The same shot that shattered the barge sliced through *Endymion*'s fore lower studding sail, the foot of the mainsail, and embedded itself in the mainmast.[27] Despite this, by 4 P.M., Hope had worked his ship into a position on *President*'s starboard quarter, where Decatur could not, without altering her course, bring any guns to bear. *Endymion*'s withering fire cut away *President*'s jib halyards at 4:10 P.M. and her main topgallant staysail sheet ten minutes later. Every British shot slammed into *President*'s hull or chewed away at her spars, sails, and rigging. The American frigate's erratic rolls caused her gunners to shoot high, and most of her return fire passed over the *Endymion*.[28] Decatur sorely missed William Henry Allen, his previous first lieutenant, now promoted to command of *Argus*, whose artillery skills were legendary. Babbit, for all his enthusiasm, was a gunboat sailor without significant broadside experience.

Positioned out of harm's way, with his bow chasers constantly galling *President*, the English skipper had the best of the early going. It was, however, an advantage steeped in irony. Henry Hope and Stephen Decatur knew and respected each other. The year before, in an act of scintillating chivalry that could qualify either one as the ideal knight, they had unsuccessfully attempted to arrange an Arthurian ship to ship duel while the Englishman had the American blockaded at New London.[29] Moreover, in February 1812, Decatur had hosted David Hope, the Briton's distant cousin and former first lieutenant of the *Macedonian*, to dinner in his home during her visit to Norfolk. Eight months later, he had again entertained young Hope—this time as a prisoner of war in *United States*, after she had captured *Macedonian* in October 1812. But, as *Endymion* and *President* closed within broadside range of each other, gunsmoke obliterated the social niceties of the situation.

Watery daylight dwindled to gloomy dusk around 5:00 P.M. In the gathering darkness, *Pomone* and *Tenedos*, after surging past *Majestic* in their race to join forces with *Endymion*, and then falling victims to the dying wind, had again begun to catch up. They now lay, along with the brig, abaft *President*'s larboard quarter about five miles distant. Hayes's sluggardly razee, dead astern of *President*, continued to fall further behind and was in danger of dropping below the horizon.

Most of Decatur's officers and men had not been off their feet since they left Staten Island 36 hours earlier. They were bone-weary and sapped of morale by the collisions with the bar and the loss of their war patrol. Realizing that he must do something to restore their spirit and vitality, Decatur came up with an inspiring, if far-fetched, idea. First outlining his solution to the officers, who whole-heartedly embraced it, he then had the master call the men aft.[30] When they assembled, he detailed his plan to engage, board, and takeover *Endymion*. Never at a loss for lower-deck language, Decatur importuned: "My lads, that ship is coming up with us. As our ship won't sail, we'll go on board of theirs, every man and boy of us, and carry her into New York. All I ask of you is, to follow me. *President* is a favorite of our country. If we allow her to be taken we shall be deserted by our wives and sweethearts." He closed with the plea: "What! let such a ship as this go for nothing! 'T would break the heart of every pretty girl in New York!"[31] His startling stratagem and daring tactics epitomized his supreme self-confidence. And, they infused fresh life into his forlorn followers. Every Jack Tar on board reflected renewed vigor. When the Commodore stood his men down, the quarterdeck resounded with the echoes of three hearty cheers.[32] As the crew dispersed, Babbit aimed one of the ship's howitzers into the hold to scuttle the ship once they captured the *Endymion*.

Despite his brave words and whimsical plan, Decatur could do little else but keep to his course and continue to absorb the punishment being meted out by the British bow chasers. His state of mind suffered further when a messenger from the gun deck reported that Midshipman Richard Dale, whose father had been John Paul Jones's first lieutenant in the American Revolution, had been hit by a 24-pound cannonball. In the sick bay, Dr. Samuel Trevett, using knife and saw, amputated Dale's pulverized foot.

Above them, in a masterful display of sail-handling and gunnery, Hope continually yawed his ship to prevent her creeping ahead, and carefully maintained her deadly position on *President*'s quarter. His manœuvreing prevented the Americans from returning anything but an occasional shot from their stern chasers—and that at the risk of being raked.

If Decatur's course to this mid-January confrontation can be traced back to New London, the events affecting *Endymion*'s condition that star-crossed night began three months earlier. Patrolling off

Nantucket, Hope launched a boat attack at the becalmed New York privateer *Prince de Neufchatel* on 10 October 1814. Led by *Endymion*'s veteran first lieutenant, Abel Hawkins, 104 British officers and sailors in the frigate's five boats assaulted, but failed to capture, the stoutly-defended privateer. In fact, the New Yorkers routed the British. Two results of this debacle affected the current battle: Hawkins, *Endymion*'s long-serving executive officer, lost his life while attempting to board the *Prince de Neufchatel*; and American guns sank *Endymion*'s yawl, severely damaged her principal cutter, and injured her launch, barge, and gig.

The total loss, when the assault party returned the following morning, was ten killed, thirty-one wounded, and thirty-six missing.[33] Sixteen officers, seamen and marines eventually succumbed to wounds received during the attack. Third Lieutenant Francis Ormond, Midshipmen Alexander Boyter and Henry B. Mathews, with part of the captured barge crew, rejoined *Endymion* from Nantucket five days later.[34] But, these officers and men had given their parole to the United States Marshall there and could not serve again until they were officially exchanged. To replace the losses she suffered, as well as men previously sent off in prizes, *Endymion* received a draft of one lieutenant, William Thomas Morgan, and sixty-two petty officers, seamen, and marines from H.M.S. *Saturn* on 30 October. Two days later, Captain Hope re-stationed his ship's company, an evolution dictated by the large group of newcomers.[35]

Unaware of Hope's problems, Decatur dealt with his own dilemma: "I had prepared my crew to board; but from his continuing to yaw his ship to maintain his position, to have continued our course under those circumstances, would have been placing it in his power to cripple us, without being subject to injury himself." He knew he must gain the initiative by engaging *Endymion* with *President*'s broadside: "It was now dusk. I altered my course to south, for the purpose of bringing the enemy abeam."[36]

He did exactly that, and the broadside battle began within hailing distance. Smoke soon enveloped both vessels and the ocean surrounding them. As usual in light conditions, the concussive effect of thirty 24-pounders killed the remaining breeze, and created an arena of eerie calm. *Endymion*'s log recorded that "at 5, 30, the enemy brailed up his spanker, and bore away, shewing a disposition to cross our bow and rake us,—put the helm hard a weather to meet this manœuvre, and brought the enemy to close action, in a parallel line of sailing."[37]

The first British broadside killed Fitz Henry Babbit. He "was standing on the coamings of the after-hatch, working the ship, Commodore Decatur being seated on the hammock cloths giving directions, when the *Endymion*'s first broadside was received."[38] A 32-pound ball from one of her carronades tore off his right leg, and he fell through the hatch, fracturing his skull. He survived for two agonizing hours. Fully aware that death lay only a breath away, Babbit dictated farewell messages to his friends, and asked that the miniature of his fiancée hanging around his neck be sent to his mother. Decatur took a moment to go below and comfort his dying first lieutenant. When he returned to the quarterdeck, he mounted the horse block to observe the *Endymion*—just as she fired another salvo, which smashed into *President*'s hull. A huge splinter struck Decatur, knocking him to the deck. He suffered a severe chest contusion and a split forehead.[39]

Yet, by five minutes after six, *President*, despite her ragged broadside and mounting butcher's bill, had seriously damaged *Endymion* aloft. Her log admitted: "Enemy now distant half musquet Shot—our Sails and rigging much Cut." But thirty minutes later, she mauled *President*'s gun deck with two raking fusillades of grape shot, after which she hauled up out of range on the American's starboard quarter, leaving a scene of incomprehensible carnage in her wake.[40] A 24-pound ball from this volley smashed into Decatur's popular fourth lieutenant, Archibald Hamilton. It cut him nearly in two. He lived long enough to shout his favorite exhortation of battle or party, "Carry on, boys! Carry on!" to the men of his division.[41] Would anyone ever forget Archie Hamilton, the son of former Navy Secretary Paul Hamilton, barging into the naval ball at Washington in December 1812 with the *Macedonian*'s battle colors draped over his shoulders? He had elegantly spread them at Dolley Madison's feet, as he advised the president of Decatur's great victory.

By 7 P.M., Hayes had no doubt about the outcome of the battle. He "haild *Despatch* and ordered her to the Admiral at New London with Intelligence," of the British capture of the United States's most famous naval leader.[42] But, despite nearly two hours of relentless cannonading, Decatur's ship was far from a toothless tiger. Hope noted, "At 7.15, the enemy shot away our boat from the larboard quarter, and the lower-main-studding-sails."[43] It was *Endymion*'s last surviving auxiliary, and the loss created a circumstance that later bedeviled both Decatur and Lumley. Since then, it has confused historians on both sides of the Atlantic.

Endymion's log noted the first significant pause in the action: "At 7,18, the enemy not returning our fire." But *President*'s guns were not silent for long. "At 7,30, the enemy shot away the larboard main-top-gallant-studding-sail and main brace."[44] By then, *President*'s gunnery, albeit poorly aimed and timed, had trashed *Endymion*'s tophamper. American small arms fire was ineffective. During the two-and-a-half-hour action, *President*'s Marines fired over 5,000 musket cartridges, but the British only lost eleven men killed and sixteen wounded, with no officers and few spar deck injuries among them.

Just before eight o'clock *President*'s junior lieutenant, 18-year-old Edward F. Howell, commanding the quarterdeck guns, peered back at the silent *Endymion* and said to one of Decatur's aides, Midshipman Christopher T. Emmett, "Well, we have whipped that ship, at any rate!" At the same instant, Howell saw a flash from the Briton's bow, "No, there she is again!" When Emmett turned to reply, Howell lay prostrate at his feet. A random piece of grape had pierced his skull, killing him instantly. Ironically, it was the last shot fired by the *Endymion*.[45]

Previous to this, Hope had been logging Decatur's manoeuvres: "At 7, 32, the enemy hauled suddenly to the wind; we trimmed sails and again obtained the advantage of giving him a raking fire, which he returned with one shot from his stern gun," adding with satisfaction, "the enemy much shattered." Then, "at 7, 58, the enemy ceased firing. Observed him to show a light," the night signal for surrender. "Called all hands to bend new sails &c. conceiving that the enemy had struck, ceased firing."[46] What Hope could not do, however, was take possession of the *President*. He did not have boat left to do so and suffered the ignominy of watching Decatur drift away from him. But, within an hour, his men had "new Courses Main Topsail, Jib Foretopmast Stay Sail and Spanker bent." Under way again, *Endymion* had nearly ranged up with *President*. Hope "observed one of our Squadron run up on the larboard beam of the Enemy and fire into her, which was not returned but the light hoisted higher in the rigging." He hailed *Tenedos* and "acquainted her with our not having a boat that Could be hoisted out."[47]

It was *Pomone* that fired into the disabled *President*. Lumley assumed that *Endymion*, by not taking possession, had been defeated. To compound his error, he misread Decatur's surrender signal: "A few minutes previous to our closing her she hoisted a light abaft, which, in night actions, substitutes the ensign;" meaning, he believed the American flag had been defiantly hoisted, which vindicated his fusillade. Decatur, in a futile escape attempt, fueled Lumley's misconception. With the wind filling again, he drove the *President* to the east under a press of sail. But, *Pomone* effortlessly caught up. As soon as she did, Lumley doused her studding sails, luffed to port, and fired his starboard broadside. In the face of this unexpected attack, Decatur, who had sent most of his crew below out of harm's way, now called them back to their guns and brought his larboard broadside to bear.[48] In response, Lumley fired several times. He then moved ahead and crossed in front of *President* with his cannon ready for a final raking volley. Decatur, "thus situated, with about one fifth of my crew killed and wounded, my ship crippled, and a more than fourfold force opposed to me, without a chance of escape left," deemed it his duty to surrender.[49] When Lumley saw him haul down the light, "we hail'd, demanding if she had surrendered—the reply was in the affirmative. The firing instantly ceased."[50]

Lumley's ill-judged broadsides killed several men who would have otherwise survived the battle. But then, the British blood was up. *Tenedos*, for example, carried so much canvas that at 11:30 she "carried away the Lower and topmast Studding Sails." But, unlike Lumley, when Hyde Parker hauled alongside *President*, he hailed her first, not last. Ironically, while Lumley crossed *President*'s "T," Parker took possession of her: "She proved to be the United States Frigate *President*, Commodore Stephen Decatur, mounting 54 Guns and 480 Men."[51] When *Tenedos*'s boats boarded the *President*, "Decatur insisted on having his sword sent to the captain of the black ship (the *Endymion*) which he had engaged, as he said he struck to her alone—and when he ceased firing, he hoisted his light higher to indicate he had struck. Notwithstanding all this, in his official dispatch he makes assertions of a contrary nature."[52]

On board *Endymion*, Hope "secured the Guns and beat the retreat."[53] At four in the morning, still without serviceable small craft, the boats of *Tenedos*, *Pomone*, and *Majestic* delivered

"Commodore Decatur, 1 Lieutenant, & 213 Seamen, part of the Crew of *President* on board."[54]

Decatur's official dispatch, written on board the *Endymion* three days after the battle, denies his surrender to that ship. He reported the following version:

> We continued engaged, steering south, with steering sails set, two hours and a half, when we completed succeeded in dismantling her. Previously to her dropping entirely out of the action, there were intervals of minutes when the ships were broadside and broadside, in which she did not fire a gun. At this period, (8:30 P.M.) although dark, the other ships of the squadron were in sight, and almost within gunshot. We were, of course, compelled to abandon her.[55]

Hope, in direct contradiction, stated in his own dispatch: "I have great satisfaction in acquainting you that we closed with the United States Frigate *President,* and brought her to close action at half past five in the afternoon, and continued in that position, for two hours and a half, when we succeeded in crippling her very materially."[56]

During his testimony to the Vice Admiralty Court at Bermuda, on 30 January, he again confirmed his surrender to the *Endymion*. Thus on 15 and 30 January, while under British jurisdiction, he extends credit to Hope, while on the eighteenth, in the all-important dispatch to the Navy Department, he claims a victory over the *Endymion*.

Two factors may have influenced Decatur's statements. The first was the high regard he held for Henry Hope. The second was his disgust with John Richard Lumley for firing the superfluous broadsides that killed several of the *President*'s people.

In a final isolated analysis, the battle between the *Endymion* and the *President* clearly was a draw—they literally fought to a standstill. Note that neither Decatur nor Hope ever claimed a complete victory. The answer to the question posed in the introduction is that neither the *President* nor the *Endymion* won their single-ship duel, despite both American and British counterclaims to the contrary. The deciding factor in war is possession of territory. Neither Decatur nor Hope captured the other's territory.

The few chroniclers who have admitted this also claim that without *Endymion*'s attack, the *President* would have escaped. Not so, British strength and positioning dictated otherwise. *President*'s repeated groundings on the Sandy Hook bar and the premonition of Captain John Hayes regarding Decatur's chosen escape route, led to "the capture of a vessel universally allowed to be the finest Frigate in the world, commanded by an officer of first rate abilities (the American Nelson he is usually called)."[57] Given those two factors, the British would have eventually captured the *President*, but Henry Hope certainly sped up the process.

    1. "Endymion 4th Rate 50, 1,277bm, 159 1/2 x 43 ft. Randall, Rotherhithe 29.3.1797. Harbour service 1860. BU completed 18.8.1868 at Devonport" (J.J. Colledge, *Ships of the Royal Navy*, 2 vols. [London, England: Greenhill Books, 1987], 1:124, hereafter "Colledge, *Ships*").

    2. For details of those events see W. M. P. Dunne, "The Inglorious First of June: Commodore Stephen Decatur on Long Island Sound, 1813," *The Long Island Historical Journal* 2 (Spring 1990), 2:201–220.

    3. Testimony of John Gallagher, *President*'s third lieutenant (*Proceedings of a Court of Inquiry held on board the United States Frigate* Constellation *at New-York, in April [11], 1815, to Investigate the Causes of the Loss of the Frigate* President *late of the Navy of the United States* [New-York: Van Winkle and Wiley, 1815], hereafter "Gallagher's testimony").

    4. Log of H.B.M. Ship *Majestic*, Captain John Hayes, R.N., 13–14 January 1815, ADM51/2543, P.R.O., hereafter "*Majestic*'s log, date." See also the logs of H.B.M. frigates *Endymion,* Captain Henry Hope, R.N., ADM51/2324; *Pomone*, Captain John Richard Lumley, R.N., ADM51/2706; and *Tenedos*, Captain Hyde Parker, R.N., ADM51/2909.

    5. Testimony of several officers (*Proceedings . . . to Investigate the Causes of the Loss of the Frigate* President, hereafter "officer's name testimony").

    6. Shubrick's testimony.

    7. Gallagher's testimony.

    8. Rogers' testimony.

    9. Rogers' testimony.

    10. Shubrick's testimony.

    11. Commodore Stephen Decatur to Secretary of the Navy Benjamin Crowninshield, 18 January 1815 (Letters Received by the Secretary of the Navy from Captains, Record Group 45, Military History Branch, U.S. National Archives and Records Administration, Washington, D.C., hereafter "Captains' Letters").

    12. "*Majestic* 3rd Rate 74, 1,623bm, 170 1/2 x 47 ft. Adams & Barnard, Deptford 11.2.1785. Reduced to a 4th Rate 58, 28–42pdr carr., 28–32 pdr, 2–12pdr in 1813. BU 4.1816" (Colledge, *Ships*, 1:216).

    13. "*Astree* 5th Rate 38, 1,085bm, 152 1/2 x 40 ft. French, captured 6.12.1810 at the reduction of Mauritius. Renamed *Pomone* 26.10.1811. BU 6.1816" (Colledge, *Ships*, 1:41).

    14. "*Tenedos* 5th Rate 38, 1,083bm, 150 x 40 1/2 ft. Chatham DY 11.4.1812. Convict hulk 4.1843. BU completed 20.3.1875 in Bermuda" (Colledge, *Ships*, 1:344).

    15. Hayes to Rear Admiral Henry Hotham, ADM1/508, 387–394, italics added, Public Records Office, U.K.

    16. Rogers' testimony.

    17. Hayes to Hotham, ADM1/508, 387–394.

18. *Majestic*'s log, 15 January 1815.
19. *Endymion*'s log, 15 January 1815.
20. *Pomone*'s log, 15 January 1815; "Nautical Anecdotes and Selections," *The Naval Chronicle for 1815: Containing a General and Biographical History of the Royal Navy of the United Kingdom; with a Variety of Original Papers on Nautical Subjects* 33:370–371, hereafter, "Naval Chronicle."
21. Decatur to Crowninshield, 18 January 1815 (Captains' Letters).
22. *Majestic*'s log, 15 January 1815.
23. *Dispatch* Brig-sloop 18, *Cruizer* class, 388bm. King, Upnor 7.12.1812. Sold 5.1836 (Colledge, *Ships*, 1:105).
24. Decatur to Crowninshield, 18 January 1815 (Captains' Letters).
25. Shubrick's testimony.
26. *Naval Chronicle*.
27. *Endymion*'s log, 15 January 1815.
28. *Endymion*'s log, 15 January 1815.
29. Decatur to Captain Thomas Masterman Hardy, R.N., and Captain Hassard Stackpole to Decatur, 17 January 1814 (War of 1812 mss., Lilly Library, Indiana University).
30. Rogers' testimony.
31. Alexander Slidell Mackenzie, *Life of Stephen Decatur, A Commodore in the Navy of the United States* (Boston: Charles C. Little and James Brown, 1846), 214–15, hereafter "Mackenzie, *Decatur*."
32. Mackenzie, *Decatur*, 215.
33. *Endymion*'s log, 11 October 1814.
34. *Endymion*'s log, 15 October 1814.
35. *Endymion*'s log, 1 November 1814.
36. Decatur to Crowninshield, 18 January 1815 (Captains' Letters).
37. *Endymion*'s log, 15 January 1815.
38. James Fenimore Cooper, *The History of the Navy of the United States of America*, 2 vols. (Philadelphia: Lea & Blanchard, 1839).
39. Mackenzie, *Decatur*, 217.
40. *Endymion*'s log, 15 January 1815.
41. Christopher McKee, "The Pathology of a Profession: Death in the United States Navy Officer Corps, 1797–1815," *War & Society* 3 (May 1985): 1:2.
42. *Majestic*'s log, 15 January 1815.
43. *Endymion*'s log, 15 January 1815.
44. *Endymion*'s log, 15 January 1815.
45. Mackenzie, *Decatur*, 219.
46. *Official Letters, With Comments, and Observations relative to the Capture of the President, American Frigate: and Concealment of Men on board that Ship; together With the Correspondence between the Secretary to the Commander in Chief, and the Editor of the Royal Gazette; and a Letter substantiating the charge of Concealment*. Selected from the Royal and Weekly Gazettes, of different dates, Bermuda, St. George, Published by Edmund Ward, 1815, italics added, hereafter "*Official Letters*."
47. *Endymion*'s log, 15 January 1815, italics added.
48. Shubrick's testimony.
49. Decatur to Crowninshield, 18 January 1815 (Captains' Letters).

50. *Pomone*'s log, 15 January 1815; *Naval Chronicle*.
51. *Tenedos*'s log, 15 January 1815.
52. *Naval Chronicle*.
53. *Endymion*'s log, 15 January 1815.
54. *Endymion*'s log, 16 January 1815.
55. Decatur to Crowninshield, 18 January 1815 (Captains' Letters).
56. Captain Henry Hope to Captain John Hayes, 15 January 1815 (ADM1/508, 391–392).
57. *Official Letters*.

Constitution's Winning Captains

Tyrone G. Martin

⚓

During the War of 1812, one American frigate, the *Constitution*, participated in three victorious engagements under three different commanding officers and two different crews. How the victorious captains reported their successes versus how the broader spectrum of participants recalled them is the subject of this paper. For reasons I hope will become apparent, they will be considered in inverse chronological order.

On the afternoon of 20 February 1815, the *Constitution*, under the command of Captain Charles Stewart, came upon the British light frigate *Cyane* and her corvette consort, *Levant*, in the Atlantic Ocean southwest of Gibraltar.[1] After a chase lasting about four hours, the fight commenced. In the four-and-a-half hours that followed, Stewart divided and demolished his enemies—and everyone's report of the battle was in essential agreement with everyone else's! In studying the available eyewitness materials, the only points of difference are the starting time and the length of time it took for smoke to clear after the opening cannonade. Stewart may have "adjusted" these to make the action appear of shorter duration and more intense, but such an assessment has no documentary support. In any event, he and his ship clearly were superior and did everything right on this occasion. Had the battle not occurred in the twilight of the age of fighting sail, this engagement would have been one for the textbooks.

Charles Stewart's predecessor in command of *Constitution* was Commodore William Bainbridge, who had been in command about three-and-a-half months when his moment of glory arrived. To that point, his career had been marked by three negative events: the loss of his first command, schooner *Retaliation*, to the French in the Quasi-War; having his second command, ship *George Washington*, commandeered as a transport by the Dey of Algiers; and losing frigate *Philadelphia*, his third command, to the Tripolines. In each case, his impetuosity was, at least in part, to blame. And in each case, political affiliations saw him through unscathed and even got him promoted to captain ahead of some more senior to him. While cruising offshore of São Salvador, Brazil, on 29 December 1812, Bainbridge spotted two strange sails upwind of him, one large and one small.[2] The larger of the two turned to close him while the other continued toward the port. Bainbridge turned to seaward, writing later that he did so because he wanted to draw his enemy away from the haven of neutral Portuguese waters. At least two of his subordinates have recorded, however, that the stranger initially was assessed as a ship of the line, which made hauling off a prudent maneuver, if not the stuff of which heroic tales are made. When it became apparent that the stranger was faster than *Constitution*, it was obvious she must be another frigate. Then Bainbridge turned back to offer battle.

Bainbridge's reporting of the details of the battle is in agreement with information from other eyewitnesses with the exception of one glaring omission: he says nothing about having been raked from astern. Both the court martial record of Lieutenant Henry Ducie Chads, the senior surviving British officer, and battle diagrams found there and among the papers of Master's Mate Charles F. Waldo, who was in charge of *Constitution*'s main top in the action, clearly show this. After twice being prevented from wearing across *Constitution*'s bows by course reversals, *Java*'s Captain Henry Lambert lulled Bainbridge into thinking he was trying it again when he suddenly wore astern and caught the Americans flat-footed. This is the critical detail as to how one of Bainbridge's wounds occurred and how the ship's wheel was shot away.

These beautifully executed diagrams not only show Lambert's raking maneuver, they also make clear how Bainbridge subsequently handled his critically damaged frigate. When, a few minutes later, a lucky shot destroyed *Java*'s jib boom and threw her into confusion, Bainbridge used the wind to wear his ship through nearly three-quarters of a circle to get to a raking position off his enemy's port quarter while she still was "in irons." Coming nearly up into the wind himself, he fired, and then let *Constitution* fall off, wearing in the opposite direction to regain speed and better control. Later, he again used what we might call a "long wear" to rake a greatly slowed *Java* from ahead, continued around to do it from astern, then fell off to the other side to rake yet again from astern. It was a masterful performance by a twice-wounded man with a wounded warship.

One can understand that a person of Bainbridge's sensitivities and record would not wish to confess to having been raked, but it is a damning fact that no historian had discovered how close *Constitution* came to defeat. It shows Bainbridge totally unprepared for the eventuality, for he made no attempt to wear parallel to his enemy and preclude the tactic while he had the opportunity. His recovery after the fact, despite wounds, shows that Bainbridge did not lose his grip on the situation. He subsequently handled his ship skillfully in gaining the upper hand and ultimately in winning the day.

Another thing Bainbridge failed to mention in his letters was the amount of damage suffered by *Constitution*: *Java* had destroyed six of her eight boats. Two of her masts were so hurt they had to be fished for the return home and replaced before she went to sea again. The main topmast had to be replaced even before the voyage home and repairs made to shot-torn sails and rigging.

Four months prior to Bainbridge's success, *Constitution* engaged in the first frigate duel of the war. When it was done, the representative of the smaller, younger service had won; her enemy gone. The victor headed for Boston to spread the good news.[3] As he neared that port, on 28 August 1812, Captain Isaac Hull, commanding *Constitution*, penned his report to Secretary of the Navy Paul Hamilton. Some 1,200 words long, it detailed weather conditions, the relative positions of the combatants when first sighted, the maneuvers prior to the close action, and an enumeration of the damage inflicted, all set on a general time scale that indicated the decisive phase lasted just 35 minutes. Having thus summarized the action, he then identified his enemy, recounted casualties, commended his officers, and forwarded a list of prisoners. Two days later, now in port, Hull rewrote his report to Hamilton, reducing it to about 500 words. Gone was most of the tactical information he had recorded earlier and emphasized was the brevity of the toe-to-toe phase of the action as he recalled it and the damage wreaked on his adversary. That done, he forwarded both versions, but appended a note to the shorter one, noting: "I have written you an account of the action in detail, but . . . it's my opinion that the less there is said about a brilliant act the better. I have therefore given you a short sketch which I would prefer having published to that in detail. I however leave it with you to do whatever you please with them." The Secretary was, not surprisingly, happy to comply with the Captain's wishes. Hull's "short report" was published and republished across the land and became the basis for the continuing popular legend—the myth—of this battle.

The close-in action actually began at 5:00 P.M., an hour earlier than Hull reported. In about twenty minutes, as Hull reported, *Guerriere*'s mizzen mast was shot away to starboard. Its wreckage, still attached to the ship, plunged and then surfaced to impale itself in the quarter gallery. Acting as a sea anchor, it slewed *Guerriere* to starboard. Seeing this, Hull attempted to luff across his foe's bows, but destroyed main braces precluded it, and *Guerriere* crashed into his larboard mizzen shrouds, destroying the quarter boat hanging there. There was no mention of collision by Hull. The American's forward motion swung the British ship astern, and she surged into *Constitution* several times, smashing Hull's gig in the stern davits.

Hull was unready for his loss of braces, and he had trouble maneuvering his ship. In time, he managed to gain a position on *Guerriere*'s larboard bow, where he unleashed at least two lethal broadsides into her. The Briton, largely immobilized by the mizzen wreckage, was unable to reply with effect. When Hull saw this, he moved in to rake her from ahead. Then, whether from a sudden surge by *Guerriere* as she cleared the wreckage, or an error in Hull's seamanship, another collision occurred, and *Guerriere*'s jib boom became snared in *Constitution*'s starboard mizzen rigging. Again, there was nothing in Hull's reports about a collision.

Both sides then successfully repulsed boarding attempts with deadly fire from their Marines. When the two ships parted, *Guerriere*'s jib boom whipped, and the resultant shock took down both her fore and main masts like dominoes. His enemy now totally immobilized, Hull withdrew to the eastward for a half hour of repairs before returning to take *Guerriere*'s surrender shortly before sunset (which was at 6:57).

Two other points are important. Nowhere in his official reports does Hull specify the respective positions of the foes as the close action began. In the paintings he subsequently commissioned from Michel Felice Corne, however, as well as in a letter he wrote nearly a decade later, he places *Constitution* to larboard. His Purser, Thomas Chew, whom he left to oversee the paintings, argued with Hull on this point but was overridden. Furthermore, the bulk of the witnesses commenting on this point also placed him to starboard.

Why did Hull do this? Perhaps because some knowledgeable individual might suspect the first unreported collision and raise embarrassing questions had he adhered to the facts. There exists a record that *Constitution* fired 953 rounds in this action. Using Hull's 35 minutes, if we exclude the ten 18-pounder rounds listed as having been expended in the initial phase, and if we further assume that the 260 stands of grape and 100 rounds of canister all were fired double shotted with round shot, we end up with each of the 27 cannons the frigate had in broadside firing every minute and 23 seconds, a tremendous rate of fire for experienced crews. Hull's crew was completed less than two months prior to the date of the action and had had only non-firing drills in the interim. It is unrealistic to accept that these men, no matter how well motivated they might have been, could have achieved and sustained this rate of fire. It is more persuasive to add an hour to the engagement, as found in British reports—and allow for periods of no firing—then one comes up with a much more realistic rate of fire.

Hull appended enclosures to each of his reports to the Secretary detailing the damages suffered by *Constitution*. (These were never published and cannot be found today.) Hull made only the briefest allusion to his damages in the body of the longer report, summed up by saying the ship was ready for action again in two hours; however, he deleted even this observation from the later, widely circulated one. A survey of the ship's log for the days following the engagement, supplemented by the observations of the participants, shows that the big American frigate had fore and main masts damaged enough to be fished and woolded. Braces and jib halyards had been shot away in the first ten minutes of the close action. Sails and much of the remaining standing and running rigging were "much cut." The crossjack yard had been snapped and the spanker gaff and boom destroyed. The band for the main chains had been broken and the chains for the main topsail yard shot away. The fore topgallant mast had been shot through the heel, and the truck at its head was gone.

Damages not affecting maneuverability included the loss of the two boats, injury to the taffrail, and a small fire in Hull's day cabin caused by a burning wad from a British bow gun at close range. While *Constitution* may have been basically ready to defend herself again in two hours, much of the trip home was spent in effecting repairs, and she certainly was in no condition to continue a war cruise. (Replacement of both fore and main masts was a priority effort under Bainbridge before he took her out of Boston in October.)

Isaac Hull was not only the victor of the day, but he later succeeded in attaining every benefit from his defeat of *Guerriere*. The earliest historians merely copied his short report as originally published. Roosevelt and Mahan struggled to describe, in their own words, the action in accordance with what the Captain had written, but, concerned with larger issues, apparently did not take the time to investigate other reporrts. A critical look at the maneuvers, considering time and distance factors and relative motion, and utilizing the eyewitness accounts from both sides, did not occur until the last quarter of the 20th century. Hull's was not the swift demolition of a powerful foe, but a rather clumsily fought action against a smaller enemy who might have carried the day had not *Constitution* been so powerfully built.

My colleagues and I have studied the battle reports of five American captains in eight actions—seven victories and one defeat—and have found only one instance in which the report is corroborated in its essentials by other participants. It appears that the majority of the officers of our young Navy, those defenders of "honor" and seekers after "glory," were perfectly willing to sacrifice "truth" in their quest. The bottom line is: if your intent is to analyze tactics or evaluate a fighting captain's actions, do not content yourself merely with his report, for you probably are not getting the whole story. In one of the cases discussed, controversy has arisen in later years as a result of writers overstepping the record in determining winners and losers. It seems to be a human condition not to be content with the way events evolve, and if the humans also are historians, then they must strive all the harder to present the truth that is at the heart of history, whatever their era of interest. In other words: *caveat historicus.*

1. Primary sources for this discussion of the *Constitution-Cyane/Levant* battle include the Court Martial Record, Captain Lord George Douglas, R.N., 28 June 1815, ADM1/5449, PRO [Captain of HMS *Levant.*]; Court Martial Record, Captain George Thomas Falcon, RN, 28 June 1815, ADM 1/5449, PRO [Captain of HMS *Cyane.*]; Chaplain Asheton Y. Humphreys, U.S.N., "Recapitulatory Journal," Lilly Library, Indiana Univ. [Thought to have been on quarterdeck during battle.]; Ltr, Captain Charles Stewart, U.S.N., to Secretary of the Navy, [?] May 1815, NA; Log, USS *Constitution*, 18 December 1814–16 May 1815, NA; Daphne D. C. Pouchin, "What It Was Like To Be Shot Up By 'Old Ironsides,' " *American Heritage*, Volume 34, Number 3 (April/May 1983). [Includes the text of three foolscap pages, apparently from HMS *Cyane*'s log, signed "Alfd L. Strangeways." Midshipman Strangeways was among the prisoners removed from *Cyane.*]; Norma Adams Price, Norma

Adams, ed. *Letters from Old Ironsides, 1813–1815*. Tempe, AZ: Beverly-Merriam Press. 1984. [The edited letters of Midshipman Pardon Mawney Whipple, U.S.N., who was assigned to the Third Division on *Constitution*'s Gun Deck.].

2. Primary sources for the discussion of the *Constitution/Java* battle include Midn Frederick Baury, USN, Journal, 28 October 1812–16 February 1813, Massachusetts Historical Society. [On quarterdeck during the battle.]; James Campbell, Boatswain's Mate, U.S.N., "Glorious Naval Victory." Broadside. Boston, c. 1813. [Gun Captain, #13 long gun during battle.]; Court Martial Record, Lieutenant Henry Ducie Chads, R.N., 23 April 1813, ADM1/5435, PRO. [Lieutenant Chads was the senior surviving officer in the *Java*.]; Amos Alexander Evans, Surgeon, U.S.N., "Journal Kept on Board the Frigate *Constitution*," repr for William D. Sawtell from the *Pennsylvania Magazine of History and Biography* (1967). [Evans was *Constitution*'s Surgeon, assigned to the cockpit in battle.]; "Journal Kept on Board the U.S. Frigate *Constitution*," in Samuel Woodworth, "The War," 3 vols. [Commodore Bainbridge's journal.]; ltr, Bainbridge to John Bullus, 23 January 1813, Fogg Autograph Collection, War of 1812, Maine Historical Society; ltr, Bainbridge to SecNav, 13 April 1813, NA; ltr Midn Henry Gilliam to Captain William Jones [the Secretary of the Navy and Gilliam's uncle], 16 February 1813, Georgia Historical Society. [In charge of *Constitution*'s mizzen top during the battle.]; Charles F. Waldo, Master's Mate, USN, Mss battle diagram, Private Collection. [In charge of *Constitution*'s main top in the battle.].

3. Primary sources for the *Constitution/Guerriere* battle are: a) Mdn Frederick Baury, U.S.N., Journal, 24 June–26 October 1812. Massachusetts Historical Society. [Thought to have been on the quarterdeck during the battle.]; Court Martial Record, Captain Richard [sic: James] R. Dacres, R.N., 2 October 1812, ADM 1/5431, PRO; Evans, Amos Alexander, Surgeon, U.S.N. "Journal Kept on Board the Frigate *Constitution*," Reprinted for William D. Sawtell from the *Pennsylvania Magazine of History and Biography*, Lincoln, Massachusetts, 1967. [Evans was *Constitution*'s Surgeon, assigned to the cockpit in battle.]; Mrs. Lilla M. Howes, ed., "Letters of Henry Gilliam, 1809–1817," *Georgia Historical Quarterly*, Vol. XXXVIII, No. 1 (March 1954), pp. 59–61. [Midshipman Gilliam probably was in charge of *Constitution*'s mizzen top.]; Letters, Captain Isaac Hull to the Secretary of the Navy, 28 and 30 August 1812, NA; Letter, Captain Isaac Hull to Purser Thomas J. Chew, October 1812. William L. Clements Library, University of Michigan. [Chew was *Constitution*'s Purser at time of battle.]; Ltr, Hull to Professor Benjamin Silliman, 29 October 1821, Yale Univ.; Ltr, U.S. Naval Observatory to author, 9 August 1984.; ltr, Lieutenant Alexander S. Wadsworth to Stephen Longfellow, 31 August 1812, MS 67-497-1, Maine Historical Society. [Wadsworth probably was in charge of *Constitution*'s First Division during the battle.]; Log, USS *Constitution*, 1–29 August 1812, Henry E. Huntington Library; Charles Morris, "Autobiography." *USNIP*, Vol. VI, No. 12 (1880), pp. 163–67. [*Constitution*'s First Lieutenant at time of battle.]; Moses Smith. *Naval Scenes in the Late War* (Boston: Gleason's Publishing Hall, 1846), pp. 30–36. [Seaman Smith was Gun Captain #1 Long Gun during the battle.]; The battle is treated in greater detail in Tyrone G. Martin, "Isaac Hull's Victory Revisited," *American Neptune*, Volume XLVII, Number 1 (Winter 1987), pp. 14–21.

The Crescent Adrift: Problems of Ottoman Maritime Power

Douglas S. Brookes

⚓

When asked to consider the history of the Imperial Ottoman Navy, maritime historians might recount a galley fleet victory or two, the defeat at Lepanto, then understandably run rather quickly into shallow waters. Thus, when preparing these remarks, it seemed best to diverge from the themes of naval architecture or seaborne strategy typically addressed at a naval history symposium, and, instead, back up to a more general question. What was the overall course of Ottoman naval history? Or, differently stated, what was the attitude of the Ottoman state toward naval power?

But it was a naval historian friend who crystalized for me the question I really want to address. One day I proudly showed him the magnificent 1910 lithograph I had purchased in Istanbul, showing the Ottoman fleet racing down the Bosphorus before the imperial palace, reviewed by the sultan's yacht, flags flying, smoke billowing. My friend said, "Ah, the Imperial Ottoman Navy—steaming off to another glorious defeat." Thus, the other question to be addressed: why did the Ottoman Empire not retain the naval strength it had wielded in the sixteenth century?

The latter question seems to demand addressing before indulging in the particulars of Ottoman maritime history. Here, after all, was an empire that straddled the Mediterranean, Black, Red, and Arabian Seas and the Persian Gulf, at the very heart of the great commerce between Europe and South Asia. Yet it never developed a commercial trading fleet of great significance. Its once omnipotent navy, the terror of sixteenth-century Europe, slumped to such an extent that the tired frigate selected in 1890 to carry the sultan's gifts to the emperor of Japan, the *Ertugrul*, did not pass Suez before requiring repairs, then foundered off the Japanese coast on her return voyage.

Clearly Ottoman Turkey did not build an enduring maritime presence because the empire did not develop an enduring native-born international commerce. This study will analyze the geographical inheritance and socioeconomic objectives of the empire in order to uncover the factors which inhibited the growth of Ottoman commerce and, hence, of Ottoman shipping protected by a vigorous Ottoman fleet.

To consider the first of our questions, let us review six centuries of maritime history in ten minutes, beginning with the Ottoman merchant marine. Ottoman commercial shipping existed throughout the centuries alongside the far vaster fleets of, first, the Italian city states, and then the Atlantic seapowers trading in the Mediterranean and east of Suez. Yet Ottoman commercial fleets never developed into rivals of European shipping concerns.

Initially, the Venetians and Genoese transported most of the Ottoman international seaborne commerce after the empire expanded to the shores of the Aegean in the fourteenth century. With the Italians in possession of large fleets ready to transport commerce to Europe, the Turks developed only a small merchant fleet of their own. Far from a sign of weakness, the Turks regarded the situation as advantageous. By leaving shipping in Italian hands, the Turks could threaten one or the other Italian city-states with cutting off their trade, as need arose. Foreign commerce seemed of prime value as a diplomatic weapon rather than an economic boon.[1]

As the empire expanded in the fifteenth and sixteenth centuries, small numbers of Ottoman merchant ships participated in overseas trade. Turkish vessels carried Eastern goods to Italy and throughout the Black Sea. They carried grain and goods to Istanbul from the Balkans, Anatolia, and the Arab provinces, and provisions from the northern provinces to Egypt. Vessels of the formerly Byzantine sailors, now under Ottoman suzerainty, transported the empire's commerce throughout the Mediterranean just as they had carried Greek trade before the Turkish conquests.

In particular, an Ottoman Christian merchant/shipowner class, mostly Greek, developed in the Balkans in the sixteenth century, as maize and coffon were cultivated for trade to Western Europe.[2] By the mid-seventeenth century, according to the Turkish traveler and author Evliya Celebi, Istanbul's merchant shipowners numbered among the empire's most prosperous citizens. They comprised two groups, both composed of Muslims and Orthodox Christians. The first captained their own vessels and were called "Black Sea Captains" or "Mediterranean Captains," according to where they traded. The latter group owned large fleets of ships trading between the empire and Europe.[3] As wars between the French and English ruined European shippers trading to Ottoman Balkan ports, Ottoman-owned fleets increased in size.[4] Yet the Atlantic seapowers always recouped their maritime position in the Levant as the wars between them ended.

East of Suez, vast quantities of spices and silk entered the empire from two sources. Part came overland through or from Persia. Arab sailing vessels transported the remainder from South Asia to the Red Sea and the Persian Gulf for transshipment westward across the Mediterranean to Europe. Yet the Ottomans never constructed a merchant fleet to haul this trade because the Arab merchant vessels filled this function well. Nor did the Portuguese effort to divert commerce around Africa disrupt the spice and silk trade seriously enough to stimulate construction of Ottoman commercial and naval fleets.

After 600, however, the transshipment trade steadily declined. The financial difficulties of the empire had led to increased customs duties on the transshipment trade in the late sixteenth century. The English and the Dutch then sought to avoid the Ottoman middleman by sailing around the empire directly to the sources of the spices and silk in South Asia. In 1603 the first East India merchant ship returned to London, barely twenty years after Englishmen had established the Levant Company for trade in Istanbul and Izmir. By 1626, England was importing Asian pepper around Africa, then selling it to the Turks.[5]

In effect, the Ottomans throttled their transshipment trade by relying heavily on the customs duties it engendered. Still, the Turkish empire did not join in the competition for overseas trade beyond the establishment of a small trading station in Sumatra,[6] nor did it attempt to develop exports of its own as a matter of state policy. The image remains of a small Ottoman trading fleet, mostly Greek and, therefore, Christian-owned in the Mediterranean, mostly Arab east of Suez, pursuing the little intra-impenal seaborne trading. For the most part, Europe transported Ottoman international commerce in European ships.

Turning now to the navy, in overview, the Ottoman fleet seemed invincible in the late fifteenth and sixteenth centuries, then slumped in efficacy once expansion of the empire stopped. External humiliation and internal reform sparked modest naval revivals in the nineteenth century. Further, self-regeneration commensurate with the empire's revived trade and new role in the Concert of Europe placed the Imperial Ottoman Navy on the verge of viable competitiveness as World War One destroyed the empire.

The Ottoman Navy began its 600-year career in 1320, as soon as the Ottomans conquered seaside territory on the Gulf of Izmit in northwestern Anatolia. With no prior maritime experience, the Ottomans borrowed maritime technology from the Italians and the Byzantines. They also profited greatly from the corsair experience of the other Anatolian Turkish principalities that they conquered throughout the fourteenth century. Because their early adversaries possessed no maritime forces of their own, however, and because the army encountered no immediate need for waterborne transport of troops, the small Ottoman warships played only minor roles in the early territorial expansion of the empire. To transport troops across the Straits from Anatolia for the wars of conquest in Southeast Europe, the Ottomans simply hired Byzantine vessels.[7]

Consequently, the outfitting of a large Ottoman fleet for the siege of Constantinople in 1453 provided a nasty surprise for the Christian defenders. The conquest of the Byzantine capital involved the first major Ottoman use of the military advantages a fleet could provide. Acknowledging the role of the navy in the victory, the Ottomans, thereafter, incorporated a large fleet into their military operations. Reflecting the supremacy of the army in Ottoman strategy, the navy could help the army by transporting troops to battle. Together they could conquer land.

Sultan Bayazit II strengthened the fleet by inviting Turkish corsairs in the Aegean to work for his navy. With their experience, the Turks overpowered most of the islands and coasts of the Aegean and Black Sea. Selim I made use of the fleet to transport troops, heavy artillery, and supplies to Egypt during his conquest of the Levant in 1516–17.

Immediately after securing Egypt and the Hejaz, however, the Turks faced a quite different opponent in the Portuguese traders/conquerors at large in the Indian Ocean. The utterly un-Mediterranean caravel sailing ships of the Portuguese, mounting powerful broadsides of cannon, represented a new threat to Turkish power. The caravels allowed the Portuguese to roam the high seas at will and bring relatively large numbers of cannon to bear on opponents. By contrast, the Ottoman fleet consisted of the traditional Mediterranean oared galley. With its low freeboard and difficulty of maneuvering under sail, the galley could not venture into the open waters of the ocean with impunity. Nor was the galley stout enough to carry more than three to five cannon, all placed at the bow. It could fight very well, however, in the calmer waters of the Red Sea, under cover of shore bases whose heavy cannon could inflict much damage.[8]

Working in tandem with the cannon of the Ottoman encampment ashore, the galleys defeated the Portuguese squadron which sailed up the Red Sea to Jedda in 1517. The Turks chased the Portuguese from the Red Sea, but could not follow them across the Arabian Sea to destroy their bases in India. From these bases, the Portuguese continued to divert a portion of the Levant spice trade around Africa to Lisbon.

The death of Selim I in 1520 left the Portuguese quandary to be resolved by his son, Suleyman the Magnificent. The new sultan's options were two: either to construct an ocean-going sailing ship fleet to pursue the Portuguese across the Indian Ocean and so warn off other potential interlopers, or to turn toward central Europe and pursue the holy war against Christendom. As one factor to be weighed in the sultan's decision, by the 1520s the Levant spice trade had resumed its old volume despite the Portuguese incursions. The Portuguese then seemed but a slight and distant nuisance, once the Ottomans secured the Red Sea approaches to the holy cities in Arabia. Reflecting the traditional Ottoman emphasis on territorial acquisition rather than the development of international trade, the sultan turned his power against Europe.

The decision not to pursue the infidel challenge on the Indian Ocean decided the future course of Ottoman naval history. The state would remain a land-based empire in which the army ranked at the center of military strategy. The navy would merely assist the army in the conquest of territory, which would then yield taxes to support the state and its military. To the Ottomans, the creation of a commercial overseas trading empire, such as the Portuguese, offered no advantageous lure. Therefore, the state never viewed the primary role of the navy as protecting the seaborne commerce of the empire. Besides, Ottoman commerce seemed relatively unthreatened in the sixteenth century. The Portuguese had made little dent in the trade entering the Ottoman lands from the east. The Italians in the Mediterranean, who carried the trade away to the west, relied on the Ottomans for their business and generally cooperated with them. Little concerned with international commerce, Ottoman naval policy did not change even when Europe robbed the empire of its Asian commerce.

As a consequence of these decisions, the oared galley remained the backbone of the Ottoman fleet. It met the needs of the fleet, confined as it was to operations in the protected coastal waters of the Mediterranean, Black Sea, Red Sea, and Persian Gulf. The long war for Crete (1644–1669), fought against the fleet of Venetian sailing ships, first induced the Porte to build a sailing navy of its own to meet the challenges posed by these new vessels. Thus, the 1682 decision to adopt the European galleon as the major warship of the navy to gradually replace the galley did not reflect neglectful tardiness in adopting advances. It represented, instead, the traditional Ottoman readiness to adopt advances in European military technology once those advances truly assisted the state in meeting its goals.[9]

Following the defeat of Venice over Crete in 1669, the Ottomans faced no serious seaborne challenges until the rise of Russian naval strength toward the close of the eighteenth century. Once again the pivotal location of the empire swept it into contact with international transit—this time at the crossroads of the expanding Russian and British empires. The remaining centuries of Ottoman naval history reflected the empire's jockeying for position in the maritime struggle between St. Petersburg and London.

The decades of naval inaction in the early eighteenth century inflicted military slovenliness and demoralization, culminating in the Russian cremation—with the assistance of Greek corsairs—of nearly the entire fleet at Ceme near Izmir in 1770. With humiliation at Russian hands again in 1791, the needs of the navy received imperial attention. Sultan Selim III initiated far-reaching naval reforms.[10] The government hired French, Swedish, and British naval architects to redesign the clumsy Turkish vessels for greater seaworthiness and fighting capability. Improvements in recruitment, training, and retention of the crews dovetailed with the new law appointing officers based on ability, not on how much money they could pay to purchase the rank.

Selim's reforms resulted in a navy which could hold its own through the Napoleonic era, the Greek wars of independence, and the Crimean War. The sultan could transform the navy, due to its non-Turkish origin, with far fewer objections from conservative elements than he could the army. When the army's Janissary Corps revolted in 1826 to protest reforms, the fleet remained loyal throughout the state-ordered massacre of the Corps. As a result of its loyalty, the navy basked in imperial favor formerly lavished on the army alone.

Perhaps encouraged by the credible performance of the fleet at Crimea, Sultan Abdulaziz oversaw a major expansion of the navy in the 1860s and 1870s. Possibly, too, the sultan's excursion through Europe in 1867 inspired him to acquire a squadron of the latest steam-powered ironclad warships. However, the fiscal crisis which gripped the empire during and after his reign took its toll on the costly new fleet. Naval expansion came to a halt following the accession of Abdulhamit II in 1876. Some observers have accused Abdulhamit of deliberately allowing the fleet to deteriorate during his thirty-two-year reign.[11] But the state had bankrupted itself in the 1870s, leaving no money for more than the occasional purchase of small warships. Nor, for all the money Abdulaziz had lavished on it, had the fleet provided much help during the Russo-Turkish War of 1877–1878. Consequently, Abdulhamit resumed the traditional Ottoman reliance on the army, and the navy rode at anchor in the Golden Horn between 1878 and 1908. Permission for a ship even to move had to be obtained from the palace beforehand.

The overthrow of Abdulhamit II in 1909 ushered in a reversal of naval policy. To benefit from the dramatic evolution in European fleets, the Naval Ministry scrapped older ships in favor of newer vessels obtained thanks to the *Muavenet-i Milliye*, the newly formed Ottoman Naval League. The League's journal spread interest in the fleet among the populace, while its money-raising campaigns at public rallies across the empire made possible the purchase of several modern warships. The supreme achievement of the *Muavenet-i Milliye* occurred when the government ordered two dreadnought battleships in England in 1913, with monies raised by the League. Britain's requisitioning of the ships while on the ways at the outbreak of World War I infuriated Ottoman opinion and helped turn the then-neutral empire toward the Central Powers.

Between 1911 and the dissolution of the empire in 1923, then, a patched-up but not yet fully modernized Ottoman fleet provided moderately successful defense of Turkish territory during the wars with, in turn, Italy, the Balkan kingdoms, the Allied Powers, and Greece.

Following this brief overview of their maritime history, the question remains, why did the Ottomans relinquish the naval competitiveness they had achieved against Europe? Turkish naval power remained quiescent after the sixteenth century not because of the usually cited reasons of decay or incompetence, but because neither military nor commercial needs arose to demand naval expansion. Decay, as we have seen, there was, but as a consequence of economic and political realities rather than as a symptom of ineptitude. This situation changed only in the late nineteenth century when the tremendous expansion of foreign trade and the new demands placed upon the state as a member of the Concert of Europe called for the creation of an expanded naval force.

What were the qualities of the Ottoman system, then, which de-emphasized the evolution of a flourishing native maritime commerce? One such quality was the Ottoman guild system. Encompassing the entire working population, the guilds inhibited individual entrepreneurship and innovation in order to guarantee steady employment for members. The goal was to eliminate competition and control prices. Changes in imperial economic goals finally led to the abolition of the guilds only in 1912.

State opposition to export also hindered maritime commerce. The Ottoman system had generally opposed exports from the beginning as not necessarily beneficial for the state—indeed, as counter to the need to provision the state. As the population of the empire expanded, the government expressly forbade the export of crucial products, in particular foodstuffs. This seemed necessary to forestall scarcity, high prices, and political unrest. This policy backfired into large-scale smuggling, however, because prices remained much lower than in Europe, and Europe was buying.[12] Izmir, in particular, evolved into a bustling center of illegal crop-selling to Europeans, since the money was good.

By inadvertently encouraging smuggling, the state's hostility to exports cost it not only the smuggled produce, but also the opportunity to earn customs duties on legitimate export. Ottoman Greek brigands prospered, but legitimate shipowners lost the opportunity to earn revenues on the transport of exports in Ottoman ships. The opposition to export also encouraged chronic piracy, primarily by the Greek brigands. The risk of piracy in turn made shipping more expensive by requiring larger crews and more armament for defense. Consequently, cargo-carrying efficiency declined.[13] Not until Greek independence did the threat of piracy in the Eastern Mediterranean recede. Until it did, legitimate Ottoman shipping remained doubly handicapped by state opposition to export and by smuggling.

With export trade discouraged, European capitalists with the money to develop overseas trade turned to other parts of the world. One product native to the empire, coffee, originally was exported from south Arabia through Cairo. After the government resumed pressure against export in the late seventeenth century, the Dutch took coffee to Java, and the French took it to the West Indies. By the 1730s, foreign coffee had swamped the Ottoman market.[14] The cotton and silk trades suffered similar fates. Whereas in the fifteenth and sixteenth centuries the empire loomed large in the trade of Europe, after 1600, the European sea powers circumvented the empire, with its resistance to exports, and established their own direct sources of supply further afield.[15]

Thus, most Ottoman foreign trade slipped away in small Greek-owned vessels as brigandage. After the empire allowed foreigners to trade under their own flags, in 1739, legitimate exports then departed in European vessels, funneled to them by European residents or their Ottoman Christian intermediaries.

Concomitantly, the capitulations awarded to certain European powers in the sixteenth century granted foreign merchants immunity from taxes and levied customs duties below what Ottoman merchants had to pay.[16] In hindsight, seemingly unfavorable to the empire, the capitulations in the short run allowed the state to protect its trade in silk and spices from diversion by the British or the Dutch in Iran.[17] But their ultimate effect was to work against the development of commerce that might be carried away in Ottoman ships, and in favor of imports brought in foreign hulls. In effect, the Muslim merchant was made to subsidize the foreign trader and his foreign ships.

Fiscal policies did not consider entrepreneurship as a necessarily desirable goal. Would-be entrepreneurs faced a discriminatory tax burden because the entire military-administrative class remained exempt from taxation. Interest rates remained high in comparison to rates in Europe, perhaps due to the shortage of coinage in circulation. Credit was difficult to obtain and expensive once obtained.[18]

The insecurity of person and property in Ottoman lands also worked against the development of industry and maritime commerce.[19] Property remained subject to imperial confiscation and to capricious extortions by governors and customs officials. Then, the economic system favored consumption of capital and not its accumulation over years for investment. Islamic inheritance law mandated division of estates among the heirs in certain proportions. This rendered difficult the transmission of large blocks of money and property through generations, promoting its dispersal or seclusion instead.[20] The practice favored the Muslim *waqf* endowment system whereby the populace could shield its resources from the grasp of the state by creating charitable trusts. However, the huge sums thereby sheltered remained essentially untapped for industrial enterprise.[21]

Political and economic insecurity had their counterpart in social insecurity. As part of its economic innovations, Europe instituted disaster management long before the Ottoman empire did. Infamous as endemic with plague, the Ottoman empire took no steps to control the disease until the navy established an isolated hospital in 1806.[22] Meanwhile, repeated plague outbursts into the nineteenth century decimated the labor supply and threatened the security of investment.[23]

Here I will discount resistance to innovation on the part of Islam as a significant factor in impeding commerce. There exist numerous examples of ready adoption of European techniques in warfare and in production when benefit accrued from adopting them.

Education did, however, remain limited in availability and restricted in scope, with literacy far below that of Europe. The resultant intellectual stagnation of the empire troubled the Turkish scholar Katip Celebi as early as 1657.[24] Eleven years later, the English traveler Paul Rycaut noted the appalling state of Turkish cartography—hardly conducive to maritime excellence, if excellence were the goal.[25] Opposition to the printing press in the empire exacerbated the tendency. The consequent reliance on handwritten manuscripts, by nature time-consuming to reproduce and prone to error in the copying, severely restricted the scope of the maritime education of ships' officers—those officers who could read at all. Lacking printed maps, quite likely the reliance on hand-copying accounted for the gross inaccuracy of Turkish charts. Without the printing press, the price of information remained high, and the empire could not share in the tremendous pool of knowledge accumulating in Europe.

Corruption thrived in the attempt to beat the system financially—a logical response to the cycles of devaluation and inflation which wracked the state after the late sixteenth century. The navy suffered in particular. The fifty years of peace between 1725 and 1775 provided little incentive to keep the fleet in fighting shape. For extra income, most officials of the naval yard at Istanbul held other jobs and rarely showed up at the yard. Essential maintenance on ships remained neglected while large sums of money intended for maintenance flowed to individual pockets instead. Perhaps most harmful of all, after the sixteenth century the post of Lord High Admiral degenerated from an appointment for qualified officers to a political plum for court favorites utterly inexperienced in the naval art and the demands of a fighting fleet.

In a similar reaction to the fiscal situation, captains and ships' officers purchased their commissions for the profit the salary would bring, a maritime variation on the tax-farming system. This meant that gentlemen who had no knowledge of the sea served as officers in the imperial navy. With the emphasis on turning a profit, officers ignored maintenance, cheated on food rations, and substituted fictitious names for deceased or discharged sailors so as to continue to collect the sailor's pay, which in turn left the ships undermanned.[26]

By the mid-eighteenth century, the quality of officers and crew so deteriorated that Ottoman vessels had to sail within sight of the coast and could not navigate at night.[27] The post-1791 naval reforms of Selim III and his successors eliminated much corruption, but as long as economic realities forced one to feather his nest where he could, the traditional modus operandi asserted itself until the last days of the imperial navy.

Finally, frequent local violence arose from the waning of central control between 1700 and 1850. In addition, all wars which involved the empire after the mid-seventeenth century, except the Crimean War, took place on Ottoman territory. Unfortunately for the Ottomans, their first and major territorial losses occurred in Europe—the most fertile and productive segment of the realm. The havoc wreaked on the economy by these wars far outweighed the fighting experience gained and strained the treasury through both expenditure and decreased revenue from territorial losses.

In conclusion, the Ottoman empire abandoned its ranking in the world's naval hierarchy and did not develop a merchant fleet seemingly commensurate with its strategic maritime location astride the crossroads of Europe, Asia, and Africa. Having enumerated the major reasons for this apparently (in the European view) negative trend, I trust that one will reject accusations of Muslim backwardness in not developing as Europe did. After all, this state and its navy survived for 600 years until militant nationalism and European economic competitiveness triggered its demise. Rather, I would emphasize that the Ottoman state deliberately chose to develop its maritime commerce and its navy in the way that it did, that is to say, *not* on the model of the European seagoing empires. A small native commercial fleet and naval force served the empire well, in accordance with its economic and military objectives, at least from the sixteenth to the eighteenth centuries.

These objectives changed over the eighteenth and nineteenth centuries, as European expansion integrated the empire into the emerging world economy at its periphery. The resulting dramatic increase in the empire's foreign trade sparked the emergence of a strengthened naval fleet, but enmeshed the empire in the competitiveness which sparked the First World War. Following the war's destruction of the familiar status quo between Europe and the Ottomans, the Turkish military installed a social and economic system which embraced the European methods of producing and trading, at the expense of the traditional Ottoman orientation to the world.

To the inheritors of the Ottoman empire in Europe, Asia, and Africa, there remained the lessons of economic integration under European direction, which the Ottomans were among the first in the world to face. Against the onslaught of European finance capital seeking raw materials and markets, the Ottoman navy could offer no defense.

1. Archival sources for this paper include: Basbakanlik Arsvi (Prime Minister's Archives), Istanbul; and the Deniz Muzesi Arsivi (Naval Museum Archives), Istanbul. Printed sources include: Ahmad, Feroz. "Vanguard of a Nascent Bourgeoisie: the Social and Economic Policy of The Young Turks 1908–1918," in *Social and Economic History of Turkey (1071–1920)* (Ankara: Meteksan Skti, 1980), pp. 329–350; Alpagut, Haydar, *Denidze Turkiye* (Istanbul: Deniz Matbassi, 1937); Ashraf, Ahmad. "Historical Obstacles to the Development of a Bourgeoisie in Iran," in *Studies in the Economic History of the Middle East* (London: Oxford Univ. Pr., 1970); Ahmad Ashraf, "Historical Obstacles to the Development of a Bourgeoisie in Iran," in *Studies in the Economic History of the Middle East* (London: Oxford Univ. Pr., 1970); Ashtor, Eliyahu. "The Venetian Supremacy in Levantine Trade: Monopoly or PreColonialism?" in *Studies on the Levantine Trade in the Middle Ages* (London: Variorum Reprints, 1978), pp. 5–53; Baer, Gabriel. "Guilds in Middle Eastern

History," in M. Cook, ed., *Studies in the Economic History of the Middle East*; G. Baer, "Ottoman Guilds: A Reassessment," in *Social and Economic History of Turkey*; F. Braudel, *The Mediterranean World in the Age of Philip II* (Vol. I London: Collins, 1972); A. Buyuktugrul, Osmanlt Deniz Harp, *Tarihi* (Istanbul: Deniz Basimevi, 1970); *Buyuktugrul*, Afif. Osmanlt Deniz Harp Tarihi (Istanbul: Deniz Basimevi, 1970); Cohen, Amnon. "Some Conventional Concepts of Ottoman Administration in the Light of a More Detailed Study: the Case of Eighteenth Century Palestine," *Social and Economic History of Turkey, 1071–1920*, pp. 187–192; Davis, Ralph. "English Imports from the Middle East, 1580–1780," *Studies in the Economic History of the Middle East* (London: Oxford, 1970); Ertugrul (Bey). *Akdeniz Hakimiyeti ve Turkler.* (Istanbul: Deniz Matbaasy, 1933); Evin, Ahmet O. "The Tulip Age and Definitions of Westernization," *Social and Economic History of Turkey*, pp. 131–45; Findley, Carter V. "Patrimonial Household Organization and Factional Activity in the Ottoman Ruling Class," *Social and Economic History of Turkey*, pp. 227–235; Gibb, Sir Hamilton and Harold Bowen. *Islamic Society and the West*, Vol. 1, pts. 1 and 2 (London: Oxford Press, 1963); Guilmartin, John F. *Gunpowder and Galleys* (New York: Cambridge Press, 1974); Gulen, Nejat. *Dunden Bugene Bahriyemiz* (Istanbul: Kastas, 1988); Hess, Andrew. "The Evolution of the Ottoman Seaborne Empire in the Age of Oceanic Discoveries, 1453–1525," *American Historical Review*, Vol. 75, no. 7, December 1970; Inalcik, Halil. "Capital Formation in the Ottoman Empire," *Journal of Economic History*, Vol. 29, No. 1, March 1969; Inalcik, Halil. "The Ottoman Economic Mind and Aspects of the Ottoman Economy," in M. Cook, ed., *Studies in the Economic History of the Middle East* (London: Oxford Press, 1970), pp. 207–18; Islamoglu, Huri, and Caglar Keyder. "Agenda for Ottoman History," in Islamoglu, ed., *The Ottoman Empire and the World Economy* (London: Oxford, 1970); Jones, E. L. *The European Miracle* (New York: Cambridge, 1981); Issawi, Charles. "Middle East Economic Development 1815–1914: the General and the Specific," *Studies in the Economic History of the Middle East*; Kasaba, Resat. *The Ottoman Empire and the World Economy* (Albany: SUNY Press, 1988); Kurtoglu, Fevzi. *Turkierin Deniz Muharebeleri* (Istanbul: Deniz Matbaasi, 1940); Ma'oz, Moshe. "Intercommunal Relations in Ottoman Syria during the Tanzimat Era: Economic and Social Factors," *Social and Economic History of Turkey*, pp. 205–10; Murphey, Rhoads. "The Ottoman Attitude towards the Adoption of Western Technology: The Role of the Efrenci Technicians in Civil and Military Applications," in *Contributions a l'histoire economique et sociale de l'Empire ottoman* (Paris: Association pour le developement des estudes turques, Collection Turcica III, 1983), pp. 287–98; Padfield, Peter. *The Tide of Empires* Vol. 1: 1481–1654 (London: Routledge and Kegan Paul, 1979); Sahillioglu, Halil. "Sivis Year Crises in Ottoman Empire," in *Studies in the Economic History of the Middle East*, pp. 230–52; Shaw, Stanford J. "Selim III and the Ottoman Navy," in *Turcica* Vol. I, 1969; and Wallerstein, Immanuel. "The Ottoman Empire and the Capitalist World Economy," in *Social and Economic History of Turkey*, pp. 117–22. For citation, see Inalcik, "Mind," p. 214.

2. Jones, p. 189.

3. Inalcik, "Capital Formation," p. 120, quoting from p. 551 of *Seyahatname* of Evliya Celebi.

4. Jones, p. 189.

5. Davis, p. 195.

6. Braudel, p. 568.

7. Gibb and Bowen, 1, 1, p. 88.

8. The lack of Ottoman crews experienced in handling the new vessels helped draw out the long war. See Gibb and Bowen, 1, 1, pp. 95ff.

9. See Guilmartin on the continued usefulness of the galley in the nineteenth century. Also, there seems no basis for the theory that Ottoman naval decline occurred in this era because the empire's timber resources ran out in the seventeenth and eighteenth centuries. See Murphey, p. 292. The lack of timber theoretically caused the Ottomans to retain the galley for coastal defense rather than develop a seagoing fleet of galleons. However, a galley fleet would not consume significantly less timber than a galleon fleet. Both Braudel (p. 142) and Shaw (p. 225) cite the chronically abundant oak, pine, and great plane trees of the Black Sea, Marmara, and Gulf of Izmit coasts.

10. See Shaw on the reforms of Selim III.

11. For one expression of this theory, see Gulen. The suspicious sultan may have mistrusted the navy for its role in the deposition of his uncle, Abdulaziz.

12. Islamoglu and Keyder, pp. 51–57. The authors conclude that large scale smuggling of raw materials to fee Europe's burgeoning industry clinched the peripheralization of the Ottoman Empire in the world economy.

13. Jones, p. 65.

14. Davis, p. 201.

15. Davis, p. 206.

16. Generally 3 percent customs duty for foreign merchants versus 5 percent for native merchants. Gibb and Bowen, Vol. 2, p. 15.

17. Inalcik, "Mind," p. 214.

18. Inalcik, "Capital Formation," p. 138.

19. Findley, p. 227.

20. Inalcik, "Capital Formation," p. 138.

21. Inalcik, "Captial Formation," p. 136.

22. Shaw, p. 239.

23. Jones, p. 181.

24. Quoted in Jones, p. 179.

25. Jones, p. 179.

26. Shaw, p. 213.

27. Shaw, p. 213.

English and American Mariners in Chile's First Squadron, 1817–18

Carlos Lopez

⚓

It is a generally accepted fact that Lord Thomas Cochrane and a team of English captains were the founders and organizers of Chile's Navy. Although nobody can deny the enormous contribution and lasting impression that Cochrane, his captains, officers, and seamen made on the Chilean Navy, the fact is, that by the time the future Earl of Dundonald arrived in Valparaiso in November of 1818 and took command of the Chilean Navy, the Chileans had already organized a squadron which had successfully engaged the Spanish Royal Navy in action. Cochrane, although hampered by the lack of funds and supplies, received a young navy in which pride, discipline and organization had already been instilled. Furthermore, the majority of the cadre of mariners and marines was either American or British, thus paving the way for a ready acceptance of English methods, English speaking captains, lieutenants and petty officers which were to bring the navy to the same standards as the British navy. This was the great accomplishment of Cochrane and his men.[1]

The very first ship of the "Patria Nueva" as the newly independent Republic of Chile was then known, was the former *Eagle*, an old American smuggler which had been captured by the Spaniards and put in their service. The rechristened *Aguila* was in turn captured by the Chileans when she entered Valparaiso on 26 February, 1817.

Although there were several Argentinean and Chilean officers who had served in the Spanish Navy, command of the brig was given to Raymond Morris of the Army of the Andes, who had previously served in the British Navy from where he had been dismissed.[2] He was a daring individual well known for his lack of responsibility, which had earned him the nickname of "el loco

Morris." His second in command was a Chilean but under them were two English officers, Lieutenants John Young (or Yung) and James Hurell.

Finding a crew for the *Aguila* proved to be no easy task. Although there were plenty of qualified seamen in Valparaiso, most refused to serve unless paid a month's wages in advance. Governor Rudecindo Alvarado, acting as "Chief of Marine," wrote to the Santiago Government, in reference to the *Aguila*'s sailing: ". . . in order to follow your orders, it was necessary and indispensable to agree to all the demands of the English seamen, the ones we can trust. They would not go aboard in spite of my threats and vigor and we had to pay them a months salary."[3] The officers were more easily satisfied. Fifty pesos were paid to each officer while Morris was given "twenty-five pesos until his salary is determined by the authorities."[4]

The first cruise of the *Aguila* was uneventful, but threatened by a Spanish blockade, the governor again communicated to Santiago on 7 July 1817 his urgent need for money. He had chartered the American brig *Rambler* and was forced to pay 600 pesos to the crew plus "200 pesos to the foreigners on board the *Aguila,* who were then signed up as sailors of the state to serve in the same ship."[5] He added that the Chilean members of the crew and the marines were not paid.

Soon Morris proved to be unreliable as he disobeyed orders and was suspended from command. He had stayed at sea too long and the governor wrote to Santiago: "I am afraid that Morris has reached the culmination of his madness, (el colmo de su locura)." But when the brig pulled into Valparaiso a few days later, Morris' faults were temporarily forgiven.[6]

Governor Alvarado's plea for English sailors was constant. On 18 July, he again requested money to hire English sailors and to charter two more American ships. Colonel Zenteno, the Minister of Marine, authorized the funds, but Alvarado's replacement decided to put an end to all these temporary activities and to start preparations to create a regular navy. The Chileans had captured a frigate and a sloop and still had to face a powerful Spanish squadron that was blockading Valparaiso. The Spanish frigate *Venganza* was accompanied by the corvette *Veloz* and two brigs.

During the last months of the Southern Winter of 1817, a serious effort was made to get the navy under a strong organization. Zenteno and O'Higgins were preparing the way for the ships that would soon arrive from Europe. Regulations were drafted, a depot was established, and a regular pay schedule adopted. The pay was to be equal for Chilean and foreign sailors. Ships could not be provided in Chile. They had to come from the United States or Europe, and naval activities were concentrated in showing the flag, mostly within the port and even that with great caution so as not to attract the attention of the blockading Spaniards.

By January of 1818, the Spanish squadron had increased its vigilance, probably being informed by spies that the Chileans were expecting the arrival of new units for the navy. Still, an American brig, the Baltimore-based *Ariel,* managed to slip the blockaders in the first days of February and anchored at Valparaiso.[7] A month later, taking advantage of a temporary lifting of the blockade, the East India frigate *Windham* managed to enter the port. This "inchimán" had been sent by Antonio Alvarez Condarco, the Chilean agent in England, to be sold to the government. She was the first large ship to join the navy. Her price had been set at 180,000 pesos; she carried 34 guns, her size was 800 tons, and she was bringing to Chile 192 experienced English sailors. The government could only offer 105,000 pesos, and for a while it looked as if the ship could not be purchased. But the merchants of Valparaiso purchased shares in the ship with the agreement that they would share in the booty. This arrangement, of course, meant that the ship would operate as a privateer, the type of enterprise that would soon make Valparaiso the leading port in the Pacific. Many English-speaking merchants were involved in the purchase of the East-Indiaman and took great interest in the naval affairs of Chile.[8]

National pride was running high, and General O'Higgins, as Supreme Director, could not accept the Spanish scorn, represented by those ships blockading Valparaiso, of his Declaration of Free Trade. He felt the time had arrived to take decisive action. Accordingly, he ordered the new governor of Valparaiso, Manuel de la Lastra, a former midshipman in the Spanish Navy, to arm the *Lautaro,* as the *Windham* was renamed, and to set sail to "capture the Spanish warships *Esmeralda* and *Pezuela,* the only two that have remained blockading Valparaiso after the withdrawal of the *Venganza.*" He added, "it is necessary to facilitate everything possible. . . . For crew you will enlist all the sailors the captain requests; the American and English agents will also be paid whatever they demand to get the ship ready for sea, taking the money from the State Treasury or borrowing it, if possible."[9]

The immediate need was to find a captain, and George O'Brien was chosen. O'Brien was an Irishman who had served in the British Navy and who, like Morris, had been dismissed for disciplinary reasons. He was in Valparaiso as pilot of an American merchantman when the frigate *Essex* was engaged by the British *Cherub* and *Phoebe*. O'Brien had volunteered his services to the British and behaved in such a gallant manner during the action that he received a letter of commendation from the *Phoebe*'s captain. O'Higgins, Zenteno and De la Lastra felt he was the best qualified of all the candidates.

O'Brien was given a full complement of English officers. His second in command was First Lieutenant J. Argent Turner; second lieutenants were Samuel Faulkner, W. H. Walker (or Waller) and William Mathews. The pilots were John Lee, John Barton and John Robinson.[10] In addition, Lieutenant Nathaniel Beley (or Bell), from the brig *Aguila*, was also on board. The *Lautaro*'s battery was increased to 44 guns and the crew to 350 men. More than a hundred had Anglo-Saxon names. Captain Biddle of the *Ontario* freely gave his advice and assistance in preparing the ship for battle. For this he would later receive a warm note of thanks from San Martin. His assistance did not extend to recruiting sailors. Getting a crew turned out to be a problem. The governor had to resort to force to get men. Sailors who had deserted foreign ships were not allowed to return but were impressed into the Chilean Navy. On 23 April 1818, all masters of merchant ships were called to the governor's house where they were told to allow part of their crews to volunteer for naval service. It was made clear that the volunteering was for a single action against the blockaders. When the masters refused to comply with the request, Chilean boats went alongside merchantmen announcing a ten dollar bonus and shares of prize money to those who enlisted.

Biddle tried to recover at least the American deserters from his ship, but the governor flatly denied it and stated: "I would not give up a single man even to an order to that effect from General San Martin or God Almighty Himself."[11] It was finally necessary to leave the *Aguila* behind and to take some of the crews of six cannon launches.

The *Lautaro* carried a full detachment of marines under the command of Captain William Miller from the Army of the Andes.[12] This selected troop was formed almost exclusively by Chilean soldiers placed on board with the mission of preventing treason and desertion by foreign sailors.[13] Not only was the *Lautaro* officered and crewed by Englishmen, but also her appearance and rigging had been changed to resemble an English man-of-war.

On the evening of 26 April 1818, the *Lautaro* put to sea, taking advantage of a temporary absence of the blockaders. O'Brien had been given strict instructions commanding him to stay off the coast, train his crew, and then return to surprise the enemy. But O'Brien was to prove more of a "loco" than Morris, who had resigned from the navy when his request to command the ship was denied. Disregarding orders, the very next day at dawn, the *Lautaro*, flying the British flag, approached the bigger and more experienced *Esmeralda*, and attempted to ram and board her.[14] The flag was hauled down and the Chilean ensign was raised before opening fire. Although O'Brien bravely led the boarding party and managed to cut down the Spanish flag, the attack failed. Turner, seeing the enemy strike the flag, thought she had surrendered to O'Brien and went after the brig *Pezuela*, abandoning about 25 men, most of whom managed to jump overboard to be picked up later, but O'Brien had been shot through the heart and died on the enemy's deck. When he realized his mistake, Turner returned and discharged at least two broadsides against the enemy. The *Esmeralda* fled with heavy damage to her rigging. The enemy had escaped, the patriot captain had been killed, but the main objective of the engagement had been achieved: lifting the blockade of Valparaiso.

On her return to Valparaiso, the *Lautaro* sighted, pursued and captured a Spanish brig. On board were important passengers whose ransom was enough to pay the shares of foreign merchants, the wages of the crew and the cost of outfitting the ship. It was a very lucky break that made up for the failure to capture or destroy the Spanish frigate.

This first battle at sea had so involved the English that the senior Spanish officer, General Ossorio, lodged a protest with the senior British officer, Captain Kickey of HMS *Blossom*. The Spanish crew of the *Esmeralda* firmly believed that they had been attacked by a shipload of Americans and Englishmen.[15] Independently of Kickey, Captain Sheriff of HMS *Andromache* protested to Chilean authorities, in the name of His Britannic Majesty, the use of the British flag and pennant and the fact that most of the *Lautaro*'s boarding crew and even one officer killed on the *Esmeralda* were dressed in the uniforms of HBM 66th Regiment.[16] The Chilean government denied the charges, stating that the use of a foreign flag was an accepted ruse of war and that the uniforms had been purchased from an East-Indiaman.

The naval combat off Valparaiso had some important consequences. First, it lifted the Spanish blockades of the Chilean coast. Second, it created an esprit de corps in the Chileans. Third, it convinced Chilean authorities that the next commanding officer must be a man of their own. The last point was especially important to O'Higgins and Zenteno. The specter of insubordination would always be with them. It was necessary to find a well disciplined officer who could be trusted to follow orders. "Locuras" could not be risked in the future. It was obvious that even if money were available to purchase ships, the men to service them could not be so easily obtained. This fact alone had deprived O'Brien of the help of the *Aguila*, which may have been decisive in the final outcome of the battle.

The shortage of sailors became acute with the arrival of the *Cumberland*, a full ship of 1350 tons, carrying 64 guns, and the purchase of the brig *Columbus*, with 16 guns. The *Cumberland* was renamed *San Martin* and purchased through a three-installment sale. Captain William Wilkinson, who had brought her to Chile, retained command of the ship by accepting a commission in the Chilean Navy as a Commander. His lieutenants followed suit: William J. Compton, George Phillips, Thomas Johnson, Robert Bell, William Wynter, John A. Green, and John Esmond. The *Columbus*, which was owned by an American, Zachary W. Nixon, was renamed *Araucano*. She also remained under the command of her former master, Charles Wooster, an American of distinguished service in the War of 1812.[17] Although the British believed that the squadron would be manned by Americans, crews became an acute problem.[18] Most of the *Lautaro* men had been hired for the one engagement, and the rich prize had provided money to pay them off. But now the situation was critical. The *San Martin* alone required 100 men to man her rigging. Under these circumstances it is no wonder that "the Patriot armed forces were delighted to impress the well-trained men from foreign warships when the opportunity offered."[19] Men without previous experience were offered two pesos for signing up. Still, not enough volunteers could be found. O'Higgins ordered a roundup of the Santiago vagrants, which produced 1,000 men who were marched in a long and disorderly column all the way to Valparaiso. These men were placed under British officers and seamen for training.

Command of the *Lautaro*, along with the title of senior officer of the squadron, went to John Higginson, a former Boston merchant who was a business associate of Henry Hill, the American Vice-Consul. O'Higgins, after consulting with the members of the Lautaro Lodge, appointed Captain Manuel Blanco Encalada as overall commander. Blanco was a Chilean trained in the Spanish Navy, where he had earned a gold medal for bravery defending the Carraca arsenal in Cádiz.[20] The new commodore was only twenty-seven years old, but he had proven to be an ardent patriot and been confined as a Spanish prisoner to Juan Fernandez Island. As a Brother in both the Masonic and Lautaro Lodges, he could be trusted by O'Higgins, San Martín, and the other members of the government to follow orders.

The appointment of the Chilean Blanco Encalada was to cause some difficulties with the English-speaking captains and officers. Chile had been fortunate in that on every new ship a skeleton crew of good seamen and officers had remained to join the navy. Without them, Chilean history might have been different because, maritime talent among the natives being almost nil, foreigners were imperative as sailors and officers. But, inevitably, the appointment of a commodore in his twenties was not well received in all quarters. Captain Higginson, who had assumed that he would be selected, was so incensed that he wrote O'Higgins, demanded the dismissal of Blanco Encalada and stated that, since he knew the young man well, he realized that no English-speaking officer would obey his orders. Furthermore, since his position was Head of Flotilla, his command was incompatible with the commodore's. According to the historian Sayago, who in 1860 may have had access to sources not available today, there was animosity among the nationalities represented, and the "diversity of language between superiors and subordinates contributed to increase this serious problem to the point where Higginson, commander of the *Lautaro*, was disrespectful to the Navy Commander in Chief. O'Higgins deposed him immediately."[21]

Higginson proved to be wrong. Blanco Encalada had the necessary qualities to establish harmony between Chileans and foreigners. He was sober, serious, hardworking, and he was described as "an officer of one of the best families in Chile and has always conducted himself with good sense and propriety."[22] Under his leadership, the ships were made ready and the crews trained while creating an atmosphere of trust and reliability among officers and men.

When it became known that a powerful squadron had left Cádiz to reinforce the Viceroy, Chilean preparations were accelerated. The ships were ready but not enough men were available to man them. Blanco Encalada wrote to O'Higgins: "We still need to attract the English sailors, the ones we must use because they are the only ones that know how to handle the rigging."[23] The Supreme Director went to Valparaiso and issued a proclamation in which he spoke of a "very rich convoy" and offered a 12 pesos bonus to foreign sailors who would sign up and eight pesos to Chileans, plus "daily rations of provisions prepared daily to the taste of each nation." [24]

It is not known if the proclamation had the proper effect, but the fact is that by mid-September the squadron had enough men to set sail. Miller, now promoted to major and in command of the marines, would later write: "Fortunately Blanco had all the necessary qualities to establish union, harmony and good order."[25] Higginson resigned and commands were assigned as follows:

Type	Name	Captain	Guns
Ship of the line	*San Martin*	William Wilkinson	64
Frigate	*Lautaro*	Charles Wooster	44
Corvette	*Chacabuco*	Francisco Díaz	24
Brig	*Araucano*	Raymond Morris	16

Commander Francisco Díaz was an Argentinean officer from the Army of the Andes who had been Blanco's adjutant. Morris, reappointed at San Martin's request, rejoined the navy and was given the command of the *Araucano*. He wasted no time in getting lost, capturing a transport, and rejoining the squadron but missed the battle at Talcahuano Bay. The squadron left Valparaiso and headed South to meet the "rich convoy," whose rendezvous points, secret signals and other vital facts were known to the Chileans thanks to a mutiny aboard the transport *Trinidad*, which ended up with the ship being turned over to the patriots in Buenos Aires.

Learning from a British whaler that the flagship of the convoy had already entered Talcahuano Bay, Blanco Encalada led his squadron into battle. He left behind the brig and the corvette and entered the port on 28 October 1818 with only the *Lautaro* and *San*

Martin. Blanco then issued a historical order: "It is necessary that the Chilean navy signalize the time of its birth by an act of glory." An act of glory it turned out to be.

The Chileans approached, again, flying the British flag. In the inner bay, the 50-gun frigate *María Isabel* was anchored. Upon coming into range, the Chilean ships changed flags and discharged their batteries. The Spanish ship responded weakly, fired one broadside but then slipped her cables and ran into the shallows. The two patriot ships luffed and fired batteries at the enemy. It was the signal for the Spanish crew to abandon ship and head for the shore. Blanco Encalada was ready and ordered two boats under the commands of lieutenants Nathaniel Bell and William Compton to board the *Maria Isabel*. They moved so fast that at least sixty Spaniards, unable to leave the ship, were taken prisoner. At the same time, Miller, with 150 marines, went directly to the beach to cut off the enemy's retreat. But reinforcements from Concepción joined the defenders and soon outnumbered the marines; supported by four field cannons, the defenders forced the major to take to his boats and return to the ships.

The *María Isabel* was firmly aground when Blanco ordered Wilkinson to take command of the prize. This experienced mariner set about to get the ship afloat. All night long the sailors shifted weight and tried to lighten ship. By noon next day, in spite of fire from shore, they were ready to try. Sail was set and a light breeze was blowing from the South. At the first attempt, the ship cleared the sandy bottom.

The three ships sailed out towards the open sea. The crews were exhausted after almost 30 hours of continuous action. Only one lieutenant, James Ramsay, was left on board with the commodore, and he was hoarse after all the shouting. The *San Martin* ran aground, and no one could direct the maneuver to get her off. Blanco did not speak English; Lieutenant Ramsay could not give orders. Wooster, who was following with the *Lautaro*, realized what had happened and, boarding one of his boats, went aboard the flagship. Since he spoke Spanish fairly well, he conferred with Blanco Encalada and then ordered the topsails brailled up, let go the foresail and pulled the ship off. He then returned to his own command. Twice more the flagship ran aground that night because orders could not be understood. Miller thought that if it had not been for a change of wind the ship would have been lost. The exhausted and inexperienced crew could do very little.

In the following days, the *María Isabel*, still flying the Royal flag, was used to deceive the incoming transports, so that only four of the twelve original transports managed to reach the Viceregal fortress at El Callao. One ship had mutinied and entered Buenos Aires. The Chileans had captured 570 soldiers, seven transports and the flagship of the convoy. The interception of this convoy is, without doubt, the most important single event in the naval wars for South American Independence. With one blow, a squadron, built from scratch, had disbanded and destroyed the most important expedition sent by Spain to recover her colonies. At the same time that the Chileans gained confidence, the Spaniards lost it. The Royal ships took only evasive action from that moment on. The Battle of Talcahuano Bay was as significant as the Battle of Maipu had been on land. It was the turning point in the Wars of Independence of South America.

The majority of the officers continued in the Chilean squadron after the arrival of Lord Cochrane and participated in the Peruvian Campaigns.[26] Some, like Esmond and Miller, would eventually join the Peruvian service; others like Wilkinson, would serve in the Chilean Navy until their deaths. Many established homes and families in Chile; and Charles Wooster, after retiring as an Admiral, would die in poverty in the California Gold Rush of 1849.

The final destinations of the crews have proven very difficult to follow. Other than some incomplete paymaster rosters, very few documents mention them. Better records have been preserved after the arrival of Cochrane, and it can be assumed that most sailors remained in the squadron until 1822. Many joined the privateers, however, and Blanco Encalada reported to O'Higgins, after returning from Talcahuano, "the sudden disappearance of 300 sailors, who, I understand, have gone to Coquimbo and other northern ports so that they can join the privateers."[27]

A lasting tradition in Chile's navy is the use of hispanicized English words: managuá (man of war); cuque (cook); guachimán (watchman); luquear (to look); michimán (midshipman); and many others.[28] As historian García Reyes aptly describes it, "the most characteristic note of these crews was the diversity of languages spoken on board. It was truly a Tower of Babel."[29]

Chilean privateers were soon to sweep Spanish merchantmen from the American Pacific Coast reaching the California coast. Cochrane would chase away or capture whatever was left of the

Royal Navy. He was also to transport San Martin's liberating Army to Peru at the same time that the coast was kept clear so that Bolivar could advance south to Peru. His task was made easier by the earlier mariners, Americans and Englishmen, who sailed Chile's First Squadron under Blanco Encalada.

A note on the sources:

The documents relating to the organization of the Chilean Navy are deposited in the Archivo Nacional de Chile in Santiago, bound in 46 volumes, under the title "Ministerio de Marina" 1817–1826. Most of the important communications, including the battle reports, have been published by Luis Uribe in his book, *Orijenes de Nuestra Marina Militar,* Vol. I, Santiago: Imprenta Nacional, 1892. A selected volume of these documents done by Professor Jorge Garín Jiménez has been recently published. The crew and officer rosters have not been published and can be found scattered through several volumes under "Fondos Varios," "Contaduría Mayor" and some under "Ministerio de Marina," already mentioned. There are thirty additional bound volumes with documents concerning the navy and an uncataloged vault at the Estado Mayor de la Armada. The spelling of English names is sometimes difficult to follow and many officers and men hispanicized their names: "Evans" for "Ibañez," "Williams" for "Guillermos," etc.

Of all the participants, only Major William Miller, later General, wrote his memoirs, John Miller, ed., *Memoirs of General Miller in the Service of the Republic of Peru,* 2 volumes, London, 1828. Nonparticipants who refer to these events are María Graham, Lady Calcott, *Journal of a Residence in Chile during the Year 1822;* J. F. Coffin, *Journal of a Residence in Chile,* Boston, 1823; and Samuel Haight, *Sketches of Buenos Aires and Chile,* London, 1829.

Eugenio Pereira Salas discusses the role played by Captain James Biddle of the *Ontario,* in his *Actuación de los Oficiales Navales Norte-Americanos en Nuestras Costas* (1813–1824), published by the University of Chile in 1935. Most Chilean historians starting with Barros Arana in his monumental *Historia Jeneral de Chile,* Vol. XI, recognize the contribution of foreign seamen. Chilean naval historians, Luis Langlois, *Influencia del Poder Naval en la Historia de Chile, desde 1810 a 1910,* Valparaiso, 1911; Rodrigo Fuenzalida Bade, *La Armada de Chile,* Vol. I, Santiago: Imprenta de la Armada, 1970; and several others, such as Sayago, Vío, and Novoa, all agree on the valuable contribution of these foreign seamen and officers. The most detailed account of the activities of the First Squadron can be found in Antonio García Reyes, *Memoria sobre la Primera Escuadra Nacional,* Santiago: Universidad de Chile, 1846. An English handwritten translation is at the Navy Department Library in Washington, D.C., under the title "Maritime Operations in the First Period of Independence (Chile)," n.d.

Several American historians have written about these events. They are best described by Donald E. Worcester, *Sea Power and Chilean Independence,* Gainesville: U. of Florida Press, 1962. From an American Navy point of view, see Robert E. Johnson, *Thence Round Cape Horn,* Annapolis: U.S. Naval Institute, 1963, and Edward B. Billingsley, *In Defense of Neutral Rights,* Chapel Hill: U. of North Carolina Press, 1967. Chapter II, "Biddle and the Patriots" is especially interesting.

British documents related to these events have been published by Gerald S. Graham and R. A. Humphreys, editors, *The Navy and South America: 1807–1823*, London: The Navy Records Society, 1962. A very superficial survey among textbooks commonly used in United States colleges and universities shows the following: Worcester and Schaeffer, *The Growth & Culture of Latin America*: "The hero of this often discouraging undertaking was Lord Cochrane." Bailey and Nasatir, *Latin America*: "To turn the navy into an 'invasion fleet' O'Higgins hired a brilliant navy officer in bad repute at home, Lord Thomas Cochrane." Lynch, *The Latin American Revolutions*: "Chile had to create a navy from nothing, to buy ships and equipment, to recruit personnel . . . to find an admiral . . . and a famous British naval officer, Thomas Cochrane, assumed command of the new squadron." Keenan and Wassermann, *A Short History of Latin America*: "He (O'Higgins), secured a number of ships in England and the United States and engaged a competent though eccentric naval officer, Thomas, Lord Cochrane." Only Hubert Herring in his *History of Latin America*, gives partial credit to the true founders: "The organization of a navy to transport the army, ably begun by Chilean Blanco Encalada, was completed by Lord Cochrane."

1. Cochrane would write after the capture of the *Esmeralda* at Callao on 5 November 1821: "We had not been on deck a minute, when I hailed the foretop, and was instantly answered by our own men, an equally prompt answer being returned from the frigate's main top. No British man-of War's crew could have excelled this minute attention to orders." Thomas Cochrane, *The Life of Thomas Lord Cochrane*, London: Richard Bentley, I, p. 186.

2. It has been impossible to determine what qualifications prevailed on O'Higgins in selecting Morris for command. Some Chilean historians believe that San Martín had incorporated him in the Army until a job could be found for him at sea.

3. Alvarado to O'Higgins, Valparaiso, 8 March 1817.

4. Ibid. Sailors were paid twenty, fifteen and twelve pesos in accordance with their experience and qualifications. For comparison purposes, the peso was then equivalent to a Spanish dollar.

5. Alvarado to O'Higgins, Valparaiso, 18 July 1817.

6. Alvarado to O'Higgins, 17 July 1817. Morris' character was the source of constant worries. He found favor with San Martin who recommended that he be hired as a commander. The decree signed by O'Higgins was issued on 7 October 1817. Unable to fit in the navy, he tried his luck in privateers and finally settled in Chile where he established a large and well known family.

7. Bowles to Crocker, on board the *Amphion*, Buenos Aires, 10 June 1818. Quoted in Gerald S. Graham, *The Navy and South America*, London, 1963. The Navy Records Society lists the *Ariel*, mounting 16 guns, as a Chilean warship. A search in the Archivo Nacional or Navy Archives has failed to produce any evidence that the *Ariel* was ever purchased by the navy, or was chartered or licensed as a privateer.

8. There seems to be enough evidence to conclude that Captain Biddle of the U.S.S. *Ontario* actively participated in the negotiations to purchase the ship. Among the shareholders of the *Windham* were two Americans, Henry Hill, the U.S. Vice-Consul at Valparaiso, and Charles Donegal.

9. O'Higgins to De la Lastra, Santiago, 20 April 1818. It seems that the agents referred to here were Donegal and Hill, who lost no time in requesting assistance from Biddle to get the ship ready for sea. But later, Hill, as Vice-Consul, was to protest the enlistment of American deserters. See Edward Billingsley, *In Defence of Neutral Rights*, Chapel Hill: U. of N. Carolina Press, 1967, pp 35–36.

10. John Robinson seems to have been the only American in this group. He had been imprisoned by the Spanish authorities in Concepción, from whence he escaped in a launch. See J.E. Coffin, *Diario de un Joven Norteamericano*, Buenos Aires: Aguirre, 1967, p. 78.

11. Billingsley, op. cit., p. 37.

12. There is some question concerning Miller's rank at this time. He is referred to as "Capitán Miller," assuming it was an Army rank, but O'Higgins had promoted him to Major at Cancha Rayada on 19 March 1818, where he had saved the field artillery train from being captured or destroyed.

13. Chilean fears of treachery by foreign sailors were not unfounded. During the first period of Independence, 1810–1812, the only attempt to create a naval squadron failed when foreign crews mutinied and betrayed the ships. When *Lautaro* went to battle stations, Miller's marines were stationed in the tops and on the yard in order to fire on either their own or the enemy's decks.

14. O'Brien's orders have been published in Luis Uribe, *Oríjenes de Nuestra Marina Militar,* Santiago: Imprenta Nacional, 1892, p. 50.

15. See Coffin, Op. cit., p. 114.

16. This was Captain O'Brien, the only officer killed in the action.

17. See Charles Lyon Chandler, "Admiral Charles Whithing Wooster," *American Historical Association Annual Report for the Year 1916,* Washington, 1919.

18. Bowles to Crocker, *Amphion,* 9 April 1817, quoted in *Navy and South America,* p. 190. "Commanded and manned chiefly by Americans."

19. Robert Johnson, *Thence Round Cape Horn,* Annapolis: U.S. Naval Institute, 1963, p. 21.

20. Blanco Encalada graduated from the Naval School at Isla de León and was commissioned midshipman by Royal Decree on 27 February 1807. He served five years in the Royal Spanish Navy. He would eventually become the first President of Chile. See Enrique Villamil, *Vida de Don Manuel Blanco Encalada,* Santiago: Universitaria, 1920.

21. Sayago, *Crónica*, p. 25.

22. Bowles to Crocker, *Creole,* Buenos Aires, 27 February 1819. Quoted in *Navy and South America*, p. 263.

23. Blanco to O'Higgins, Valparaiso, 24 July 1818.

24. Uribe, *Orijenes*, p. 115.

25. John Miller, *Memorias*, I, p. 37.

26. Only four of these original officers were among those who returned with Cochrane on 12 June 1822 at the end of the war in Peru: Wilkinson, Granville, Craig, and Winter. Esmond, Prunier, Young, and Robinson joined the Peruvian Navy. From two lists attached to a communication, Cochrane to Minister of Marine, O'Higgins at anchor in Valparaiso, no date, but probably 13 or 14 June 1822. Wooster refused to serve under an Englishman and temporarily "retired" from the Navy while Cochrane was the commander in chief.

27. Quoted by Uribe, *Oríjenes*, p. 58. It should be noted that practically all privateers were commanded by English or American captains: Brown, Budge, Mc Kay, James, Coles, Illingsworth, Seymour, MacGilvrey, to name a few.

28. For a more detailed discussion see Carlos López, "Algunos vocablos de origen inglés en el vocabulario marítimo chileno," *HISPANIA* 51: Dec. 1968, p. 868.

29. García Reyes, *Memoria*, p. 8, Sayago, in his *Crónica*, p. 24, states that O'Higgins served as personal interpreter in negotiating some of the contracts with the sailors.

"To Preserve and Not Destroy": The U.S. Navy and Fugitive Slaves in the Civil War, 1861–62

Barbara Brooks Tomblin

⚓

On a warm mid-July day in 1861, Flag-Officer Silas Stringham, the commanding officer of the Union Navy's Atlantic Blockading Squadron, received a most unusual communication from Oliver Glisson, commanding officer of the USS *Mt. Vernon*. Glisson reported that on the morning of July 15th he had ordered one of his officers to take a boat crew to investigate reports of a small boat adrift near Stingray lighthouse in the Rappahannock River. To the officer's surprise, the lighthouse was occupied by six black slaves who had deserted from shore and had taken shelter in the lighthouse during the night, leaving their boat adrift to avoid detection.[1] The six escaped men told Glisson that there was "much excitement" ashore among the black population, as it was rumored that the whites were arming the blacks with the intention of putting them in the front lines. Many blacks were deserting, they told Glisson, and two boats had put out from shore the previous night in hopes of being picked up by some vessel.

Lacking specific orders on such a situation, Commander Glisson had taken the six black deserters on board the *Mt. Vernon* and was giving them rations and awaiting further instructions.[2] The following day Glisson reported the men's names and asked how he was to dispose of the runaway slaves and any future cases and concluded his report with a note of urgency, "They say if they should be returned they would be murdered."[3]

Commodore Stringham sent Glisson's report on to his superior, Navy Secretary Gideon Welles, with a cover letter in which Stringham argued that the Navy should accept the fugitive slaves' reports as valid. He told Welles that, were he in Glisson's position, he would have done exactly as the commander had done—received the fugitive blacks and taken care of them until he had heard from the Department.[4]

Stringham concluded his letter with a prophetic statement: "If negroes are to be used in this contest, I have no hesitation in saying they should be used to preserve the Government, not to destroy it. These men are destitute; shall I ration them? They may be serviceable on board our storeships."[5]

The U.S. Navy had not encouraged black slaves to escape from their owners and seek refuge on Federal warships, but it was the opinion of the officer responsible for enforcing the Union blockade that the U.S. Navy should not only accept responsibility for the fugitives but take advantage of the situation!

The arrival of fugitive slaves on board the USS *Mt.Vernon* in July 1861 was not, as Stringham predicted, an isolated incident. In the next year, hundreds of black slaves, including women and children, sought the aid and protection of Union naval vessels whenever they appeared in southern rivers and sounds. The policy of the Navy Department toward these fugitives was tentative at first, but, by the end of 1862, had become a broad policy that included the use of fugitive slaves as laborers, laundresses, river pilots, and intelligence sources, the establishment and active protection of "contraband" colonies, and even the enlistment of black men into naval service.

Navy Secretary Gideon Welles set the tone for the Navy's initial, official policy in his reply to Commodore Stringham's letter of July 18th. Welles explained that the government's policy was not to invite or encourage this class of desertions, and yet he said, "under the circumstances no other course than that pursued by Commander Glisson could be adopted without violating every principle of humanity." The Secretary felt that to return the slaves would be "impolite as well as cruel" and suggested that Stringham pursue his idea of using them on Union storeships.[6]

The Navy's original policy about receiving and using escaped slaves was based on the Navy Department's suspicion that the Confederacy was employing blacks in their war effort against the Union. This was the same argument used by General Benjamin F. Butler to justify his refusal to return three fugitive slaves to a Virginia militia officer after his forces had occupied the Hampton, Virginia, area in May 1861. Butler argued that the fugitive slaves had crossed into Federal lines and were, therefore, "contraband" property liable to confiscation in time of war. Not only did General Butler deliberately violate the provisions of the Fugitive Slave Law, he also used the able-bodied blacks who came in increasing numbers into Federally controlled areas near Fortress Monroe as labor.[7]

Official Confederate use of black slave labor gave Union officials ample reason for confiscating slaves as property, but the paid employment of black labor demanded further justification from Federal authorities. A persuasive argument was developed early in the war by Commodore Silas Stringham, who observed that often the escaped slaves who sought refuge on Union naval vessels were without proper clothing. In a clever turn of bureaucratic maneuvering, Stringham used their condition as a pretext for employing them in Union service and paying them in the form of a clothing ration for their labor.[8]

By September of 1861, the number of fugitive slaves subsisting at navy yards or on board Federal warships so increased that the Navy Department found it necessary to adopt regulations in regard to them. On September 25, 1861, Welles authorized Silas Stringham's successor, Louis Goldsborough, to enlist persons of color for naval service under the same regulations and forms of other enlistments and yet at no higher a rating than "boys" at a compensation of $10 a month and one ration per day.[9]

The following May 15, 1862 the flag officer commanding the South Atlantic Blockading Squadron, Samuel F. DuPont, issued General Order No. 11 authorizing his commanders to enlist contrabands in the naval service. The order stated that "Hot weather makes it advisable that acclimated persons be employed on board ships in the squadron to do such duties as involve exposure to sun and heat such as boat service and work in enginerooms." DuPont instructed commanding officers to ship contrabands, with their consent, on naval vessels, rating them as boys at 8, 9, and 10 dollars a month with one daily ration.[10]

By the time Samuel DuPont authorized the actual enlistment of blacks, the U.S. Navy had been forced, by the course of wartime events, to move beyond the reception and temporary care of fugitive slaves to the establishment and protection of several colonies of "contrabands." Ironically, expansion of naval policy toward fugitive slaves was not deliberate, but the result of a resounding Union victory—the capture of Port Royal Sound by a Union flotilla on November 7, 1861. This objective required Union forces under General Thomas Sherman to first secure the strategic island of Hilton Head which guarded the entrance to Port Royal Sound.

Port Royal's capture made the Confederate position on the numerous sea islands north of Savannah, Georgia, untenable, and many southern plantation owners, realizing they were all but defenseless against the Yankee invasion, fled the city of Beaufort and other coastal areas. When Lieutenant Daniel Ammen took the gunboat *Seneca* upriver to Beaufort, he found the city practically deserted of its white inhabitants. What Ammen did see were "hundreds of negroes on the wharf and on the streets; all the scows were in requisition and were being loaded with furniture and personal effects of all kinds, provisions, and lumber to erect sheds elsewhere; on the part of the negroes it was an exhibition of wild confusion and great joy; they imagined that they were setting out on a picnic for life." The black slaves remaining in Beaufort told Captain Ammen that all the whites had left the island and that "many slaves had been shot by their masters while making an attempt to escape while being driven to the Port Royal ferry to be taken to the mainland."[11]

The Navy's delay of several days in occupying Beaufort had given the plantation slaves the opportunity to come into Beaufort and ransack the town. One white owner who returned to his Beaufort home on November 8 found one of his slaves, a woman named Chloe, "seated at Phoebe's piano playing away like the very Devil and two damsels upstairs dancing away famously."[12] According to other eyewitness accounts, including those of the slaves themselves, plantation hands who had come into Beaufort in the wake of the whites' evacuation were responsible for the looting.

These unfortunate incidents of plundering and disorder in Beaufort prior to the Union occupation were accompanied by alarming reports of Southern slave owners coercing or even shooting slaves who would not accompany them in their flight from the Union invasion. Black informants gave convincing testimony to Union officials and naval officers that slaves had been shot resisting removal, and others had been burned to death in their cotton houses. Although some were undoubtedly exaggerated, these stories of mistreatment and coercion against the slaves may have prompted many Union naval officers to later react with alarm to rumors or contraband reports of white slave owners returning to the sea islands to recover or shoot former slaves.

General Sherman ordered temporary "contraband camps" set up for these black laborers at Beaufort and Hilton Head Island. Jurisdiction of the contrabands became the responsibility of chief quartermaster Captain Rufus Saxton. In addition to the hundreds of slaves who had fled their masters, an estimated 8,000 black slaves remained on their plantations in areas now occupied by Union forces. Although now "defacto freedpeople," most were willing to work for their former drivers, but in the meantime could no longer depend on their old masters for food and clothing. Those former slaves who were able helped themselves to provisions in pantries and storehouses, but this was only a temporary solution to the problem of fashioning new life in freedom. Abandoned by their Southern owners, many of the new freedpeople faced a winter without adequate clothing or food.

To solve their dilemma some former slaves on the South Carolina sea islands turned for assistance to a visible and expedient source— Union navy gunboats. The first officially recorded incident of freedmen seeking succor from the U.S. Navy's vessels off the sea islands followed the Union occupation of Port Royal by less than a month. In response to a request from General Sherman for assistance in taking Tybee and Wassaw Islands at the entrance of Wassaw Inlet, Flag-Officer Samuel F. DuPont ordered four U.S. Navy vessels, under the command of Commander Percival Drayton, to St. Helena Sound on December 5, 1861. When Drayton's ship, the sloop USS *Pawnee*, anchored off Otter Island in the Sound, blacks from shore came on board and informed him that Confederate troops were located up the Ashepoo River near Mosquito Creek. Twice, Drayton took the 240 ton side-wheeler *Vixen*, the 90 day gunboat *Unadilla*, and the medium screw *Isaac Smith* up the Ashepoo. The second time he landed on Hutchinson's Island where he discovered the rebels had recently burned all the black slaves' houses, overseers' houses, outbuildings, and picked cotton. "The scene was one of complete desolation; the smoking ruins and cowering figures which surrounded them, of those, negroes who still instinctively clung to their hearthstones, although there was no longer shelter for them, presented a most melancholy sight, the impression of which was made even stronger by the piteous wailing of the poor creatures, a large portion of whom consisted of the old and decrepit," he wrote DuPont.[13]

Drayton's little flotilla went on to explore the Coosaw River and with just the small side wheel gunboat *Vixen*, continued on to the entrance to Beaufort Creek, where he anchored off a plantation. Going ashore, Commander Drayton learned the cotton house had been burned and many of the blacks taken away. However, on the beach he found numerous black refugees from Hutchinson's Island lined up with all their household effects: "Some of them begging to go to Otter Island, saying that they had neither shelter nor food." Needless to say Drayton felt compassion for them and took the homeless former slaves back with him, leaving 140 of them on Otter Island. When Drayton and the *Pawnee* sailed back to Port Royal, he left this fledgling contraband colony in charge of Lieutenant Commander J. W. A. Nicholson, who remained in St. Helena Sound with *Dale* and *Isaac Smith*.[14]

And so, without setting out to establish a colony of former slaves on Otter Island, in December 1861, the Union Navy found itself quite unexpectedly responsible for the care and protection of over one hundred former slaves. The task of supervising these "contrabands" fell to Lieutenant Commander Nicholson, who immediately set out to find provisions for the new colony. On December 10th Nicholson took 40 men and some marines in boats from the sloop *Dale*, followed by twenty contrabands in boats, up the river to reconnoiter and to get potatoes. The expedition also yielded some corn, a corn mill, two horses, and one cart "to make the contrabands more comfortable."[15]

On December 11th Nicholson formally turned the island and fort over to the Army under the command of Colonel Welsh. The Navy's responsibility for the protection of Otter Island, however, did not end with the transfer of command ashore. On December 12th Lieutenant Commander Nicholson took his naval force up the Ashepoo River to locate a house previously ascertained as rebel headquarters. Encountering mounted rebel pickets, Nicholson dispersed them with 8 inch shell and rifle shot from the *Isaac Smith*. He then stood up the river and landed *Dale's* marines to burn the Confederates' quarters.[16]

Nicholson's aggressive patrolling allowed the contraband colony on Otter Island to remain relatively free of rebel harassment. However, more fugitive blacks greeted Commander Drayton's vessels when he took an expedition up the North Edisto on December 16th. This resulted in the collection of nearly 150 blacks "in a great state of alarm" who fled to the Union vessels when they appeared in the river. Evidently the rebels' hasty evacuation that morning had caused great consternation among the black population, many of whom then sought refuge on the Union naval vessels. They were in turn deposited on the point of Edisto Island and Lieutenant T. A. Budd of the USS *Penguin* ordered to assist them.[17]

By the end of December, this small colony of former slaves had grown to between 700 and 900 persons. Although Lieutenant Ammen of the *Seneca* reported they had built huts and "appeared contented," he feared they would soon run out of provisions. Ammen also told Flag Officer DuPont that there were gangs of rebel cavalry rumored to be operating on Wadmelaw, John's, and parts of North Edisto Islands whose "principle, if not sole, object is to drive the negroes into the interior."[18]

This continuing threat to the contrabands led the U.S. Navy to engage in more riverine operations to intimidate rebel forces and, whenever possible to secure provisions for the contraband colonies. For example, on January 4, 1862, Lieutenant Budd took a raiding party in the three masted schooner USS *Penguin* up the North Edisto to Bear's Bluff, dispersed some rebels, and captured 100 bushels of corn for the contraband colony, which now numbered almost a thousand persons.[19]

This cache satisfied the colony's need for food but not for security. On January 23rd Lieutenant Alexander C. Rhind, who had relieved Ammen in the Sound, received word that Confederate troops had landed on Edisto Island and were "moving off and shooting blacks." Rhind got underway immediately in the 775 ton *Crusader* and steamed up the river to Pines Wharf, where he discovered the rebels had fled but 150 blacks remained. He collected them and proceeded upriver to Steamboat Creek where another party of fugitive slaves had gathered. *Crusader* took a total of 320 of them back to the colony, but Rhind reported that more were constantly coming in.

Ten days later Rhind's ship was fired on by rebel troops along the river bank, and he returned fire with a howitzer which had been placed on a flatboat. When the flatboat's bows gave way, Rhind ordered *Crusader* to fire into the village, behind which 250 Confederates were rumored to be hiding. All these enemy activities led Lieutenant Rhind to recommend that Edisto Island be occupied by Union troops, and, in February 1862, the army sent a garrison force to occupy North Edisto Island. On February 10, 1862, Flag Officer DuPont warmly congratulated Lieutenant Rhind on his occupation of the waters of North Edisto and went on to express his pleasure "that you are giving proper and kind attention to the contrabands" and promised to send him a rifle gun and boat for a twelve pound howitzer.[20]

In March 1862 Union naval vessels helped to establish another colony of fugitive blacks at St. Simon's Island. While conducting operations in St. Simon's Sound, S. W. Godon's ship, the 1,461 ton screw sloop *Mohican,* was approached by contrabands who sought refuge on board the vessel. Godon reported, "it now became necessary to obtain food for these people, as by now they mustered over forty men, women, and children, and both my provisions and those of the *Pocahontas* were getting low." To supply his growing brood, Godon stopped at Colonel's Island where he found 150 bushels of corn, a quantity of peas, and sweet potatoes. He landed the contrabands with their corn and tools on St. Simon's island, which was not occupied by rebel troops. Godon told Flag Officer DuPont that St. Simon's was a "fine, rich island, about ten miles long," and he thought a gunboat at either end and a marine battalion might be sufficient to secure the island from rebel attack.[21]

Having established these "contraband colonies," the U.S. Navy now found itself responsible for defending them, for the Federal troops garrisoning these islands in the spring of 1862 were always in danger of sudden enemy attack. To secure these sea islands and protect the contrabands, the Army was dependent upon the Navy for support in the form of transport for reinforcements, naval gunfire, and even naval landing parties.

For example, on March 29, 1862, the USS *Dale* responded to a request from Colonel Henry Moore, the commander of the troops on Edisto Island, for help in repelling a rebel attack on the island. Lieutenant Truxtun of the USS *Dale* offered to send Colonel Welsh a twenty-man marine guard, his boat howitzer, and a crew of 13 men. Also coming to the army's assistance was Lieutenant Rhind in the three masted bark *Crusader,* which went up Steamboat Creek on the 29th to take off some troops of the 59th Pennsylvania Regiment cut off from Little Edisto Island.[22]

Union naval officers like Alexander Rhind seemed to welcome the opportunity to aid the Army and to have a chance for action against the enemy which often eluded those responsible for the monotonous task of enforcing the blockade. But those same naval officers had varying responses to their other important task, that of protecting these "contraband" colonies on the sea islands. Many officers commanding Union naval vessels, men like Percival Drayton, seemed deeply moved by the plight of the fugitive slaves. In a letter to his brother Heyward on January 10, 1862, Percival

Drayton justified his actions on the behalf of fugitive slaves after the Port Royal invasion, saying, ". . . I cannot enter coolly into a discussion of the legal points of the question, and obliged when in sight of a mother wailing over the loss of her child to look upon them as persons not things."[23]

In fact, navy officials seemed shocked by the condition of the black slaves they saw on abandoned sea island plantations. Samuel F. DuPont, by his own admission a conservative on the question of slavery, wrote: "Oh my! What a delusion—there are no swine in Massachusetts not better cared for. The Dahomeys and Congos are better off—these cotton lords who have been boasting of their wealth and power, will you believe it, have never spent a dollar in ameliorating the condition of these people physically." When DuPont complained to a fellow officer about the lack of even common decencies for the slaves on a plantation he had visited, the officer replied, "Why sir, those slaves are living in luxury compared with the general run!"[24]

Some of the young commanders of Samuel DuPont's South Atlantic Blockade Squadron took a genuine, if paternalistic, interest in the "contrabands." One, Acting Volunteer Lieutenant H. St. C. Etyinge of the USS *Shepherd Knapp*, wrote to DuPont on August 11, 1861, that, after attending Divine service on board his vessel, he went ashore "among my dependent contrabands on Otter Island, and read them the morning service of the Episcopal church. I never saw poor humanity more pleased with the consolations of the Divine promises, and when they thanked me after service I could not repress a tear of joy in having been instrumental even in limited good."[25]

Others, like Alexander Rhind, had less positive experiences with the former slaves. To DuPont, Lieutenant Rhind expressed his frustration and suspicion of the contrabands: "The negroes on Botany Bay Island are in such numbers and leading such an idle and improvident life here that I fear, unless they are speedily removed, disease and want will appear among them. At present they have a sufficiency, but I have learned from experience with them that they destroy or trade away much of their provision. If I go anywhere to enable them to collect corn or potatoes they begin to plunder the houses of furniture and other articles entirely useless to them."[26]

Not only did some of the contrabands have a tendency to plunder, their sheer numbers could often deplete a Union naval vessel of her provisions and water, as Oliver Glisson discovered in August

1861 while on patrol in the Rappahannock River. Glisson reported to Silas Stringham that as of August 22nd he now "had sixteen negroes onboard that they are consuming our water and provisions faster than I think is desirable." Clearly uncomfortable with his shipload of fugitive slaves, Glisson asked Stringham if he could send a spare vessel up the river to take them off.[27]

J. W. A. Nicholson found himself in a similar situation in the St. John's River in mid-June 1862 when his flotilla was besieged by fleeing blacks. Finding that he could not accommodate all of them on board, Nicholson had to dispatch the little 192 ton *Uncas* to Fernandina with some of the fugitives. In all, Nicholson said he took on forty-three blacks, including twelve children and four free blacks. Unlike Glisson, however, Lieutenant Nicholson could see the positive aspects of the situation and wrote DuPont, "the banks of the river as far as one can see is planted with corn. They say corn enough in Florida for all of the Southern rebel states. If we carry off their darkies they can not gather it; one consolation."[28]

As the war progressed and the appearance of fugitive blacks became a more common situation, some naval commanders coped creatively with the task of providing for these often unwelcome "guests." For example, S. W. Godon, of the USS *Mohican*, was so anxious about feeding the contrabands on St. Simon's Island that he ordered one of his vessels, the 220 ton, single screw USS *Madgie*, and thirty contraband stevedores to Barret's Island where a cache of rice was rumored to be stored. Godon took 630 bushels on the *Madgie* back to St. Simon's and ordered her to return to Barrett's Island with a 12 pound howitzer to seize a rebel schooner. Acting Master's Mate Meriam promptly found the schooner *Southern Belle* and seized her along with a cargo of 3,000 more bushels of rice. *Madgie's* successful expedition motivated Godon to report on June 26, 1862, "The colony improves, the crops grow finely, and the people are contented. Their large supplies on hand now by the addition of the rice leaves them nothing to fear on that head."[29]

Examples like that of S. W. Godon's rice expedition leave little doubt that the need to supply and protect contraband colonies afforded many a naval officer the perfect excuse for some aggressive patrolling or even perhaps the chance to take a prize.

Although on occasion the necessity of protecting the fledgling contraband colonies from rebel harassment confined the movement and options of Union warship, in general, Flag Officer DuPont was supportive of the Union experiment to settle former slaves on abandoned plantations and even took a personal interest in the colonies. However, the withdrawal of troops from the Department of the South for service with the Army of the Potomac left the sea islands more vulnerable to harassment by the rebels.

In St. Helena Sound, for example, after the withdrawal of Union forces on Otter Island, the sloop *Dale* was left alone to protect the numerous contrabands. The 566 ton *Dale*, a sailing vessel commissioned in 1840, was not a real substitute for Union army troops on shore, and her 32 powder guns failed to prevent one of the most serious attacks on the sea islands.

Lieutenant Truxtun gave Flag Officer DuPont a graphic account of this incident, during which 300 rebel troops attacked Mrs. Marsh's plantation on Hutchinson's Island, surrounded the house and chapel, and murdered the occupants in cold blood. "At early dawn they fired a volley through the house. As the alarmed people sprang nearly naked from their beds and rushed forth, frantic with fear they were shot, arrested, or knocked down." Truxtun said the rebels took off a number of chickens, set fire to the buildings, and fled. Having been alerted that there was a fire on the island, Truxtun had taken a party up to the plantation in boats and now filled the same boats with as many of the "panic stricken" people as possible. Many of the 100 fleeing slaves were women and children. Some of them were seriously injured, including one man riddled with bullets and a very pregnant woman who had dislocated her hip leaping from a second story window.[30]

In light of this action, Lieutenant Truxtun urged the Navy Department to send more light draft steam vessels and troops to defend that portion of the coast. He wrote, "The Department will perceive by the narrative how much the gunboats are looked up to by the contrabands for their defense and how much they are feared by the enemy for attack." And Truxtun reminded DuPont that for months the contrabands had quietly been cultivating crops on the islands under Union protection and offered his opinion that "the Government is bound by every principle of justice and policy to shield them from these barbarian inroads."[31]

The situation of the sea islands after the withdrawal of so many Union troops for McClellan's peninsular campaign put the Union Navy in a difficult position. Samuel DuPont confided to his wife, "I have written you how shamefully the poor contrabands are abandoned on these islands, after remaining or rushing to our protection. Truxtun has sent another load today since the descent on Hutchinson's Island—but the truth is we have not a military force to hold what the Navy has taken in a proper way—making a show of at least protecting loyal people."[32]

Indeed, by mid July, the number of rebel parties marauding the sea islands had increased, but Truxtun's plea for more troops to protect the contrabands on the islands went unheeded in the wake of Union Army troop withdrawals. A rebel reconnaissance of Hutchinson and St. Helena islands was interrupted by Truxtun in the little 30 ton schooner *Wildcat*, but he was unable to block their retreat. The disappointed Truxtun tried twice more to find the rebels but was frustrated by his inability to remain up the river overnight due to the danger of malaria. Lieutenant Truxtun then requested a steam vessel that he could steam up the river "just long enough to show her sight of Fort Chapman, I am sure we should here no more of these visits in the cornfields and poultry yards of the negroes."[33]

DuPont sympathized with Truxtun's frustrations and sent him the light draft steamer *Hale* "to enable you to scour the waters in your vicinity, and if possible, to capture these marauders."[34] Rebel raiding parties continued to harass the sea islands, however, and General David Hunter was finally faced with the unpleasant task of evacuating the garrison on Edisto. On July 11, 1862, he ordered the island commander, General Horatio Wright, to remove his troops whenever transportation could be arranged and to consult with Mr. De La Croix "as to the best means of collecting all the negroes within our lines and on the adjacent islands, and forwarding them to these headquarters."[35]

And so, with much regret to be abandoning such rich farm land and crops, the superintendents of the contrabands on Edisto gathered up about 1,600 of the former slaves, together "with their pigs, chickens and personal effects," and they were ferried across to St. Helena Village where they spent the remainder of the war. One of the refugees, Maria Middleton, recalled that they were taken off in large flatboats camouflaged with tree branches to conceal them from the Confederates.[36]

The evacuation of Edisto was lamented by many of the Union officials. Samuel F. DuPont's wife wrote to Henry Winter Davis on August 2, 1862, that the admiral regretted "extremely" the abandonment of "such valuable property to the raids of the secessionists." When Edward Pierce protested to the Secretary of the Treasury Salmon Chase about the abandonment of beautiful Edisto Island and the Lincoln Administration's lack of support for his experiment in black labor at Port Royal, Chase blamed "McClellan's infatuation" and the President's very conservative opinions on the role of blacks in the war effort.[37]

Confederate pressure on the sea islands continued during the summer of 1862. In mid-July Volunteer Lieutenant Irvin B. Baxter, in the 116 foot bark *Gem of the Sea*, foiled an attempt by about 500 rebels to cross from Georgetown in boats to Pawley's Island and proceed from there south to North Island to attack some 700 contrabands, including women and children, on the south end of the island. Operating from Winyah Bay, Baxter's force destroyed a rebel salt works, evacuated all those persons who wished to leave Georgetown, and dispersed rebel soldiers who returned the sailors' fire.[38]

The threat to the North Island contraband colony so concerned Flag-Officer DuPont that he ordered Lieutenant George Balch of the USS *Pocahontas* down to Georgetown, South Carolina, for added protection of the contrabands until General Hunter could despatch a steamer to transport the contrabands to Port Royal. Du Pont also instructed Lieutenant Balch to select 100 of the "best" contrabands for public service and have the medical officer look after them. The War Department evidently fulfilled its promise to send a steamer to North Island to evacuate the former slaves, for in his report Lieutenant Balch praised both Captains Baxter and Gregory for their zeal and energy and said, "they have been indefatigable in aiding in every way the embarkation of nearly 1,700 contrabands."[39]

Rebel activity in the sea islands continued to challenge the Navy, and by late summer 1862 the future of contraband colonies off the Southern coast was problematical. In mid-August Captain J. R. Goldsborough of the USS *Florida* reported to DuPont, recently appointed a rear admiral, that despite destroying all the boats on St. Simon's to cut off their means of escape, Confederate soldiers continued to wage a guerrilla war against Federal forces. Goldsborough said he had armed all the contrabands and landed more men from the *Florida* every night, but the rebels eluded him and he "did not think the feeble military force now stationed on the island at all adequate to its protection."

Rear Admiral DuPont expressed his approval of Goldsborough's handling of the situation on St. Simon's, but informed him that there was a rebel attempt to run the blockade off Georgia and that he needed every available vessel to guard all the various entrance points. "If the colony on St. Simon's should require more protection," said DuPont, "it will have to be given by the army."[40]

Samuel F. DuPont was a realist, and he wrote Lieutenant Etyinge on August 18, 1862, "The importance of your position I am fully aware of, but it impossible for the Navy alone to hold the islands bordering the waters of St. Helena sound and as the Army has withdrawn their forces from the fort on Otter Island, I do not propose to occupy it with sailors."[41]

In August and September, in the wake of General McClellan's failed James River campaign and the Army's retreat to the banks of the Potomac, further troop withdrawals from the South were ordered. These withdrawals compelled General Hunter to abandon the contraband colony on St. Simon's island. For the former slaves who had been settled and encouraged to plant crops on the island, it was a tragic development. By the fall of 1862 the entire contraband colony, some 4,000 blacks, had been uprooted and transported with the Navy's assistance to Port Royal. Here the impoverished refugees were unable to plant new crops, for the season was too advanced.

Those former slaves left on the sea islands were now responsible for their own protection. General Rufus Saxton armed some of the men and assigned them to picket duty to protect the remaining contraband colonies. On October 26, 1862, black pickets on St. Helena fired on two boat loads of rebels attempting to land on the island, forcing the Confederate raiders to flee. By November 1862 black troops of the First South Carolina Volunteers were available to assist in the defense of the sea islands, so General Saxton decided to send an expedition up the river on the steamer *Darlington* to "prove the fighting qualities of the negroes (which some have doubted) and to bring away the people from the mainland, destroy all rebel salt works, and to break up the rebel picket stations along the line of the coast."[42]

On November 12, 1862, a clearly delighted Saxton reported that the expedition had been very successful, making thirteen landings, driving in rebel pickets, and destroying rebel salt works. All hands he said reported that the black soldiers had "fought with coolness and bravery and would have done credit to veteran soldiers." The success of the mission prompted Saxton to recommend that a flotilla of light draft vessels with 100 black soldiers on each vessel be sent up the numerous rivers of the southern coast. "These boats should go up the streams, land at different plantations, drive in the pickets, and capture them if possible. The blowing of the steamer's whistle the negroes all understand as a signal to come in, and no sooner do they hear it than they come in from every direction." Saxton felt certain that if such a plan were undertaken, "we could soon have the complete occupation of the whole country." Although Saxton did get the authorization to enlist blacks into the military and many black regiments were eventually organized and proved themselves to be capable fighters, his plan to occupy the South by sending ships with black troops up southern rivers was too ambitious and never realized.

General Saxton's plan may not have been implemented, but his envisioning of such a bold scheme is fitting tribute to the men and ships of the U.S. Navy who, although without adequate ground troops and not always able to guarantee the protection of contraband colonies from rebel attack, could and did establish the precedent of aggressive patrolling and joint army-navy small unit operations on which Rufus Saxton's concept was based. Their role in freeing, caring for, and defending fugitive black slaves in the South during the Civil War has been overlooked by historians of the Port Royal experiment, but was certainly taken into account at the time and should not be forgotten.[43]

1. Commander Oliver S. Glisson to Flag-Officer Silas Stringham, July 15, 1861, U.S. Navy Department, *Official Records of the Union and Confederate Navies in the War of the Rebellion*, 30 vols. (Washington, D.C., 1894–1914), 1st Series, Volume VI, 8, hereafter cited as *ORN*.
2. Oliver S. Glisson to Silas Stringham, July 15, 1861, *ORN*, Vol. VI, 8.
3. Glisson to Stringham, July 17, 1861, *ORN*, Vol. VI, 8.
4. Silas Stringham to Hon. Gideon Welles, July 18, 1861, *ORN*, Vol. VI, 8.
5. Ibid.
6. Gideon Welles to Silas Stringham, July 22, 1861, *ORN*, Vol. VI, 10.
7. Benjamin F. Butler, *Autobiography and Personal Reminiscences of Major General Benjamin F. Butler* (Boston, 1892). In *Contraband to Freedman: Federal Policy Toward Southern Blacks 1861–5* (Westport, Conn., 1973), Louis F. Gerteis argues that Butler's policy was "a long way from emancipation," but that it was a step in that direction and one that appealed to men like Blair who were firmly opposed to general emancipation," see 12–13.
8. Silas Stringham to Gideon Welles, August 17, 1861, *ORN*, Vol. VI, 92.
9. Gideon Welles to Louis Goldsborough, September 25, 1861, *ORN*, Vol. VI, 252. For a discussion of black enlisted men, see Herb Aptheker, "The Negro in the Union Navy," *Journal of Negro History* 32 (April, 1947), 169–200. The best description of the U.S. Navy's relationship with contrabands is Benjamin Quarles, *The Negro in the Civil War* (New York, 1953), 89–93.

10. Samuel F. DuPont, General Order No. 11, May 15, 1862, *ORN*, Vol. XIII, 5.
11. Daniel Ammen, *The Old Navy and the New* (Philadelphia, 1891), 33–34.
12. Willie Lee Rose, *Rehearsal for Reconstruction: The Port Royal Experiment* (New York, 1964), 102.
13. Percival Drayton to Samuel F. DuPont, Dec. 9, 1861, *ORN*, Vol. XII, 388–89.
14. Drayton to DuPont, Dec. 9, 1861, *ORN*, Vol. XII, 388–390.
15. Lieutenant J. W. A. Nicholson to Samuel F. DuPont, Dec. 13, 1861, *ORN*, Vol. XII, 392–93.
16. Ibid.
17. Drayton to DuPont, Dec. 21, 1861, *ORN*, Vol. XII, 405–6 and Ammen, *Old Navy*, 356.
18. Ammen to DuPont, Dec. 29, 1861, *ORN*, Vol. XII, 431 and Ammen, *Old Navy*, 357.
19. Lieutenant T. A. Budd to Samuel F. DuPont, Jan. 14, 1862, *ORN*, Vol. XII, 463 and enclosure to W. B. Wright to T. A. Budd.
20. Lieutenant A. C. Rhind to Samuel F. DuPont, February 7, 1862, *ORN*, Vol. XII, 520, and DuPont to Lieutenant Alexander C. Rhind, Feb. 10, 1862, *ORN*, Vol. XII, 540. On February 5, 1862, DuPont instructed Rhind to keep a close watch on all enemy movements in the waters off North Edisto and informed him that as the "possession of North Edisto was of great importance" a regiment was being sent there for future joint operations, *ORN*, Vol. XII, 536.
21. Commander S. W. Godon to S. F. DuPont, March 30, 1862, *ORN*, Vol. XII, 633–34. The planters on St. Simon's had abandoned their plantations in December 1861 after the Union invasion, but 1,500 Confederate troops under Colonel Carey Stiles remained on the island. General Robert E. Lee, assigned to supervise the defenses of the coast, ordered them evacuated in February 1862. War Department, *A Compilation of the Official Records of the Union and Confederate Armies* (Washington, 1880–1901), 70 vols., series 1, XII, 487 (hereafter cited as *ORA*). See also T. Conn Bryan, *Confederate Georgia* (Athens, Ga., 1953), Chapter V.
22. Lieutenant Truxtun to DuPont, March 29, 1862, *ORN*, Vol. XII, 675, and Lt. Rhind to DuPont, April 3, 1862, *ORN*, Vol. XII, 676–7. For Union troop dispositions on Little Edisto and Otter Island, see Brig. Gen. H. G. Wright to Capt. A. B. Ely, April 21, 1862, *ORA*, XIV, 335.
23. Percival Drayton to Heyward Drayton, January 10, 1862, in Drayton Family Papers, Pennsylvannia Historical Society.
24. John D. Hayes, editor, *Samuel Francis DuPont Letters, A Selection from His Civil War Letters* (Ithaca, N.Y., 1969), Vol. 1, 281.
25. Lieutenant H. St. C. Etyinge to DuPont, August 11, 1862, *ORN*, Vol. XIII, 249.
26. Lieutenant A. C. Rhind to Samuel F. DuPont, Feb. 7, 1862, *ORN*, Vol. XII, 521.
27. Lieutenant O. S. Glisson to Flag Officer Silas Stringham, August 22, 1861, *ORN*, Vol. VI, 107.
28. Lieutenant J. W. A. Nicholson to Flag Officer Samuel F. DuPont, June 17, 1862, *ORN*, Vol. XIII, 424.
29. Commander S. W. Godon to Samuel F. DuPont, June 26, 1862, *ORN*, Vol. XIII, 142–43. The vessel changed her name from *Northern* to *Southern Belle* and was said to belong to a Mr. Stevens who Godon did not know for certain was in the rebel

army, so he decided to leave the schooner there should Stevens "prove himself free from suspicion."

30. Lieutenant Truxtun to Samuel F. DuPont, June 13, 1862, *ORN*, Vol. XIII, 95–97.

31. Ibid. The Army had already evacuated troops from Otter Island, and on May 24, 1862, the Assistant Adjutant-General C. W. Foster, at army headquarters on Edisto, directed Col. Welsh of the 54th Pennsylvania Volunteers to take a company to Otter Island on the steamer *Honduras* and remove "the horses, ammunition, shot, shell, implements, and all other property remaining there." *ORA*, XIV, 346.

32. Samuel F. DuPont to Mrs. DuPont, June 19, 1862, in *Samuel F. DuPont Letters*, Vol. 2, 124. In early June 1862 the army evacuated most of its troops from Edisto Island. According to H. G. Wright, the remaining garrison was composed of the Fifty-Fifth Regiment Pennsylvannia Volunteers, one squadron of Massachusetts cavalry, and two field artillery pieces with a detachment of the Third Rhode Island Regiment to serve them. Wright told Lieutenant Alexander Rhind he had instructed Colonel White not to occupy the entire island but to attempt to hold the depot of supplies near the wharf only. He also commended Rhind on his assistance in getting the troops across to the other side of the Edisto River. H. G. Wright to A. C. Rhind, June 3, 1862, *ORA*, Vol. XIV, 348.

33. Lieutenant W. T. Truxtun to Samuel F. DuPont, July 8, 1862, *ORN*, Vol. XIII, 185.

34. Samuel F. DuPont to Lt. Truxtun, July 15, 1862, *ORN*, Vol. XIII, 192.

35. Major General David Hunter to the Honorable E. M. Stanton, July 11, 1862, and Hunter to H. G. Wright, July 11, 1862, *ORA*, series 1, Vol. XIV, 363–64. General Hunter says he has sent six regiments to Ft. Monroe and will send "four more as soon as transportation arrives." Hunter lists the exact regiments in his letter to Stanton on July 12, 1862, *ORA*, Vol. XIV, 364.

36. Rose, 182–83.

37. Rose, 182–83. She says Edisto "became a no man's land that was raided sporadically by scouting parties from each army." In November 1862 DuPont reported to General Saxton that 60 contrabands remained on North Island totally dependent upon Union naval vessels for provisions. Saxton promised to send a vessel to take them off and said he expected to re-occupy Edisto Island where he would have room for 2,000 contrabands. See *ORN*, Vol. XIII, 463.

38. Lieutenant Irvin B. Baxter to S. F. DuPont, July 15, 1862, *ORN*, Vol. XIII, 193. For defenses and Confederate activities in Georgetown, see George C. Rogers, Jr., *The History of Georgetown County, South Carolina* (Columbia, S.C., 1970), especially Chapter XVIII. Rogers says, "Although showing some restraint, the Federals were making the lives of the leading planters miserable" and claims the Federals knew where the "great secessionsists" lived, 402.

39. Lieutenant Balch to S. F. DuPont, July 25, 1862, *ORN*, Vol. XIII, 212–13.

40. Samuel F. DuPont to J. R. Goldsborough, August 11, 1862, *ORN*, Vol. XIII, 248.

41. Samuel F. DuPont to H. St. C. Etyinge, August 18, 1862, *ORN*, Vol. XIII, 263–64.

42. Brigadier General Rufus Saxton to Major General Ormsby Mitchel, Oct. 26, 1862, *ORA*, Vol. XIV, 189. General Mitchel replaced General David Hunter who was

called north to testify in a court martial, but returned to the Department of the South at the end of the year. Ormsby Mitchel contracted yellow fever and died suddenly on Oct. 30th at Beaufort. For DuPont's comments on General Hunter and on Mitchel's death, see *SFDP Letters*, Vol. II, 216, 268, and 271.

43. Brigadier General Rufus Saxton to Honorable E. M. Stanton, Nov. 12, 1862, *ORA*, Vol. XIV, 190. Saxton sent Mansfield French to Washington to plead the case for his plan to arm blacks. See Rose, 190–91, and Dudley Cornish, *The Sable Arm: Negro Troops in the Union Army, 1861–65* (New York, 1956), 53–55. For an excellent introductory essay and selection of documents on blacks in the Union Army, see Ira Berlin, ed., *Freedom: A Documentary History of Emancipation 1861–1867*, series ii, "The Black Military Experience" (Cambridge, 1982). In organizing and gaining government support for black regiments, General Saxton accomplished what Hunter had tried and failed to do earlier in 1862.

The Union Sailor–Confederate Deserter Alliance in Florida

George Buker

⚓

At the time of its formation early in 1862, no one would have guessed that the East Gulf Blockading Squadron would create a civil war along Florida's west coast. Flag Officer William McKean was mortified to find that his command could not operate against the enemy because all of the important positions in the Gulf of Mexico, i.e., New Orleans, Mobile, and Pensacola, were assigned to Flag Officer David Farragut's West Gulf Blockading Squadron. McKean's coast, with minor exceptions, was desolate of commercial shipping and had few harbors, rivers, or bays deep enough for oceangoing vessels.[1] Yet the East Gulf Blockading Squadron organized and directed Florida's refugees and contrabands (escaped slaves) in partisan conflict against the Confederacy. However, this paper's focus is limited to the importance of the squadron's alliance with Confederate deserter bands in Taylor and Lafayette counties. This alliance was the precursor for the later recruitment of Floridians to be employed in a civil war within the state.

The East Gulf Blockading Squadron, guarding the Florida coast from St. Andrew Bay on the west to Cape Florida on the east, was the only squadron not to have any major actions to emblazon its wartime duty. Although Florida had about fourteen hundred miles of coastline, its three strategic military installations, Fort Pickens at Pensacola, Fort Jefferson on Dry Tortugas, and Fort Taylor on Key West, were always in Union hands, and this was the only blockade zone where there was no large established enemy seaport. The squadron guarded several excellent harbors at Cedar Key, Tampa Bay, and Charlotte Harbor, as well as small, active ports at St. Marks and Apalachicola, but because of the scanty population, these ports were of only minor importance during the war.

When the sailors raided the mainland, they found sympathizers ashore among the Floridians. Ship captains used these refugees to aid in cutting out blockade-runners, in harassing the enemy, and in destroying valuable coastal saltworks. As the number of loyal Floridians increased, the captains provided shelters on offshore islands protected by their ships' guns. Soon refugee centers were established on Hurricane and St. Vincent Islands, Cedar and Egmont Keys, and Usseppa Island from St. Andrew Bay to Charlotte Harbor.

But some Floridians seeking the blockaders in 1863 preferred to remain on shore near their homes. These men included Confederate deserters and conscript layouts (draft dodgers) who banded together to protect themselves from conscript officials who periodically swept the country gathering up draft evaders and deserters. With this group the blockaders established partisan combat actions on shore. When times were propitious, these men, supported by the navy, rose up in armed conflict; when times were ominous, they remained anonymous within the larger civilian community.

Lieutenant Commander David Harmony of the *Tahoma* built up a fine rapport with the deserter bands along his section of the coast. He had contact with four bands: William Wilson Strickland's group based at the mouth of the Econfina River, James Coker's band located on the Fenholloway River, William White's men on the Steinhatchee River, and another group of fifty men on the Suwannee River. Under Harmony's guidance, the first three bands organized themselves into quasi-military companies of eighty men each.

Private Strickland, Second Florida Cavalry, CSA, deserted the Confederacy on 5 June 1963. He gathered a group of men and established his camp at the mouth of the Econfina River on Snyder's Island near the east bank. His camp was almost inaccessible, surrounded by a marsh that was inundated at high tide. There Strickland and his men took up their frontier farmer-herdsmen duties raising crops and tending cattle.

On 18 November 1863, Strickland established contact with the blockaders when he sent a load of beef out to the *Stars & Stripes*. Both the officer and enlisted messes made purchases. Three weeks later, six members returned with fresh beef and sweet potatoes. Four men took the oath of allegiance to the United States and elected to remain aboard. Two days later, the other two cast off for the Econfina, only to return the next day with four more who desired to leave the Confederacy. Traffic between the Econfina men and the gunboat continued. On 22 December, four more came out to take the oath of allegiance. Later, their boat was dropped astern while they spent the night aboard ship. The next day they returned to the Econfina. On 15 January 1864, their sloop came alongside with more potatoes and beef to sell.[2]

In February, the pattern of events changed. Strickland no longer just sold beef and provisions to Union ships and brought out those desiring to leave the Confederacy; now, under the blockaders' guidance, Strickland engaged in armed opposition to the Confederacy. On 4 February 1864, he told the captains of the *Stars & Stripes* and the *L. S. Chambers* of his planned attack on the enemy. Next day he skirmished with a cavalry unit, captured four, killed three, and wounded one. Four days later he sent his prisoners out to the anchorage where the *Stars & Stripes* and the *Tahoma* were swinging on their chains. Captain Harmony took them aboard his ship. The men remained only long enough to turn over their prisoners and to pick up provisions.[3]

On 16 February, Harmony sent his executive officer, Acting Master Edmund C. Weeks, with eleven sailors, ashore to enlist the aid of Strickland and Coker in an expedition against extensive saltworks located between Warrior River and Point Edwards, a desolate section of the coast. Ninety-six Floridians joined him in a successful raid which destroyed a large number of saltworks. Wesley Bishop was the only casualty when he accidentally discharged his shotgun, putting some buckshot in his leg. At the conclusion of the action, four of the refugees returned to the ship with Weeks.

The next day Weeks brought provisions back to the men on the Fenholloway. When he returned to the *Tahoma* again, he brought Wesley Bishop back for medical treatment and a prisoner captured during the saltworks attack.[4] By now it was standard practice for both Strickland and Coker to turn their captives over to the blockaders. Eventually, these prisoners of war ended up under army control in Key West.

On the morning of 8 March 1864, Captain Coker came aboard the *Tahoma* to pick up supplies. In the afternoon Captain Strickland visited the ship for his provisions. That evening the ship anchored off the Ochlockonee River, where Acting Master Weeks took a boat party on an expedition upriver. He was joined by men from both bands, who remained with him on the river for two days. Obviously, the blockaders not only gave aid but planned operations with the partisans.[5]

Confederate Brigadier General William M. Gardner saw the danger of these bands and issued a circular stating that he had ample forces to move into Taylor and Lafayette counties to punish these men. He said that anyone found bearing arms would be shot. Further, he stated that he would gather up the deserters' families, send them into the interior, and destroy their property.

Two days after the general's circular, Strickland captured three men: a father and son who had aided some cavalrymen in capturing and killing two Union men and a third man who was home on furlough. Strickland turned all three over to Harmony to be shipped to Key West.[6]

Ultimately, the rebel sweep through Taylor and Lafayette counties fell upon Lieutenant Colonel H. D. Capers. After a thorough investigation, Capers determined that a deserter camp was situated at the mouth of the Econfina River. Recent rains had been heavy, adding to the inaccessibility of the region, when Capers ordered Major Charles H. Camfield to take a detachment of cavalry down the east bank of the Econfina. At the same time, the Twelfth Georgia Battalion moved out along the east bank of the Aucilla River.

On 24 March Capers found the dissidents' deserted camp. The hide-out consisted of a few temporary huts which led him to believe that the men spent most of their time in their homes, gathering at the camp for their raids and for mustering during emergencies. Therefore, Capers issued orders to destroy the homes on the east and west banks of the Econfina and Fenholloway rivers where the deserters lived.[7]

When Capers got to Strickland's farm, he found a wealth of information. Here in the leader's home was a copy of the rules of conduct for the Independent Union Rangers of Taylor County signed by thirty-five men, which provided positive proof of the involvement of Strickland and his neighbors. In addition, there were two thousand rounds of ammunition for Springfield muskets, as well as barrels of flour from the United States Subsistence Department. There were many lesser items on the premises, all indicating that Strickland had been in constant communication with the blockaders. The items Colonel Capers found were the result of many visits by Strickland to the Union ships offshore.

Capers set about gathering up the women and children and destroying their property. While he burned the deserters' homes, several of Strickland's men ambushed one of his cavalry units four miles northwest of present-day Perry. In the ensuing skirmish, two cavalrymen were killed and two wounded. Three of the deserters were captured, two of whom were listed on Strickland's muster roll. On his return to headquarters, Capers was forced to stop to rest his soldiers who were exhausted from their march through densely wooded swamps, where water, at times, was so deep that they had to remove their cartridgeboxes to keep their ammunition dry.[8]

Before his departure, Capers left a letter for Strickland with his father-in-law. The following day Strickland answered the colonel, presenting the deserters' case in a rough but eloquent manner: "I cannot control my men since they saw you fire our house, I cannot control them any longer. I ain't accountable for what they do now." He went on to say that he had done his duty, and now he was through with the war. All he wanted was to remain with his father-in-law to help him raise stock. If the Southern government would permit him and his men to remain at home and not fight, they would be willing to raise stock for the Confederate forces. "But they will not go into war if you had as many again men and dogs . . . so I remain a flea until I get a furlough from headquarters, and when you put your thumb on me and then raise it up I will be gone." Strickland thanked the colonel for treating his wife kindly and said that "it was not her notion for me to do as I was doing." But he threatened that if the government did not grant his men permission to live peacefully in Taylor County, it had better move "the steers out of the adjoining three counties." He concluded with thoughts for his family, now in Confederate hands: "So here is my love for the good attentions for my wife and child. If the war lasts long enough and you will raise him to be a soldier he will show the spunk of his daddy."[9]

In the meantime, the wives and children rounded up by Colonel Capers were taken to Camp Smith, about six miles from Tallahassee. Less than two weeks earlier, the planters in the area had been called upon by the state to build nine double-pen log houses. Each house had two large rooms with fireplaces and a passageway joining the rooms. There were doors and shuttered windows, but no panes of glass.[10] All during construction, the local citizens were curious, but no answers were forthcoming until military wagons began discharging the families of the suspected deserters.

Susan Eppes of Tallahassee described in some detail the workings of the "wagon brigade," as she termed the operation. The wagons, under military escort, were taken to suspected regions ("god-for-saken country," in Eppes's words), where the women were told to pack up. Some women sullenly complied, but others ranted and cursed the soldiers and obstinately refused to pack. If they did nothing, the drivers packed for them before all moved on. As the wagons departed, the buildings were torched.[11]

When the South lost the Mississippi River, cutting off its source of western beef, it turned to the cattle ranges of south Florida to supply its armies with meat. Primarily to stop the flow of beef, Admiral Theodorus Bailey, East Gulf Blockading Squadron, prevailed upon General Daniel P. Woodbury, District of Key West and Tortugas, to enlist his squadron's Floridian allies to strike inland beyond the operating range of his sailors. Both men were headquartered at Key West. Their commands were strikingly similar: the squadron was among the least desirable commands because its backwater duty offered little opportunity for naval action or glory; the district was a small occupational command designed to keep the vital forts of Key West and Tortugas under Union control, but offering no opportunity for military action or glory. Admiral Bailey and General Woodbury commiserated with each other over their isolation. Both men were eager to enlarge the scope of their activities. Thus, Woodbury accepted Bailey's offer immediately.

What excited Woodbury most was Captain Harmony's list of seventy-three men in one of the deserter bands working with him. Woodbury asked Harmony if it would be possible to recruit these men for his U.S. Second Florida Cavalry. Harmony replied that, although he had worked with the Floridians and had directed some of their operations, he doubted very much if they would be willing to enlist, for the refugees did not want to leave home.[12]

Woodbury sent soldiers north to the *Tahoma* to evaluate the navy's operations. When they arrived on 16 March 1864, Harmony sent them to Coker's camp on the Fenholloway. A week later Woodbury brought his staff to Harmony's anchorage to continue negotiations. The next day the general visited Coker and remained overnight. Then he returned to his transport to await further developments.[13]

Two days later, there was a flurry of activity on the *Tahoma*. Woodbury came aboard at 1 P.M. Shortly thereafter a refugee boat came alongside with a message from William White's group. At 2:40 P.M. a refugee sloop brought out more deserters. Woodbury began his all-out campaign to convince the Floridians to enlist in his Second Florida Cavalry. The next day the general led soldiers, sailors, and refugees back to the Fenholloway to continue negotiations. Woodbury remained two days with the Floridians before returning to his transport.[14]

Circumstances favored General Woodbury, for not only had Lieutenant Commander Harmony established contact with and helped organize the deserters, but Confederate actions also played into his hands when the rebels swept through Taylor and Lafayette counties burning homes and driving the women and children off to confinement at Camp Smith. In fact, Woodbury arrived aboard the *Tahoma* the day before William Strickland's house was burned. After the house burning, many members of both bands were willing to enlist. Woodbury sent his recruiters into Taylor County where between 6 and 10 April 1864 seventy-seven men enlisted in his Second Florida Cavalry.[15]

But who were these men that took to Florida's swamps in defiance of Confederate authority? Susan Eppes referred to them as "an enemy we had with whom we were unable to cope, the diabolical deserter . . . these men, who were so treacherous and disloyal belonged to a peculiar class; they were, for the most part the descendants of criminals, who had taken refuge in the bays and swamps of the Florida coast."[16] But an examination of extant records provides less emotional information about them.

Most of their Confederate service records are too sketchy to gather much information, although that is not always the case. John R. B. Brannon, born in Madison County, Florida, worked as a farmer until he enlisted. Private Brannon, Company M, Second Florida Infantry, was twenty-one when he joined the army. A year later he was wounded at Sharpsburg, Maryland. After a two-week stay in the hospital in Richmond, Virginia, he was released to recuperate. The last entry in his service jacket, dated December 1862, states that he was "on wounded furlough in Florida."[17] The next record of Brannon is on William Strickland's roll.

As soon as the war broke out, James A. Martin of Jefferson County, Florida, enlisted as a private in Company C, First Florida Infantry. He fought at Murfreesboro, Tennessee, where he received a slight jaw wound. Later, stationed at Brewton, Alabama (a hotbed of deserter and layout bands), he deserted, only to show up six months later in Strickland's band.[18]

Wyche Fulford, Jackson Sapp, and William Stanaland were family men: Fulford had eight, Sapp four, and Stanaland three children.

All three men were saltmakers exempt from military service.[19] But when the Exemption Act of 17 February 1864 removed saltmakers from the exempted list, the three joined Strickland's band.

The men in Strickland's band were probably all Southerners: fourteen born in Florida, twelve in Georgia, three in South Carolina, two in North Carolina, and four whose birthplaces are unknown. Many may have been neighbors. Twenty-four were listed in the 1860 Florida census; sixteen lived in Taylor County, six in Jefferson County, and two in Madison County. Seven were in their teens, eleven in their twenties, five in their thirties, eight in their forties, and one in his sixties. Three men's ages are unknown.

Union sources indicate that Strickland's band was larger than the thirty-five men carried on the captured muster roll. Lieutenant Commander Harmony reported being in contact with two companies of eighty men each, who, at his suggestion, elected a captain and three lieutenants for each unit. Strickland was one of the captains.[20]

Further circumstantial evidence may be drawn from the ship's logs listing men traveling with known members of Strickland's band. On several occasions Snyder's sloop brought out members to the *Tahoma*, indicating that Snyder was affiliated with the group. Once, when Strickland stayed aboard the *Tahoma*, the log recorded that three men of the company remained, and one of them, Jordan, was not on the muster roll.[21]

The log of the *Stars & Stripes* often listed visits of the refugee boat from the Econfina River. Charles Martin came out with John Nichols and William M. Snipes on one occasion, and another time Paul Poppell accompanied George W. Green; only Martin and Poppell were on Strickland's roll. These events indicate that the muster roll of Strickland's Independent Union Rangers was not complete.[22]

It is more difficult to locate members of James Coker's group, for there are no extant records of his organization. Yet circumstantial evidence provides the names of a few men. First, there were his two brothers, Allen and William. James and William Coker enlisted as privates in Company A, Eighth Florida Infantry. Fifty-five days later both deserted. In April 1864, when the Union army enlisted men in Taylor County, the two younger Cokers, William and Allen, became privates in the U.S. Second Florida Cavalry; why James Coker did not also join is not known.

There is strong circumstantial evidence for believing that Charles Dunn, George Tales, L. E. Brook, I. L. Kale, and Wesley

Bishop were members of Coker's band. When Acting Master Weeks of the *Tahoma* returned from a four-day salt raid, he brought the first four men back with him. The next day they returned to the Fenholloway River with provisions for Coker's company. When Weeks again returned to the ship, Bishop was with him, seeking medical treatment for his gunshot wound. It is reasonable to assume that all five men belonged to the Coker band.[23]

Thirteen other men could have been from Coker's group. In December 1863 Charles Martin and three others from Strickland's band came out to the *Stars & Stripes* and remained overnight. They departed for the Econfina River after another refugee boat was seen in the distance beating its way toward the gunboat. The *Stars & Stripes* heaved up its anchor and steamed over to bring the boat back in tow to its anchorage. That Strickland's men left before the other boat arrived could imply that the men in the second boat were from another group. That the gunboat had to steam over to pick them up could mean that it came from the more distant Fenholloway River.[24]

The Coker and Allbritton families provided six of the twenty-one men, and there is a possibility that the Woods family supplied another three men associated with the Coker band. Two of the three Allbritton brothers had served in the Confederate army. James Allbritton deserted from the hospital at Lake City. A year later, George Allbritton was reported "absent sick."[25] Nineteen-year-old John Allbritton never enlisted for Confederate service. It could not be determined if the three men named Woods were from the same family. Twenty-two-year-old Thomas J. Woods enlisted at St. Marks as a private in Company G, Fifth Florida Infantry. He was captured by Union forces in combat operations in Virginia and exchanged during a prisoner-of-war swap. Less than six months later, Woods was wounded and brought to a military hospital in Richmond. In March 1863, he received a ninety-day furlough to report to a Florida hospital. Woods did not return to Confederate military service.[26] A year later, in Taylor County, he enlisted in the U.S. Second Florida Cavalry. Henry Woods enlisted in the First Florida Cavalry, and six months later he found a substitute and was released. His discontent must have been for other reasons than a dislike for military service, for during his career in the U.S. Second Florida Cavalry, he rose to the rating of sergeant.[27]

Second Lieutenant John Woods's Confederate service record reveals a man one would not expect to find among the deserters of Taylor County. When he submitted his resignation, he had a surgeon's certificate of disability. In his letter to his commanding general he wrote: "I am now forty-five years old, have served in the Indian Wars of Florida for more than six years and in the present war since its commencement, having been eight years a soldier and in resigning feel that I have fully discharged my duty to my country." Why he changed his allegiance between the time of his resignation in January 1863 and his enlistment in the Union army in April 1864 is not known. Although he enlisted as a private in the U.S. Second Florida Cavalry, his military experience enabled him to rise to the rank of captain.[28]

Private Samuel J. Godwin, Company I, Ninth Florida Infantry, spent very little time between deserting and enlisting. He left Camp Dade, Florida, on 1 April 1864 and enlisted five days later in the U.S. Second Florida Cavalry.[29]

By the end of April, encouraged by his success recruiting among the deserter bands, Woodbury turned to enlisting men from the navy's refugee camps. His recruiter, Lieutenant Thomas Hunter, made a thorough trip up the west coast. First, he stopped at Fort Myers, the U.S. Second Florida Cavalry's first mainland post. The fort was manned by Floridians from the Usseppa Island refugee camp and layouts from south Florida's cattle frontier. Captain Henry A. Crane (former Acting Master's Mate of the East Gulf Blockading Squadron), one of the first refugees in the Second Florida Cavalry, detached some of his men to go to the navy's Egmont Key camp in Tampa Bay to help recruiting. Next, Hunter went to Cedar Key where Captain Charles E. Fleming of the *Sagamore* had 250 refugees living under his protection. Hunter went ashore to begin enrolling Floridians. At St. Marks, Hunter visited Captain Harmony who took him to his St. Vincent Island refugee camp. Here Hunter continued recruiting. When Hunter contacted Captain William R. Browne of the *Restless* off St. Andrew Bay, it was by now a familiar story. Browne took him to his Hurricane Island camp where again he recruited Floridians. Near the end of May his recruiting efforts were:

Ft. Myers	158
Cedar Key	102
St. Vincent	112
St. Andrew	56
Key West	4
TOTAL	432

With the exception of Key West, all of these localities had been refugee camps established by the East Gulf Blockading Squadron. Ultimately, the Second Florida Cavalry recruited 739 soldiers.[30]

Meanwhile, Governor John Milton felt that the gathering of the disloyal families at Camp Smith was a mistake. He believed that people who were not disloyal also lost their homes, and he pointed out that this act in no way stopped the violence and lawlessness in those regions; on the contrary, such actions further alienated the men and put an additional barrier between them and the Confederacy. He also believed that many of the disloyal were from other states and that the gathering and imprisoning of these women and children had no effect on those out-of-state men.[31] The governor was correct in believing that the action alienated many of the men. Moreover, information on their enlisting in the U.S. Second Florida Cavalry found its way back to their wives at Camp Smith.

At first, there was apprehension in the capital that an effort to free their families would bring the deserters swooping down on Tallahassee, but as time went on and nothing threatening happened, the citizens relaxed. Soon the people began to bring food to the near destitute prisoners at Camp Smith.[32] The lessening of tension over reprisals led the wives to petition the governor to be allowed to join their menfolk.

Earlier, the military had offered to let the women and children go through the lines to the Federals if they desired, but the governor had objected. Now the women petitioned him to change his mind. Pointing out that they were homeless and separated from their providers, they asked him to withdraw his objection to their "being sent to the Blockading Vessel, to seek our Fathers, Husbands and Brothers." They told the governor that they knew that most of their men were "still on the coast and [we] believe that we could soon be re-united with them."[33] The petition was signed by twelve women, most of whom were from Taylor and Lafayette counties. Among them, four were wives of men in Strickland's group and another signee was the wife of a member of William White's Deadmans Bay band. Upon receiving the women's request, Governor Milton relented and not only allowed them to leave but had them escorted to the blockading vessel off St. Marks on 19 July 1864.[34] Thus ended one of the better-documented episodes among the deserter bands in Florida.

General Woodbury completed the organization of his Florida regiment by requesting the services of Acting Master Edmund C. Weeks. When Admiral Bailey released Weeks on 16 July 1864, the general appointed him a major and gave him command of the Second Florida Cavalry. Woodbury explained his concept of the strategy and tactics to be employed: never occupy a position where the enemy could reach him without employing boats; always select bases on islands which could be protected by the squadron's ships; and the primary objective of the unit was to raid the mainland and stop the flow of cattle from south Florida to the Confederate armies in the north. Finally, he wrote: "You have men under your command familiar with every part of Western Florida, send them out by fours, with orders to travel nights, hide by day, communicate with Union people for information etc.; at least one man in each four should have on the common dress of the country, so that leaving his arms with his comrades, he may talk with the people of the country without exciting suspicion."[35] Of the twenty-seven officers assigned to this regiment, sixteen were former naval officers or refugee partisan leaders, and the bulk of the enlisted men were Floridians who had ties with the blockaders.

The formation of deserter bands on Florida's west coast allowed the East Gulf Blockading Squadron to establish guerrilla operations within Florida. Without the squadron's aid, these dissenting Floridians would not have been able to challenge the state's military forces or disrupt its home front. And it must be noted that the Taylor and Lafayette counties' deserter bands did not become militarily active until after they had established contact with the blockaders.

Although all blockading squadrons had contacts with refugees, only the East Gulf Blockading Squadron utilized these allies to foster a civil war on its shores. The squadron's creation of the Second Florida Cavalry elevated the blockader-refugee alliance from guerrilla to conventional warfare. Additionally, the Second Infantry Regiment, U.S. Colored Troops, fought beside the blockaders and refugees. Together these three units, spearheaded by the Second Florida Cavalry, carried the war into Florida. The refugees made cattle raids up the Caloosahatchee River, two strikes up the Peace River to Fort Meade, a temporary occupation of Tampa, the destruction of Brooksville, a deep probe into St. Andrew Bay, a strike at St. Marks, and other skirmishes too slight to record. In brief, the Floridians were Confederate Florida's most active foes from St. Andrew Bay to

Charlotte Harbor. Florida Governor John Milton recognized their efforts when he said: "Deserters and disloyal persons have constituted the most efficient force the enemy has had upon our coast to conduct raiding parties, supply the enemy with beef and enable them to increase their forces with runaway slaves."[36] The uniqueness of the East Gulf Blockading Squadron's wartime role was its organization of, and support for, Florida's civil war on the Gulf Coast, and it began with its blockader–Confederate deserter alliance.

1. U.S. Navy Department, *Official Records of the Union and Confederate Navies in the War of the Rebellion*, 30 vols. (Washington, D.C.: GPO, 1894–1927), I, 17:217–18 (hereafter cited as ORN).

2. USS *Stars & Stripes*'s log, 18 Nov., 8, 10, 22, 23 Dec. 1863, 15 Jan. 1864, National Archives, RG 24, Records of the Bureau of Naval Personnel (hereafter cited as [ship's name], log, and date).

3. Ibid., 4 Feb. 1864; USS *Tahoma*, log, 9, 14 Feb. 1864; Harmony to Bailey, 9 Feb. 1864, enclosure in Woodbury to Stone, 15 Feb. 1864, NA, RG 393, U.S. Army Continental Commands, 1821–1920, Department of the Gulf, Letters Received.

4. USS *Tahoma*, log, 16, 17, 21–23 Feb. 1864; ORN, I, 17:649–50.

5. ORN, I, 17:651; Letter Books of Admiral Theodorus Bailey, NA, RG 45, Naval Records Collection of the Office of Naval Records and Library, 7:4621.

6. USS *Tahoma*, log, 20 Mar. 1864; Bailey to Woodbury, 6 Apr. 1864, NA, RG 393, U.S. Army Continental Commands, 1821–1920, District, Key West & Tortugas, Letters Received.

7. U.S. War Department, *The War of the Rebellion: A Compilation of the Official Records of the Union and Confederate Armies*, 130 vols. (Washington, D.C.: GPO, 1880–1901), I, 53:316–18 (hereafter cited as OR).

8. Ibid.; William T. Cash, "Taylor County History and Civil War Deserters," *Florida Historical Quarterly*, 27 (1948): 50.

9. OR, I, 53:319.

10. Susan Bradford Eppes, *Through Some Eventful Years* (1926: rpt. Gainesville: University of Florida Press, 1968), 223.

11. Ibid., 221–23.

12. OR, I, 35, pt. 2:14.

13. USS *Tahoma*, log, 16, 23–26 Mar. 1864.

14. Ibid., 28, 30, 31 Mar. 1864.

15. Companies C and D service records, U.S. Second Florida Cavalry, NA, RG 95, Records of the Adjutant General's Office, Compiled Service Records of Volunteer Union Soldiers from Florida (hereafter cited as RG 95, Ser. Rec.).

16. Eppes, *Through Some Eventful Years*, 223–24.

17. Brannon, NA, RG 109, War Department Collection of Confederate Records, Compiled Service Records of Volunteer Confederate Soldiers from Florida (hereafter cited as RG 109, Ser. Rec.).

18. Martin, RG 109, Ser. Rec.; Georgia Lee Tatum, *Disloyalty in the Confederacy* (Chapel Hill: University of North Carolina Press, 1934), 63–64.

19. Cash, "Taylor County History," 46.
20. USS *Tahoma*, log, 22 Feb. 1864.
21. Ibid.
22. USS *Stars & Stripes*, log, 23 Dec. 1863, 4 Feb. 1864.
23. USS *Tahoma*, log, 21–23 Feb. 1864.
24. USS *Stars and Stripes*, log, 22–23 Dec. 1863.
25. Ser. Rec. of James and George Allbritton, RG 109.
26. Woods, ibid.
27. Woods, ibid.
28. Ibid.; Woods, RG 95, Ser. Rec.
29. Godwin, RG 109, Ser. Rec.; Godwin, RG 95, Ser. Rec.
30. Woodbury to Stone, 27 May 1864, NA, RG 393, District of Key West, Letters sent (hereafter cited as DKW, rec. or sent).
31. OR, I, 53:349–51.
32. Eppes, *Through Some Eventful Years*, 221–23.
33. Letter of Petition, 7 July 1864, reprinted in Cash, "Taylor County History," 54–55.
34. John E. Johns, *Florida During the Civil War* (Gainesville: University of Florida Press, 1963), 167.
35. Woodbury to Weeks, RG 393, DKW, sent.
36. Governor John Milton, Letter Book, 142, Division of Archives, History, and Records Management, Tallahassee, Florida.

Temptations for the Small Navy of a Great Power: The Case of Austria-Hungary

Lothar Höbelt

⚓

The second half of the 19th century saw a permanent revolution in naval technology: For almost two centuries, in the "Age of Fighting Sail," the fundamentals had remained the same. That still necessitated some sort of periodic rearmament as the life-span of individual wooden ships was less than that of the technology as a whole. On average that meant that ships-of-the-line had to be rebuilt every 20 to 50 years, depending upon a series of factors from maintenance to climate. After the 1850s that situation was turned on its head. Naval vessels might still be serviceable (even though, in the transition period, wooden hulls did not take kindly to steam-engines and their emissions) but were often already becoming obsolescent by the time they entered service. In the period from 1848 to World War I, almost every decade was marked by thorough-going innovations that transformed the face of the main combat units. The screw-driven steam ships in the 1880s, the advent of Krupp armour and quick-loading guns in the 1890s and finally, the dreadnought in the 1900s. (Apart from that—and on a slightly different level because its impact did not always directly affect battleship construction—torpedo-boats and submarines made their impact felt.)[1]

It needs to be pointed out that the pace of these developments was not just much more rapid than before. It was also much more rapid than that of contemporaneous developments in the technology of warfare on land. Here the main steps were the introduction of breech-loading rifles in the 1860s, of repeating rifles in the 1890s and the (comparatively slow) diffusion of machine-guns until WW I. What there was of an armament race on land was more concerned with quantitative expansion than qualitative leaps. States tried to use fully the manpower available by enlarging their intake of recruits and to improve their ability to move troops around quickly by building strategic railways. In both these respects, there were natural limits imposed by geographical and demographic factors that could not easily be overcome. One result was that the main item of the army estimates continued to be pay and food. Another was that the ranking of the great powers on land changed only very slowly if at all. True, Austria-Hungary and France fell behind Germany and Russia as time went by. But this was a gradual and almost imperceptible shift brought about by profound forces that politicians were more or less powerless to control.

With sea-power, on the other hand, that was a different matter. Naval expansion did not, as it were, spring almost automatically from universal military service and its logistical corollaries. Its growth was much more intimately linked to political determination and strategic decisions. True, natural limitations could not be overlooked entirely: At its most basic, you needed access to the sea, a warm sea, perhaps (Russia´s perennial problem), or one where you could not easily be bottled up. Having to do without a sea-faring population might also be considered a draw-back. Industrial clout obviously played its part once it came to producing your own up-to-date weapons systems. But on the whole, naval ports could be created almost from scratch (like Sebastopol and Pola); the numbers of personnel required were not prohibitive and steamers no longer required the same daring skills as a sailing-ship anyway. Up-to-date ships could, at a pinch, even be bought from abroad, as Italy, Turkey, and Chile amongst others all demonstrated. The main constraining factor seemed to be financial. A small state could not easily afford the resources needed to keep up with the big powers. Even countries that had been traditional naval powers when that position more precisely reflected a country´s socio-economic status and trading interests, like the Netherlands or Denmark, no longer bothered to join the race.

The big continental powers, on the other hand, were given a chance to enter that race on favourable terms, or at least without suffering from any disadvantages as late-comers. If they chose to do so, they could simply outspend many of the traditional naval powers, thus decisively upsetting the local balance of powers at sea within a comparatively short span of time. In the Baltic, Prussia, which had been almost defenceless against its small neighbour Denmark in 1864, built a navy around the turn of the century that was to scare even the British. In the Black Sea, Russia, which had previously been debarred from having any fleet at all, radically changed its position vis-a-vis Turkey by building a squadron of modern battleships in the 1880s. Austria-Hungary had had its first famous bout of "Flottenpolitik" even earlier, in the 1860s. She returned to it in the 1890s, at about the same time as her German ally. Let us look a little closer at the particular circumstances governing these choices.

Even though the Habsburg Empire had long had some access to the Adriatic (at Trieste, Fiume or the Uskok port of Zengg), in naval terms, it was heir to one of the traditional naval powers: Venice (including its possessions along the Dalmatian coast-line). It is only fair to say that prior to 1848 Austria did not really treasure this heritage. It was only when Austrian domination on the Italian peninsula was challenged by the Risorgimento and its allies at the Court of Savoy that naval power came to be appreciated by Vienna. The siege of Venice in the summer of 1849 was a show-piece of the usefulness of naval forces in subduing the rebellious "Mistress of the Seas."[2]

A turning-point was reached when Italy actually achieved unification in 1860. Until then Austrian naval rivalry had been carried on with the Kingdom of Sardinia, a small state by any standards (5 million inhabitants to Austria's almost 40) that was heir to Genoa as Austria was heir to Venice. Now Sardinia has been transformed into Italy. The Regno d'Italia was not yet considered an equal by the European Pentarchy; its great power status remained disputed; alpine barriers to its North even restricted the nuisance value of its army in any big-scale confrontation on land. But Italy possessed one of the longest coastlines of Europe; even internal communications depended upon coastal traffic; it had a large reservoir of sea-faring people; and the nucleus of quite a respectable navy in the combined forces of Sardinia, Naples and Tuscany. Even if General Staffs contemptuously dismissed the Italians, they certainly looked set to become a sizeable power in naval terms.

After 1860, Austria thus faced a choice: The Habsburgs could refuse to compete with the Italian navy at all, relying instead on their black-and-yellow regiments to keep in check their unruly neighbours to the south. This was a view that was popular with some of the army top brass (like Archduke Albrecht, the victor of Custozza). In the beginning there was even another strand of wishful thinking from another quarter: An arms race with Italy was unnecessary because the "Regno d'Italia" would fall apart again anyway.

For a number of political reasons, however, Austria did decide to enter the arms race, partly out of considerations of prestige and because of the danger of parts of Dalmatia being cut off from the rest of the monarchy; last but not least probably because of the august person of the Naval commander, no less than the Emperor's brother, the Archduke Ferdinand Maximilian (the future Emperor of Mexico). What converted this decision into a feasible and worthwhile option, however, was technological change. It was the express aim of Austrian naval policy "to substitute quality for quantity."[3] In 1860, when Italy achieved its unification, the first ironclad entered service. In 1861 and 1862 Austria ordered no less than five of these armoured frigates in order to be able to fight a successful battle against the Italians "as early as next spring." Austria did not manage to keep that momentum up beyond 1863, but the initial investment paid off—thanks to Bismarck, who hastened the coming of the next conflict. Tegetthoff's victory of Lissa in 1866 was the result—even if that victory was far from inevitable and was, indeed, based on more than a pinch of good fortune![4]

Contrary to his own—often quoted—moanings, Tegetthoff used the prestige acquired at Lissa to single-mindedly pursue his vision of a powerful armoured battle fleet after 1868, when he was at the helm of the Austrian navy, until his untimely death in 1871. Those three years resulted in a thorough and wrenching process of modernisation at the expense of all the non-armoured elements of the fleet (like coastal fortifications, patrol ships, and even the marines—who were far from enjoying anything like their present-day reputation). Even though Italy stopped its naval expansion programme after 1866, Austria continued to lay down new battle ships until 1871. When that fleet was ready—by the time of the Oriental crises in the mid-1870s—Austria's navy was equal not just to that of Italy, but also to that of France. The ranking of the Mediterranean naval forces had changed dramatically: The down-swing proved to be just as sudden.

The next round in the Mediterranean arms race was sparked by tension between Italy and France; it centred on the turret-ship, an ironload armoured with just one or two super-heavy guns that returned to artillery its superiority over steel-armour. Once the first of the new breed, the *Duilio*, showed up in 1880, it condemned the whole of the Austrian fleet to obsolescence. This time, though, the Austrians refused to compete. Their attention had been turned eastwards. Staving off the potential Russian "steam-roller" in the plains of Galicia was now accorded priority, while Italy was to be converted into an ally by means of the Triple Alliance, theoretically, at least.[5] In addition to that, torpedo boats now seemed to offer a cheap way of providing for coastal defence. There is an interesting parallel with developments in Germany where Caprivi, who entered office as head of the admirality in the same year as Max von Sterneck did in Austria (1883), also stopped the building of battleships—and for very much the same reason: Because no one seemed to be able to tell with any degree of certainty what the battleship of the future was going to look like. Continued construction of such "mastodons" appeared to be money ill spent.[6]

However, this commitment to what the French called the "Jeune Ecole" was never as whole-hearted as Tegetthoff's single-minded expansion of the ironclad squadron had been. It soon ran aground when technical difficulties cropped up (like torpedo boats turning out to be too small to be sea-worthy). Moreover, the Austrian version of the Jeune Ecole, despite its catchword of economy, was not devoid of expensive white elephants that helped to undermine confidence in Sterneck's leadership, e.g., his beloved half-breed ram cruisers that were supposed to substitute speed for armour. It can safely be assumed that from the very beginning there was a strong undercurrent of scepticism about Sterneck's experiments from within the navy itself, where the longing for the days of the battle fleet had never died out. By the 1890s, that scepticism burst into open opposition.

The decisions reached in the first few years of the 1890s—even if less prominent in historical annals than the building of the fleet than won Lissa—are noteworthy for more than one reason. For one thing, they provide us with, perhaps an even more striking attempt by the small navy of a great power to catch-up with its more powerful neighbours by exploiting a window of opportunity that technical improvements seemed to have opened for it. What is fascinating about this attempt is both that it was half-hidden and that it did its best to stretch meagre resources by a subtle combination of options offered by modern technology. It was no longer the fairly straightforward leap of ironloads over wooden hulls. The battleships laid down by the Austrians in the 1890s, the *Monarch* class, posed as coastal defence boats. Their displacement was originally planned to be no more than 3000 to 4000 tons; they finally came to almost 6000 tons. That was still small, but then they could afford to be. Their radius of action was confined to the Adriatic. They did not need to have big coal-bunkers. Their guns were of a comparatively small calibre, only 9.4 inch. But then they were quick-firing: Calculations purported to show that they could fire five to six times as often as the 12-inch guns favoured by the Italian navy. A memorandum, from as late as 1905, spelled out the implications of that choice for Austrian battle tactics. At ranges under 2000 yards, the Italians would be swamped by Austrian shells; at long range (5000 yards or more), on the other hand, hits were considered to be improbable anyway. True, there remained a danger zone in between, but for a decade or so that was considered to be a calculated risk worth taking.[7] These pocket battle-ships—including their two successor squadrons that again carried no larger calibre than 9.4 inch—seemed to provide good value for a comparatively modest outlay of money.

The other thing that is striking about this turn-around in naval policy is the way it came about. The re-birth of the battle fleet was politically approved by the Joint Ministerial Council of the Habsburg Monarchy in February 1893. (Under the fairly complicated Constitution set up in 1867, the Joint Ministerial Council was composed of the Foreign Secretary, the Minister of War and Finance, plus the Prime Ministers of Austria and Hungary—the two autonomous "halves of the Empire.") What had preceded it, though, was a successful campaign by most of the navy's ranking officers against the plans of their anti-armour commander, Sterneck. That revolt of the admirals formed part of the never-ending naval debate of speed vs. protection, as each side sought to digest the latest technological developments in the race between guns and armour. The arguments of course resurface over and over again. To cite but the most prominent, in the early twentieth century Lord Fisher's views were to repeat some of Sterneck's pet theories (with one notable exception, though: Belief in ramming had finally been laid to rest in his period.) In terms of cliques and factions within the navy, that constellation contained an exquisite irony: The leadership of Tegetthoff's "band of brothers" had devolved upon Sterneck, his trusted lieutenant and the commander of his flagship at Lissa. But it was the navy's number two, Admiral Max von Pitner, who had occupied a similar position under Tegetthoff's great rival Pöck, who helped restore the battle-fleet to its former paramount position.

In the summer of 1891, after the Emperor himself had taken part in naval manoeuvres, Sterneck was invited to present his plans for future naval expansion. However, when Sterneck turned up at the Emperor's summer retreat in Ischl a few weeks later to present his ideas, the head of the Emperor's Military Chancellery, General Bolfras, poured cold water on his over-optimistic expectations. Obviously, Pitner and his associates had succeeded in bringing their objections to the Emperor's notice—and found a favourable hearing. It was by no means certain that torpedoes would be as effective a means of defence, as Sterneck claimed, Bolfras advised the Emperor. Sterneck soon realised that the tide had turned. In the Joint Ministerial Council, in September 1891, he faced hostile criticism from his nominal superior, the Minister of War. Rather than being approved, his draft estimates were referred back to a committee of experts headed by Pitner. The expansion plan finally adopted as a result of their deliberations differed greatly from Sterneck's original version: Whereas Sterneck wanted two cruisers for every armoured ship (and no less than nine torpedo-boats), Pitner's committee almost completely omitted the cruisers and contented itself with little more than three torpedo-boats per battleship. Belief in the tenets of the Jeune Ecole had clearly come to an end in the Austrian navy.[8]

That process of concentrating all the resources of the navy on the expansion of the battle-fleet was sped up after Sterneck's death in 1897 (just as Tirpitz's programme got into its stride in Germany, too). For half a dozen years, no more cruisers or torpedo-boats at all were ordered, but every year saw the launching of a new battleship (the *Habsburg* and the *Archduke* class). By 1904 Austria had once again drawn level with Italy in that respect. (1904 was also the year when relations between the two nominal allies took a turn for the worse. The Austrians even feared an Italian "Port Arthur"—a surprise attack on their naval port of Pola to mark the opening of hostilities—and bargained for their own form of reassurance treaty by concluding a neutrality agreement with Russia.)[9]

There is another parallel between Austrian *Flottenpolitik* in the 1860s and the late 1890s: Both reached their high-water mark during a transitional period in the monarchy's constitutional life. In the 1860s the largest appropriations had been sanctioned during the very first year of the *Reichsrat*. As parliament asserted itself—thus strengthening the hand of the Minister of Finance, Ignaz Plener—appropriations fell off, and they did so even more after Maximilian left for Mexico in 1864. In the 1890s it was the other way around: Increased spending on the navy fell into a period of parliamentary retreat. Between 1897 and 1906, the parliamentary mechanism of the Dual Monarchy—complicated as it was—was hardly ever in working order. The Lower House of either the Austrian or the Hungarian half of the monarchy was immobilised by obstruction. That made it impossible for the army to increase its annual intake of recruits, but it gave the executive more leeway to spend money on the navy.[10]

Just as Germany indulged in her politically counterproductive naval rivalry with Britain, so Austria-Hungary engaged in a no less intense, if more discreet, competition with her nominal ally Italy—with political implications that were more ambivalent. At least these efforts could still be halfway plausibly portrayed as being directed at France and Russia (which German expansion by then no longer could). Put together, the Austrian and Italian navies might indeed threaten France's communications with its North African Empire—on paper, at least. A case could thus be made for Austrian naval expansion, even if one did not subscribe to the corrosive distrust of Italy so prevalent in the ruling circles of the Habsburg monarchy—a scepticism that in hindsight seems justified and yet came close to being a self-fulfilling prophecy.[11]

That naval race, of course, entered its final phase with the dreadnought. At that time neither Austria nor Italy were in the forefront of naval development. Austria, in fact, missed her chance once again to leap-frog her competitors by laying down the first all-big-gun battle ship in the Mediterranean. Instead, over the objections of their technical experts, in the summer of 1905, they chose to disregard the lessons of Tsushima, which had taken place only a few weeks before. But old habits died hard. "Never change a winning team," seemed to be the order of the day. The man who, probably more than any other individual, was responsible for that decision was Admiral Julius von Ripper, Pitner's successor as the navy's number two. He himself had even been an eye-witness of an earlier naval engagement that pointed the other way—namely that off Santiago de Cuba in 1898 where the intermediate artillery had in fact performed well against lightly armoured but elderly opponents.[12] By 1905, however, lots of 9-inch guns, combined with only two pairs of 12 inch, was an option that had lost its rationale now that big guns could be reloaded just as quickly. And those were to be the ships that were started one-and-a-half years after the *Dreadnought* was launched—

even though it must be admitted that they were also almost exact contemporaries of the French *Danton* class.

In the end, Italy started to lay down dreadnoughts earlier, but, thanks to the superior efficiency of its Trieste buildings yards, Austria finished hers sooner. By the end of 1913, Austria possessed two dreadnoughts to Italy's one, and the Austrian fleet, for the time being arguably the most powerful in the Mediterranean, was proudly paraded around the Levant only a few weeks before the shots of Sarajevo. When considering the parallel with Germany, one should take note that Germany had already started reducing the pace of its building programme after 1908 (even if the political benefits of that slow-down—a relaxation of tension with Britain—came too late to be of any use during the July crisis of 1914). Both Tirpitz and the Austrians had in fact put their trust in a pre-dreadnought fleet. That they had to start all over again was far less welcome to them than one might have expected from "up-start navies." Austria, however, accepted that challenge much more whole-heartedly than the Germans did.[13] In Germany, the pendulum had swung back towards giving priority to armaments on land by 1911. In Austria-Hungary, on the other hand, as well as in Russia[14], naval outlays continued to demand an ever larger share of military expenditure.

Only actual war stopped Austria from building another squadron of four even stronger dreadnoughts. The support for military expenditures engendered by the sense of almost permanent crisis during the Balkan Wars—with its recurrent mobilisations of the Austrian army—was astutely hi-jacked by Admiral Haus in 1913 when he won permission to go ahead with plans for his new squadron of super-dreadnoughts.[15] Compared with the needs of the army—whose structural weaknesses (in particular, the lack of an adequate supply of trained reserves) were to be glaringly exposed during World War I—Austria can indeed be said to have indulged in another luxury fleet.

Significantly though, it was a top-heavy fleet, the most top-heavy fleet in the world after Germany and Britain—measured according to its ratio of dreadnoughts to overall tonnage. Once it was set upon that course, there was no turning back. Little attention was given to the torpedo arms, or to the U-boats whose proponents had a hard time persuading their superiors of the merits of their case. (In return, even protection against underwater weapons was given fairly low priority when building the battleships; tests were conducted only perfunctorily.) Austrian U-boats remained small and coastal-bound throughout most of World War I. Notwithstanding the case of Captain Trapp, who (apart from a successful second marriage years later) also happened to be the first U-boat commander to ever sink an enemy ship at night,[16] they took little part in the exploits of the Pola-based German U-boat fleets. The submarine's revolutionary potential was never properly recognised. To sum up briefly and maybe a little bit unfairly: There had been some interest in the *Jeune Ecole* and the potential of "Guerrilla warfare at sea" in the 1880s when the torpedo arm still went through its teething troubles. Now that it had come of age, it was seen as a fad whose time had passed. Apparently, battleships were what a great power felt compelled to build, even if its navy continued to be a small one.

1. For basic information on naval vessels, see Robert Gardiner (Ed), *Conway's All the World's Fighting Ships 1860–1905*, London 1979; Robert Gardiner (Ed.), *Conway's All the World's Fighting Ships 1906–1921*, London 1985.

2. For the early history of the Austrian navy, see Lawrence Sondhaus, *The Habsburg Empire and the Sea: Austrian Naval Policy 1797–1866*, Purdue UP 1989.

3. Quotes are taken from Archduke Maximilian's statement in the Ministerial Council of 19 September 1861 in *Die Protokolle des österreichischen Ministerrates 1848–1867*, Vol V/2, Vienna 1981, pp. 376 f.

4. The sinking of the Italian flag-ship only came about because a chance hit had previously damaged her rudder; another Italian ship apparently blew up because of sloppy fire-fighting procedures. For further details, see the literature quoted in my brief history of the Austro-Hungarian Navy: *Die Habsburgermonarchie 1848–1918*, Vol 5: *Die Bewaffnete Macht*, Vienna 1987, pp. 687–763.

5. For Italian ships, also see Giorgio Giorgerini and Augusto Nani, *Le Navi di Linea Italiane 1861–1961*, Rome 1966.

6. On the Jeune Ecole, see Theodore Ropp, *The Development of a Modern Navy: French Naval Policy 1871–1904*, Annapolis 1987; Volkmar Bueb, *Die junge Schule der französischen Marine: Strategie und Politik 1875–1900*, Boppard 1971; for its application in Austria, see Sterneck's diary: Lydia v. Sterneck and Jerolim v. Benko (Ed.), *Max Freiherr von Sterneck: Erinnerungen aus den Jahren 1847–1897*, Vienna 1901; on the Austrian torpedo arm: Franz Ferdinand Bilzer, *Die Torpedoboote der k.u.k. Kriegsmarine von 1875–1918*, Graz 1984. I have tried to sum up developments in an article for *Etudes Danubiennes* 4 (1988), pp. 147–156: Von der "Jeune Ecole" zur Flottenpolitik.

7. KA (Kriegsarchiv = Austrian War Archives, Vienna), B 684, Nachlaß Jedina v. Palombino, Memo of Captain Boeckmann, April 1905.

8. KA, MKSM (Records of the Military Chancellery) 1891 66–5/6, 17 July 1891; PK/MS (Records of the Navy Section of the Ministry of War) 1891 IX-5/11, 20 July 1891; PK/MS 1892 IX-5/1, 19 December 1891; PK/MS 1892 IX-5/9, 7 November

1892; Sterneck diary, pp. 266–270; some information about the new ships was also divulged in the Annual Report for 1894: Jahrbuch der k.u.k. Kriegsmarine für 1894.

9. In the Meeting of the Common Ministerial Council on 23 April 1904, Francis Joseph himself alluded to the danger of being exposed to a surprise attack like Russia in the Far East ("einer Überrumpelung ausgesetzt wie Rußland in Ostasien"). See Haus-, Hof- und Staatsarchiv Wien, PA (Political Archive) XL 295, protocols of the Council Meetings.

10. After the Compromise with Hungary in 1867, legislation had to be approved by both the Austrian und Hungarian parliaments, raising the number of recruits who belonged to that sphere; when obstruction raised its head, the executive felt justified in authorizing expenditure and passing the budget by decree, not however in changing existing laws. For further information see: Lothar Höbelt, Parliamentary Politics in a Multinational Setting: Late Imperial Austria, *Working Papers in Austrian Studies* 92–6, Minneapolis, Center for Austrian Studies, 1992, 15pp.

11. On the larger strategic picture, see Paul G. Halpern, *The Mediterranean Naval Situation 1908–1914*, Cambridge, Mass. 1971; Mariano Gabriel, *Le Convenzioni Navali della Triplice*, Rome 1969.

12. For details, see Erwin Sieche, *Die "Radetzky" Klasse, Österreich-Ungarns letzte Vor-Dreadnoughts*, Graz 1984, p. 5; Ripper's ship—in fact, one of Sterneck's ram-cruisers, the *Maria Theresia*—had almost been mistaken for a Spanish one during the battle of Santiago de Cuba.

13. See the latest two studies on the pre-war naval policy of the Central Powers: Michael Epkenhans, *Die Wilhelminische Flottenrüstung 1908–1914*, Munich 1991; Milan N. Vego, *The Anatomy of Austrian Sea Power 1904–1914*, PhD Thesis, Washington 1981.

14. Dominic Lieven, *Nicholas II.*, London 1993, p. 174.

15. See KA, B 241–5/VIII, diary of Admiral Anton Haus; Paul Halpern is now working on a biography of Admiral Haus, the Austrian naval commander from 1912 to 1917.

16. Trapp's "U5" sank the French cruiser *Leon Gambetta* in the Straits of Otranto on the night of 23 April 1915. On Austrian submarines, see Wladimir Aichelburg, *Die Unterseeboote Österreich-Ungarns*, 2 vols., Graz 1981.

Luxury Fleet: The Austrian Navy and the Battle of Lissa, 1866

Geoffrey Wawro

⚓

The hagiography embracing Admiral Wilhelm Tegetthoff, who steered Austria's ironclad fleet to victory in the Adriatic waters around the island of Lissa (Vis) in July 1866, has tended to make serious analysis of the Austrian naval program in the 1860s difficult. In Admiral Tegetthoff, the Habsburgs found an icon every bit as useful as Field Marshal Joseph Radetzky, Austria's savior in 1848–49. Both were simple, brave men who first routed the bureaucrats of Vienna, then whipped the Italians into the bargain. Though Tegetthoff truly was a remarkable man, it must be said that the ironclad squadron he commanded was a marginal asset and one which scarcely affected the outcome of the Austro-Prussian-Italian War of 1866. How else to explain the fact that less than a month after its victory at Lissa in July 1866, Austria was forced to cede the splendid port of Venice and all Venetia to the Kingdom of Italy?

Indeed, looking at its meager results in the war of 1866 and, later on, in the two Balkan Wars and the First World War, it is difficult to say just what Austria's fleet was supposed to accomplish. Economically, it did little to develop the Austrian seacoast. The ports of Dalmatia—Zadar, Split, Dubrovnik, and Kotor—some of the best natural harbors in the Mediterranean and unquestionably superior to anything on the Italian shore of the Adriatic—were still undeveloped in the 1860s. "What might the Americans have made of these first-rate ports?" an Austrian war ministry official complained after a discouraging tour of Istria and Dalmatia in 1866, where he remarked the poverty of the region and the lack of infrastructural improvements under Habsburg administration.[1] Likewise, Austria's fleet did little to promote Austrian trade, which continued to follow the Danube and the railways, not the Trieste-based Austrian Lloyd. Though Navy advocates promised that Austrian trade would follow the Habsburg flag, the actual picture of Austria's Mediterranean trade in the 1860s was uninspiring, owing to the underlying structure of Austrian commerce.[2] The state-owned Danube Steamship Company made far more money plying between Germany and the Black Sea than did the state-owned Austrian Lloyd. The same was true of Austria's railways, which earned 220 times the profit of the Lloyd in 1865.[3]

All in all, Austria was not even close to being a maritime power in the 1860s and, given its chronic shortage of capital and enterprise, it had little maritime future. Anton Ryger, a Liberal deputy in Austria's Reichsrat, or parliament, smote the Navy lobby's pretensions in 1862:

> Count Mensdorff [Austria's foreign minister] says that our maritime trade requires naval protection. Is maritime trade our main source of trade? No. Railroads are the key to our prosperity. They convey the bulk of Austrian trade and don't depend on a fleet for protection. Moreover, our shipping is not even competitive! We have an impoverished, cramped seacoast that produces no export products and is altogether without an infrastructure to move export articles to the ports. The Navy has no colonies to serve, no foreign basing agreements and apparently precious little sense!

He finished with a thrust at Emperor Franz Joseph Habsburg's wide-eyed naval pamphleteers: "As for the so-called 'Levant and Balkan trade,' we can already make our way there overland, by road and rail. We don't need a fleet for that."[4]

Ryger was seconded by the Reichsrat's Finance Committee, which blasted Franz Joseph's navalist ambitions: "Austria's maritime trade is too insignificant to merit a battle fleet for its protection. Even were Italy to master the Adriatic for a time, it could scarcely extort more money from us [in ransom] than the Navy itself is already doing with its annual budget appropriations of ten to twelve millions!"[5] Even Admiral Bernhard Wüllerstorf, as keen a proponent of the Austrian fleet as there was, had to agree: "Austria should be able to export grain, wine, tobacco, lumber and hides all over the world, but we just don't have the necessary low-cost infrastructure . . . connecting our Danubian provinces with our Adriatic seacoast." The Danube, not the Adriatic, he concluded, was the "natural and historical trade artery from Austria to the Black Sea and the Levant."[6] For this reason, a Liberal deputy dismissed the Austrian fleet in 1862 as just "the latest of the Army's fantasies, a pretty little summer palace (Lustschloss) cresting the waves.... The Army has run out of room on land and wishes to extend its projects into the sea."[7]

In terms of strategy, Austria's fleet figured hardly at all in the European balance-of-power except insofar as it weakened the monarchy's military deterrent by diverting scarce resources from the land army.[8] The Austrian emperor had little need of a fleet to defend his Adriatic crownlands for five reasons. First, Austria was already shielded by the contours and desolation of its Dalmatian coast, which made enemy landings difficult and hardly sustainable.[9] Second, Britain and France, concerned with defending their own maritime interests, were committed to leaving the eastern shore of the Adriatic in Austria's relatively weak hands. They were loath to see a powerful Italian nation-state, already in possession of the world's third largest ironclad fleet, established in the Balkans.[10] Third, with 50,000 garrison troops in Croatia and a mobile army of 250,000 camped in Venetia, the Austrian Army would be more than equal to any Italian landing on its Adriatic coast for the simple reason that so long as Austria held the Quadrilateral fortress group around Verona, the Italians would be forced to deploy their main army there.[11]

The fourth reason why Austria had little need of an iron fleet to defend its Adriatic seacoast in the 1860s was that opinion in Dalmatia was already decidedly anti-Italian. Dalmatia's Croats and Italians alike feared an Italian conquest, which Zadar's Nazionale conjectured would reduce Dalmatia to the status of "Italy's Algiers," a colonial backwater.[12] The Turkish Empire, suzerain of Albania, Montenegro, Bosnia and Hercegovina, the provinces bounding Austrian Dalmatia, was no less reliable, and this was the fifth factor virtually ensuring Austrian control of Dalmatia and its islands with or without a battle fleet.[13] In the 1860s, the Ottomans were as worried about Italian expansion in the eastern Mediterranean as the Habsburgs and, in 1866, actually agreed to put their fleet and 80,000 troops at Austria's disposal to interdict Italian landings in Albania or Dalmatia.[14]

Thus, even had the Habsburg Navy been a lean fighting machine, it would have been something of a luxury given the ample insurance provided by the Austrian land army and its allies, not to mention the perennial budgetary problems of the monarchy. The fact that the Navy was not lean at all, but was, on the contrary, quite inefficient made it an even more dubious expenditure. Far from being the "Brave Little Ship That Could" praised by nostalgic historians, the Austrian Navy was proportionately even more bureaucracy-ridden and wasteful than the land army. In 1862, a typical fiscal year between the wars of 1859 and 1866, 44 percent of Austria's naval personnel budget (635,000 of 1.44 million florins) went to *Behörden und Ämter*, the naval bureaucracies at Vienna and Pula, the latter being the fleet's arsenal, base and administrative center on the Adriatic. When pressed to reduce its personnel, Austria's admiralty responded in 1865 not by retiring superfluous officials, but by furloughing 2,000 sailors, the very men it most needed to man its growing battle fleet. In all, nearly half of the Austrian Navy's personnel budget went to functionaries.[15] Needless to say, this acquisitive naval apparatus was a goad to a Reichsrat already worried by the high cost of shipbuilding. In 1862, a Liberal deputy complained: "We spent eighty million florins on the navy ($1.08 billion) between 1850 and 1860 alone, and now you want thirteen million more. . . . What happened to all the money we gave you in the past?"[16]

Ultimately, then, it seemed that Franz Joseph's 53 million florin ($716 million) navy program for the 1860s was launched less for sound strategic reasons than from a combination of archducal patronage, bureaucratic self-interest and the untempered enthusiasm of the Habsburg Navy's advocates. Though the Reichsrat vetoed ironclad appropriations in 1861 and 1862, Franz Joseph went ahead and decreed the construction of five ironclad frigates anyway, entrusting the new fleet to his brother, Archduke Maximilian, the erstwhile governor of Lombardy, whose career had come to an embarrassing standstill in the hiatus between Austria's cession of Milan to the Italians in 1859 and the archduke's own departure for Mexico in 1864.[17] The Army war ministry, which viewed the Navy not as an interservice rival, but as yet another spending tap to be turned on full blast, was comfortable with Maximilian's doctrine of station ships, which was the Navy's equivalent of the Army's fortress cordon. Marshal Hess and Admirals Ludwig Fautz and Friedrich Pöck—the Navy mandarins in Vienna and Pula respectively—all planned to employ Austria's ironclad squadron not as a high seas fleet, but as a fixed chain of Stations-Schiffe along the Dalmatian littoral. Hess, who described the fleet as "an iron wedge, an impassable cliff driven into the sea to separate the Italians and the

Slavs and dissipate revolutionary forces," even went so far as to resolve this bizarre cordon theory into "a defensive ratio of one ironclad per every 75 to 90 kilometers of Austrian coastline."[18] There were no "blue water" operations in this fleet's future; in the event of war, the Austrian squadron would simply be attached to the Austrian Army of Italy as though it were an infantry corps, a fact that may have explained Franz Joseph's curious appointment of Archduke Leopold Habsburg to head the Navy Inspectorate in 1862. Leopold was an infantry general.

In the end, perhaps only this sort of "archducal thuggery"—as the Good Soldier Svejk would have put it—could account for Franz Joseph's construction of a battle fleet in no way justified by the slack levels of Austrian maritime trade, the poverty of Dalmatia and the unlikelihood of naval cooperation with the defensive, fortress-based land army. Indeed, one of the Navy's own, Admiral Wüllerstorf, questioned the very purpose of Austria's high seas fleet: "Although the Adriatic used to be one of the world's great highways and the source of Venetian power," he wrote, "today it has lost much of its importance as a result of new naval technologies and the emergence of new seapowers."[19] Tegetthoff concurred on this point, noting that Lissa—the rocky island near the mouth of the Adriatic gulf, known as the "Gibraltar of the Adriatic" in the age of sail—had lost its strategic function in the new era of coal-fired warships, which could give Lissa and its obsolete martello towers a wide berth.[20] This was precisely what the Reichsrat's Finance Committee had in mind when it concluded in 1863 that "even if Italy did control the Adriatic, it would hardly matter, for nowadays the Adriatic is strategically unimportant and its domination by any power offers few advantages."[21]

Why then all the fuss about the naval action in the waters around Lissa on 20 July 1866? For two reasons: first, because it was one of the only bright spots in Austria's otherwise dreary war effort against the Prussians and the Italians; and second, because Austria won the battle by the most unorthodox means, steaming under the guns of a more powerful Italian fleet to attack it with the ram.

The fact that the battle of Lissa almost never happened has in no way diminished the vigor with which it is celebrated in Austria. Upon the outbreak of war in June, Franz Joseph had formally attached his fleet to Archduke Albrecht Habsburg's South Army, which was deployed defensively in Venetia. Though there had been hopeful talk after 1859 of using a powerful fleet, as Marshal Hess put it, "to open a second operations line" into Venetia and to assail the flank of any Italian army operating inside Austria's Quadrilateral fortress group, this in fact had not happened.[22] Instead, Austria's new ironclad squadron had hunkered down behind a torpedo barricade at Pula. A sortie in June down to the Ancona Roads came to nothing when the Italians refused to engage, and Tegetthoff withdrew without firing a shot.[23] Austrian parliamentary deputies who had actually voted for naval appropriations must have felt cheated when, after an initial defeat in late June, the Italian Army had regrouped in July, thrust over the lower Po and advanced all the way to Slovenia, apparently heedless of the threat the Austrian fleet was supposed to have presented to its seaward flank.

If the Austrian Navy disappointed the high hopes which had been pinned on it, the Italians cut an even worse figure. In 1866, theirs was the third most powerful fleet in the world, thanks to French loans and the haste with which the Italian government had expanded its iron fleet after national unification in 1861. Against Austria's seven ironclad warships, the Italians could muster thirteen. Among these, pride of place went to the *Re d'Italia* and the *Re di Portogallo*, 6,000 ton monsters built in New Jersey. On their gun decks, they each mounted twenty-four rifled ninety-pounders and a pair of the latest Armstrong 300-pound rifles, the closest thing the armaments industry had to a ship-killer. Though armored from stem to stern with six inch plates, they could still speed up to thirteen knots. (Tegetthoff's flagship, by comparison, could manage only eight.)

At least as frightening as this duo was Italy's monitor, the *Affondatore*, which was still under construction in an English yard when the war began. *Affondatore* weighed 4,000 tons, was plated with five inches of iron and carried two Armstrong 300-pounders in its twin turrets. None of Austria's warships could challenge these prodigies. Indeed, technically, Tegetthoff's seven clads were equal only to the rest of the Italian iron fleet: five 4,000 ton broadside frigates and two 2,700 ton rams, all armed with a mix of ninety- and 150-pound rifles.

Though both sides were trailed into action by their old wooden fleets, naval experts were in no doubt that any Austro-Italian naval action would be decided by the ironclads. Austria's two strongest frigates—*Erzherzog Ferdinand Maximilian* and *Habsburg*—were, like Italy's *Affondatore*, still unfinished when war broke out. Since

Prussia impounded the Krupp rifles destined for these two ships, they had to be hastily reequipped with smoothbore forty-eight-pounders instead, as did Austria's four other 3,500 ton clads. This fact alone may have persuaded Tegetthoff to attack the Italians with the ram, for his obsolete guns would scarcely dent their armor.

When all was said and done, the battle of Lissa was essentially a *political* battle that had little impact on the outcome of the Austro-Prussian-Italian War, for it was fought on the very day when Austrian and Prussian negotiators were putting the finishing touches to a cease-fire that would end the conflict. Indeed, Italy attacked Lissa primarily for reasons of national prestige. The Austrians had crushed the Italian land army at Custoza in June, and, one month later, with an armistice imminent, the Italian government had hurriedly ordered Admiral Carlo Persano to sea on 16 July, a full two weeks after the decisive battle of Königgrätz in Bohemia. Italy's aim, as Naval Minister Agostino Depretis put it, was a demonstration of Italian *"padronanza del mare,"* command of the sea, nothing more.[24] There would be no landings in Dalmatia because there were insufficient troops to land, and because Emperor Napoleon III of France, concerned about the rapid growth of national Italy in the years since 1859, had threatened to intervene on Austria's side if the Italians attempted to annex more than Venetia.[25]

Italy's rushed deployment around Lissa at the end of July 1866 partly accounted for the disaster which would shortly befall it. Persano's fleet sailed from Ancona without detailed charts, with no information on Lissa's defenses and without landing troops. After covering the fifty sea miles to Lissa, the Italians deployed around the island on 17 July and blasted it for thirty-six hours, raining 5,000 shells on Lissa's garrison of 1,800. Despite this early success, the mission ultimately went off as badly as Churchill's Gallipoli expedition in 1915, for at the very moment when Persano ought to have disembarked landing troops to round up Lissa's shell-shocked garrison, he discovered that he had no landing troops and only then applied for them, on 19 July, four days after he had sailed.[26]

In the meantime, Admiral Tegetthoff had learned of the Italian attack and, after much hesitation, had decided finally on 19 July to sail to the relief of Lissa. His squadron steamed through the night and hove into sight of the Italian fleet and the beleaguered Austrian forts at 8:00 the next morning. Spying Tegetthoff on the horizon, Admiral Persano collected his warships and formed a line of battle in order to develop his full broadsides against the oncoming Austrians. Though Persano expected Tegetthoff to do the same, the Austrian admiral noted the long odds arrayed against him, formed his squadron into compact wedges instead and ran at the Italian line in double echelon, his seven ironclads in the front rank, his wooden frigates and gunboats 1,000 yards behind. This maneuver nullified in a matter of minutes Italy's advantage in mobility and firepower and transformed the engagement into a cut-and-thrust melée. Indeed, Tegetthoff saw fit to issue only three orders throughout the entire battle: "Clear for battle; close distance," "full speed," and "ironclads run against the enemy and sink him."

After much backing and filling inside the clouds of fog and gunsmoke which shrouded Persano's column, Tegetthoff finally spotted a likely target broadside on and plowed his flagship into it. It happened to be the pride of Persano's fleet, and it sank within four minutes, taking the *Re d'Italia*, most of its crew and what was left of Italian morale with it. The Austrians succeeded in crippling two more Italian frigates before Persano capitulated, steaming back to Ancona after damaging several Austrian ships, but sinking none.

The day was unquestionably Tegetthoff's, but what did it all mean? Austria's victory at Lissa was less a tribute to Habsburg seapower than to Italian ineptitude. Noting that the *Re d'Italia* had been sent to the bottom only after her rudder had been blown away by an Austrian broadside and only after several missed ram strokes, a British naval officer ascribed Persano's defeat to the incompetence of Italy's officers and crews, who ought to have avoided the Austrian rams by alterations of speed or course and then punished Tegetthoff's inferior fleet with their big guns.[27] In truth, the fact that Tegetthoff was able to rout a far heavier fleet armed with more than twice his firepower testified to the unworthiness of his opponent that day. The Italians made little use of their rifled guns, their superior frigates or their dreadful monitor. As the *London Times'* naval correspondent concluded after the battle: "What can be said . . . of sailors who allowed their ships to be run down by enemies inferior in speed and nearly every facility for manoeuvring?"[28]

In conclusion, the Austrian Navy of the 1860s lacked a purposeful strategy. Just as the Army continued to maintain Vauban-era forts long after they had outlived their usefulness, the Navy maintained wooden hulks it would never use.[29] And while the Navy laid down million florin ironclads, Austrian shipping foundered on the shoals of Dalmatia because Emperor Franz Joseph Habsburg did not authorize an update of Austria's 1820 coastal survey until February 1866![30] This kind of *Schlamperei* was probably not accidental, for ultimately the Habsburg Kriegsmarine justified itself as a useful sub-economy of the Habsburg war ministry, as yet another magnet for military appropriations. It did not need to fight. The Navy's creation of heavily bureaucratized sea district commands and naval stations, which soaked up supernumerary Army officers and war ministry Beamten, became an end in itself. This might begin to explain why, in 1859, the Austrian fleet, recipient of eighty million florins ($1.08 billion) in the 1850s, skulked in port and did not dare engage a French squadron, and why, in 1866, Franz Joseph delivered the Navy into the cautious hands of his uncle, Archduke Albrecht, commander of South Army. Albrecht peremptorily ordered Tegetthoff to keep the fleet behind the torpedoes of Pula and avoid risky attacks on Italian shipping. The Army's brave talk, in the interwar period, of using the fleet to open a "second operations line," a sea route to Venetia parallel to Vienna's Southern Railway that would both menace the Italian right and funnel reinforcements into the Quadrilateral forts, was never realized.[31] Indeed in July 1866, Austria's fleet did nothing to slow the Italian Army as it pushed past Venice toward Vienna.

Thus, Tegetthoff's much ballyhooed victory at Lissa, though an enterprising tactical feat, did not deliver the strategic goods, which had been promised in the early 1860s when Franz Joseph had begun diverting public funds to pay for an iron fleet. Those who would protest that sums expended on the Navy in the 1860s were trivial in comparison with those lavished on the land army in this period might reflect on the fact that a mere fraction of the fifty-odd millions spent on Admiral Tegetthoff's naval squadron would have sufficed to rearm the entire Austrian land army with breech-loading rifles and instruct it in Prussian-style infantry tactics, the two main things which had stood between the Habsburg Army and ultimate victory in Bohemia and Venetia. If the Navy did supply more "bang for the buck," these were none the less wasted "bucks." For the victory at Lissa was little more than a slap to the Italians and a tonic to an Austrian Empire reeling after its defeat at the hands of the Prussian Army. This, of course, explains why it bulks so large in Austrian official and unofficial historiography to this day. Still, the Austrian Republic's need to reconstruct a "useful past" from a record of military failure ought not distract us from the essential fact that Lissa did little to affect the outcome of the war of 1866. Emperor Franz Joseph's Adriatic squadron may thus with some justification be pronounced a "luxury fleet."

1. Valentin Streffleur, "Österreich am Schlusse des Jahres 1866," *Österreichische Militärische Zeitschrift* (ÖMZ) 1 (1867), p. 17.

2. Marshal Hess promised in 1864 an "Austrian merchant marine that... will grow from 400 million florins ($5.4 billion in 1994 dollars) to one billion florins ($13.5 billion) in assets within twenty years." k.k. Herrenhaus, *Stenographische Protokolle über die Verhandlungen des Herrenhauses* (Vienna: k.k. Haus-Hof-und Staatsdruckerei, 1864), 2. Session, 10. Sitzung, January 13, 1864, p. 530.

3. The Danube Steamship Company had twice as many steamships and made six times as many voyages, shipping eleven times as many goods as the Adriatic Lloyd. k.k. statistisches Central-Commission, *Statistisches Handbuchlein des Kaiserthumes Österreich für das Jahr 1866* (Vienna: k.k. Hof-und-Staatsdruckerei, 1868), pp. 38–39.

4. k.k. Abgeordnetenhaus, *Stenographische Protokolle über die Verhandlungen des Abgeordnetenhauses (SPA)* (Vienna: k.k. Haus-Hof-und Staatsdruckerei, 1862), 1. Session, 132. Sitzung, June 18, 1862, p. 3120.

5. Cited in [Hugo Kerchnawe], *Die Vorgeschichte von 1866 und 19??* (Vienna, Leipzig: C.W. Stern, 1909), p. 58.

6. Bernhard Freiherr von Wüllerstorf und Urbair, k.k. Contre-Admiral, "Über die Wichtigkeit des adriatischen Meeres für Österreich und dessen Verteidigung," ÖMZ 4 (1861), pp. 366–68.

7. SPA, 1. Session, 132. Sitzung, June 18, 1862, pp. 3116–19.

8. As a parliamentary critic pronounced in June 1862: "What good is even a thousand ship navy and a million man army with thousands of guns if there will be no money left over for basic training, maneuvers, ammunition and food?" SPA, 1. Session, 132. Sitzung, June 18, 1862, p. 3120.

9. There was no Dalmatian coastal railroad to supply or expand hostile beachheads, and what roads there were in Austria's poorest province were not suitable for large troop movements, nor was there enough food and water in Dalmatia to supply a large-scale military occupation. Any Italian invasion would have had to grope inland for the Drina river, where it would gradually have been cut to pieces by brigands, Turks or Austrian garrison troops. Moreover, as a Liberal deputy pointed out in 1862, the Dalmatian archipelago itself formed "a natural, protective wall thanks to its narrow, treacherous canals and shallow, difficult waters." Wüllerstorf, "Über die Wichtigkeit des adriatischen Meeres," p. 366. SPA, 1. Session, 132. Sitzung, June 18, 1862, pp. 3120–21.

10. After Solferino, when the fate of Venetia was still uncertain, Earl Cowley had written Lord John Russell from Paris: "To give the Venetian state and seaboard to Sardinia would be an error . . . regretted by England. . . . The true policy of England with regard to Northern Italy . . . is to favor the creation of an independent Lombardo-Venetian Kingdom, whose sympathies should incline toward Austria not France." Even the Palmerstonite Liberals, though more sympathetic to Italy,

agreed that France must be kept off the Adriatic shore at all costs. Would England ever have consented to a Piedmontese Dalmazia? Probably not. As Zadar's Nazionale opined in June 1866: "Neither France, England, nor Russia would allow Italy to get a footing in the East to become a factor in the future division of the Great Sick Man." Cited in London, Public Record Office (PRO), Foreign Office (FO) 7/714, Dubrovnik, June 19, 1866, Paton to Bloomfield. The Cowley quotation in: Michael Joseph McDonald, "Napoleon III and his Ideas of Italian Confederation, 1856–1860" (Ph.D. diss., University of Pennsylvania, 1968), p. 163.

11. In this context, the argument against a fleet was put simply by Austria's Colonel Karl Moering in 1862: "Leipzig and Waterloo, not Abukir and Trafalgar, dictated the last world peace [in 1815]." Col. Karl Moering. k.k. Generalstab, "Über die nächsten Aufgaben der k.k. Kriegsmarine," ÖMZ 1 (1862), p. 137.

12. Vienna, Haus-Hof-und-Staatsarchiv (HHSA), Informationsbüro (IB), Karton 364, BM 1866, 33, Venice, June 12, 1866, Polizeirat to Belcredi. And Vienna, Kriegsarchiv (KA), Kriegsministerium (KM) 1866, Centralkanzlei (CK), Karton 253, 57-14, Zadar, May 19, 1866, FML Philippovic to GdC Mensdorff.

13. Austria in the 1860s effectively controlled Montenegro and Hercegovina, which Italy's General Giuseppe Garibaldi hoped eventually to use as a base for a drive inland and up the Dalmatian coast. Franz Joseph paid the Prince of Montenegro 21,000 florins ($283,000 in 1994 dollars) per annum, in the years after 1859, for his complicity, so much lucre that in 1865 Britain's minister in Dubrovnik pronounced Montenegro and Hercegovina "Austria's bulwark" against Italian expansion in the Adriatic. PRO, FO 7/699, #13, Dubrovnik, June 17, 1865, Paton to Russell. KA, Militärkanzlei Seiner Majestät (MKSM) 1866, 59-1/2, Zadar, Jan. 25, 1866, FML Philippovic to Belcredi.

14. HHSA, Politisches Archiv (PA) XII, Karton 85, #22a, #25b, #30c, Constantinople, April 24, May 8, 25, 1866, Prokesch to Mensdorff. KA, KM 1866, CK, Karton 253, 57-14, Vienna, May 15, 1866, GdC Mensdorff to FML Franck.

15. *SPA*, 1. Session, 133. Sitzung, June 20, 1862, pp. 3130, 3152. *SPA*, 3. Session, 58. Sitzung, May 8, 1865, p. 1604.

16. *SPA*, 1. Session, 132. Sitzung, June 18, 1862, p. 3115.

17. Lothar Höbelt, "Die Marine," in Adam Wandruszka and Peter Urbanitsch, *Die Habsburger Monarchie 1848–1918*, 6 vols. (Vienna: Verlag der österreichischen Akademie der Wissenschaften, 1973–89), vol. 5. Lawrence Sondhaus, *The Habsburg Empire and the Sea* (W. Lafayette: Purdue, 1989), pp. 210–13.

18. In 1864, Hess concluded that "according to this defensive ratio . . . we need seven more ironclad ships of the line." Austria's merchant marine minister was more specific, asking parliament for a cordon of station ships at Venice, Trieste, Pula, Zadar, Dubrovnik, Castelnuovo, Klek and Lissa. Stenographische Protokolle Herrenhaus, 2. Session, 19. Sitzung, Jan. 13, 1864, pp. 331–36.

19. Wüllerstorf, "Über die Wichtigkeit des adriatischen Meeres," pp. 365–66.

20. L.S.-Kapitän Wilhelm von Tegetthoff, "Zur Würdigung des Aufsatzes: 'Zur Marine-Frage,'" *ÖMZ* 1 (1862), p. 421.

21. Cited in Kerchnawe, p. 58.

22. *Stenographische Protokolle Herrenhaus*, 1. Session, 66. Sitzung, July 9, 1862.

23. *New York Herald*, July 19, 1866.

24. John Knox Laughton, *Studies in Naval History* (London: Longmans Green &

Co, 1887), pp. 169–72. Theodore Ropp, "The Modern Italian Navy," *Military Affairs* (Spring 1941). Angelo Iachino, *La Campagna Navale di Lissa 1866* (Milan: Il Saggiatore, 1966), pp. 269–72.

25. Italy had no troops to land in Dalmatia because, in the third week of July 1866, the entire Italian Army was engaged in South Tyrol and on the Tagliamento. French pressure on Italy in July and August 1866 is clearly documented in *Documenti Diplomatici presentato al Parlamento dal Ministro degli Affari Esteri il 21 Dicembre 1866* (Florence: Tipographia dello Stato, 1866).

26. P.H. Colomb, *Naval Warfare* (London: W.H. Allen, 1899), p. 430. Iachino, p. 363.

27. William Laird Clowes, *The Royal Navy*, 7 vols. (Boston: Little Brown, 1903), vol. 7, p. 24.

28. *Times*, August 21, 1866.

29. In 1864, Count Leo Thun, who was fighting a losing battle in the Austrian senate for funds for his education ministry, wondered aloud: "Is there not some contradiction in our budgeting 395,000 florins ($5.3 million) to refurbish wooden ships of the line if they are considered obsolete?" *Stenographische Protokolle Herrenhaus*, 2. Session, 19. Sitzung, Jan. 14, 1864, pp. 334–41.

30. KA, MKSM-HR 1866, Karton 341, 66-7/1, Vienna, Feb. 21, 1866, "Vortrag des Kriegsministers."

31. *Stenographische Protokolle Herrenhaus*, 1. Session, 66. Sitzung, July 9, 1862.

Philo McGiffin and the Chinese Navy

Paul W. Bamford

⚓

Philo Norton McGiffin (1860–1897) was a maverick student at the Naval Academy at Annapolis; he mixed mischief with good deeds but did graduate, finally. Yet he was not appointed as an officer for a variety of reasons, in part because only a small proportion of the men graduated from the Academy were actually commissioned as officers in the U.S. Navy.

Unemployed, McGiffin sought and was fortunate and persuasive enough to obtain an appointment in the Navy of Imperial China (Northern Squadron) from Viceroy Li Hung-Chang (1885). During the next decade, as one of the small group of foreigners in Li's naval contingent, McGiffin proved himself to be competent and reliably loyal to Li. Unlike some others, McGiffin enjoyed direct contact with the Viceroy and earned a relatively favored position as a loyal and effective servant of Li's purposes. In Li's employ, McGiffin appears to have been involved in at least five different assignments on orders of the Viceroy. First, McGiffin proved himself by competent and effective discharge of instructional responsibilities at the *Tien Tsin* training school. Then McGiffin was sent on an "intelligence" mission abroad to Korea in 1886 (then considered a dependency of China) to map certain portions of the coastline; he also visited Japan, afterward reporting to Li on his total mission. Third, McGiffin was dispatched to England with a mission to bring back foreign-built warships purchased for Li's "Northern Squadron,"[1] mission commander Admiral William Lang (1887).[2]

After his return, McGiffin was allowed to undertake the establishment of a new naval officer training school to be set up at Wei-Hai-Wei; after much delay, a small school was set up. Finally, having served ten years in China by 1894, McGiffin was granted permission to take home leave to travel to the United States, but when war broke out with Japan, he cancelled the requested leave and applied for sea duty as an officer in Li's "Northern Squadron."

McGiffin was given nominal rank as Commander and assigned to the *Chen Yuen*, one of the two 7400-ton German-built (1883) ironclads (called battleships) in the Northern Squadron. Those two were China's most heavily armored and armed warships, each ship with two pairs of 12.2-inch guns. They proved to be very formidable when elements of the Chinese and Japanese navies met on 17 September 1894 and the Battle of Yalu ensued. China's two battleships distinguished themselves, one of them under the de facto command of McGiffin, who assumed a leadership role after *Chen Yuen's* designated Captain was incapacitated early in the engagement. Functioning as captain of the *Chen Yuen*, McGiffin must have performed those duties with increasing difficulty during much of the five-hour battle as the many wounds he incurred took their toll: he sustained blast injuries (partial blindness and deafness), severe burns and multiple wounds from fragments and splinters, but was assisted by Chinese fellow-officers, especially by a certain Yang Yung Ling. Notwithstanding terrific and sustained pounding, the armor of the two Chinese battleships enabled them to survive the hammering from Japanese guns; unfortunately for the Chinese battleships, their offensive power was disadvantaged by the poor quality and short supply of shells (and other ammunition) for 6-inch, and especially for their formidable 12.2-inch guns.[3] Yet both fleets sustained serious losses. At dusk, both sides seemed disposed to break off the engagement. The surviving Chinese ships reached Port Arthur.

McGiffin, badly burned and wounded, was taken aboard the USS *Monocacy*,[4] where he received medical treatment for some weeks, then spent time in further recovery ashore. Notwithstanding impaired hearing and vision and other wounds, he gave interviews, wrote reports and drafted some letters or news releases to be telegraphed, though some of them were censored or withheld from publication (or transmission) through the influence of another foreign officer, William F. Tyler.[5]

Finally, in early 1895, with a $5,000 "dead or alive" reward for his capture reportedly being offered by the Japanese, he resigned his commission and slipped away with the help of friends, taking passage at Shanghai on a ship bound for America.[6] Arriving, he spent time first at home (Washington, Pa.) with family, doing interviews with reporters from regional papers and writing. But persistent problems with wounds moved him to decide to travel to New York City to seek more medical care. There again he met reporters, and probably with secretarial help, managed to finish and submit (by May of 1895) the manuscript of his article on the Yalu fight. He also lectured on that subject at the Naval War College in their 1895 Sessions.[7] He even tried to hold some paying jobs along the way and was optimistic enough to announce in the fall of 1895 that he still hoped to return to China, but also said that a lot of medical problems remained: head injuries were causing ongoing, agonizing problems and much more "doctoring" was in store, he said.[8] Later, in a letter to a friend, McGiffin reported "that the doctors had urged upon him a certain operation." Commenting on the prospective surgery, McGiffin said, "'I know that I will have a piece of about three inches square cut out of my skull, and (have) this nerve cut off near the middle of the brain, as well as my eye taken out (for a couple of hours only, provided it is not mislaid and can be found). . . . As a result of this operation others have told me—I forget the percentage of deaths, which does not matter but—that a large percentage have become insane. And some lost their sight."[9] He joked about the medical prospects, but realized that they were ominous. Soon after that letter was written, with severe pains worsening and more cranial surgery in prospect, he decided to end his struggle by suicide and did so February 11, 1897.[10]

Understandably, by then the "McGiffin Story" had occasioned many reports in western Pennsylvania newspapers, and coverage in New York papers as well, reporting on his physical condition, wartime experiences and opinions about the late War (often called the "Corea War" at the time). McGiffin was the only known American participant in a naval battle recognized as an opportunity to deepen understanding of the changes taking place in naval technology. Hence McGiffin did well to compose and publish, in the *Century Magazine*, his detailed eye-witness "untechnical description" of the battle.[11] His recollections are still considered an important eye-witness account. In their time they elicited immediate (perhaps too hasty), yet generally very favorable commentary from many commentators, including no less an authority than the premier naval historian of the epoch, Alfred Thayer Mahan.[12] Shortly afterward, several other articles, and many discussion papers by American and foreign naval officers, were printed in the *Proceedings* of the United States Naval Institute and elsewhere;[13] many of the commentators drew lessons from the Yalu battle and included favorable reference to McGiffin's already well-known views and *Century* essay.

But general interest in McGiffin faded quickly in 1897. The *New York Daily Tribune*'s notice that "The Yalu Hero (is) a suicide" was followed a month later by the report of a jury of inquiry and coroner's verdict confirming that McGiffin's death was, indeed, simply a suicide. Any residual popularity probably evaporated soon after McGiffin's last wishes, expressed in his diary, were publicly described.[14] McGiffin's name thereafter disappeared from the newspaper indices.

The first extensive posthumous essay on McGiffin was published about a decade later in the form of an article from the pen of his loyal boyhood friend, the journalist Richard Harding Davis. The Davis essay was an admiring, popular piece of work, but, unfortunately, it was neither an accurate and balanced account of McGiffin's career, nor a credit to Davis as a reporter.[15] Yet the Davis article, widely circulated, with its many omissions and faults, helped to entrench the pattern of journalistic misrepresentation set by a few earlier (and brief) articles and encyclopedia entries. Later, numerous others appeared, but few of the authors seemed to find and use serious documentation. Thereafter, the readily available Davis essay was much used and cited by those who prepared "brief lives" for publication. For the 90-odd years of this century, the authors of non-documented articles and essays on McGiffin, including some by writers reputedly possessing serious historians' skills, habitually reproduced the mistakes of predecessors. Even the historian-editors of the *Dictionary of American Biography* simply reprinted, without change and as late as 1961, the defective article appearing in the previous edition.[16]

Perhaps it was impatience with the multiple faults found in existing publications that led the McGiffin family to sanction the willingness of a family member to undertake a longer, more serious biography of P. N. McGiffin. Lee McGiffin agreed to take on the task.[17] She volunteered, composing a literate, obviously well-intentioned short (160 page) account of McGiffin's life and career, entitled *Yankee of the Yalu* (1968).[18] It is the only biography we have. But professionally, Lee McGiffin was a newspaper-woman and author of children's books. She had at least a dozen of those, and prizes for some of them, to her credit when her McGiffin biography saw print. She readily acknowledged heavy dependence on the family collection of Philo's papers, but did not, probably could not in her circumstances, make significant use of other more distant documentation, such as books and articles published abroad and little-known but potentially enlightening Chinese language sources.[19]

Members of the McGiffin family and also members of the historical professions in the People's Republic of China and both England and the USA have been cooperative and very helpful, as have archivists and library staff, in responding to my enquiries for McGiffin materials. Numerous articles and books have been published in the last forty years by historians dealing with China's naval development, and work is continuing in preparation for an international Centennial Conference on the Sino-Japanese war of 1894-95, sponsored by the Institute of Historical Studies, Shandong Academy of Social Sciences, Jinan, Shandong, PRC, headed by Professor Qi Qizhang. Hence a new biography of PN McGiffin might now be undertaken using recent publications and new documentary finds.[20]

1. For China included two small cruisers, 2300 tons each (the *Chi Yuen* and the *Ching Yuen*); two other vessels, built in Germany (called "coast defence vessels"), of 2900 tons each (the *King Yuen* and *Lai Yuen*), were also completed and acquired this same year (1887) and presumably were acquired and delivered to China by another contingent of the expedition. Cf ship lists published in articles cited below by McGiffin and Frank Marble.

2. William M. Lang, Captain in the British Navy, adviser to Li Hung-Chang, left China in 1884 to avoid the French War, returned and was reemployed in 1886; led the expedition of 1887 to acquire and bring to China the four ships that were built in England and Germany. Resigned in 1890.

3. On the short supply of 12.2 inch shell: Philo Norton McGiffin, "The Battle of the Yalu," *Century*, 1895, 601; William F. Tyler, *Pulling Strings in China* (London, Constable, 1929), 39-43, w/note; John L. Rawlinson, *China's Struggle for Naval Development, 1839-1895* (Cambridge, Harvard, 1967), 148-150. Tyler remarked that "The very serious factor for the Chinese ships was the outrageous lack of ammunition."

4. The first *Monocacy*, sidewheel-gunboat, 850 HP, 255'X35'X9', schooner-rigged; cp1 190; dp. 1,370; launched 1864; speed 11.2 k.; a.6 guns; Asiatic Sta., 1866-1903. *Dictionary of American Naval Fighting Ships* (Washington, D.C., Navy Dept, CNOpns, 1969), IV, 417; K.J. Bauer & S.S. Roberts, *Register of Ships, USN, 1775-1990* (NY, Greenwood, 1991), 82; *List and Station Report, Officers & Warrants, USN, Active List* (Washington, D.C., 1894), Asiatic Station, USS Monocacy. (Michael J. Crawford, Head, Early History branch, Naval Historical Ctr., kindly provided these and other details).

5. Tyler was born in 1865, about five years younger than McGiffin (born 1860). Both were ambitious, strong contenders in the maneuvering for favor and position in Li Hung-Chang's Northern Squadron. At Yalu (1894) they apparently held unequal but concurrent positions in the two battleships, McGiffin the *Chen Yuen*, Tyler in the *Tin Yuen*. McGiffin had won repeated favors and promotions in his

decade of work for Li, then earned distinction in the Yalu fight. Both men showed they understood some of the larger significance of the battle, causes and characteristics and outcome. Tyler, also highly intelligent, acted then and later to forestall and denigrate McGiffin. Writing thirty-five years afterward, Tyler said that "after the Yalu battle . . . the first thing I did on arrival (in port) was to take precautions about McGiffin. I knew he would become a Yalu-maniac and send telegrams galore, so I arranged for a censorate and was only just in time to stop a (McGiffin) message to the world at large that we had won a glorious victory." Tyler, *Pulling Strings in China*, 57. cf. 58–60 *passim*. Tyler's good connections with the dominant Anglo-German contingent of foreigners in Chinese service, and luck enabled him to pull many strings! With McGiffin wounded and out of contention and many officer slots open after Yalu, Tyler advanced to a command position in the siege of Wei-Hai-Mei. None of McGiffin's subsequent publications or reported public statements known to this writer indicate he believed either side, or any ship, could be credited with "glorious victory" at Yalu, the notion Tyler's *post-facto* writing ascribed to McGiffin.

6. According to Lee McGiffin (work cited below), McGiffin was literally smuggled to Shanghai with the help of friends.

7. Robert Seager II and Doris D. McGuire, eds., *Letters and Papers of Alfred Thayer Mahan* (Annapolis: Naval Institute Press, 1975), II, 416 w/notes.

8. *New York Daily Tribune,* September 29, 1895, 13.

9. Quoted from Richard Harding Davis, "Captain Philo Norton McGiffin," in *Real Soldiers of Fortune* (New York, Collier, 1906), 173–174.

10. Report of Suicide, *New York Daily Tribune*, Feb 12, 1897, 1.

11. Philo N. McGiffin, "The Battle of the Yalu: Personal Recollections by the Commander of the Chinese Ironclad *Chen Yuen*," *Century Magazine*, 1895, 585–604, illus. In publishing his article, McGiffin offered a "disclaimer" of any pretension to making "a professional report," but his article was, in fact, both technical and professional. This article was commented on favorably by various contemporary naval writers (see notes 12 and 13 below); however, a contrary view was expressed by William Tyler in his 1929 book, referring to McGiffin's "articles giving wondrous but entirely imaginary descriptions of what he had seen and done, and illustrations of himself with his many bandaged wounds." Tyler, *Pulling Strings*, 58.

12. Alfred Thayer Mahan, "Lessons From the Yalu Fight," *Century Magazine*, 1895, 629–632. (Mahan's comments on the McGiffin article appear in the same periodical). Robert Johnson, editor at *Century Magazine*, had requested a 2000-word comment from Mahan on the McGiffin article; Mahan wrote almost 4000 words, with a favorable judgment on the McGiffin article overall. Mahan was not only willing but anxious to comment on McGiffin's article, partly for economic reasons perhaps (ATM was paid by the word). Yet Mahan was obviously interested professionally, and it would be surprising if Mahan himself did not have a hand in arranging for McGiffin's later visit to the Naval War College, where McGiffin's scheduled lecture was expanded into a series of three lectures given to the War College officers between June and October 1st, 1895. *Letters and Papers* (Mahan), Vol II, 416–418 w/notes; Robert Seager II, *Alfred Thayer Mahan, The Man and His Letters* (Annapolis, Naval Institute Press, 1977), 327–328. William Tyler admitted that McGiffin "Lectured at the American staff college and succeeded in being taken quite seriously for a time." Indeed, he was taken *very* seriously. A published *Abstract*

of the official War College report on the 1895 Session referred to the McGiffin lectures as "timely and critical observations on the practical conduct of modern naval warfare" that "cannot be referred to at length . . . (because) many of his remarks as given to the officers of the War College" were "confidential." Abstracts provided by Evelyn M. Cherpak, Head, Naval Historical Collection, Naval War College, with letter dated 25 January 1994. Yet McGiffin's inveterate critic, William Tyler, persisted in his enmity, describing McGiffin as "a curious case of partial brain affection; but," said Tyler, McGiffin "was queer even before the fight" at Yalu. Tyler, *Pulling Strings*, 58.

13. The following analyses of the battle and of McGiffin's article in the *Century Magazine*, and discussions of the general subject were printed in the *United States Naval Institute, Proceedings* for 1895, on the pages indicated: Frank Marble (Ensign, USN), "The Battle of the Yalu," 479–497, 510–521. Discussion papers were presented by: Lt. Commander Richard Wainright, USN, 499–500; Lt. William F. Halsey, USN, 501–506, (Sec'y CinC Asiatic Sta); Asst. Constructor Y. Wadagaki, 506–507 (Imp JN, Yokasuka Nyard); Lt. William P. White, USN, 507–509 (*USS Charleston*, Asia Station).

14. *New York Daily Tribune*, Feb 12, 1897; "The Yalu Hero (is) a Suicide," 1 col 3; March 11, 1897, Inquest and Coroner's Report, 12, col 6; April 10, 1897, "The Faith of Commander McGiffin," extract from McGiffin's last Diary entry, 5, col 5.

15. The Davis essay, "Captain Philo Norton McGiffin," 147–175, was disjointed, designed in the dramatic Davis style to be popular, claiming (without evidence) that "almost all those Chinese officers in the Chinese-Japanese War were his (McGiffin's) pupils." In his 28-page essay, Davis included 4 pages of pictures, 4 pages discussing McGiffin's mischief while a student at Annapolis, and a 7-page quotation from one of McGiffin's letters to his Mother. Even the Davis title was in error; McGiffin was not captain. At Yalu he had official rank as Commander and referred to himself as such.

16. In the years after his suicide, essays and encyclopedia articles on McGiffin (with many mistakes of fact or interpretation) included the following (samples): Park Benjamin, "The Story of Philo McGiffin," *Army & Navy Journal*, vol. 34, No. 25, Feb 20, 1897; A. T. C. Pratt, *People of the Period* (1896) 2 vols; *The National Cyclopedia of American Biography* (N.Y.: James White & Co, 1898), Vol XXV; J. Lossing, *Harper's Encyclopedia of United States History* (1902), 10 vols. More recent essays also included exaggeration and errors: *Who Was Who in America* (1607–1896) (Chicago, Ill., 1950), "Revised Edition" (1967), 417; *Dictionary of American Biography* (Editor, Dumas Malone), (1961), VI, pt 2, 48–49 (reprinting defective article by Carroll S. Alden, from the 1930's edition); *The Harper Encyclopedia of Military Biography* (N.Y.: Harper-Collins, 1992), 469.

17. Lee McGiffin, b. 1908, married (1937) Norton McGiffin (historian). She was a columnist and fashion editor with newspapers in Syracuse and Buffalo, NY, 1931–37; then free-lance magazine writer and author of books for children from 1937; she had won prizes for her children's works (over a dozen published), ten with Dutton & Co. Her last book was *Yankee of the Yalu* (1968) (*Contemporary Authors*, Permanent Series, 431).

18. Full title: *Yankee of the Yalu: Philo Norton McGiffin, American Captain in the Chinese Navy, 1885–1895* (N.Y.: Dutton, 1958), 160 pp.

19. Lee McGiffin, in her Preface, referred to help received with "Mandarin" translation, perhaps of Philo McGiffin's Chinese name. She appended a list of books as bibliography, but did not provide footnote references to her sources (most of them family letters and papers, unpublished). Her book seems never to have received a scholarly review. It also was seldom purchased by college and public libraries, though some copies were donated to libraries and placed in the "juvenile" section. A "lumina" computer survey of holdings in US and Canadian libraries reveals a total of under 125 copies in college, university, and public libraries.

20. Among the Chinese scholars publishing in the field whose work has come to my attention are the following (all published in Chinese, of course): Jiang Ming, *Fleet With the Dragon Flag: The Rise and Fall of the Modern Chinese Navy* (Shanghai: Jiaotong University Press, 1991); Qi Qizhang, *The Northern Squadron* (Shandong: Remin Press, 1981); Zhang Xia et al. (Editors), *The Chinese Navy in the Late Ching Dynasty: Historical Data* (Beijing: Maritime Press, 1982). A number of English language works have also appeared in the years since John Rawlinson published his now classic work on *China's Struggle for Naval Development, 1839–1895* in 1957; some are listed in Samuel C. Chu's article, entitled "The Sino-Japanese War of 1894: A Preliminary Assessment from the U.S.A.," 20 pages with extensive documentation. A very recent book "traces the career of a Chinese government official who built the country's first modern naval academy and dockyard," is by David Pong, *Shen Pao-Chen and China's Modernization in the Nineteenth Century* (Cambridge University Press, 1994), 412 pages (not yet seen).

Teddy's "Ollie" and the Teflon Admiral: William S. Sims vs. Robley D. Evans in Theodore Roosevelt's Navy

James R. Reckner

⚓

More than a quarter century ago Samuel P. Hays examined the municipal reform movement in Pittsburgh, Pennsylvania, during the Progressive Era.[1] Hays concluded that 48 percent of the reformers were professional men whose interest in reform, for the most part, "stemmed from the inherent dynamics of their professions." They were men "in the forefront of acquisition and application of knowledge." They were not the older professional men seeking to preserve the past against changes; they were in the vanguard of professional life, actively seeking to apply expertise more widely in public affairs.[2] How accurately this seems also to describe that small group of officers who sought reform in the United States Navy in the early years of this century! One need only substitute "naval affairs" for "public affairs."

Hays found that 52 percent of Pittsburgh reformers were businessmen who directed "new" industries, which "had come to dominate the city's economic life";[3] Similarly, naval reformers largely were the advocates of the new technologies within the navy. According to Hays, "the most visible opposition to [municipal] reform and the most readily available target of reform attack was the so called [political] 'machine.' "[4] To line officer reformers, the "bureau system," the navy's "machine," was responsible for much of the navy's ills. Power was decentralized; as *The Navy* reported in 1907: "No provision of law exists for any coordination. All [eight] bureaus have equal standing; and each is independent, subject only to the Secretary of the Navy,—free to proceed in its own way, according to the Chief's ideas of the needs and interests of the service.... Each element in constructing and equipping a ship is provided for,—except the single, controlling influence necessary ... to adapt the vessel most perfectly to her purpose."[5] Each chief, through long years of service as chief of a specific bureau, in essence, was in command of his own "machine" consisting of officers owing loyalties to the specific bureau, which at times over-rode the larger loyalty to the navy.

The drama of the municipal reform effort, Hays reported, "lay in the competition for supremacy between two systems of decision-making." One involved "wide latitude for the expression of grass-roots impulses," the other "grew out of the rationalization of life which came with science and technology, in which decisions arose from expert analysis and flowed from fewer and smaller centers. . . ." The same was very much true for the navy. To use labels applied by William S. Sims, the "conservatives" sought to preserve the bureaucratic procedures of the past, while the "insurgents" sought more scientific and systematic arrangements, not just for the improvement of gunnery and the design of battleships, but for management of the navy itself in the form of a modern naval general staff. To quote Hays one final time, "Those who espoused the former looked with fear upon the loss of influence which the latter involved, and those who espoused the latter looked only with disdain upon the wastefulness and inefficiency of the former."[6] Commander Albert L. Key, one of Sims's close friends and a former aide to President Roosevelt, described this phenomenon much more bluntly:

> My cry is to give the "young" officers—the misguided youths under 55, a chance, and down with the senile incompetent old grafters on the retired list, or about to retire, who must devote the whole of their time to a hopeless defense of their errors of administration while on the active list.[7]

The stormy relationship between Rear Admiral Robley D. Evans and Lieutenant Commander (much later Admiral) William S. Sims during the first decade of the twentieth century illuminates well this struggle.

After George Dewey, Rear Admiral Robley D. Evans was the most widely known active duty naval officer of the Theodore Roosevelt era. A Civil War veteran, one of the few still serving, contemporary journalists compared Evans's "grim, brown, square-jawed countenance" with the battleships he commanded; his "coarse, almost savage mouth" suggested an older age of "hand-to-hand cutlass fighting and close, fierce ship grapplings."[8] Evans had acquired considerable institutional strength through marriage to a sister of his Annapolis classmate, Henry C. Taylor, and, as a result of early entry into the Naval Academy and advancement related to Spanish War service, he reached the rank of rear admiral at the then remarkably early age of 55. This gave him an unprecedented seven years in flag rank—longer than any other officer of the period—during which he served as commander-in-chief of the Asiatic and later the Atlantic Fleet.[9]

Evans understood well the power of positive publicity. In 1901, he published his autobiography, *A Sailor's Log*,[10] and nine years later, a second autobiographical volume, *An Admiral's Log*.[11] He was remarkably popular with the general public. When assigned to escort the German Prince Henry on a tour of the United States in 1902, the "popular enthusiasm" for Evans was "a marked feature of every crowd all along the route."[12] But *A Sailor's Log*, published while Evans was still on active duty, particularly upset former Secretary of the Navy William E. Chandler with its claim that he had bent to political pressure to have Evans removed from a position in the Light House Service while he was Secretary in 1884. On the contrary, Chandler told Secretary of the Navy John D. Long, Evans was one of the few officers he ever encountered who claimed favors of the administration because he was a Democrat. He summarized Evans's account of his life in a brief passage heavily laden with cynicism:

> [W]hen I read his frank admissions that he, almost alone, in 1882, changed our naval construction from wooden to steel ships, and thus originated our new Navy; in December 1897, induced Assistant Secretary Roosevelt to provide the fleet in Cuban waters with torpedo boat destroyers and guard boats; and above all, on July 3, 1898, commanding the battleship *Iowa*, discovered Cervera's fleet coming out of Santiago harbor and destroyed it, I feel that liberal allowances should be made by all true Americans for any mistakes . . . which may be made by our greatest self-confessed and self-recorded hero of the War of 1898.[13]

Evans subsequently received a public reprimand for his criticism of Chandler,[14] after which the former Secretary privately dismissed Evans as "a braggart and an ass."[15]

A Sailor's Log, published about six months before the Schley court of inquiry and while Rear Admiral Winfield Scott Schley was still on active duty, also fueled the flames of the Sampson-Schley controversy with Evans's negative portrayal of Schley's actions during the Baltimore incident of 1891 and his suggestion that Schley might have warranted a "dreadful court-martial sentence" had

Cervera escaped from Santiago during the "retrograde movement" in 1898. For the pro-Schley *Baltimore American*, this was proof positive that Evans belonged to "the Sampson-Crowninshield-Long clique." To the Baltimore paper, Evans merely endeavored in *A Sailor's Log* "to boost the fortunes of Admiral Sampson and show his hatred for Admiral Schley."[16]

Unfortunately, no significant collection of Evans's papers remains; the biographer is compelled to supplement the questionable autobiographies with what few papers may be found in official records and other related collections. The picture that emerges from such sources is one of a man of short temper and long memory, adept at bureaucratic manipulation, and willing to claim full credit for the achievement of others. Charles S. Sperry, a future C-in-C of the Atlantic Fleet, shared many hours with Evans during Evans's tour as C-in-C on Asiatic Station. He found Evans a "pleasant companion";[17] therefore, his private observations are illuminating.

Concerning Evans's flagship, the battleship *Kentucky*, Sperry noted, "Evans has made [Captain Charles H.] Stockton's life a burden. . . . Evans is nervous and meddlesome, and interferes and makes comments all over the ship."[18] "Evans is not the man he is popularly supposed to be. . . . He is rash and intemperate."[19] Five years later, Rear Admiral Charles M. Thomas also took note of Evans's Atlantic Fleet flagship, the battleship *Connecticut*. After witnessing a heated public argument between the flagship's captain and the admiral's chief of staff, he wrote to his wife Ruth Simpson Thomas [the daughter of yet another admiral], "The consensus of opinion is that 'things' are rather unharmonious on board the Flagship of the Commander-in-Chief."[20]

Evidence of Evans's intemperance is not difficult to find. He traveled to Asiatic station on board the steamship *Gaelic* in April 1902 to take up his assignment there. The *Gaelic* reached Honolulu after midnight on April 16, but, following standard practices, was not boarded by a health officer to grant pratique until 7:40 A.M. According to the captain of the vessel, "the Admiral became incensed over his having been delayed." However, when the health officer did appear and granted clearance, Evans was in no hurry to leave the ship. But his ill-temper over the perceived delay remained. When *Gaelic* returned to sea, Evans officially reported the medical officer to the Secretary of the Treasury, a measure which generated considerable unpleasantness and correspondence.[21]

A slight to Evans, once noted, was rarely forgotten. When the Paymaster General of the Navy refused to provide Evans with 12,000 pairs of newly modified uniform trousers for the men of his squadron because 20,000 of the older style were still in stock, Evans placed the Paymaster General on report to the Secretary of the Navy. Paymaster General A. S. Kenny responded by placing Evans on report to the Secretary for failing to observe navy regulations which required Evans to provide him a copy of the original report.[22] The issue was seemingly resolved when the Judge Advocate General of the Navy reported that neither officer's report was sustainable.[23] Clearly, though, the incident was not forgotten.

During the following year, a general court martial on Asiatic Station found an assistant paymaster, an officer of the paymaster general's corps, guilty of drunkenness and "scandalous conduct tending to the destruction of good morale," but assigned a relatively mild sentence. As the convening authority, Evans reviewed the findings and, dissatisfied, returned them to the court for reconsideration, criticizing the leniency of the sentence. The court stood by its decision, and Evans then approved the findings, but, in so doing, he singled out the three junior officers of the court, including two assistant paymasters, saying that "the disgraceful conduct of Paymaster Nicholson [the subject of the court martial] was less reprehensible than that of those members of the court who succeeded in arriving at the sentence awarded, and thereby bringing the honor of a court martial into disrepute."[24] This was a criticism that even the normally friendly *Army & Navy Journal* found "unbecoming" of the admiral.[25]

One of the paymasters so criticized, Henry E. Biscoe, appealed to the Secretary of the Navy[26] and, ultimately, to the President, both of whom upheld Evans.[27] Hardly had Biscoe's appeals been resolved when Evans went on the attack. When a shortage of supplies was discovered on board Paymaster Biscoe's ship, Evans ordered a court of inquiry. The court recommended nothing more for Biscoe than a reprimand and that the commissary steward receive a general court martial. Instead, the enlisted man was disrated by his commanding officer for falsehood, then served as the principal witness against Biscoe at the general court martial ordered by Evans against the recommendation of the court of inquiry![28] The duty of Admiral Evans's new court was clear: Biscoe was found guilty and ordered reduced 50 numbers in seniority.

Biscoe's civilian lawyers filed a formal brief appealing his sentence,[29] and Biscoe's father-in-law, Theodore Roosevelt's uncle, Robert B. Roosevelt, approached the President for redress.[30] In the end, by direction of the President, Secretary Moody remitted the sentence of the court and issued a letter of reprimand to Biscoe.[31] As for Evans's role in the affair, President Roosevelt observed that Evans may have "allow[ed] his vindictiveness to cloud his judgement."[32] Moody, in response, told the President that he had "always thought that Admiral Evans indulged the sharpness of his pen too much." But, he added, "There should also be taken into account the larger fact, not comforting at all to this accused or his friends, I fear, that Admiral Evans left the Asiatic Fleet in a high degree of efficiency."[33] In essence, Evans's mistreatment of Paymaster Biscoe was excused as the unfortunate, yet necessary, side effect of Evans's demand for efficiency.

Evans's connection with Rear Admiral Henry Clay Taylor provides an interesting insight into how the naval bureaucracy actually worked during the early years of the twentieth century. Widely hailed as the navy's leading strategist and thinker of the period, Taylor had served as President of the Naval War College and had been responsible for the founding of the General Board. On 24 April 1902 he became Chief of the Bureau of Navigation and de facto principal advisor to Secretary William H. Moody.

Among the many contentious issues within the Navy Department and Congress during the Theodore Roosevelt years was the location of coaling stations, those bases vital to extending the operating radius of the growing battlefleet. Similarly, bitter struggles occurred over the evolving designs of battleships, including such issues as the adoption of superposed turrets and design of the 13,000 ton *Idaho* class (*Idaho* and *Mississippi*). While the official discourse on these topics is well outlined in the appropriate records of the National Archives, the personal aspect is equally enlightening.

"Evans and Taylor have been fighting [Rear Admiral Royal B.] Bradford [Chief of the Bureau of Equipment] all along the line and he has been hitting back," Commander Charles S. Sperry confided to his wife. "Bros in law [Evans and Taylor] have been opposing B's [Bradford's] coaling stations and he has been opposing their battleship designs." Unable to overcome the honest and outspoken Bradford through frontal assault, Taylor attempted a flanking maneuver: "Taylor has gotten the Secy to accept [Captain William]

Swift as the ultimate wisdom and he is solemnly digesting a retinue of coaling stations for the whole world which is evidently not expected to agree with Bradford's vision. . . . [Senator Eugene] Hale has been backing Bradford, and got Frenchman's Bay Coal Depot, and [Secretary of the Navy] Moody intimates that Hale is a jobber, etc., etc."[34]

One of the important functions of the Bureau of Navigation was the issuance of orders for all naval officers. Thus, when brother-in-law Evans was sent to the Asiatic Station, Evans's son-in-law, Lieutenant Commander Charles C. Marsh, was ordered to the Orient as naval attache to Peking and Tokyo. And Evans's own son, Ensign Franck Taylor Evans, a young man with a major drinking problem and a temper possibly even worse than the admiral's,[35] was ordered as an additional aide to his father. As Evans was the only flag officer on duty afloat with a third junior officer on his personal staff,[36] it seems clear that young Evans was assigned to keep him under his father's protection. Also accompanying the admiral to Asiatic Station was the female branch of the Evans clan, which established residence in Japan: Mrs. R. D. Evans, the Evans's unmarried daughter Virginia, Mrs. Marsh, Ensign Evans's wife Gertrude, and Dora Taylor, Rear Admiral Taylor's unmarried daughter.[37] Their presence in Japan, perhaps, sheds some light on Evans's plan, rejected by the Navy Department, to station the Asiatic battleship squadron, including his flagship, in Nagaski during the Russo-Japanese War, although Evans later reported to the Secretary of the Navy that his "idea in placing the battleships at Nagasaki was to have a proper force near at hand in case of trouble at Tientsin or Peking which is always threatening."[38]

It was widely understood that Evans and Taylor conspired to further each other's career. The general outline of the scheme that emerged was that Evans, upon completion of his tour as C-in-C of the Asiatic Fleet, would return home to a temporary position awaiting the end of Taylor's term as Chief of the Bureau of Navigation. When Rear Admiral Albert S. Barker, C-in-C North Atlantic Fleet, retired in March of 1905, Taylor would take that position and Evans would be nominated for the bureau chief slot.[39] In the meantime, Taylor enlisted Admiral Dewey to urge passage of the bill creating two vice admirals for the navy: the rank to be held by officers who held the command-in-chief of either the Asiatic or North Atlantic Fleets. "Both Taylor and Evans cultivated Dewey highly. It was evidently Taylor's policy to exalt Dewey in order that Dewey in return might exalt him," a disgruntled Rear Admiral Charles D. Sigsbee later wrote.[40]

In due course, Evans returned to the United States and accepted the presidency of the Lighthouse Board as his "holding" position. Unfortunately for the grand scheme, while on a tour of the Great Lakes, Admiral Taylor died of peritonitis on 26 July 1904.[41] On the level of strategic thinking, the navy's loss was great; Taylor had been the navy's "mastermind," Reginald R. Belknap wrote.[42] And Rear Admiral J. B. Coghlan confided to Taylor's widow, "We of the Navy feel that a great light has gone out, and left us to grope in semi-darkness."[43] Taylor's demise could not have been less well timed for Evans, who was then suffering one of many recurring bouts of illness related to his Civil War wounds. He was "not in the best of health and his assignment as chief of the Bureau of Navigation was not contemplated for several months, by which time he hoped to have regained his strength."[44]

Unfit to take charge of the Navy Department's principal bureau, Evans had to stand aside while Rear Admiral George A. Converse was awarded the prize. Given Evans's vindictive nature, his failure to gain this most influential staff position probably was a stroke of good fortune for the navy. But if the Bureau of Navigation chiefship was now out of Evans's reach—the appointments were for four years—new vistas unfolded in the North Atlantic Fleet.

By September of 1904, Evans had mounted a campaign to gain the command originally slated for his brother-in-law. "Intimate friends" announced that Evans "would not be averse" to return to sea in command of the fleet.[45] On 8 September Admiral Dewey discussed command of the North Atlantic Fleet with the Secretary of the Navy,[46] and, although there were a number of candidates for the prized position, at least one, Rear Admiral Sigsbee, was convinced that Evans's selection was the fruit of Dewey's support.[47]

Evans assumed command of the North Atlantic Fleet on 31 March 1905. Three months later, Lieutenant Reginald R. Belknap, an officer on the fleet flagship, USS *Maine*, confided to his wife that the fleet still hadn't shaped up.[48] That little changed in that respect throughout the period of Evans's command is suggested by notes made by Captain Nathan Sargent in the summer of 1907. Sent to the fleet to observe operations for the General Board, Sargent recorded, "Simple evolutions rather raggedly done. . . . Evidence of very little drills." And, illustrative of Evans's abrasive command style, "During exercises C in C's criticisms of commanding officers rather severely made by wireless."[49]

Little noted by historians were a pair of fleet accidents during Evans's tenure as commander-in-chief which reflect upon his leadership. On 7 January 1906, five battleships of the Atlantic Fleet[50] got underway from New York harbor. Sailing down channel during an unusually low tide at "standard" distance of 400 yards from foremast to foremast, at twelve knots, there was little margin for error. When, negotiating a bend in the channel, the number two ship, the *Kentucky*, ran aground; the *Kearsarge*, next in line, maneuvered to avoid the *Kentucky* and also ran aground. The *Alabama*, astern of the *Kearsarge*, attempted to swing clear of the two grounded ships, and in so doing, collided with the *Kentucky*.[51] Fortunately, all three ships avoided major damage. The press was quick to allocate blame: "The responsibility is wholly on Rear Admiral Evans—unless he can show that the *Kentucky* was, at the time of the grounding, unavoidably out of her proper position. This is not very likely, as he has recently been peremptorily suspending captains by signal from the flagship for deviating from their proper places."[52] "Admiral Evans should be put on his defense—and no scapegoat substituted," the *Independent* concluded.[53]

But Evans escaped censure; Rear Admiral Converse, in his official endorsement of Evans's report of the accident, defended Evans's selection of formation for leaving port, saying it was "the only one in fact which could be used and still retain the semblance of a formation."[54] Immediately after the grounding and collision, Evans ordered a court of inquiry, which inquired into the actions of the individual ships but did not question the orders issued by the commander-in-chief. In the end, the court concluded that none of the commanding officers was to blame for the accident, responsibility for that having been assigned to an "incompetent helmsman" aboard the *Kentucky*![55]

When yet another battleship collision occurred, this time while maneuvering in a dense fog off Newport, Rhode Island, in July, 1906, President Roosevelt turned his attention to the problem.[56] The President correctly attributed the earlier New York accident to "Evans' mistake in taking the ships out in intricate and dangerous navigation in too close order."[57] Evans, the President asserted, should learn that the idea of training was "to enable people to take risks, and yet that the risks should not unnecessarily be taken." Yet despite this criticism, Roosevelt added in his own hand at the end of the letter, "But Evans is a first class man."[58] Even obvious failure did not diminish Evans's aura. Concerning the Newport collision, the President told Secretary Bonaparte that "Evans should explain about sending out those ships in close order in the fog."[59] Yet the president of the court of inquiry into that collision, Captain Benjamin F. Tilley, did not even interview Evans, limiting his inquiries to the actions of the two battleships involved.[60]

Throughout Evans's years as an admiral, the "astonishingly handsome"[61] William S. Sims was a relatively junior officer.[62] His accomplishments during the Theodore Roosevelt presidency have been exceptionally well presented by Elting E. Morison;[63] however, Morison paid scant attention to the Sims-Evans relationship.

There can be little doubt that Sims's efforts to convert the navy to "continuous aim" firing encountered significant resistance, all of which has been documented elsewhere. But Albert Niblack, Sims's predecessor as Inspector of Target Practice, tried to assure Sims that "there was no conspiracy, no ring, no desire to curb you, turn you down, discredit you or anything of the kind."[64] One of Sims's many faults, however, was that he equated even honest opposition to his reforms with conspiracy, and, increasingly, he labelled those who resisted, "enemies." And, not unlike Evans, Sims had an unfortunate habit of alienating many people with "language and a manner that [were] unnecessarily harsh." As Bradley A. Fiske advised him, "They say you are your own worst enemy."[65] But Sims saw it differently: "The criticism would be just if it is assumed that the ridicule and sarcasm were not entirely necessary. I am perfectly certain they were, and I used them deliberately."[66]

Sims had been very fortunate that Rear Admiral Taylor was his superior in Washington when he first became Inspector of Target Practice. Taylor "deplored Sims' virulence," but "never allowed that to stand in the way of using Sims's valuable services and intelligence." But, whereas Taylor controlled Sims, Taylor's successor, George A. Converse, was "intimidated" by Sims's contentiousness; he "hardly endured" Sims and was "all but vigorously opposed to him."[67]

Before Taylor's untimely death, when Evans had been preparing to take over the Bureau of Navigation, he had pressured Taylor to order Sims to sea.[68] Evans's desire to put Sims to sea related to Sims's gunnery work. The initial reforms, which Sims had begun while on Asiatic Station, had still been in progress when Evans assumed command there. Evans, in his official reports and personal correspondence, had created the impression that he had initiated this work.[69] To continue Sims as Inspector of Target Practice with Evans as Chief of the Bureau would undermine Evans's claims.

But events, on occasion, follow an unpredictable course. Admiral Taylor had died unexpectedly; at the time, Evans was too sick to replace him, and so Sims managed to stay on as Inspector of Target Practice. But when command of the North Atlantic Fleet became available, Evans got it. Thus, Sims, having barely avoided termination of his gunnery duties by Taylor's death, now had to cooperate with Evans as the new commander-in-chief. And he now viewed Evans as one of his principal "enemies" within the service.

By 1906, Sims had convinced himself that Evans's "sinister influence" with the late Admiral Taylor was the reason why no official record of his remarkable gunnery achievements had been included in his record of service.[70] And in conversations with army Brigadier General Henry G. Sharpe, he learned that Evans had claimed, on a number of occasions since 1902, that he had invented the system of "continuous aim" firing which Sims had championed.[71] But within the service, the truth was almost universally known. Commander William S. Benson, a future Sims antagonist, in 1906, expressed the hope that Sims's "phenomenal work" would be recognized, and said he would be "delighted to lose a number" in seniority to have Sims advance.[72]

By March of 1907, Evans was again suffering from complications from his Civil War wounds.[73] At this point, Sims saw his opportunity to act. In a memorandum to the President, sent outside the Navy Department chain of command, Lieutenant Commander Sims detailed Rear Admiral Evans's failure to carry out the Navy Department's wishes concerning practice of the General Board's Battle Plan No.1 throughout 1905 and 1906 and his intention not to carry out the practice during the spring maneuvers of 1907.[74]

Evans's normal tour in command of the fleet was scheduled to expire on 1 April 1907. "He is incapaci[ta]ted by chronic illness for the arduous duties of the position," Sims told the President. The second in command, Rear Admiral Charles H. Davis (Senator Henry Cabot Lodge's brother-in-law and, therefore, politically influential in the Roosevelt administration), was nearing retirement.[75] And the two remaining flag officers with the battleship fleet "have just been ordered as divisional commanders and . . . are in no way fitted to take up the work of training our battle fleet . . . in battle tactics."

Sims suggested that the real problem was that "the most important commands were obtained largely through personal and other influences," with the result "that the administration of the fleet by officers so selected is a personal one, often to the extent of a total disregard of the important tactical studies made by the War College and the General Board," as in the case of Evans.[76]

Immediately after having, in effect, put Evans on report to the President, Sims, as Inspector of Target Practice, headed south to join Evans for the annual target practice. Upon his arrival at Guantanamo, an understandably tense Sims reported to the admiral.[77] Evans asked whether Sims had seen reports in the *New York American* that the decision had been made to relieve him of command. Sims replied that he had not seen that article, but understood that a similar one had appeared in the *Philadelphia Bulletin*. At the end of this tense discussion, Evans looked directly at Sims and said, "Some 'white mouse' [read Sims] has been talking to the President, and I'd just like to know who it was."[78] Evans, no stranger to intrigue, eventually concluded that certain members of the General Board had conspired to have Rear Admiral Caspar F. Goodrich replace him, but that by April the intrigue had failed and "only the rotten smell of it" remained. Evans questioned the General Board's motives and concluded, with remarkable arrogance, "Of course, the [General] Board must know that they are on trial before the service and not I!"[79]

A few days later, Evans, in the course of an after-dinner discussion, said that Sims had been able to effect his reforms "through the President's friendship" and added: "If any one of us had attempted to do the same thing in the same way we would probably have been court-martialled." Privately, Sims noted, "Observe that the last remark assumed that 'we' knew how to do it, but were too subordinate to take the unusual (and insubordinate) measures I am supposed to have employed."[80]

By the summer of 1907, President Roosevelt had made the decision to send the Atlantic battleship fleet on its famous cruise around the world. Interestingly, Sims and Evans were in agreement in opposing the cruise. Evans, Sims noted, "is very much opposed to the Pacific cruise, in fact says violent things against it—that it is political, to catch the Pacific vote, and is also due largely to the influence of Jim Bennett's Russian mistress (though he designated the lady by a less conventional name)."[81]

Sims felt that Evans agreed to the cruise because to object would be to risk being relieved of command by the President, who was determined that the cruise would go forward. In fact, Evans's health was a source of growing concern. In May he temporarily relinquished command to Rear Admiral Davis,[82] and an October series of public denials that Evans was ill again suggested just the opposite.[83] Removing Evans from command was discussed in a Cabinet meeting. "The opinion of the President and his Cabinet was that Evans is in no condition for the job, but that it would be the better policy to let him go and make the 'try,'" rather than risk a newspaper sensation before the sailing of the fleet.[84]

During his years as Inspector of Target Practice, Sims had continued to examine and criticize the design of America's new battleships. These reports he had sent to the Navy Department through the normal chain of command, where they eventually reached the Board on Construction, only to languish. Sims's increasing frustration with his inability to effect changes in battleship designs led him to further criticism of the organization of the Navy Department itself, for, in his view, it was the faulty department organization that made possible the perpetuation of design errors in the battleship fleet.

By late 1907, Sims had concluded that he would be unable to effect change within the organization, and, therefore, when Henry Reuterdahl, a noted marine artist and American editor of *Jane's Fighting Ships*, approached Sims to clear an article on the battleship design errors and the need for reorganization within the Navy Department, Sims agreed to permit Reuterdahl to publish information he had earlier provided. The resultant article, "The Needs of Our Navy," appeared in the January, 1908, edition of *McClure's Magazine*,[85] which went on sale shortly after the Atlantic battleship fleet departed for its highly publicized cruise to the Pacific.[86]

The public outcry raised by Reuterdahl's criticisms led Senator Eugene Hale, Chairman of the Senate Naval Affairs Committee, to hold hearings into the alleged battleship defects. This confrontation pitted Sims and his friends against Sims's own immediate superior in the Navy Department, Rear Admiral George A. Converse. Converse, along with Chief Constructor of the Navy Washington L. Capps, had been tasked with rebutting the Reuterdahl claims.

When Sims and his "insurgent" friends seemed to be proving the validity of the criticisms, a development unanticipated by Senator Hale, the committee went into executive session and then adjourned without issuing any findings.[87] The reformers, frustrated in their efforts, would seek one more test before the end of the Theodore Roosevelt presidency.

While Sims and his friends fought a bitter bureaucratic battle in Washington, Evans was fighting an equally bitter health battle as the fleet circumnavigated South America. Although the *New York Times*, on the eve of the fleet's departure, described Evans as an "efficient survival of the Civil War" who was "looking younger every day,"[88] nothing could have been further from the truth. At the fleet's first port of call, Trinidad, Rear Admiral Charles M. Thomas recorded that Evans was "Not at all well, worn and tired in appearance and manner."[89] He was unable to attend the officers' Christmas reception the next day,[90] and, as the fleet sailed south to Rio de Janeiro, his condition worsened. His chief of staff, Captain Royal R. Ingersoll, confided to Rear Admiral Charles S. Sperry that "for the first time the admiral seemed to lose his grip," and one night Ingersoll "was afraid he could not live." Sperry was "alarmed"; he had never seen Evans "look so ill and frail."[91] A plan was hatched to relieve him if his health did not improve while the fleet was in Punta Arenas, Chile, but at the last minute he apparently showed some signs of recovery. Nevertheless, Thomas reported that Evans had "taken so many opiates to relieve pain that it has knocked out completely his stomach, so that he is now unable to eat solids and is living on milk."[92]

Thomas, who performed all social functions in Evans's place, thought it "criminal" to the navy and the fleet that Evans retained command.[93] But it seemed unlikely that Evans would willingly give it up: "he is the greatest Cormorant for Power that I have ever seen," Thomas recorded.[94] The reason Evans was permitted to stay was obvious to Thomas: "No other man in the Navy but Evans would be kept in command of a fleet a single day, in his condition, but the prestige of his name goes a long way."[95]

By the time the fleet reached Magdelena Bay, Mexico, Evans's condition had further deteriorated. On 30 March he headed north to recuperate at the Paso Robles health resort, while the fleet conducted target practice. But, even in this situation, he refused to relinquish command, choosing, rather, to take leave.[96]

The American public received daily announcements from Paso Robles indicating a gradual improvement in health,[97] but when the fleet reached Santa Cruz and Evans rejoined it for his triumphal entry into San Francisco, he clearly had not improved:

> Admiral Evans was met at the wharf by a launch from the flagship. Four picked seamen lifted him from the train, placed him in an invalid's chair, and rolled him to the launch. He walked down the ladder to the launch, leaning on a crutch and aided by two seamen, who assisted him at every step. When the launch was alongside the *Connecticut* ropes were lowered and attached to a chair, and the Admiral was hoisted to the deck.[98]

"[I]n another minute," *Current Literature* noted, "the Commander of the greatest fleet in American history was again on deck and again in command."[99] That the "Commander of the greatest fleet in American history" was an aged invalid incapable of exercising effective command elicited no unfavorable public comment; such was Evans's remarkable popularity.

The next day Evans "led" the combined Atlantic and Pacific Fleets to a tumultuous welcome in San Francisco. Evans, who had criticized Rear Admiral Montgomery Sicard for retaining command in 1898 when a younger, more healthy man might have rendered better service in the crisis immediately following the sinking of the *Maine*,[100] had himself retained command of the fleet for four months while totally incapacitated. During that period, the fleet had undergone a most important operational test while Evans's chief of staff, Captain Royal R. Ingersoll, ran the affairs of the fleet and Rear Admiral Charles M. Thomas met all of the extensive social requirements during port visits.[101]

In San Francisco, Evans finally relinquished command. At a farewell dinner at the St. Francis Hotel, he excoriated Sims and the other reformers who had so publicly criticized battleship design faults. "It is not armor belts or waterlines that win battles," he claimed. "It is the men who shoot the straightest and hardest and can stand punishment the longest. If you have such men ... it makes no difference whether the armor belts are of leather or wood, or eggshells, or anything else."[102]

The location of armor belts had been one of the substantive issues of the recently aborted Senate hearings into battleship defects. Evans's own view of armor belt location apparently had evolved considerably during the cruise to the Pacific. In August 1907, commenting on reports that American battleships, when fully laden, often had their armor belts either awash or completely submerged, he expressed the belief that such belts were "a mistake" unless they were so placed "as to give maximum protection possible by waterline armor when the fleet goes into action. This is not possible when the waterline armor belt is submerged, or nearly so."[103]

In his formal report of the cruise, Evans concluded that even with "smooth seas, and practically no wind, the swell at times caused such rolling and pitching as to expose the lower portion of the armor belt even at heavy load, hence the lower limit of armor should not be raised."[104] In essence, although Evans had publicly conceded that the upper level of the armor belt was too low, he now observed that the lower level of the belt wasn't low enough!

This was Evans's final formal report, and it caused anguish for Sims and his friends, who were even then preparing for a major struggle over the design of the new dreadnought battleship *North Dakota*, which, Lieutenant Commander Frank K. Hill reported, would also float lower in the water than calculated when she was ready for battle.[105] Evans's report was a valuable tool in limiting change to the *North Dakota* class design: a total of four ships.

But even as Evans underwent surgery and then went on the retired list in August of 1908, Sims and the "insurgents" did battle with their "enemies" at the Newport Conference (July–August 1908). In the end, reaction prevailed in the short-term, with the majority at the conference voting to not significantly alter the *North Dakota* plans. But in the long term, the navy benefitted from the conference decision that future battleship designs would be reviewed by a board of sea-going line officers before their approval.[106]

In the final days of the Roosevelt administration, Evans, now retired, embarked on a highly publicized lecture tour, and published a series of critical articles in *Hampton's Magazine* that attempted to refute Sims's criticisms as publised by Reuterdahl.[107]

Sims, who had fearlessly campaigned for reform of gunnery, improvement of battleship designs, and, perhaps most importantly, for reform of the Navy Department organization, was rewarded during Theodore Roosevelt's final days as president. When Sims advised Roosevelt that none of the many reports he had made throughout what had been a full decade of intense effort had been entered into his record,[108] the President ordered the Navy

Department to assemble them and attach them to his service record along with a presidential letter of commendation.[109] And in an extraordinary measure, Roosevelt had Navy Regulations, which limited command of battleships to captains, altered to permit the newly promoted Commander William S. Sims to assume command of the battleship *Minnesota*.[110]

Sims had successfully used his command of the navy's new technology to affect changes on a broader scale. He used the influence he gained through his extraordinary achievements in gunnery to campaign for improvement in battleship design procedures and reorganization of the Navy Department. In the process, Sims also actively promoted himself. He became the most widely known junior officer of the navy and had a devoted following amongst junior officers. As Commander William S. Benson wrote, "There is a very strong feeling among many officers of the service . . . that there is but one God and the Inspector of Target Practice is his prophet."[111] But within the service, his campaign for reform during the Theodore Roosevelt years had also exposed his personal flaws, which became so critical after World War I, and ensured he would never take the helm as Chief of Naval Operations.

Despite his remarkable energy and the breadth of his reform endeavors, Sims had been unsuccessful in his efforts to unseat Evans. Within the rigid military structure of the navy, success in that endeavor was unlikely in any case. Evans was not one of the ordinary run of flag officers of the period; his largely self-generated popularity further worked against any effort to discredit him.

After Evans's death in 1912, Navy Chaplain Father Matthew C. Gleeson wrote, "it might be well if some citizen with a passion for accuracy would . . . write our public librarians, and have both the *Sailor's Log* and the *Admiral's Log* fittingly shelved among prominent works of fiction. As long as they are looked on as volumes plentifully besprinkled with fact, well-meaning men . . . will be constantly using them as reference books."[112] But no such correction ever occurred, and Evans's reputation survived the many professional criticisms within the service. In the process, he became a hero to a whole generation of young Americans, including Franklin D. Roosevelt, who in 1931 wrote: "His will always be a household name among those of us who love the Navy and its glorious record; his will always be a personality which will live in the traditions of the Service."[113]

1. Research for this paper was made possible by the Navy Historical Center's grant of the Secretary of the Navy's research chair in naval history for 1991–1992. I gratefully acknowledge this invaluable support.
2. Samuel P. Hays, "The Politics of Reform in Municipal Government in the Progressive Era." *Pacific Northwest Quarterly* 55, no. 4 (Oct. 1964): 160.
3. Ibid.
4. Ibid., 162.
5. "The Bureau System," *The Navy*, 1, no. 10 (Oct. 1907): 35.
6. Hays, 168–169.
7. Albert L. Key to William S. Sims, 3 April 1908. William S. Sims Papers, Navy Historical Foundation collection, Library of Congress (hereafter, Sims Papers).
8. Richard W. Turk, "Robley D. Evans: Master of Pugnacity," in James C. Bradford, ed., *Admirals of the New Steel Navy: Makers of the American Naval Tradition, 1880–1930* (Annapolis: Naval Institute Press, 1990): 73–74, quoting "The Adventurous Career of 'Fighting Bob' Evans," *Current Literature* 42 (January 1907): 35.
9. Promoted to rear admiral, 11 Feb. 1901; C-in-C Asiatic Fleet, 29 Oct. 1902–21, Mar. 1904; C-in-C North Atlantic Fleet, 31 Mar. 1905–9 May 1908. Dates from Naval Historical Center Operational Archives, "ZB" File, Box 74. For a brief summary of Evans's career, see William B. Cogar, *Dictionary of Admirals of the U.S. Navy*, vol. 2 (1901–1918) (Annapolis: Naval Institute Press, 1991): 84–85. The most recent biographical treatment of the admiral is Richard W. Turk, "Robley D. Evans: Master of Pugnacity," 73–96.
10. Robley D. Evans, *A Sailor's Log: Recollections of Forty Years of Naval Life* (New York: D. Appleton & Co., 1901).
11. Robley D. Evans, *An Admiral's Log: Being Continued Recollections of Naval Life* (New York: D. Appleton & Co., 1910).
12. *Army & Navy Journal* 39 (8 March 1902): 668.
13. William E. Chandler to John D. Long, 15 July 1901. John D. Long Papers, Massachusetts Historical Society (MHS). Also published in *Army & Navy Register* 30 (17 Aug. 1901): 128.
14. Assistant Secretary of the Navy Frank H. Hackett to Evans, 9 Aug. 1901. *Army & Navy Register* 30 (17 Aug. 1901): 128.
15. Chandler to Long, 13 Aug. 1901. Long Papers, MHS.
16. "The Conceit of 'Fighting Bob': A Sailor's Log a Record of Self-Glorification." *Baltimore American*, 5 May 1901, 33.
17. Sperry to Edith M. Sperry, 4 Aug. 1902. Charles S. Sperry Papers, Navy Historical Foundation collection, Library of Congress (hereafter, Sperry Papers).
18. Sperry to Edith M. Sperry, 6 Nov. 1902. Sperry Papers.
19. Sperry to Edith M. Sperry, 11 Dec. 1902. Sperry Papers.
20. Charles M. Thomas to Ruth S. Thomas, 25 Dec. 1907. Charles M. Thomas Papers, Navy Historical Foundation collection, Library of Congress (hereafter, Thomas Papers).
21. Evans to Secretary of the Treasury, 17 April 1902. This and related correspondence is contained in National Archives, Record Group 80, entry 19, case 14662. Such documents hereafter cited as: NA, RG 80:19/14662.
22. A.S. Kenny to SecNav William H. Moody, 17 Nov. 1902. NA, RG 80:19/15136-2.

23. NA, RG 80:19/15136-2. See also, *Army & Navy Register* 33 (10 Jan. 1903): 1.

24. Asiatic Fleet General Court Martial Order No. 22, 7 Aug. 1903. Published in *Army & Navy Journal* 41 (26 Sep. 1903): 90.

25. "Encroachments of Executive Authority." *Army & Navy Journal* 41 (3 Oct. 1903): 114.

26. NA, RG 24:88/4161-1. See also, *Army & Navy Register* 34 (24 Oct. 1903): 3; (14 Nov. 1903): 2; (21 Nov. 1903): 12, 20.

27. Captain John E. Pillsbury (Acting ChBuNav) to Biscoe, 12 Jan. 1904. NA, RG 24:88/4161-1.

28. Paymaster General of the Navy to SecNav, 23 June 1904. Samuel McGowan Papers, Navy Historical Foundation Collection, Library of Congress (hereafter, McGowan Papers). By comparison, when Evans was president of the General Court Martial of Commander Benjamin F. Tilley, accused of drunkenness and gross immorality when Governor of American Samoa, he refused to permit enlisted men to testify against the officer, even though they were the principal witnesses still on station.

29. A copy of the appeal is contained in the McGowan Papers.

30. Robert Barnhart Roosevelt had taken the young TR into his law offices when TR had decided at one point that he wished to study law. William H. Harbaugh, *The Life and Times of Theodore Roosevelt* (New York: Oxford University Press, 1975): 25.

31. Moody to BuNav, 30 June 1904. NA, RG 24:88/4161-10.

32. TR to Moody (Private), 20 Feb. 1904. William H. Moody Papers, Haverhill Public Library, Haverhill, Mass.

33. Moody to TR, 25 June 1904. Attached to TR to Bonaparte, 30 Nov. 1906, in Charles J. Bonaparte Papers, Library of Congress. The Biscoe case became a cause celebre and was extensively reported in service journals. See, for examples, *Army & Navy Register* 35 (27 Feb. 1904): 2; (19 March 1904): 2; (9 April 1904): 4; (22 April 1904): 3; (14 May 1904): 2; (21 May 1904): 2; (11 June 1904): 2–3. Moody's findings were published in *Army & Navy Register* 36 (2 July 1904): 4, and Biscoe's public reprimand in *Army & Navy Register* 36 (9 July 1904): 5.

34. Sperry to Edith M. Sperry, 21 Nov. 1902. Sperry Papers.

35. The young Evans had had eight reports filed against him in 1901 alone: four for drunkenness, one for disrespect to the executive officer of his ship, three for either leaving the ship without authority or failing to return to the ship at the time ordered. More spectacular misdeeds followed in 1908 immediately after he lost his father's protection. See SecNav Truman H. Newberry to Attorney General, 2 March 1909. NA, RG 80:19/26282-26:2). According to Sims, Franck Evans was "an utter swab and should have been dismissed long ago—and would have been if he had not been protected by his father." Sims to Anne Hitchcock Sims, 3 Oct. 1908. Sims Papers.

36. See, for example, List and Station of the Commissioned and Warrant Officers of the Navy of the United States, etc., July 1 1902 (Washington, D.C.: GPO, 1902): 70–76.

37. "Americans in Japan," *Army & Navy Journal* 40 (6 Sep. 1902): 16. See also, *Army & Navy Journal* 41 (26 Sep. 1903): 93.

38. Evans to SecNav, 27 Feb. 1904. NA, RG 45:464/"OO", Box 470.

39. *Army & Navy Register* 35 (30 Apr. 1904): 2; (18 June 1904): 3; *Army & Navy Journal* 41 (18 June 1904): 1097; (25 June 1904): 1121. Sims called this "the Taylor-Evans family-combination scheme." Sims to Anne Hitchcock Sims, 30 March 1907. Sims Papers.

40. RADM Charles D. Sigsbee to Edward R. Johnstone, 23 Feb. 1905. Johnstone was connected with the *Minneapolis Times*. Sigsbee Papers, SC16148, box 35, New York State Historical Society, Albany, NY (hereafter, Sigsbee Papers, NYSHS).

41. Asst. SecNav Charles H. Darling to TR, telegram, 27 July 1904. NA, RG 24:88/2780-42.

42. Reginald R. Belknap to Julie Belknap, 8 April 1905. Belknap Papers, Naval War College manuscript collection 103, series 1, box 8, folder 7 (hereafter, Belknap Papers).

43. RADM J. B. Coghlan to Mrs. H.C. Taylor, 28 July 1904. Taylor Papers, Navy Historical Foundation collection, Library of Congress.

44. *Army & Navy Register* 36 (30 July 1904): 3.

45. *Army & Navy Journal* 42 (10 Sep. 1904): 37.

46. *Army & Navy Journal* 42 (10 Sep. 1904): 29.

47. Sigsbee to Edward R. Johnstone, 23 Feb. 1905. Sigsbee Papers, NYSHS.

48. R.R. Belknap to Julie Belknap, 29 June 1905. Belknap Papers, series 1, box 8, folder 8.

49. Sargent notebook, entries for 26, 27 Aug. 1907. Nathan Sargent Papers, Navy Historical Foundation collection, Library of Congress.

50. The North Atlantic Fleet was officially redesignated the United States Atlantic Fleet on 1 Jan. 1906. Charles J. Bonaparte to Evans, 1754/225, 28 Dec. 1905. NA, RG 45:464/"OO", Box 473.

51. For reports of the individual ships involved, see NA, RG 45:464/"HK", Box 183. For a personal account, see Reginald R. Belknap to Julie Belknap, 8 Jan. 1906. Belknap Papers, series 1, box 8, folder 12.

52. "A Damaged Squadron," *Independent* 60 (11 Jan. 1906): 122.

53. Ibid., 123.

54. 2nd Endorsement to Evans to SecNav, No. 56-D, 7 Jan. 1906. NA, RG 45:464/"HK", Box 183.

55. "Naval Collision." *Army & Navy Register* 39 (30 June 1906): 4. The commanding officer's responsibility for employing an "incompetent helmsman" during critical navigation was not addressed.

56. Official correspondence relating to this collision is contained in NA, RG 45:464/"HK", Box 183.

57. TR to Charles J. Bonaparte, 6 Aug. 1906. Charles J. Bonaparte Papers, Library of Congress.

58. Ibid.

59. TR to Bonaparte, 16 Aug. 1906. Bonaparte Papers, LC.

60. For text of the opinion of the court of inquiry, see *Army & Navy Register* 40 (8 Sep. 1906): 18. Tilley, whose career had been saved by Evans's shoddy 1901 general court martial proceedings over charges that Tilley, as governor of American Samoa, had regularly been drunk and had behaved in a scandalous manner in public with Samoan women, would naturally be disinclined to pursue Evans's responsibility. For a detailed description of Tilley's transgressions as governor, see

Edward J. Dorn to Secretary of the Navy, 17 May 1901 [letter not sent], and "Memorandum of a conversation with Comdr. B. F. Tilley on May 17th 1901." Both in Edward J. Dorn Papers, Navy Historical Foundation collection, Library of Congress.

61. Elting E. Morison, *Admiral Sims and the Modern American Navy* (Boston: Houghton, Mifflin, 1940): 15.

62. Lieutenant, 1 Jan. 1897; lieutenant commander, 21 Nov. 1902; commander, 1 July 1907. Cogar, *Dictionary of Admirals of the U.S. Navy* 2:255.

63. Elting E. Morison, op. cit.

64. Albert P. Niblack to Sims, 7 Dec. 1902. Sims Papers.

65. Bradley A. Fiske to Sims, 18 March 1905. Sims Papers.

66. Sims to Anne Hitchcock Sims, 2 July 1905. Sims Papers.

67. Reginald R. Belknap to Julie Belknap, 8 April 1905. Belknap Papers, series 1, box 8, folder 7.

68. For discussions of this, see Sims to Homer C. Poundstone, 23 June 1904, Sims to Bowman H. McCalla, 23 June 1904, Sims to unidentified captain, 19 August 1904, and Sims to Anne Hitchcock Sims, 30 March 1907. All Sims Papers.

69. See Sims to unidentified captain, 19 Aug. 1904, and Robley D. Evans to Henry C. Taylor, 11 Sep. 1902. Both Sims Papers.

70. Sims to Anne Hitchcock Sims, 31 July 1906. Sims Papers.

71. See, for example, Sims to Anne Hitchcock Sims, 14 July 1906, 18 July 1906. Sims Papers. On 12 October 1906 Evans told Navy Chaplain Matthew Gleeson, "I organized [the present system of gunnery training] in China in 1902, and have brought it up to its present state of efficiency." Sims to Anne Hitchcock Sims, 13 Oct. 1906. Similarly, in 1906, Lt. I. V. Gillis formally proposed the engineering competition program adopted by the Atlantic Fleet in 1908. Yet Evans "allowed the world to believe that he had evolved it in his own brain." I.V. Gillis to Sims, 7 Sep. 1908. Sims Papers.

72. Commander William S. Benson to Sims, 12 Nov. 1906. Sims Papers.

73. These wounds were suffered storming Fort Fisher in 1865. The nature of his ailment was variously described as rheumatism and rheumatic gout. For indications of this recurring illness, see Charles S. Sperry to Edith M. Sperry, 28 Nov. 1902, Sperry Papers, *Army & Navy Journal* 41 (31 Oct. 1903): 213, and *Army & Navy Register* 38 (7 Oct. 1905): 11.

74. Sims memo to the President, March, 1907. For a later critical public discussion of the lack of battle practice for the Atlantic Fleet, see, "Have We Any Battle Tactics," *The Navy*, 1, no. 6 (June, 1907): 12–13. This article claimed that the fleet had had a total of ten hours of battle practice—all prearranged—since the war with Spain nearly ten years earlier. Writing to his wife, Sims reported that the article reflected what the President had earlier been told. Sims to Anne Hitchcock Sims, 22 June 1907. The President had been briefed by Catholic Navy chaplain Matthew C. Gleeson, both about the state of battle practice and Evans's attitude toward it, which the President termed "incomprehensible." Sims to Anne Hitchcock Sims, 12 March 1907. Sims Papers.

75. Approaching retirement notwithstanding, Senator Lodge had appealed directly to Secretary Charles J. Bonaparte to appoint his brother-in-law to the command-in-chief should Evans step down. H.C. Lodge to Bonaparte, 2 Nov. 1906. Bonaparte Papers, Library of Congress.

76. Sims Memorandum for the President, February 1907. Sims Papers.
77. Sims to Anne Hitchcock Sims, 9 March 1907. Sims Papers.
78. Sims to Anne Hitchcock Sims, 11 March 1907. Sims Papers.
79. Evans to Charles S. Sperry, 11 April 1907. Sperry Papers. The General Board-Evans conflict eventually reached the press. See *Army & Navy Register* 42 (28 Sep. 1907): 6 and (5 Oct. 1907): 7.
80. Sims to Anne Hitchcock Sims, 14 March 1907. Sims Papers.
81. Sims to Anne Hitchcock Sims, 13 Sep. 1907. Sims Papers.
82. *Army & Navy Register* 41 (11 May 1907): 9.
83. See, for example, *New York Times,* 14 & 16 October 1907, and *Army & Navy Journal* 45 (19 Oct. 1907): 161.
84. Charles M. Thomas to Ruth S. Thomas, 20 Dec. 1907, quoting Henry Reuterdahl. Thomas Papers.
85. Henry Reuterdahl, "The Needs of Our Navy," *McClure's Magazine* 30, no. 1 (Jan. 1908): 251–263.
86. For a detailed treatment of the world cruise of the Great White Fleet, see James R. Reckner, *Teddy Roosevelt's Great White Fleet* (Annapolis: Naval Institute Press, 1988).
87. The best treatment of these hearings is contained in Morison, *Admiral Sims and the Modern American Navy,* 184–199. But see also, Reckner, *Teddy Roosevelt's Great White Fleet,* 61–75. A transcript of the Hearings was published; see, U.S. Senate, *Hearings Before the Committee on Naval Affairs, on Bill S.335* (Washington, D.C.: GPO, 1908).
88. *New York Times,* 15 Dec. 1907.
89. Charles M. Thomas to Ruth S. Thomas, 24 Dec. 1907. Thomas Papers.
90. Charles M. Thomas to Ruth S. Thomas, 25 Dec. 1907. Thomas Papers.
91. Charles S. Sperry to Edith M. Sperry, 14 Jan. 1908. Sperry Papers.
92. Charles M. Thomas to Ruth S. Thomas, 2 Feb. 1902. Thomas Papers. Ironically, while Thomas grappled with Evans's illness, in a skit performed by the "Larboard Watch" at the 23rd Gridiron banquet, joking reference was made to Evans's health: "What were Admiral Evans' orders?" "Those weren't orders. They were prescriptions." *Army & Navy Register* 43 (1 Feb. 1908): 16.
93. Charles M. Thomas to Ruth S. Thomas, 14 Jan. 1908. Thomas Papers.
94. Charles M. Thomas to Ruth S. Thomas, 13 Feb. 1908. Thomas Papers.
95. Charles M. Thomas to Ruth S. Thomas, 16 Feb. 1908. Thomas Papers.
96. Not surprisingly, Evans made no mention of his illness in his account of the cruise until he actually left the fleet for Paso Robles. For his account, see Robley D. Evans, "Admiral Evans' Own Story of the American Navy." I. "The Cruise of the Atlantic Fleet to the Pacific Coast." *Hampton's Magazine* 21, no. 4 (Oct. 1908): 403–419; II. "Hampton Roads to Trinidad." *Hampton's Magazine* 21, no. 5 (Nov. 1908): 577–90; III. "Taking the Fleet for a Fight or a Frolic: Trinidad to the Straits of Magellan." *Hampton's Magazine* 21, no. 6 (Dec. 1908): 719–729; and IV. "My Last Days with the Atlantic Fleet: Straits of Magellan to California." *Hampton's Magazine* 22, no. 1 (Jan. 1909): 33–40. See also, chapters 29 to 32 of Robley D. Evans, *An Admiral's Log: Being Continued Recollections of Naval Life.*
97. See, for examples, *New York Times,* 2 April–3 May 1908.
98. *New York Times,* 6 May 1908.

99. "The Big Battleships at San Francisco." *Current Literature* 44 (June 1908): 591–2.

100. Evans, *A Sailor's Log*, 405–406.

101. Captain (later Rear Admiral) Royal R. Ingersoll was the father of Admiral Royal E. Ingersoll of World War II note. The added strain of performing Evans's social duties likely contributed to Rear Admiral Thomas's death by heart attack on 3 July 1908 while dining at the Del Monte Hotel, Monterey, which building is now the Navy Postgraduate School's officers' club. "Rear Admiral Thomas Dead," *New York Times*, 4 July 1908. Thomas's daughter Emily had earlier married a future famous naval officer, Harry E. Yarnell. See *Army & Navy Register* 34 (19 Sep. 1903): 8.

102. *New York Times*, 10 May 1908.

103. "Answers to The Navy's Criticisms of Our Fleet." *The Navy* 1, no. 8 (Aug. 1907): 14. See also, "Admiral Evans on Naval Armor." *Literary Digest* 36 (4 Apr. 1908): 469.

104. Evans to SecNav Metcalf, no. 910, 17 March 1908, and Naval Constructor R. H. Robinson to Evans, 4 March 1908. Both NA, RG 80:19/25107-21:1. Robinson maintained a diary with technical and personal observations throughout the cruise. See Robinson Papers, New York Historical Society, New York City. See also, "Admiral Evans' Report on the Needs of Our Ships," *Scientific American* 98 (13 June 1908): 422–423.

105. Hill to Secretary Metcalf, 15 June 1907. NA, RG 80:19/24667.

106. For a detailed account of this conference, see James R. Reckner, *Teddy Roosevelt's Great White Fleet*, 126–137.

107. These articles include, "Dangers That Threaten Our Battleships in Action: Exaggeration of the Weaknesses of Turrets, Gun Ports, Powder Magazines, and Ammunition Hoists Refuted." *Hampton's Magazine* 22, no. 4 (April 1909): 485–492; "Handling Big Guns and High Explosives on Our Battleships." *Hampton's Magazine* 22, no. 3 (March 1909): 362–371; "Our Undermanned Navy—And Congress: Dearth of Battle Ship Officers Makes a New System of Promotion Imperative." *Hampton's Magazine* 22, no. 5 (May 1909): 651–659; and "Superiority of Our Navy: Answers to Various Critics." *Hampton's Magazine* 22, no. 1 (Jan. 1909): 41–48.

108. Sims to TR, 13 February 1909. Sims Papers.

109. TR to Secretary Truman H. Newberry, 16 February 1909. Sims Papers. In response, see Newberry to Sims, 18 February 1909, Sims Papers, and Sims to Newberry, 23 February 1909 (a 29 page typewritten summary of Sims's reports), Sims Papers.

110. TR to Newberry, 27 February 1909. Text also printed in New York *Sun*, 27 February 1909.

111. William S. Benson to Sims, 14 March 1909. Sims Papers.

112. Matthew C. Gleeson to Sims, 26 August 1913. Sims Papers.

113. Edwin A. Falk, *Fighting Bob Evans* (New York: Jonathan Cape, 1931). Foreword by Franklin D. Roosevelt, p. viii.

Tirpitz and the Origins of the German Torpedo Arm, 1877–1889

Patrick J. Kelly

⚓

There exists a vast literature on the Imperial German Navy in the era after 1897 when Tirpitz began the buildup which made the German fleet the world's second largest. Relatively much less has been written about Tirpitz's earlier career, which included the creation, virtually from scratch, of German torpedoes, the boats to fire them, and the strategy and tactics of their use. This article examines Tirpitz's leadership in this field, how what he learned then substantially served as a model for much of his later momentous work, and how, by 1889, the German Torpedo Arm had become a world leader.

When David Farragut commanded, "Damn the torpedoes, full speed ahead," the obstacle he dared to pass was an uncleared field of floating mines. After the Civil War, many navies began to experiment with ways to improve this weapon by making mines mobile. The first idea was to put one at the end of a spar and use it as an exploding ram; a second, the Harvey tow torpedo, put a floating charge on a tether attached to a boat, with the intention of turning away at the moment of attack and striking the target like a swinging fist. Both these methods required almost suicidal daring on the part of the hapless crews of improvised 10 knot torpedo boats. Nevertheless, by the early 1870s, Russia, France, England, Germany, Italy, Austria-Hungary, and even Norway were gingerly trying out variations of these weapons. The possibility, even if remote, of sinking expensive battleships with relatively cheap torpedoes was too tempting to resist, especially for the smaller navies.

Another, more promising, approach was the self-propelled "fish" torpedo. A retired Austrian naval officer developed a primitive mobile torpedo in 1860, but the Austrian Naval Ministry rejected it in 1864. An English engineer, Robert Whitehead, director of the Firma Stabilimento Tenico in Fiume, pursued the idea. In 1867 the Austrian government bought Whitehead's patent and began experiments with it under his direction in Fiume. By 1868, he had added a significant improvement, a depth-stabilization device which was meant to keep the torpedo from inconveniently sinking. In 1869 a delegation from the North German Navy visited Fiume. At first they were unimpressed, but in 1873 the Imperial German Navy joined the other navies which purchased torpedoes under license from the Austrian government and Whitehead.[1]

In 1872 a reorganization in the German Navy led to the appointment of the energetic General Albrecht von Stosch as its first Chief of Admiralty. He was given control over both the military and the administrative sides of the navy. The choice of a soldier rather than a sailor was a controversial one inside the navy, but Stosch, a successful commander in the Franco-Prussian War, was highly respected by the Emperor and the Crown Prince, who supported him in many of his later conflicts with Bismarck. With a few minor exceptions, the navy had not distinguished itself in the war.

Stosch set clear strategic goals, which included coastal defense and protection of German trade and citizens abroad. In 1873, he enlisted Reichstag support for a ten year program which proposed to expand substantially the armored force of the navy and which included an initial request for 28 small torpedo vessels. He made strenuous efforts to free the navy from dependence on foreign contractors and introduced army drilling methods into the navy, which did not endear him to some of the more complacent officers.[2]

Stosch set up, in 1873, a Torpedo Experiment Commission under *Korvetten-Kapitän* Alexander Graf von Monts, who ordered the first 100 torpedoes from Whitehead and, from an English yard, *Zieten*, a large 1170-ton torpedo vessel which was especially designed to test the Whitehead torpedo.[3] By 1876, when *Zieten* was completed, disappointing experiments with the spar and tow torpedoes persuaded the Admiralty to focus greater attention on the Whitehead torpedo.

On January 1, 1877, Stosch appointed a 27 year old *Kapitän-Leutnant*, a young man without powerful connections who had a good, but not spectacularly distinguished, service record, to be the officer in charge of detonators and warheads in the Torpedo Commission. There is no contemporary evidence to suggest that anyone regarded this as other than a routine placement. His name was Alfred Tirpitz.[4]

Tirpitz's first task was to accompany the officer then in charge of torpedo development, *Korvetten-Kapitän* Carl Heusner, to Fiume to learn about torpedo construction. Stosch had confidence in Tirpitz because in May 1877 he had already decided to entrust him in the following spring with command of *Zieten* and to lead further experiments on the Whitehead Torpedo. On September 18, Stosch witnessed Tirpitz, as torpedo officer of *Zieten*, score three direct hits with practice torpedoes at a stationary target 730m away.[5] Stosch still had his doubts and polled a group of officers, including Tirpitz, about the torpedo's feasibility. Tirpitz's written response impressed the gruff Stosch so much that he called it "exemplary."[6]

Although Tirpitz had less than a year's experience with torpedoes, this document anticipated, to a remarkable degree, both the future course of torpedo development and ideas which were to characterize his work when he moved to a much larger stage in 1897. Perhaps influenced by the frustrating experience of sitting impotently in Wilhelmshaven aboard the *König Wilhelm* during the war with France, he began by using words he would also use much later:

> It is characteristic of battle on the open sea that its sole goal is the annihilation of the enemy. Land battle offers other tactical possibilities, such as taking terrain, which do not exist in war at sea. Only annihilation can be accounted a success at sea.[7]

He then addressed the question of which ship types would be the best for this purpose. 1877 was a time when the use of steam had thrown into confusion time-honored tactical principles, and when, in the conflict between guns and armor, the latter was at least temporarily ascendant.[8] If a torpedo could be built which would strike under the waterline, the most powerful armored battleship might be annihilated. "Compared to the gun it is a very cheap means of destruction." Such a task would be almost impossible for spar or tow torpedoes and: "The Whitehead torpedo is . . . the first that promises military feasibilty."

There followed a sober discussion of the unripe character of the Whitehead torpedo. One problem was that torpedoes built for the Adriatic tended to sink in the Baltic because the specific gravity of the seawater there was different. Another was that single screw torpedoes were hard to keep on a straight course; but Tirpitz was confident that a well-designed double screw would solve the problem. Weak boilers greatly limited range and external parts tended to break under the stress of launching from a tube. Firing tests from a moving ship had just begun and were fraught with pitfalls. To deal with these technical complexities, he recommended the establishment of a group of specially trained torpedo mechanics and engineers.[9] He estimated that with a double screw torpedo the probability of hitting a 30m wide stationary target at 750m was about 90 percent. In the identification of these and other nettlesome problems, he set almost the whole agenda for the next 3 or 4 years of torpedo experiments.

On the question of a delivery system for the torpedo, he believed that, in the event of imminent war, *Zieten* could already pose a threat to enemy warships, but he shrewdly observed:

> If war were to come now there are too many unknown factors and I can only promise success if I assume that the mere existence of the torpedo would have a moral effect on the enemy and influence his manoeuvers.

He rejected, for the moment, a general introduction of the torpedo to the warships of the navy, but to try it on a few ships would have the advantage that "the whole front (i.e., sea officers) would come in contact with the new weapon." Another way would be to equip the steam powered auxiliary boats of the large ships with torpedo tubes.

Finally, he raised the concern which would dominate his work throughout the 1880s: Should Germany develop special ships with the torpedo as their principal weapon? He dismissed the idea of building more 1170 ton *Zietens* because they would be too large, expensive, and vulnerable to gunfire. Instead, such vessels should be as small, fast, and cheap as possible and be designed to operate in coastal waters.

This memorandum marked Tirpitz's public debut as a thinking man in a navy where rough-and-ready sea dogs were the norm. His ideas were clear, balanced, and logical. He criticized the helter-skelter methods other navies were using to introduce the weapon and advocated the calm, systematic, incremental and empirical approach which would become the hallmark of his entire career. Despite his junior rank and middle class origins, and Stosch's continued, though abating, skepticism about the torpedo, the young Tirpitz had made his initial mark. Now it remained for him to actually carry out his daunting mission.

Events in the Russo-Turkish War seemed to make his remarks somewhat prophetic. In December 1877 and January 1878, Russian boats fired Whitehead torpedoes at Turkish ships. On the first attempt, they malfunctioned, but on the second, a Turkish sentinel boat was sunk in the harbor of Batumi. This was the first combat success of a Whitehead torpedo, and it sparked a frenzy of torpedo boat building and experiments in virtually all the navies of Europe.[10]

In March and April 1878, Stosch sent Tirpitz on his own to Fiume to try to arrange with Whitehead the return of unsatisfactory torpedoes ordered the previous year. This was his first opportunity to negotiate independently with a contractor. To Stosch's joy, Tirpitz got Whitehead to take back half of them. He also investigated a new detonator and conducted experiments with various types of tubes.[11] Thereafter, during his work in the Torpedo Arm, Tirpitz would conduct ever more complex negotiations with a great variety of suppliers to the navy. Upon his return to Kiel in May, he became Director of Torpedo Development and assumed command of *Zieten*. Heusner went to Berlin to take overall command of the torpedo department at the Admiralty. In practice, this meant the young officer had autonomy in his work, though Stosch kept a watchful and supportive eye on him and took his side in bureaucratic conflicts with the Kiel Dockyard. As Tirpitz put it many years later: "Since I was 29 I have had the good fortune to be employed uninterruptedly in positions of independence."[12]

In his end-of-season report as commander of *Zieten*, Tirpitz noted that officers of several navies were achieving promising results, but that the torpedo was still in its initial stages. "The great expectation . . . which discovery brings with it is not realizable at the first stage of the process." But the idea will soon "come to life in a practical form." "The torpedo will only be critically significant to the conduct of war after a further development period whose duration will have to be measured in years."[13] Despite this cautious statement, Stosch was pleased enough to write:

> I am happy about the report of the commander of *Zieten* on the current status of the torpedo experiments. These experiments finally and for the first time are being carried out in systematic order according to objective principles. I want to express my appreciation to *Kapitän-Leutnant* Tirpitz for this.[14]

The first public firing of a loaded torpedo took place on June 26, 1879 in the Wiecker Bight, with the old paddle-wheel *aviso* (dispatch boat) *Preussischer Adler*, a survivor of the Federal Fleet of 1848, as the target. Its hull was coated with iron for the occasion. Tirpitz and Torpedo Engineer Voigt loaded two torpedoes, each with 20kg of explosives, into a steam pinnace. Tirpitz fired the first one, which hit the target from 200m and exploded, although it ran on the surface for most of the way. The observers, who included Rear Admiral Franz Kinderling, Chief of the Baltic Station, and a number of other senior officers, said the shot was a failure because the torpedo did not run at its designed depth of 3m. Tirpitz replied that this was done deliberately because he wanted to see if the detonator would explode on the surface. He then fired the second torpedo, which ran true at the right depth and blasted the target again. The senior officers sheepishly offered congratulations. Tirpitz was learning to meet the opposition head-on.[15] This success probably helped to restore Stosch to the good graces of the Crown Prince, who had felt Stosch partially responsible for the disastrous collision of two armored ships in the English Channel the year before. Tirpitz again won Stosch's gratitude.[16] As a result of these experiments, Stosch decided to put aboard all large warships steam pinnaces armed with torpedoes.[17] For the moment, Tirpitz deemphasized his idea of torpedo boats which would operate independently of the large ships.

The use of steam pinnaces was put to the test in the squadron maneuvers of July 26–27, 1880. The fleet, which consisted of five armored ships and an *aviso*, anchored for the night in Tromper Wiek and secured itself with nets, watch boats, and searchlights against an attack by torpedo-armed pinnaces. The attack came early in the morning of the 27th, and predictably failed because the squadron was on full alert and well protected.[18] Though the test seemed biased, it also suggested the difficulty of attacking a fleet at anchor near the shore. This raised again the possibility that fleets would have to be attacked at sea, which could only be done by boats larger and more seaworthy than the pinnaces.

The next day, the fleet inspection by the Crown Prince at Friedrichsort near Kiel, saw one of Tirpitz's greatest triumphs. Before the experiment, the Crown Prince visited *Zieten* and returned to the Imperial Yacht *Hohenzollern* to watch. *Zieten* withdrew for a distance, then came steaming at full speed (16kn) into the harbor. At 400m Tirpitz fired a single torpedo from an underwater tube. The *Barbarossa*, an old barracks ship, was hit amidships. A cloud of smoke, mingled with smashed bits of wood, erupted into the air. For a moment, the ship did not move. Then it sank slowly with a huge hole in its side.[19]

This test, the first public one to fire from an underwater tube, created great enthusiasm in the Admiralty for further development of torpedoes. It seemed to prove both that large ships could effectively fire torpedoes and that small, swift, relatively cheap boats bigger than the pinnaces might be feasible.[20] It was also an enormous display of confidence by Tirpitz that he was willing to risk failure before such a prestigious audience. On Stosch's behalf, Tirpitz's nominal superior at the Admiralty, Graf Schack von Wittenau, wrote:

> The Chief gave me the mission to write to you that the news made him very happy. To lead and carry out a military manoeuver with such skill and success as you have is excellent. He only regrets that, due to the circumstances of the day, he could not tell you this personally.[21]

In August 1880, the new protected corvette *Blücher* (3400 tons) was put into service to replace *Zieten* as the mother ship for torpedo experiments. Its guns and armor were removed to make way for a great number and variety of torpedo tubes. *Blücher* was to serve as the torpedo training ship for the majority of German sea officers for a generation.[22] The tender *Ulan* was added to Tirpitz's command to relieve *Blücher* of routine tasks.[23]

At the end of 1880, Kapitän-Leutnant Hunold von Ahlefeld and Leutnant zur See Georg Alexander Müller joined the Torpedo Commission. They were among the first and (later) most famous members of what soon became known as the "Torpedo Gang."[24] Tirpitz put them to work immediately on *Blücher* with a typically ambitious program for 1881. This included, among other things, practice with bow, stern, broadside, and underwater tubes, each of which had its own idiosyncrasies. Instinctively uncomfortable with a single supplier and consistent with Stosch's desire that Germany become self-sufficient in material, Tirpitz began to experiment with the first German-made torpedoes. These were made of bronze to inhibit rusting and offered the promise of being cheaper, faster, and of longer range than the Whitehead model.[25]

The policy of incremental change, painstaking work, and winters spent digesting the lessons of the previous year to prepare for the next, was beginning to bear fruit. This was demonstrated once again in Kiel harbor in spectacular fashion, this time with Kaiser

Wilhelm I present. At the annual fleet review and inspection on September 17, 1881, the Torpedo Commission took center stage. Orchestrated to the minute, *Ulan* and four steam pinnaces in flotilla formation swept close past the Imperial yacht and fired their torpedoes unerringly at an anchored target.[26] Then *Blücher*, under Tirpitz's command, at full speed, fired one of the new bronze torpedoes at 400m range. It blew up and sank the old barracks ship *Elbe*. Ten sheep had been placed aboard the target to test the force of the explosion. Two that were within ten meters of the blast had their legs broken.[27] In recognition of his outstanding service, Tirpitz was promoted to Korvetten-Kapitän on the spot, a very unusual honor.

Although work continued on the further development of the torpedo, and no one doubted by 1882 that they had a role to play in future wars, Tirpitz and the Admiralty began to focus more directly on an appropriate way to deliver them. With the consent of the Reichstag, which in general liked cheap torpedo boats and was more susceptible than he to the "torpedo craze" that was sweeping Europe, Stosch modified the naval building plan of 1873 to provide for 10 large and 12 small torpedo boats.[28] As a result, a number of steam pinnaces were laid down to carry on large warships and the firm Weser of Bremen was commissioned to build the seven boats of the Schütze class, four of which were completed by the summer of 1882. These were larger, at 56 tons, than the earlier spar torpedo boats and similar to the French Normand type. The crews were kept at only 13 men because of the persistent shortage of officers, which permitted only one per boat.[29] Tirpitz thought too many of these boats were built before enough experiments were performed to determine the right type. They had been ordered as a hasty response to a Russian war scare in 1882.[30]

On the night of September 10–11, 1882, came the first torpedo boat manoeuver against a fleet outside a harbor. It became known as "the Battle of Fehmarn Sound." Vice Admiral Carl Batsch, Chief of the Baltic Station, scripted the general scenario, which gave the torpedo boats the main role. The plan assumed that an "eastern power" declared war on Germany on September 10. On the same morning an enemy squadron of four armored frigates and an *aviso*, under *Kapitän zur See* Wilhelm von Wickede, left Danzig, perhaps to attack Kiel harbor.[31] The forces defending Kiel were *Blücher* and three small ships which served as *avisos*, plus a group of four Schütze class torpedo boats under *Kapitän-Leutnant* Paul Jaeschke.[32] The defending *avisos*, under Tirpitz's command, were to patrol Fehmarn Sound, a strait about 15km wide between the German island of Fehmarn (which was about 80km east of Kiel harbor) and the Danish island of Lolland. The attacking torpedoes boats were to conceal themselves close to shore at the Marian Light on Fehmarn Island. If the defending *avisos* spotted the enemy at night, they were to light a signal which would order the torpedo boats to attack them from behind. Wickede had considerable discretion about whether to pass the Sound by day or night, about what formation to use, and about whether to pass the Sound on the German side, the Danish side, or in the middle.[33] The defending forces also had several options, which depended on where and when the enemy tried to force the Sound.

Tirpitz left Kiel on September 10 upon the declaration of "war" and that night spread his *avisos* across the 15 km width of the Sound. *Blücher*, the fastest, he stationed as near to the Danish shore as possible without losing sight of *Ulan* (commanded by Leutnant zur See Hugo Pohl), the next ship in the picket line.[34] Pohl spotted the enemy at about the same time *Luise*, the other *aviso*, gave the signal.[35] Wickede's "attackers" were screened in front by an *aviso* and four torpedo boats. Upon receiving the signal, Jaeschke's four boats steamed out at full speed from Marian Light and took the squadron from the rear.[36]

In his post mortem, Stosch credited Tirpitz's screen with spotting the enemy quickly and criticized Wickede for hugging the German shore, precisely where he would be most vulnerable to torpedo attack. The referees awarded the torpedo boats with a hit on the rear of the frigate *Preussen*. Another boat claimed a hit on the *Kronprinz*, but this was adjudged dubious. The torpedo boats escaped unscathed, although their attempt to attack the squadron the next day near Kiel was not successful. Stosch, who previously on occasion had skeptically referred to the torpedo boats as *"Blitzboote,"* concluded that "the best defense of the harbor is to take the offensive, and the whole fleet should throw all its force against the enemy."[37] Even though he still saw the cannon as "the king of weapons," the "battle" was such a tremendous success for the torpedo that he dropped his final hesitancy about sea-going torpedo boats. It still remained to be tested whether *Schütze* type boats were the right kind, but after the fall manoeuvers, Tirpitz was able to convince Stosch to support more torpedo boat experiments and to put funds for 18 more boats in the next year's estimates. These manoeuvers also enhanced Tirpitz's reputation within the navy and weakened the opposition of some of the senior admirals to the new weapon.[38]

The navy's Stosch era ended with his resignation on March 20, 1883. He was worn out by his frequent conflicts with Bismarck.[39] Stosch had laid the groundwork for a plausible system of active coastal defense with fortified harbors, torpedo boats, and enough armored ships to form a "sortie fleet" to break a blockade by anyone but the British. When he left, Germany had the world's third largest navy, and perhaps (qualitatively, at least) the world's best torpedo force. Though many had resented the appointment of an army man in 1872, most of the naval officer corps, including Tirpitz, regretted his departure.

To the shock of the navy, Stosch was succeeded not by the capable Admiral Batsch, but by another general, Leo, Graf von Caprivi, whom the admirals saw as an enemy of the navy.[40] Caprivi's time as Chief of the Admiralty (1883–1888) was dominated by his obsession that "next fall" a two-front war would break out with France and Russia. Since large armored ships took a long time to construct, Caprivi built none, except for some coastal defense ships (the Siegfried class). By 1888 the German navy was only the world's sixth largest. On the other hand, Caprivi was an ardent torpedo boat enthusiast. These were cheap, could be built quickly, and were very popular in the Reichstag.[41]

Tirpitz had fought hard for six years to get Stosch to see the value of torpedo boats; now, ironically, with no effort at all, he got a superior more enthusiastic than he. Tirpitz, who had never considered torpedo boats a substitute for a battle fleet, spent the next six years trying to moderate Caprivi's fervor.[42] In 1883, the Schwarzkopf firm in Berlin began to mass-produce bronze torpedoes under a licensing agreement with Whitehead. Characteristic of his later dealings with contractors, Tirpitz opposed giving Schwartzkopf a monopoly:

> Because a share-holding company which has a monopoly easily pays too much attention to its annual dividends, and not enough to the development of the product; because of the tendency towards home-production that was growing in the larger foreign navies, no foreign money would have come to Germany as a compensation for us; and finally, because the most important experimental work on the water could not be done by the firm, but was our own prerogative.[43]

He therefore encouraged the development of the navy's Torpedo Depot at Friedrichsort near Kiel as a possible competitor to Schwarzkopf. The company even suggested he buy some of its shares, which quickly trebled because of its navy contracts. "Naturally, I did not buy any shares, and would have dismissed any official who acted otherwise."[44]

In the summer and fall of 1883, torpedo experiments continued and the *Schütze* class was completed. Wickede, again the Squadron Chief, grumbled that torpedo exercises were taking too much of the fleet's precious summer manoeuver time.[45] Perhaps partly in response, it was decided for the first time to keep *Blücher* in commission in Kiel over the winter to train more officers and men in the technical aspects of handling the balky torpedoes.[46] After some discussion, Tirpitz managed to gain the winter command (Tirpitz commanded *Blücher* in the summer) for a long-time member of the "Torpedo Gang," Kapitän-Leutnant Max von Fischel, instead of Paul Jaeschke.[47] Tirpitz spent the winter, as usual, shuttling between Kiel and Berlin, assessing the prior year's work and planning for the next. Almost certainly, he helped Caprivi prepare his proposals for the naval estimates in the Reichstag.

Caprivi was not alone in his "torpedo intoxication." From the mid-1870s to the late 1880s and beyond, the French *Jeune École*, led by Admiral Théophile Aube, struggled to redefine naval strategy, with the torpedo boat as a centerpiece.[48] Aube confronted the awkward question of how to defeat the British at sea when their economic resources and historical commitment to traditional forms of sea power were substantially greater than France's. Aube thought the solution lay in technological change. The "mastadons" of British [and Italian] battleships could be defeated by the "microbes" of French torpedo boats. A sustained blockade of the French coast could be rendered impossible by night attacks on the blockaders with swift, small, and cheap torpedo boats. One well-aimed shot could sink a vastly more expensive battleship. Once the blockade was broken, swift commerce raiders would strike ruthlessly at Britain's achilles heel, its trade-based national wealth and its dependence on foreign sources for food. Even modest success in commerce warfare would cause maritime insurance rates to skyrocket and paralyze trade. France could thus hope to win a *guerre industrielle*. In 1884–85 such ideas were seductive, even compelling. Younger officers in France were attracted to torpedo and cruiser warfare because they offered opportunities for initiative and independent command, which previously had been monopolized by a hidebound, aristocratic officer corps.[49] At that time, Aube's disastrous term as Minister of Marine (January 1886 to May 1887) lay in the future. The gross inadequacies of French torpedo boats were not yet apparent.[50] The French also greatly underestimated the amount of political will and stability needed to carry out a coherent naval program.

Caprivi sought to gain a consensus within the navy for a fleet based solely on coastal defense and torpedo boats. In 1883, he cancelled Stosch's program. In January 1884, he convened a meeting of senior admirals (Blanc, Knorr, Wickede, and Monts) to suggest Germany might entirely abandon building armored ships in favor of torpedo vessels. The admirals argued vainly for the replacement of existing armored ships, at least.[51] In March 1884, Caprivi submitted his program to the Reichstag. In the accompanying memorandum, he admitted that the fleet ultimately could not do without some armored ships; but because of uncertainty about the type of battleship which could survive torpedo attack, "a navy like ours cannot afford the luxury of failed experiments." The navy would have to await the experience of other countries' experiments before committing Germany's resources to a particular type. Meanwhile, since war with France and Russia could come at any time, the navy would have to rely on existing forces and additional torpedo boats, which could be built quickly. To Caprivi's surprise, the Reichstag accepted, almost without discussion, his whole program for 150 torpedo boats over a period of years.[52]

To Tirpitz fell the task of deciding which kind of torpedo boat to build.[53] Consistent with his later views, he feared building a huge number of boats simultaneously because, if he made an incorrect choice, Germany would wind up with a fleet of quickly obsolescent vessels. Partly as a result of the tests described below, in 1886, the prospective number of boats was cut from 150 to 70.

There was substantial disagreement even about how large the new boats should be. Germany had shallow river mouths and shoaled coasts. Some officers wanted a greater number of boats with a draft small enough to operate easily in such waters. Others favored fewer vessels of a larger type, which could operate alongside the armored squadron in the North Sea and the Baltic and participate in a fleet action. The upper limit in size would be determined by cost and by the chronic officer shortage, which only permitted one officer per boat. Tirpitz favored the larger type because he wanted them to sail with the fleet; but he saw the need for extensive experiments before the skeptics could be convinced. In the spring of 1884, the Admiralty awarded contracts to the English firms Thorneycroft and Yarrow, and to the German firms Weser, Vulkan, and Schichau to build sample boats of varying designs.[54] By September 1884, the Thorneycroft, Vulkan, Weser, and two Schichau boats had completed their trials and were ready for rigorous high seas testing.

The five boats and *Blücher*, with Tirpitz in command, sailed from Kiel to Cuxhaven in good weather.[55] The Weser boat had difficulties even on the westward journey and had to drop off at Christiansand in Norway. As the four other boats and *Blücher* arrived at the mouth of the Elbe, the two S (Schichau) boats collided. One, commanded by *Leutnant zur See* August von Heeringen,[56] had its rudder bent. The other sprang a leak. A potential disaster seemed to be looming for the test. Since it was not possible to repair them in Cuxhaven, Tirpitz tried to use materials aboard *Blücher* to make good the damage. As the repairs were under way, a report came that bad weather was coming. A more faint-hearted (or less ambitious) officer might have been deterred; Tirpitz saw the storm as the opportunity he had been awaiting to test the boats in rough weather. On September 27, *Blücher* and the four remaining boats (Heeringen's and the other S boat; Pohl, aboard the Thorneycroft; and Paschen aboard the Vulkan) set off for Kiel. That night a storm came up from the SSW. The first day went well, but the storm got worse, and at night Heeringen signalled *Blücher* that the mechanical controls of his damaged rudder were failing. Instead of turning back, Tirpitz boarded Heeringen's boat in the darkness and heavy weather, and tried to jury-rig a manual rudder. Soon after, *Blücher*, now under Ahlefeld's command, lost sight of Tirpitz's boat in the darkness and dangerous seas. Since the other S boat was leaking due to collision damage, and Vulkan and Thorneycroft were in trouble in the force 8–9 winds, Ahlefeld was compelled, with a heavy and fearful heart, to seek shelter in Christiansand harbor.

From there, he sent a worried telegram to the Admiralty that Tirpitz's boat had become separated during the storm. Ominously, nothing was heard from it. The next day Ahlefeld began anxiously to search along the Danish coast. At last, early in the morning of the 29th, a telegram arrived in Kiel from Frederikshavn, a Danish port on the east side of Jutland, that Tirpitz had arrived safely there with a damaged rudder. He and Heeringen looked so battered and filthy that at first they were refused hotel accommodations there. When he heard the news, Ahlefeld was so relieved that he looked in a mirror to see whether his hair had turned gray.

In the storm, the Vulkan boat had proven itself only marginally seaworthy, with insufficient range. The Thorneycroft was technically very good, but not seaworthy enough. The S boat, though far from perfect, had demonstrated the sea-keeping qualities to survive a very bad storm. Also, it had good range and economical engines. One could argue that Tirpitz, who had favored the S boats from the beginning, had loaded the dice in their favor by his brave and ruthless behavior during the storm. Nevertheless, "storm night" became a legend in the navy, and Tirpitz used it successfully to press his point that torpedo boats could and should be able to sail with the fleet in the North Sea and the Baltic.

On December 6, 1884, Caprivi issued contracts for 22 S boats.[57] Within a few years Schichau gained a monopoly which lasted well into the 1890s.[58] This created problems for Tirpitz which foreshadowed his later conflicts with Krupp, who would have a monopoly of armor and heavy guns once the great fleet buildup began after 1898.[59] Nevertheless, torpedo boat construction was simple and cheap enough for there to be a plausible threat to use other contractors, so Schichau could be kept in line.

In 1884, Caprivi gave Tirpitz another particularly welcomed mission to develop torpedo boat tactics further and to begin preliminary study of fleet tactics, which had been seriously neglected in the German navy as in most others.[60] This too was consistent with Caprivi's belief that war was imminent.

Tirpitz began with the formation of the navy's first experimental torpedo boat division [6 units]. Caprivi hectored Monts, the Commander of the Exercise Fleet for 1884:

> The training of crews for battle and the thoughts of the whole squadron should be directed towards war. . . . This is to be the opposite of "parade training." The time for exercises is short and should be used to the utmost for battle training.

He also ordered a reduction in Stosch-style military drills and urged practicing night attacks, and even boarding exercises![61] The summer and fall of 1884 saw the first systematic development of individual and group torpedo boat tactics, including signaling and gunnery.[62] Tirpitz spent the whole winter digesting these lessons and preparing for the next year's exercises.[63] He also went on his honeymoon.[64]

While Tirpitz was away, until the end of January, after convoluted intrigues within the Admiralty, Graf Schack finally retired. Tirpitz replaced him as head of the Torpedo Department of the Admiralty.[65] Although Caprivi's confidence in him had always given him direct access to the top, an intermediary, even a token one like Schack, sometimes created bureaucratic problems. The reshuffling, though it increased Tirpitz's power, left some important administrative problems unresolved. The Imperial Dockyards were sometimes uncooperative; and the power to have the final word on torpedo boat design still had to be shared with the Admiralty's Construction Department and with the private contractors.[66]

Tirpitz tried hard to preserve secrecy about many aspects of torpedo work. In the fall of 1884, his old comrade, Korvetten-Kapitän Iwan F. J. Oldekop, wrote to him to get more information about German torpedo development, so he could keep a knowledgeable eye on comparable British work.[67] Tirpitz took almost six months to reply in a way which gives a rare insight into the interaction of his personal and service life:

> You must once give wing to your fantasy and put yourself in the position of a young husband on his honeymoon. Then you will forgive me that I did not answer your friendly letter of last October. When I returned here, I found such a flood of business that I hardly knew what to do. But I will try to make up for it now.

He admitted frankly to Oldekop that the new *Germania* and British built Yarrow boats were failures, but that the Thorneycrofts were better than the S boats in some respects. He still believed that the efficient engines and bad-weather endurance of the S boats should tip the scales in favor of the latter.[68] An observer might also speculate that their German origins did not hurt either.

By then it was also becoming clear that a divisional structure required the leader's boat to be larger than the others to accommodate administrative, seamanly, and command tasks.[69] The first thought was to use "mother ships," such as *Blücher*, *Zieten*, or some of the newer *avisos*, to lead the divisions.[70] The drawback of this approach was that the leader would then not be present at the crucial moment in battle when the division actually attacked.

By 1885, there were two divisions organized into a flotilla, which undertook an ambitious program of exercises for the summer.[71] Tirpitz led the flotilla on intensive individual and group manoeuvers. They focused alternately on picket duty with the armored squadron, while another group would stalk the big ships by day and try to attack them by night.

In December, Tirpitz reported the results of the year's work.[72] He argued that the torpedo boats should always operate in divisions, not individually or attached to particular large ships. "Almost without exception, individual deployment miscarried." Boats steaming in divisions were the best way to provide reconnaissance for the fleet and to attack an enemy formation. He felt that as long as Germany had mobile torpedo boat divisions it would not be possible for an enemy fleet to maintain itself in German waters. He admitted this could change over time: "measures beget countermeasures." Substantial command and control, as well as range problems for boats operating with the fleet, remained to be investigated. He admitted frankly that there was no war experience with torpedo boats, and no one could say with any certainty what would happen in a real battle; but he concluded that by testing realistic torpedo exercises, Germany had gained about a one year lead on other navies. Nevertheless, senior fleet officers had to pay more attention to the risks, opportunities, and potential of the torpedo arm. That winter, Tirpitz lobbied vigorously with Caprivi to solve his administrative problems by the establishment of a Torpedo Inspectorate, which would be responsible only to the Admiralty:

> The existence [of the Torpedo Inspectorate] will have a desireable effect on the dockyards. . . . It would not mean complete autonomy of fabrication, but we will achieve complete independence from the private firms, which seems to me absolutely essential for our torpedo development. . . . I believe now is the right moment to move in this direction and this is only possible by a decisive break with the old dockyard organization. Things are very bad in the dock-yards.[73]

On April 1, 1886 Caprivi set up the Torpedo Inspectorate, which gathered all aspects of torpedo development under one office. It included procurement, control of construction, training, weapons, manpower, and maintenance. In cooperation with the North Sea and Baltic Stations, two special torpedo detachments supplied men both to the torpedo boat divisions and for torpedo service on all the ships of the fleet armed with them.[74] This clarification freed Tirpitz from most of the administrative problems and competence conflicts with other organizations.

By 1885, the type question for torpedo boats was largely resolved for the duration of Tirpitz's service as Inspector. Between 1885 and 1889, another 35 S boats were built in addition to the six from 1884.[75] The non-Schichau boats were gradually put in reserve or used for training. The S boats ranged between 98 and 113 tons with a top speed of about 20 knots and three torpedo tubes, two on deck and one in the bow, above water, since underwater tubes had not proven feasible. They had sufficient range to cruise with the armored ships, though coal consumption went up enormously at high speed. Always mindful that "measures beget countermeasures," Tirpitz experimented [S 32 in 1886] with armor because quick-firing light artillery on armored ships was gradually improving. The six tons of armor slowed the boat too much, but this failure led to a rearrangement of the coal bunkers, which provided a degree of protection.

Another experiment was successful, but had a perverse outcome. In 1887, Schichau delivered the first two boats which, unlike tenders, could lead the torpedo boat divisions into battle.[76] These were 300 tons, with 7 officers and 39 men, and an armament, besides three torpedo tubes of six 3.7 cm guns. The division leader, relieved of the task of ship command, could devote his full attention to the division of six to eight boats. The additional guns were designed to attack or defend against enemy torpedo boats. Without fully realizing it, Tirpitz had built the world's first torpedo boat destroyers. Ironically, his great adversary of later years, Sir John Fisher, in 1892, designed superior 27 knot boats for the same purpose. Thereafter, through the war, Britain retained superiority in this ship type.

By 1886, with a large number of homogeneous boats organized into divisions, more sophisticated work began with formation steaming, signalling, and coordinated attacks. In contrast, the armored squadron lacked any but the simplest notions of tactics.[77] The rules of 1876 were still in effect. The only battle signals permitted were "open fire" and "attack the enemy." There was a vague idea of closing with the enemy to bring about a melee, wherein captains should "act according to circumstance." The sinking in a collision of the armored ship *Grosser Kurfürst* in 1878 had left squadron commanders paralyzed with fear. As the growing skill of torpedo boat commanders permitted ever more daring manoeuvers, captains of large ships looked on in amazement mingled with horror. Caprivi hoped the example of the torpedo boat flotilla would inspire the others, but he was disappointed. During the 1886 manoeuvers, Wickede, the squadron commander, complained to Caprivi that Tirpitz had too much independence in directing the flotilla. Caprivi replied icily: "My dear excellency, there is only one indispensable man in the navy, and that is Tirpitz."[78]

Caprivi's pressure and the example of the handy torpedo boats began slowly to attract favorable attention among some older navy men. Rear Admiral Carl Paschen, squadron chief in 1887, noted that the torpedo boat portion was the most interesting part of the exercises, and suggested senior officers study it for possible application to handling the larger ships.[79]

In 1887, Caprivi's confidence in the torpedo boats was such that he assigned them a lead role in an offensive war plan. It provided for a coup de main by the torpedo boats and the armored squadron against the French Northern Fleet in Cherbourg before it could be reinforced from the Mediterannean. The plan had many questionable assumptions, including the indispensable benevolent neutrality of Britain, since the Germans would need to refuel in the Channel.[80] Nevertheless, it was the first coherent war plan which took note of the growing capabilities of the torpedo force.

To continue to improve tactics, in January 1888, Caprivi sent a questionnaire to a number of senior officers. A hypothetical German fleet of 12 armored ships and 3 torpedo boat divisions would face an enemy of about the same strength, approaching in line abreast formation. Some officers did not take it seriously. Knorr, who was abroad at the time, later wrote: "I was happy that this . . . mostly purposeless exercise passed me by."[81] Caprivi wanted to know what formation the German fleet should adopt and how it should attack. Most officers answered in a literal and uninspired fashion.[82] Tirpitz seized the moment to write a 200 page response which answered the questions directly, but added lengthy elaborations which addressed a variety of contingencies and gave him license to discuss some lessons of his torpedo work.[83] Though his answer was by far the most comprehensive, the advice given would not pass muster by later standards. For example, he advocated steering towards the enemy in line ahead formation, which would leave the German fleet vulnerable to having its T capped.

More important than the response was the cover letter.⁸⁴ A "clarifying consensus" about tactical questions in the officer corps was necessary, the only way "working together among ships" was possible:

> I personally believe, although it is not a conclusive belief, that such a consensus is achievable in peacetime and that this possibility would substantially improve our chances in case of war because the qualities necessary to do this—system, perseverance and a military vision—can be found in a not insignificant degree in our national character. . . . We should spread out the systematic and programmatic work over several years.⁸⁵

He proposed that critical questions be addressed empirically and one at a time in the squadron exercises. Each answer would lead to other questions to be answered in turn. Three or four years, he estimated, would be necessary to reach substantial results. This is exactly the process Tirpitz put into practice in 1892, when he became Chief of Staff of the High Command and put fleet tactics on a firm footing. Since this is the same method he used to develop the torpedo arm, it is easy to see here its influence on his later work.

On June 15, 1888, Prince Wilhelm ascended the throne upon the successive deaths of his grandfather and father. Also a grandson of Queen Victoria, the young man had shown a lively interest in naval matters from an early age. The torpedo arm had not escaped his attention. In 1884, he had witnessed a torpedo shooting exercise aboard *Blücher*.⁸⁶ In 1886, he visited the first Schichau division boat.⁸⁷ Along with his brother, *Korvetten-Kapitän* Prince Heinrich, commander of a division of torpedo boats, he sailed to England for his grandmother's jubilee in June 1887 aboard the new *aviso*, *Blitz*, with Tirpitz in command. To the amazement of British torpedo experts, the flotilla accompanied *Blitz* across the North Sea. The boats made a striking impression with their range and seaworthiness. This occasion marked the true international debut of the German torpedo arm. It was also the first chance for Tirpitz to have sustained personal contact with the future emperor.⁸⁸

Wilhelm II had every intention of leading the navy personally. Caprivi understood this and resigned three weeks after the succession because he did not share Wilhelm's well known passion for a large navy. He also knew a dismantling of the Admiralty was coming.⁸⁹ Monts was named as his replacement. He, and some other senior officers such as Knorr, had long resented the independence of

Tirpitz and the young officers in the torpedo arm. When Monts, at the fall manoeuvers, dismissed the torpedo flotilla as "parade ships," Tirpitz asked to be relieved and given a sea command.[90] He was ordered to stay on until March 25, 1889, when the planned reorganization of the navy would be complete. Wilhelm II wanted to devolve the Admiralty into three organizations: an Oberkommando to assume the command function; a Reichsmarineamt to handle administration and to deal with the Reichstag; and a Naval Cabinet for personnel matters.

Tirpitz had quickly realized such a measure would likewise split the Torpedo Inspectorate into its command and administrative parts. Throughout the winter of 1888–89, Tirpitz made desperate but unavailing efforts to save the Inspectorate as it had been.[91] His promotion, on schedule, to *Kapitän zur See* on November 24, 1888, was small consolation for what he feared was the destruction of his twelve years of strenuous and determined effort, despite a superb qualification report: "he has served with extraordinary distinction. He inspired his subordinates with enthusiasm for their work and shows a particular zest for the initiative."[92] Tirpitz, fearful that all his work had been for naught, took command of the armored ship *Preussen*, which, ironically, his torpedo boats had "sunk" at the "Battle of Fehmarn Sound."

Were German torpedo boats the Best in the World in 1889? The leading authorities on the German navy agree that the German torpedo arm was the best at that time.[93] Perhaps even more significantly, Theodore Ropp, the historian of the French Navy, believes the same.[94] Ropp states that the 58 ton torpedo boats built by Admiral Aube in the late 1880s were a "complete failure." Arthur J. Marder, the great historian of the Royal Navy, does not address the point directly, but notes that on a cruise in the Channel in 1887, within a space of three weeks, 19 of 23 British torpedo boats had serious mechanical problems. In sheer numbers, Britain, France, and Russia had as many or more; but Germany seems to have gained an advantage in usable high seas torpedo boats. Due to Tirpitz's unstinting efforts, Germany also had a qualitative edge.[95] As noted in the text above, after 1892, Britain surged into the lead in usable destroyers, a type superior to the German torpedo boat, and never relinquished it. It remains to be established why Tirpitz, in complete control of German ship design after 1897, did not build ships as good as British destroyers.[96]

In 1918, Tirpitz wrote:

> I spent the best eleven years of my life in the torpedo section among "our black comrades, of the wild and daring chase." We were bound to our imcomparable crews by ardour and mutual comradeship in storm and danger. We officers of the torpedo section constituted a corps within a corps, the united spirit of which was everywhere recognized, but also envied and opposed.[97]

In 1937, Admiral Adolf von Trotha, a close collaborator of Tirpitz after 1906, but too young to have been in the Torpedo Gang, wrote of Tirpitz's method of managing men:

> From the first day an officer would be appointed, Tirpitz would make great demands. This soon showed if a man was up to the job. If his ideas and work methods were satisfactory, Tirpitz soon opened to him his innermost thoughts. But if there was no meeting of the minds or—the worst case—he proved to be a person who remained stuck on trivialities or administrative questions, Tirpitz would set him aside and find another way.[98]

It is widely known that during the torpedo years Tirpitz developed a cadre of younger officers, many of whom in later years became important and influential in the navy; but, except for a few obvious examples like Heeringen, Müller, Pohl, and Braun, no one has identified who they were. Here is not the place to attempt a collective biography of the Torpedo Gang. Rather, it is a first, tentative listing of those this author has identified who, because they served in the torpedo arm when Tirpitz led it and later served under him in other assignments, might be considered a part of the Torpedo Gang. Much further work would be necessary to compile anything like a definitive list.

The list of 24 includes no less than ten men who served under Tirpitz at the OKM, all the commanders of the High Seas Fleet from 1913 to 1918 (Ingenohl, Pohl, and Scheer), and five of the six Chiefs of the Admiral Staff between 1902 and 1915 (Büchsel, Fischel, Heeringen, Pohl, and Bachmann). During the war, of course, Tirpitz had bad relations with Müller, Pohl, and Ingenohl. Büchsel, who generally had good relations with Tirpitz except for a brief period after 1908, was only marginally a torpedo man. Fischel, who was very close to Tirpitz in his torpedo days, battled Tirpitz for institutional reasons when he was Chief of the Admiral Staff. Only

Heeringen[99] and Bachmann remained close to Tirpitz during their terms as Chiefs of the Admiral Staff.

The inclusion of some on the list may be the result of simple coincidence of assignment. Nevertheless, pending further research, it is plausible to include in the Torpedo Gang Ahlefeld, Bachmann, Fischel, Ingenohl, Jaeschke, Truppel, Winkler, and Zeye, along with Braun, Heeringen, Müller, and Pohl, as mentioned above.[100] Taken together, during the prewar years, they constituted a talented and formidable "mafia."

In conclusion, a detailed study of the torpedo years affirms the judgment of Volker Berghahn, whose book on Tirpitz's later work is still the single most important:

> Tirpitz was from the beginning an unusual sea officer. In the breadth of his interest for technical, political, and "philosophical" problems, and in his piercing and cool intellect he seems to have far surpassed his comrades. . . . Not the least of his many noteworthy characteristics was his unsurpassed sense for the systematic, and the tenacity with which he pursued his goal, once he recognized it.[101]

The development of the Whitehead torpedo, a viable type of torpedo boat, and the strategy and tactics that went with them demonstrated the combination of vision, painstaking empiricism, and ruthless energy characteristic of his later work.

As he was to do with Wilhelm II, Tirpitz courted, manipulated, and, when necessary, discreetly stood up to Stosch and Caprivi, his principal superiors. He persuaded an often reluctant Stosch of the value of the torpedo and pushed him towards the beginnings of a "blue water" strategy. He retained a genuine, though not uncritical, respect and affection for Stosch even after the latter's death.[102]

Tirpitz took Caprivi's obsession with coastal defense, demonstrated the lack of viability of small torpedo boats, and steered Caprivi ever so subtly towards more of a high seas orientation. As Batsch, his mentor in cadet days [and no torpedo enthusiast], noted in 1891, "It was an unfortunate accident that your splendid programmatic talent should be joined together with Caprivi's ambition."[103] In writing this, Batsch inadvertently identified the one point at which the two men's interests coincided. In contrast to Caprivi, Tirpitz never lost sight of the idea that Germany needed a battle fleet. At the same time he stayed on friendly personal terms with Caprivi even after he left the Admiralty in 1888.[104] Tirpitz, until the war, was very skillful in the management of his superiors. In 1891, Caprivi, by then Imperial Chancellor, told Tirpitz that Wilhelm II saw in him the future of the navy.[105]

After 1892, and particularly after 1897 when he became State Secretary of the RMA, Tirpitz demonstrated a ferocious *Ressorteifer*.[106] With Wilhelm II's gullible assistance, he abolished the OKM and balkanized the navy. Eight or more officers reported directly to the Emperor, a choatic situation not conducive to orderly procedure. Until the war, when matters slipped beyond Tirpitz's control, he made certain the Admiral Staff was weak and without much influence. With no Chief of Admiralty or Commanding Admiral [Head of OKM] to contend with, he was able, until 1914, to be the Emperor's most important naval adviser by far.

It is worth contemplating to what degree this tendency was present during the torpedo years. In his Tirpitz biography, Michael Salewski argues that "as Torpedo Inspector at least, Tirpitz was no Ressortegoist."[107] He correctly points out that, for all Tirpitz's enthusiasm for the torpedo arm, he never lost sight of the ultimate goal of a battle fleet. Tirpitz had little respect for uncritical torpedo enthusiasts like the French Admiral Aube. He recognized during the torpedo years, though perhaps not later, that torpedoes and torpedo boats, like cut flowers, had a short usable lifespan and needed to be improved continuously in the light of rapid technological advance: "measures beget countermeasures."

Nevertheless, even in the torpedo years, *Ressorteifer*, at least in ovo, was present, though in nothing like the magnitude of the post-1897 period. The creation of the Torpedo Inspectorate in 1886 gave him a virtually self-contained sphere, which embraced all peacetime aspects of the torpedo arm and freed him from vexatious outside interference. This was a kind of small-scale model of the later all-embracing Navy Laws, whereby he fended off meddling from other elements of the navy and played the Emperor and the Reichstag off against each other in bravura fashion. In 1888, the resignation of his patron, Caprivi, left his carefully constructed organization in disarray. Despite his brilliant successes and growing reputation, the torpedo arm was too small a base, and his seniority in a tradition-riddled navy did not provide him the power to preserve his work. Things would be different after his great triumph of 1898, when the Navy Law made him indispensible to an Emperor hungry for the prestige of a world-class navy. Only then did he have the institutional base and seniority to carry his cherished battle fleet idea close to completion.

A Note on the Sources:
I am grateful to Drs. Fleischer and Granier, and Herr Moritz of the *Bundesarchiv-Militärarchiv* [BA-MA], in Freiburg, and to the staff of the *Niedersächsiches Staatsarchiv* [NS SA], in Bückeburg, for their friendly assistance in the fall of 1990. Dr. Wilhelm Deist of the *Militärgeschichtliches Forschungsamt* in Freiburg kindly gave me access to its library, plus a memorable evening of hospitality on the day of German unification. Rolf Hobson [Trondheim] and Matthew Kelly read the manuscript and provided some valuable suggestions. Dr. Raffael Scheck [Bowdoin] pointed out some useful materials. All translations and, of course, all errors are my own.

In the notes below, all documents are from the BA-MA Freiburg, except for a few from the NS SA, which are duly designated. Documents preceded by RM are from the official Admiralty files. Documents preceded by N are from the private papers [*Nachlass*] of the individuals named in the note. N 253 indicates the document is from the Tirpitz *Nachlass*.

Approximate rank equivalents to the U.S. Navy for the 1880's: [the system was somewhat different later]: *Leutnant zur See*=Lieutenant; *Kapitän-Leutnant*=Lieutenant Commander; *Korvettenkapitän*=Commander; *Kapitän zur See*=Captain.

1. On the early history of the torpedo see, e.g., Albert Röhr, "Vorgeschichte und Chronik des Torpedowesens der deutschen Marine bis zum Ende des 19 Jahrhunderts," Schiff und Zeit 7, pp. 47 f; Hans Hildebrand, Albert Röhr, and Hans-Otto Steinmetz, *Die deutschen Kriegschiffe*. 7 vols., Herford, Koehler, 1979–83, VII, pp. 81–85; Elmer Potter, Chester Nimitz, and Jürgen Rohwer, eds. *Seemacht* (German edition). München, Bernard und Graefe, 1974, pp. 241 ff; Hans Hallmann, *Der Weg zum deutschen Schlachtflottenbau*. Stuttgart, Kohlhammer, 1938, p. 22; and Theodore Ropp, *The Development of a Modern Navy: French Naval Policy 1871–1904*, Annapolis, US Naval Institute, 1987, pp. 110 ff.

2. On Stosch's appointment and work at the Admiralty, see Wolfgang Petter, "Deutsche Flottenrüstung von Wallenstein bis Tirpitz." pp. 13–262, in *Handbuch zur Deutschen Militärgeschichte*, Manfred Messerschmidt [ed.], München, VIII Deutsche Marinegeschichte der Neuzeit, 1977, pp. 101–28; and Frederic Hollyday, *Bismarck's Rival: A Political Biography of General and Admiral Albrecht von Stosch*. Durham, Duke UP, 1960, chs IV–VI.

3. Röhr, p. 49; Hildebrand, VI, 71.

4. Biographical information on Tirpitz's years in the torpedo arm has hitherto been based almost solely on two sources, his memoirs, Alfred von Tirpitz, *Memoirs*, 2 vols., reprint of 1919 ed., New York, AMS Press, 1970, pp. 46 ff; and Ulrich von Hassell, *Tirpitz*, Stuttgart, Belsersche Verlag, 1920, pp. 94 ff. Biographies of Tirpitz with some substantial, though largely derivative, treatment of those years include: Michael Salewski, *Tirpitz. Aufstieg - Macht - Scheitern*, Göttingen, Musterschmidt, 1979, pp. 17 ff; Baldur Kaulisch, *Alfred von Tirpitz und die imperialistische deutsche Flottenrüstung. Eine politische Biographie*, Berlin (East), Militärverlag der DDR, 1982,

pp. 27 ff, which is surprisingly good, if one ignores its gratuitous ideological overlay; and Hallmann, pp. 22 ff, 103 ff.

5. N 253 14, 3. Stosch to Tirpitz, May 16 1877; Hildebrand, VI, 71.

6. Hassell, pp. 94 ff; N 253 330, 1–10. Tirpitz to Stosch, October 12, 1877: "Opinions about the Fish Torpedo and about the present status of the Torpedo Question." All quotations below are from this document.

7. Here is not the place to debate Tirpitz's views as a strategic theorist. Rolf Hobson [Trondheim] is completing a very interesting dissertation which is a comprehensive reexamination of Tirpitz as strategist.

8. See, e.g., Potter, ch 16.

9. This was done in 1879. See RM 1 2839, Cabinet Order of July 8, 1879; Röhr, p. 50; See also the personal recollections of Torpedo Engineer Voigt in RM 8 76, 128 ff.

10. Potter, pp. 243 ff.

11. For the correspondence on this trip, see N 255 2 [Diedrichs Nachlass], Tirpitz to Diedrichs, February 12, 1878; N 253 14, 6–31. There is currently a controversy on Tirpitz's later relationships with contractors. See Michael Epkenhans, *Die Wilhelminische Flottenrüstung, 1908–1914: Weltmachtstreben, industrieller Fortschritt, soziale Integration*, München, Oldenbourg, 1991; and Gary Weir, *Building the Kaiser's Navy: The Imperial German Naval Office in the von Tirpitz Era 1890–1918*, Annapolis, MD, Naval Institute Press, 1992.

12. Tirpitz, I, 46.

13. N 253 14, 32–35. Tirpitz to Baltic Command [Rear Admiral Kinderling], November 8, 1878.

14. RM 31 453. Stosch to Baltic Command [Admiral Kinderling], July 29, 1878; See also Stosch's letter of commendation to Tirpitz, May 1, 1879, N 253 10, 43.

15. On this episode, see Hildebrand, V, 57 ff and VI, 71. There is a fascinating eye-witness account of this by Torpedo Engineer Voigt in RM 8 76, 121 f, on which this narration is based. Hildebrand implies that *Zieten* fired these shots, but Voigt's evidence and other indirect evidence from 1880 convince this author that the shots were fired from the pinnace.

16. Hallmann, p. 18. See also N 253 40, 14f, Graf Schack to Tirpitz, November 12, 1879 and Carl-Axel Gemzell, *Organization, Conflict, and Innovation: A Study of German Naval Strategic Planning 1888–1940*. Lund, 1973, p. 58.

17. Röhr, p. 50; Hallmann, p. 23.

18. See RM 1 24 for a description of the attack and the referees' comments. See also A. Tesdorpf, *Geschichte der kaiserliche deutschen Kriegsmarine*, Kiel, Lipsius, 1889, pp. 212 ff. For a similar attack tried the following year, see Credner's report of an attack on August 9, 1882, RM 1 327, 262 f.

19. Testorpf, p. 214; Hildebrand, I, 123, and VI, 71; for Voigt's account, see RM 8 76, 123; Hallmann, pp. 22, 103.

20. The first two large ships to be armed with torpedoes were the corvettes *Prinz Adalbert* and *Ariadne* in 1881, Röhr, p. 50.

21. N 253 40, 16f, Schack to Tirpitz, August 1, 1880. Schack had succeeded Heusner at the Admiralty in 1879. Stosch could not be present because to be greeted publicly by the Crown Prince would have been regarded as an insult by Bismarck, who was feuding with Stosch at the time. See Hollyday, chs V and VI.

22. See Hildebrand, I, 150 ff. For one year's example of the role of *Blücher* in training the officers of the fleet, see Tirpitz's notes, probably from April 1881, in RM 31 39.

23. Hildebrand, VI, 20.

24. Ahlefeld later worked closely with Tirpitz in the Reichsmarineamt. Despite his obvious competence, he had some bizarre ideas. Until the 1890s at least, he was an ardent advocate of the ram. See, e.g., NS SA Dep. 18 Nachlass Trotha: Trotha's Notes on Ahlefeld. Müller became Chief of the Naval Cabinet in 1906.

THE "TORPEDO GANG" The form used below lists each officer's name; year of birth; years in the torpedo service while Tirpitz was there [1877–89]; years in the *Oberkommando der Marine* [OKM] when he was Chief of Staff [1892–95]; years in the *Reichsmarineamt* [RMA] while Tirpitz was there [1897–1916]. Listed last is each officer's final service rank and the most important position he ever held. A few of them also served with Tirpitz when he was Chief of the Cruiser Squadron in East Asia [1896–97]. These are noted where applicable. Almost all of the data below are from: Hans Hildebrand [ed.], *Deutschlands Admirale 1849–1945*, 3 vols., Osnabruck, Biblio, 1988–1990.

Hunold von AHLEFELD [1851]; Torpedo: 1880–91; OKM 1893–96, RMA 1902–07; Vice Admiral and Chief of the Baltic Station 1907–08.

Otto BRAUN [1864?]; Torpedo: 1885–87; OKM 1892–95; Died in a typhoon on July 23, 1896, as *Kapitän-Leutnant* and commander of the gunboat *Iltis*, part of Tirpitz's cruiser squadron in East Asia.

Gustav BACHMANN [1860]; Torpedo: May–August 1884; OKM 1892–94, RMA 1897, 1907–10; Admiral, Chief of the Admiral Staff, 1915.

Wilhelm BÜCHSEL [1848]; Torpedo: Summer 1881; RMA 1895–99, 1900–1902; Admiral, Chief of the Admiral Staff, 1902–08.

Carl [von] COERPER [1854]; Torpedo: 1881–03; RMA 1897–8, Naval Attaché in London 1898–1903, 1904–07; Admiral, Chief of Baltic Station, 1912–14.

Harald DÄHNHARDT [1863]; Torpedo: 1887, 1888; RMA 1895–99, 1899–1900, 1904–16; Vice Admiral, Head of Estimates Department at RMA.

Karl DICK [1858]; Torpedo: 1885; OKM 1893–96, RMA 1910–16; Admiral, RMA Dockyard Director.

Max [von] FISCHEL [1850]; Torpedo: 1879–80, 1881–84, 1887–89; OKM 1889–92, RMA 1895–1900; Admiral, Chief of the Admiral Staff, 1909–11.

August von HEERINGEN [1855]; Torpedo: 1884, 1886–69; OKM 1893–96, RMA 1897–99, 1899–1900, 1903–07; Admiral, Chief of the Admiral Staff, 1911–13.

Heinrich, PRINCE OF PRUSSIA [1862]; Torpedo: April–September 1887; No other service under Tirpitz; Grand Admiral, Chief of Baltic Forces, 1914–18.

Albert HOPMANN [1865]; Torpedo: 1888–89; OKM 1895–97, RMA 1911–15; Vice Admiral, Chief of Staff, Baltic Station.

Paul JAESCHKE [1851]; Torpedo: 1880–86; Kapitän zur See, Governor of Kiautschau, 1899–1901.

Friedrich [von] INGENOHL [1857]; Torpedo: 1888; OKM 1892–94, RMA 1897–1901; Admiral, Chief of the High Sea Fleet, 1913–15.

Günther von KROSIGK [1860]; Torpedo: 1884, 1887–89; RMA 1913–14; Admiral, Chief of Baltic Station, 1915–18.

Georg Alexander [von] MÜLLER [1854]; Torpedo: 1879–82, 1884–85; OKM 1892–95; Admiral, Chief of the Naval Cabinet, 1906–18.

Hugo [von] POHL [1855]; Torpedo: 1882–85; RMA 1895–98, 1901–03; Admiral, Chief of the High Seas Fleet, 1915–16.

Max ROLLMANN [1857]; Torpedo: 1883–84, 1884–89; RMA 1901–04, 1907–13; Vice Admiral, Chief of III Squadron, 1910–12.

Wilhelm SCHACK [1860]; Torpedo: 1885–86, 1887; RMA 1896–99, 1901–04; Vice Admiral, Inspector of Coast Artillery, 1911–13.

Reinhard SCHEER [1863]; Torpedo: January to May 1888; RMA 1897–1900, 1903–07, 1911–13; Admiral, Chief of High Seas Fleet, 1916–18.

Ludwig [von] SCHRÖDER [1854]; Torpedo: 1885–88; OKM 1895–98; Admiral, Chief of Marine Corps in Flanders, 1914–18.

Rudolf SIEGEL [1852]; Torpedo: 1879; OKM 1889–94; *Kapitän zur See*, Naval Attaché in Paris, 1895–1907.

Oskar [von] TRUPPEL [1854]; Torpedo: 1887–88; OKM 1894–97, RMA 1899–1901; Admiral, Governor of Kiautschau, 1901–11.

Raimund WINKLER [1855]; Torpedo: 1887–89; OKM 1892–95, RMA 1906–11; Vice Admiral, Department Head in RMA.

Hugo ZEYE [1852]; Torpedo: 1885, 1886–88; RMA 1901–03; Vice Admiral, Inspector of Torpedo Forces, 1903–09; Commander of Kaiser, Tirpitz's flagship in East Asia, 1896–98.

25. Space considerations do not permit a detailed discussion here of the technical aspects of torpedoes. For a sample, see RM 31 39: "Torpedo and Exercise Plan for May to July 1881."

26. Nachlass Eduard von Knorr, N 578 9, 94.

27. The best account, Voigt's, is in RM 8 76, 86 f and 124. See also Testdorpf, p. 224; Hildebrand I, 151; Hallmann, p. 23. For the program of the torpedo firing, see RM 31 183, Program for the Fleet Manoeuvers, September 17, 1881, appendix 12. See also Nachlass Knorr, N 578 9, 104.

28. Röhr, p. 50.

29. Hildebrand, VII, 83 ff.

30. See N 253 15, "Concerning the Development of the Torpedo Arm," written by Tirpitz in April 1889. This is a very important document for understanding how his ideas about torpedo boat type evolved.

31. For the plan, see RM 1 327, 108–124, Batsch to Stosch, August 27, 1882.

32. Later Governor of Kiautschau. See Hildebrand, III, 119.

33. Knorr, for one, did not regard Wickede highly: "He was from the Austrian Navy and not enough of a seaman. . . . He was an enormous windbag and saw his main mission to be the exercise of 'Turks' for the inspections." N 578 9, 94 f.

34. See Tirpitz's Report of September 11, 1882, RM 1 327, 154 f. The map above, in Tirpitz's hand, is also in this document.

35. For Pohl's account, see RM 1 327, 168 f. Pohl later served under Tirpitz in the *Reichmarineamt*. During the war, he was successively Chief of the Admiral Staff and Chief of the High Seas Fleet.

36. For reports of two of the torpedo boat commanders, see RM 1 327, 170–174.

37. See RM 1 2862, 49–68, Stosch's Report on the Fall Manoeuvers of September 10–11, dated September 23, 1882.

38. Hallmann, pp. 24, 104. See also Tirpitz's retrospective memo of April 1889, N 253 3.

39. Hollyday, ch. 6. An interesting and little known insight into the origins of the feud comes from the Nachlass Knorr, N 578 9, 123 ff. Knorr claimed Stosch told him that the conflict began during the Franco-Prussian War, when Stosch arrested one of Bismarck's adjutants for insubordination. Bismarck took it as an attack on his authority.

40. See, e.g., Nachlass Knorr, N 578 9, 127–134. Knorr concluded, after a conversation with the Emperor, that Caprivi had received the position because the army wanted to get rid of him. Tirpitz was distantly related to Caprivi. They were both cousins of Köpke, an official of the *Cultus Ministerium*. N 253 327, 100 f. Rudolf Tirpitz [Alfred's father] to Marie Tirpitz [Alfred's wife], August 25, 1897. There is no evidence that Tirpitz used this faint family connection to gain special treatment.

41. For an overall view of Caprivi's stewardship of the navy, see Petter, pp. 128–138; Hildebrand, I, 31 ff; and Ivo N. Lambi, *The Navy and German Power Politics, 1862–1914*, Boston, Allen and Unwin, 1984, ch. 2. Hobson's dissertation makes a very plausible case that, given its premises, Caprivi's was the first genuinely systematic strategy the German navy had up to this time. Even Tirpitz [I, 37 f], who was very critical of Caprivi for building no real armored ships, admitted that Caprivi had a clear set of priorities and a coherent program. He intended to construct large ships once the short term coast defense problem was solved.

42. Tirpitz, I, 54, Hassell, p. 51.

43. Tirpitz, I, 49 f. See also Röhr, p. 50; and Hildebrand, VII, 82. See also Tirpitz's "Notes about the Self-Fabrication of Torpedoes," n.d., but almost certainly 1888–9, N 253 14, 302 ff.

44. Tirpitz, I, 51 f.

45. RM 1 335, Wickede to Caprivi, September 1, 1883. See also Nachlass Knorr, N 578 9, 130.

46. For the winter training program, see RM 31 307, Tirpitz to Chief of the Baltic Station [Wickede], September 19, 1883.

47. See ibid., and Caprivi to Wickede, November 16, 1883, in the same file.

48. On the *Jeune École*, see Volkmar Bueb, *Die junge Schule der französischen Marine: Strategie und Politik 1875–1900*, Boppard am Rhein, Harald Boldt, 1971 passim; Ropp, chs 9–10; Potter, pp. 249 f; and Petter, pp. 131 f. This section has particularly profitted from the dissertation-in-progress of Rolf Hobson [Trondheim]. The starkest statement of the *Jeune École's* ideas came in a series of articles by Admiral Aube's unofficial publicist, Gabriel Charmes, in: *Revue des deux Mondes: La réforme de la marine* I: *"Torpilleurs et cannoniéres"* [Dec. 15, 1884], pp. 872–906; *La réforme de la marine* II: *"La guerre maritime et l'organisation de la force navale"*, [March 1, 1885], pp. 127– 68; *La réforme de la marine*, III: *"Défense des côtes,"* [April 15, 1885], pp. 770–806. See also Tirpitz's evaluation of their ideas in N 253 3, 23–28. What follows is my synthesis of these sources.

49. Ropp, p. 48.

50. In a test voyage across the Bay of Biscay in February 1886, which was accounted a "success," after 20 days at sea, "the crews were so worn out from seasickness and the lack of warm food that there could be no question of their inability to fight at the end of the trip." Ibid., p. 176. The conclusion was that they could never be used on the high seas for any extended period.

51. Hallmann, p. 25. See also Ekkard Verchau, "*Von Jachmann über Stosch und Caprivi zu den Anfängen der Ära Tirpitz*," pp. 54–72, in Herbert Schottelius and Wilhelm Deist [eds.], *Marine und Marinepolitik 1871–1914*, Düsseldorf, Droste, 1972, p. 67.

52. See Petter, pp. 132 ff; and Hallmann, pp. 25 ff. Tirpitz's role in drafting this program is unclear because contemporary evidence is lacking. It would be very surprising if Caprivi did not consult him, but it is unlikely, because of his low seniority among other things, that he was the major force behind this initiative. In his draft of Tirpitz's biography, Michaelis claims that much later officials in the *Reichsmarineamt* told him Tirpitz had been its driving spirit. See Nachlass Michaelis, N 164 2. Caprivi, already a "true believer" in torpedo boats, would not have needed more than technical advice from Tirpitz to put together such a proposal.

53. The analysis that follows is based upon part of the memo Tirpitz wrote in April 1889. "On the Development of the Torpedo Arm," N 253 3, 1–18. The contemporary documents agree with his analysis.

54. For the construction data, see, Eric Gröner et al., *German Warships 1815–1945*, Vol. I: *Major Surface Vessels*. Annapolis, US Naval Institute, 1982, pp. 152–55; and Harald Fock, *Fast Fighting Boats 1870–1945: Their Design and Use*, Annapolis, Naval Institute Press, 1974, I, 13 ff

55. Sources on the cruise that followed are in RM 31 237; N 253 15, 9 ff; and Hassell, pp. 99 ff. The fullest and most vivid account is Voigt's. He was aboard Blücher. See RM 8 76, 136 f.

56. Heeringen later became one of Tirpitz's closest collaborators in the *Reichmarineamt* and elsewhere. He finally rose to be Chief of the Admiral Staff from 1911 to 1913.

57. N 253 14, 123 f.

58. N 253 15, 7–13.

59. On this point, see Epkenhans and Weir.

60. Tirpitz, I, 54, 64 ff; Ropp, p. 30; Hallmann, pp. 104–109.

61. See RM 1 337, 12–17, Caprivi to Monts, March 20, 1884.

62. For the extensive March to November correspondence on these points between Caprivi and Tirpitz, see RM 1 337; RM 31 465; and RM 31 237, which contains the order to officially establish the experimental torpedo boat division on August 1.

63. See, e.g., RM 31 308.

64. On November 18, 1884, he married Marie Lipke.

65. See, e.g., N 253 408, 68 f, von Reichenbach to Tirpitz, November 19, 1884; N 253 197, 17 f, Ahlefeld to Tirpitz, January 2, 1885; and N 253 14, 116–121.

66. See, e.g., N 253 197, 15 f, Ahlefeld to Tirpitz, January 15, 1885; N253 14, 175, Tirpitz to Ahlefeld, September 3, 1885; ibid., p. 187, Tirpitz to Schickau, September 2, 1885; and N 253 15, 7 f.

67. N 253 408, 50 f, Oldekop [in effect, the Naval Attaché in London] to Tirpitz, October 13, 1884. The fact that Oldekop had to ask for basic information seems significant.

68. N 253 408, 52, Tirpitz to Oldekop, April 3, 1885; See also N 253 15, 9.

69. N 253 197, 15 f, Ahlefeld to Tirpitz, January 15, 1885.

70. N 253 408, 7f, Jaeschke to Tirpitz, March 11, 1885; and N 253 15, 34f.

71. See RM 31 237, Goltz to Caprivi, March 27, 1885. For the most detailed description I found of the technical aspects of 1885-vintage torpedo boats, see RM 31 465, "Draft of Instructions for Military Personnel of Torpedo Boats," April 19, 1885.

72. N 253 14, 210–220, Tirpitz to Caprivi, December 18, 1885.

73. N 253 14, 271. Tirpitz's notes on reorganization, n.d., but between February 9 and March 15, 1886.

74. On the work of the Inspectorate, see RM 27 III 16; RM 1 2674; N 253 14, 276 ff; N 253 15, 39–41; Hildebrand, VII, 84; Hallmann, p. 104; Petter, p. 133; and Herbert Graubohm, *Die Ausbildung in der deutschen Marine von ihrer Gründung bis zum Jahre 1914*, Düsseldorf, Droste, 1977, pp. 96, 187.

75. For technical specifications, see Hildebrand, VII, 86 f; Gröner, I, 152–8; and N 253 15, 13 ff.

76. On these boats, see Potter, p. 244; Hildebrand, VII, 85; Gröner I, 166 f; and RM 253 15, 35–9. When he left the Torpedo Inspectorate in 1889, Tirpitz was trying to get an even bigger boat to be a flotilla leader. See, e.g., the correspondence with Rear Admiral Friedrich Hollmann in late 1887 in N 253 204.

77. Ropp, p. 30; Hallmann, pp. 107 ff.

78. N 253 258, Captain Adolf Mensing [ret.] to Tirpitz, May 9, 1921. Mensing specifically wrote that the quote was verbatim. On the 1886 manoeuvers, see RM 1 253 and RM 1 338, 36–9, Caprivi's observations about the fall manoeuvers October 11, 1886. See also Hildebrand, I, 116 f.

79. Hallmann, p. 109; N 253 14, 321–334; N 253 16, 33f, Caprivi to Tirpitz, December 14, 1887. For the 1888 manoeuvers see RM 1 339.

80. Lambi, ch. 2; Petter, pp. 137 ff.

81. Nachlass Knorr, N 578 11, 123 ff.

82. For a summary of the answers of all the respondents, see N 253 35, Report of the Ship Examination Commission, March 13, 1888.

83. The response is in N 253 35 and N 253 58.

84. N 253 58, 129–37.

85. Ibid., p. 131.

86. Hildebrand, I, 151.

87. Kaulisch, p. 40.

88. On this trip, see Hildebrand, I, 149; RM 1 2717, 71–90; and N 253 14, 52. See also Tirpitz's later account of this in N 253 104.

89. See Caprivi to Tirpitz, June 26, 1888, in Hassell, p. 53.

90. Tirpitz, I, 57; and Petter, p. 144.

91. See N 253 14, 295–9, and 341 f; and especially his valedictory memorandum of February 21, 1889, in ibid., pp. 350–360; see also Tirpitz, I , 57.

92. RM 2 827, 14, January 1, 1889.

93. Salewski, p. 22; Hallmann, p. 107; Gemzell, p. 59; Petter, p. 129; and Berghahn, pp. 60 ff.

94. Ropp, Ch. 10 and p. 236.

95. For a rough numerical comparison, see Potter, p. 244. For more detailed comparative information, see Robert Gardiner [ed.], *Conway's All the World's Fighting Ships 1860–1905*, London, Conway Maritime Press, 1979. Perhaps the best existing comparative analysis for that particular point in time is one Tirpitz himself did in 1889. See N 253 15, 18–30 and 49–56.

96. There is a fascinating clue to the answer to this question in Nachlass William Michaelis, N 164 4, 29–40. Michaelis was a department head in the Admiral Staff, 1910–13. He wrote that Tirpitz simply refused to believe unimpeachable evidence that by then British torpedoes were better than German ones.

97. Tirpitz, I, 67.

98. Nachlass Adolf von Trotha, NS SA Tr Dep. 18, L 40. Trotha's notes on Tirpitz's life, March 16, 1937.

99. Nachlass Michaelis, N 164 4, 29–40, demonstrates how submissive Heeringen had to be to Tirpitz to stay in the latter's good graces.

100. It is possible that Scheer also should be on the short list. Walter Freiherr von Keyserlingk, a battleship commander in the wartime High Seas Fleet, noted in the 1930s: "[Scheer] was in on the early development of the torpedo weapon under Tirpitz and was one of those young officers on whom their experience with this weapon had a decisive influence. From then came his close relationship with Tirpitz." Nachlass Keyserlingk, N 161 9, 39 ff.

101. Berghahn, p. 58.

102. See their 1892–96 correspondence in N 253 320 and 321. Final word on the Stosch-Tirpitz relationship will perhaps be provided in Ekkard Verchau's long awaited Stosch biography.

103. N 253 407, 16–20, Batsch to Tirpitz, n.d. Unfortunately, the first page of the letter is missing from the folder, but from the context it is unmistakable that it was written just before Tirpitz became Chief of Staff in the OKM in January 1892. Batsch was the admiral who all in the navy had thought should succeed Stosch in 1883.

104. See, e.g., their correspondence in N 253 16, 33 f and 38 ff.

105. Hassell, p. 56.

106. The term *Ressort* means sphere of action, or area of competence in a bureaucratic sense. *Eifer* means jealousy or possessiveness. On this term, see, e.g., Patrick J. Kelly "The Naval Policy of Imperial Germany, 1900–1914," dissertation, Georgetown University, Washington, D.C., 1970, passim; and Gemzell, chs. 1–2.

107. Salewski, p. 23.

Preparing for War:
Admiral William H. Standley and the Struggle to Build Auxiliaries for the Navy

Thomas Wildenberg

⚓

Throughout the 1930s the United States Navy waged an unrelenting series of legislative campaigns to obtain money from Congress to rebuild and modernize the fleet. Aided and abetted by Carl Vinson, the venerable Chairman of the House Naval Affairs Committee, the hierarchy within the Navy Department successfully induced Congress to authorize and provide funding for the construction of relatively large numbers of warships and aircraft. Funding for urgently needed fleet auxiliaries proved more difficult to obtain, albeit some headway was made in the late 1930s when a limited amount of money was allocated for the construction of a few specialized Navy tenders.

Although the U.S. Navy was chronically short of funds throughout most of this era, it never lost sight of the logistic needs of the fleet. Indeed, a comprehensive blueprint for logistic support was regularly included as one of the "Contributory" plans prepared for War Plan Orange. While the exact details of the logistic plan varied from one version of "Orange" to another, several hundred merchant vessels were always included in the list of ships assigned to service force, then known as the Train, which was to accompany the Fleet across the Pacific in order to render the full range of logistic services normally provided by a naval base.[1] Because the navy could not afford to maintain large numbers of noncombatants in peacetime, strategists in War Plans [a division of the Office of Naval Operations] formulated a program for the wholesale acquisition and conversion of large numbers of merchant ships in the event of a national emergency. This strategy sufficed so long as the United States maintained a strong merchant marine.

As the level of shipping and shipbuilding fell during the Depression, however, the Navy became increasingly concerned over the deterioration of the U.S. merchant fleet. It recognized that the lack of such vessels would severely impair the Navy's ability to implement War Plan Orange. The magnitude of this problem began to surface after Admiral William H. Standley's appointment as the Chief of Naval Operations (CNO) on 1 July 1933.

Standley was intent on continuing the efforts initiated by his predecessor, Admiral William V. Pratt, to promote the construction of new ships by pushing for an annual building program which would "not only provide for replacement of ships as they become obsolete," but would also keep the "Navy modernized and up-to-date."[2] The only prewar CNO to have served as top war planner, it appears that he was also quite concerned about the Navy's plans for war, for he immediately requested an updated operations plan [Plan O-1 of Orange] from the commander in chief of the U.S. Fleet.[3] The tentative plan which emerged from the fleet called for a rapid deployment to the Philippines, which Miller has aptly dubbed "Through Ticket."[4] According to this plan, the main element would consist of "a small, compact force, composed exclusively of vessels that have been in full commission and have been maintained at the highest degree of readiness."[5] The Train would now be "kept to an absolute minimum."

Though the plan proposed by the fleet was not favorably received by Standley, it must have raised questions concerning the ability of the its aging auxiliaries to fulfill their role in time of war. As a former Director of War Plans, Standley was fully aware of the importance of the Train and its importance to the successful implementation of Orange. Troubled by the obsolescence of the vessels assigned to the Train, he immediately recognized the need to procure modern auxiliaries which were capable of keeping up with the battle force. As a first step towards this end, it appears evident that Standley (via the Secretary of the Navy) directed the General Board to review the military characteristics for the various types of auxiliaries in the Navy.[6] As was customary, these were then circulated to the various bureaus for their "comments and recommendations" before any action was taken by the General Board.

Standley's efforts to strengthen the logistic needs of the Fleet were not limited to the acquisition of additional auxiliaries for the Navy. He also lobbied for a strong merchant marine whose ships could be quickly converted in time of war into a variety of auxiliary cruisers, airplane carriers and scouts.[7] For several years War Plans had been compiling an updated list of merchant ships which would be required "in a war involving the maximum naval effort."[8] The number of ships needed by the Navy was immense—well over one thousand vessels were listed. It appears that Standley forwarded this information to the United States Shipping Board Bureau within the Department of Commerce along with a request from the Navy to study the problem of rebuilding the American Merchant Marine.[9]

J. W. Barnett, Acting Chief of the Shipping Board's Division of Loans and Sales, realized that a building program of the magnitude needed to fulfill the Navy's needs could only be accomplished by standardizing all aspects of a ship's design. He, therefore, recommended that a program be established within the Division of Loans and Sales to develop standard designs for merchant vessels which could be quickly constructed during a national emergency. Since the Shipping Board did not have its own design staff, Barnett suggested that a technical unit be established within the Division and asked for authority "to engage the services of a competent Naval architect, and four to six experienced ship draftsmen and estimators."[10] On March 12, 1934, the Navy made a formal request [probably by Standley while acting Secretary] to proceed with the program outlined by Mr. Barnett with the stipulation that the designs for standard merchant ships were to be produced in accordance to the characteristics suggested by the Navy.[11] Although the Shipping Board would be responsible for the program, it was understood that the designs would be approved by the Navy and that the Bureau of Construction and Repair, the Bureau of Engineering, as well as "any others involved or interested in the program," would lend their cooperation and technical assistance. (Note the veiled reference to WPD.)

In view of the close relationship of the program to the Navy Department, a special joint committee was formed to study the design requirements of the various classes of ships and to provide technical guidance as the work progressed. It was composed of a number of naval officers as well as several representatives of the Division of Loans and Sales and had the following objectives: First, to develop designs of the various types of merchant ships that would be acceptable to the Department of Commerce and the Navy Department as bases for construction loans. Second, to develop basic designs that would be useful to designers and ship owners as a guide to features in merchant ships which would make the latter adaptable to naval auxiliaries without interfering with their commercial peacetime use.

Third, to have available designs of standardized vessels which could be built in large quantities during a national emergency when requirements for merchant tonnage would be greatly expanded.[12]

The Joint Board for the Standardization of Merchant Vessels, as it was called in the Navy, held its first meeting on April 23, 1924 and immediately began the task of developing standard plans for a tanker, a cargo vessel, and a combined cargo and passenger vessel.[13]

In the previous month, Standley's effort to rebuild the Navy had been rewarded with the passage of the Vinson–Trammell Bill. Signed into law on March 27, the Act authorized a continuous program of new construction and replacement which would increase the size of the Navy up to the limits set by the London Treaty. Though this Act merely authorized the replacement of obsolete warships, it was a watershed in naval legislation, by-passing the need for yearly approvals previously needed to authorize new construction.[14] Buoyed by the passage of this bill, Standley resolved to obtain an auxiliary building program legislatively similar to the Vinson–Trammell Act, i.e., one which would provide blanket authority to bring the number of auxiliaries up to strength.

In an apparent effort to elicit support for constructing these ships, Standley requested that the General Board "study the Navy's needs in auxiliaries . . . and present a program for [the] yearly procurement including replacement, which [would] bring the Navy to proper strength in [these classes]."[15] The Board's report, issued on 16 June 1934, was not particularly helpful. It recommended against building any new auxiliaries at that time, fearing that funds for such ships would be diverted from the construction of major combatants. The General Board believed "that all money available for new construction should be devoted entirely to the construction of the Treaty limited classes."[16] In the Board's opinion, the number of auxiliaries in the Navy was sufficient "to meet the needs of a treaty navy operated on a peacetime basis." Although it agreed that the Navy needed these ships, the General Board opposed the diversion of funds to "minor Combatant vessels" until quotas in the treaty classes had been obtained. The Board was reluctant to add the cost of auxiliaries to the treaty building program already authorized, since the extra expenditures would only provide ammunition for those in Congress opposed to "preparedness" spending. According to the replacement schedule proposed by the General Board, no new auxiliaries would be laid down until 1940![17]

Originally formed in 1900 as an advisory board to the Secretary of the Navy, the Board's influence on policy matters had greatly declined, especially after Admiral Pratt became CNO.[18] Not surprisingly, Standley chose to disregard the Board's recommendations and pushed ahead with plans to establish a continual program of auxiliary construction to supplement the combatant tonnage authorized by the Vinson–Trammell Act. In retrospect, Standley, who later characterized his concerns for "continual construction" as a "pet hobby," was misled by the ease with which the Navy had obtained authorization and funding for its shipbuilding programs of FY (fiscal year) 1934 and FY1935.[19]

Both Standley and Claude A. Swanson, the ailing Secretary of the Navy, underestimated the political pressures which were mounting on the Administration to adopt a balanced budget.[20] Although Swanson shared the Board's apprehensions concerning Congress's reluctance to spent more money on the Navy, he disagreed with the Board's recommendation to delay the construction of auxiliaries. In November he wrote President Roosevelt stressing the "need of ships which are outside of the treaty categories,—these being those auxiliaries which must go with the Fleet to care for the logistic requirements."[21] Included in Swanson's letter was a tentative schedule for laying down or acquiring 23 auxiliary ships over a three year period. In his letter Swanson proposed that they be financed with a grant from the Public Works Administration [as had been used to fund the treaty building programs of FY 1934 and 1935], rather than through the Navy's regular budget.[22] Swanson believed that another allocation from the Public Works Administration would preserve "the desired balance" in the Navy's building program and would further increase employment within the shipbuilding industry.

Unfortunately for the Navy, the anticipated rate of re-employment had fallen far short of the pace initially forecast by the Department to justify the inclusion of ships in the NIRA's public works program. Although the Department attempted to rectify these problems, the slow pace of job growth within the industry further aggravated Secretary of the Interior Harold Ickes. One of the Navy's foremost antagonists, Ickes advised against funding auxiliary construction via the NIRA. President Roosevelt chose to heed this advice, and all naval shipbuilding funds were removed from the proposed relief budget for FY1936.[23]

After the use of PWA funds was denied, Swanson asked the Department—Standley was in London for the second session of preliminary discussions prior to the forthcoming naval conference—to draft an authorization bill along with a list of auxiliaries which were intended for inclusion as part of the Navy's regular budget.[24] He submitted this proposal to the Bureau of the Budget for evaluation in the spring of 1935.[25] Swanson's bill was not enthusiastically received by the Bureau of the Budget's Director, Daniel Bell. Daniel Bell, the incumbent director of the Bureau of the Budget, was reluctant to approve additional shipbuilding expenditures; he counseled the President against including any more funds in the Administration's financial package for the coming year. Bell advised Roosevelt that it was would be an inopportune time to present such a measure before Congress.[26] Roosevelt agreed with Bell's assessment, and the auxiliary bill was quietly dropped from further consideration.

Nevertheless, by the middle of 1935, the lack of modern auxiliaries had become the most serious deficiency in the Fleet.[27] Admiral Joseph M. Reeves, Commander-in-Chief, U.S. Fleet, was so concerned about this situation that he included a strong message to this effect in his annual report to the Secretary of the Navy. Issued in the early part of October 1935, it contained the following statement:

> There are many deficiencies in our Fleet today that should be rectified as soon as time and funds permit . . .
>
> First—Faster vessels of the Train are urgently required. Most of our auxiliaries that were designed for a comparatively high speed have to be satisfied with two or three knots less. . . .
>
> Second—The Construction of suitable tenders specially designed to facilitate the operation of patrol planes is an urgent necessity . . .
>
> Third—The replacement of our obsolete submarines is considered of primary importance.[28]

As the 1936 legislative year approached, the Department again drew up an auxiliary construction bill which it intended to present before Congress. Although the Navy was clearly in need of new auxiliaries, the prognosis for the passage of any such legislation during the spring of 1936 was not good. "The Department's internal bureaucratic structure was exceptionally weak at this point, and its relationship to its traditional Congressional spokesmen was strained."[29] While Standley was away attending the London Naval

Conference, Swanson's health worsened; then, to further complicate matters, Henry Roosevelt, the Assistant Secretary of the Navy, died in February. The simultaneous absence of the three highest officers within the Navy Department seriously weakened the Navy's ability to guide its legislative program for FY 1937 through Congress.

The chances for an early passage of the auxiliary vessel bill were further weakened when Park Trammell, Chairman of the Senate Naval Affairs Committee, died, causing further delays in the legislation process which would have introduced the needed bill. The demise of an auxiliary construction bill for FY1937 was ultimately assured after Standley's return from the London Conference. In view of Japan's withdrawal from the treaty system and Britain's intention to replace overage battleships, Standley decided to redirect the Navy's efforts towards securing funds for two new battleships.[30]

Though the Naval Appropriation Bill for FY1937 was the largest ever allocated in peace time, Standley was stung by a presidential order requiring all government departments to set up substantial reserves for funds which would be liable for cuts. To achieve the necessary savings, Standley was compelled to order a series of economies in fleet operations over the next two years. Aggravated by the cutback in operating funds and the formation of a "coterie of officers" who seemed to be excessively influenced by Roosevelt, Standley unexpectedly decided to retire at the end of 1936 and was succeeded by Admiral William D. Leahy.[31]

Although Standley failed to obtain a program for the orderly construction of auxiliaries, his efforts to encourage a strong merchant shipbuilding program were repaid with the passage of the Merchant Marine Act of 1936. This act established the development and maintenance of a strong merchant marine as the declared policy of the United States and provided subsidies for stimulating the merchant marine, including payments for the cost of certain "National Defense Features" which the Navy deemed necessary for converting merchant vessels into certain types of auxiliaries which were expected "to accompany the Fleet in time of war."[32]

Though the Navy Department was not directly involved in the legislative activities surrounding this act, there can be no doubt as to the lobbying efforts and assistance provided by the Navy. The Department "was intimately involved in virtually every aspect of the activities on Capitol Hill," and there is ample evidence to demonstrate that Navy personnel provided technical assistance to the Chairman of the Senate Commerce Committee.[33]

Though the Merchant Marine Act of 1936 was not perceived as a major breakthrough in naval funding at the time of its passage, it was to have an immense influence on the Navy's ability to quickly obtain auxiliaries during its rapid build up just prior to, and during, the first months of World War II. But for the moment, let us not forget that balancing the budget was still the Administration's primary concern during 1936, and no funds were committed that year to the construction of merchant vessels.

In 1937 the Department, now under Leahy's leadership, once again prepared a building program for auxiliaries intended for inclusion in the budget for FY1938. It was similar to the program which had been prepared previously, though the total number of auxiliaries had been reduced from 54 to 48 ships.[34] If enacted, the proposed measure would have authorized the construction of all 48 over a ten year period. This time around, Bell objected to the long range provisions of the bill. He preferred to limit the number of ships authorized only to those which could be started during the next fiscal year. Once again Roosevelt agreed with Bell and declined to approve the ten year replacement program wanted by the Navy. After much discussion and readjustment between the Department, the President, and Bell, Roosevelt decided to approve construction of the first six ships.[35] The bill which emerged from Congress (H.R. 6550) authorized the Navy to construct the following vessels:

Ships Authorized—H.R. 6550

Hull No.	Name	Type	Displacement (tons)
AV-4	*Curtiss*	Seaplane Tender	9,300
AD-14	*Dixie*	Destroyer Tender	9,000
AM-55	*Raven*	Minesweeper	600
AS-11	*Fulton*	Submarine Tender	9,000
AT-64	*Navajo*	Fleet Tug	1,150
AO-22	*Cimarron*	Oiler	8,000[36]

Signed into law on 30 July 1937, it became known as the Auxiliary Construction Act of 1938.

The Navy was far from out of the woods in its endeavors to acquire modern auxiliaries, however, as it now had to obtain funding before contracts could be let and construction begun. Roosevelt was in a frugal mood by this time, having requested all departments to economize in an effort to balance the budget for the coming year.[37] Thus, when the Third Deficiency Appropriation Act for FY1938 was passed on 25 August, it restricted the availability of funds for only two of the six vessels authorized. The House's decision to limit expenditures for only two ships was, no doubt, a result of Roosevelt's economy drive. In addition to restricting the total funds available, the Act limited the total cost for each vessel and its armament to the amounts set forth in the final estimates submitted by the Bureaus to the House Committee on Appropriations.[38]

Because the appropriation did not specify which ships were to be built, the Navy had to decide which of the six ships authorized it wanted to build. Obviously, it was in the Navy's interest to select two of the larger types, as these were more costly than either the mine sweeper or the tug. Captain J. S. Woods, the acting director of war plans, was asked to provide information on which ships were needed the most.[39] He immediately prepared a five page memorandum for the CNO detailing the Navy's requirements in the four remaining types.

According to Woods the most urgent need was for an additional seaplane tender. As he explained, the Navy was rapidly acquiring large numbers of the long range patrol bombers (including 176 PBY's) authorized under the Vinson–Trammell Act and already had 198 in operation. Another 30 of these large flying boats were to be delivered within the next two years, yet the number of seaplane tenders in service wasn't even enough to service those aircraft presently "afloat." The Navy only had two large seaplane tenders, *Wright* (AV-1) and *Langley* (AV-3), plus nine small tenders (AVP's) of the Lapwing class in commission. The latter could only service six patrol planes each, while the large tenders were capable of handling 24 planes. Thus, the total number of patrol planes which could be serviced afloat was only 102 versus the 198 planes available for duty. Assuming that all the old tenders, large and small, remained in service, the Navy still had an immediate need for four additional large seaplane tenders. Hence, Woods recommended including this type as one of the two auxiliaries to be built.[40]

Woods's report showed that the Navy was also desperately short of destroyer tenders. In the event of a major war, WPD believed that there would be an immediate need for six destroyer tenders in addition to those carried on the Navy list. Only the *Whitney* (AD-4) and the *Dobbin* (AD-3) were considered satisfactory. The others, "due to low speed and general machinery undependability, would be a distinct handicap in mobile operations."[41]

The need for submarine tenders was not quite as critical, according to Woods, as there being an immediate need for only two of this type. In as much as the plans for the destroyer tender were nearly complete, and to avoid any delay in starting construction, Woods recommended that the destroyer tender be the second ship selected. As for the need for new oilers, the ten tankers included in the long-range building program, then being formulated by the U.S. Merchant Marine Commission, were more than suited to meet the Navy's needs in the event of war.

While the auxiliary construction bill was still before Congress, Commissioner Emory S. Land suggested that the Maritime Commission assume the responsibility for securing tankers which were capable of meeting the Navy's requirements, including the need for high speed.[42] Land, the only member of the Commission nominated for a six year term, had just retired from the Navy after achieving the rank of Rear Admiral (CC) and serving as Chief of the Bureau of Construction and Repair. Once described as the "cleverest politician" produced by the Navy, Admiral Land had been instrumental in securing passage of both the NIRA and the Vinson–Trammell Act.[43] Because of his long experience in naval ship construction and wide knowledge of the shipbuilding industry, he was placed in charge of construction and all other technical activities.

Instead of building the vessels directly, Land proposed that the Commission simply subsidize the cost of providing tankers with the increased power that would be required for high speed, which he estimated would cost between $300,000 to $700,000 per ship. If the Commission could convince the oil companies to proceed on this basis, then the total cost of the Commission's tanker program would come to substantially less than the 28 million dollars already budgeted in the Commission's proposed shipbuilding program. If the oil companies would also agree to include gun foundations, magazine spaces, and other requirements desired by the Navy, then there would be no need for the Navy to develop its own oiler and the commission "would be in a position to request the proper authorities not to build this 'ideal' unit."[44] In his memorandum to the

Chairman of the Maritime Commission, Land asserted that it would be "far better" for the Maritime Commission to build tankers instead of the Navy and noted that "a good talking point" would be the 8 or 9 million dollars which could be saved in the Navy's budget. Within a week Admiral Land's proposal to divert funds from the construction of one naval oiler to the construction of ten or more high speed merchant tankers was presented to Admiral Leahy, CNO. Initially opposed to the idea, Leahy was soon convinced of its value to the Navy. That fall the Maritime Commission began to discuss the construction of high speed tankers with various oil companies. Early in December a tentative agreement had been reached with the Standard Oil Company of New Jersey to build twelve high speed tankers with the government paying the cost of the larger engines needed to provide the increased speed wanted by the Navy.

Contracts for these vessels were signed on January 3, 1938, thus initiating construction of the twelve high speed tankers which would later enter naval service as *Cimarron*-class fleet oilers. The ink was hardly dry before Admiral Leahy advised the Commission that the Navy Department wanted to acquire the first of the tankers constructed immediately upon its completion.[45] Included in its budget estimates for the coming year (FY1939) was the cost of the four auxiliaries authorized in 1938 but not funded, and it is clear that Leahy intended to acquire one of the Commission's oilers as soon as possible.[46] Four days after Leahy's letter to the Commission, on 21 January 1938, the House of Representatives passed its version of the annual naval bill for FY1939.[47] It exceeded all previous peacetime appropriations for the Navy in the nation's history and included funds for all the four of the auxiliaries requested by Leahy.

Actual construction of the first twelve "National Defense" tankers ordered by the Maritime Commission began on April 25, 1938.[48] On that date the keel for the first of these vessels, the *Cimarron*, was laid at the Chester yards of the Sun Shipbuilding and Dry Dock Company. On the following day, Roosevelt signed the Naval Appropriation Act for FY1939. More than 140 million dollars was appropriated for new ship construction, including funds for one mine sweeper, one submarine tender, one fleet tug, and one oiler.[49] By then both houses of Congress were nearing agreement on a billion dollar naval expansion bill which would become known as the Second Vinson Act. Introduced in early January by Carl Vinson, the proposed bill would increase the size of the Navy by twenty percent.

On the very day Vinson first presented the measure, Roosevelt delivered a special message to Congress stressing the need to maintain military strength in both oceans and in regions far beyond American shores.[50] In addition to forty-six combatants, the final version of the Bill (Public Law 528) authorized the construction of twenty-six additional auxiliaries, including: three destroyer tenders, three large seaplane tenders, seven small seaplane tenders, one repair ship, four fuel tankers, one mine-layer, three mine-sweepers, and two fleet tugs.[51]

Thus, in just two short years the Navy received authorization to build a total of 32 new auxiliaries, representing a 40 percent increase in the Base Force [formally the Train].[52] The Navy would also benefit from the Maritime Commission's building program, which was just getting underway. Before the year was out, the Maritime Commission was to let contracts for 49 ships: 12 tankers, 34 cargo vessels, and 3 combination passenger/cargo types. Each was designed for a minimum sustained speed of 16½ knots, then considered extremely fast for a merchantman. Over two-thirds of these vessels would later be purchased by the Navy and converted into a number of different auxiliaries.[53]

Although all of the auxiliaries authorized for the Navy during this period participated in World War II, none proved more vital than the twelve high speed *Cimarron*-class tankers originally ordered by the Standard Oil Company of New Jersey. Built to a design developed within the Bureau of Construction and Repair, they were ideally suited to accompany the fleet and were soon acquired by the Navy for conversion to fleet oilers.[54] It is important to note that this particular class of ships played a critical role in stopping the Japanese at Midway, since it is unlikely that the Battle of Midway, nor the carrier raids which preceded it, could have been conducted had these tankers not been available to provide fueling at sea.[55]

These unique vessels also played an important part in Operation Torch, albeit in a role much different from that for which they were originally designed. Though the Navy was desperately short of oilers at the start of the war, the need for carriers was even greater. To alleviate this shortage, the Navy decided to convert four of its *Cimarron*-type oilers into auxiliary aircraft carriers. Quickly converted into escort carriers of the *Sangamon* class, they were rushed to completion in order to participate in Operation Torch, where they provided air cover for the allied invasion of North Africa.

As for the large tenders authorized in 1938, though their completion prior to the outbreak of hostilities facilitated mobilization and speeded the development of similar types during wartime, their contribution to the early war effort was not critical. The disastrous attack on Pearl Harbor, coupled with major changes in naval strategy after 1939, eliminated the urgent need for this type of ship. Of greater importance were the fast merchantmen conceived by the Joint Board for the Standardization of Merchant Ships laid down by the Maritime Commission before 1941. It is difficult to see how the Navy could have carried out the worldwide range of operations conducted in 1942 without the logistic support provided by these vessels.

The Navy's role in promoting the concept for the standard merchant types, which were to become the hallmark of the Maritime Commission's prewar shipbuilding efforts, is largely unknown. While most historians credit Roosevelt for initiating the emergency shipbuilding program, they have overlooked the earlier efforts of the Navy and Maritime Commission under the leadership of Rear Admiral Emory S. Land, USN (Ret.). Although Admiral Land is justly credited for overseeing the rapid construction of large numbers of merchantmen, most scholars have neglected Standley's efforts to encourage the development of a strong merchant marine. In the author's judgment, Standley deserves more credit for this effort than is generally acknowledged. The extent of Standley's influence on the passage of the Merchant Marine Act of 1936 is difficult to access. Nevertheless, it most be pointed out that the Navy, under his direction, was adamant in recommending the establishment of a merchant shipbuilding program which would permit "the constant replacement of existing vessels in the United States Merchant Marine with modern vessels of gradually increasing speed capabilities."[56]

It is unlikely that the exact nature of Standley's involvement in the passage of the Merchant Marine Act of 1936 will ever be revealed. The measure did not involve the Navy directly and any action taken by Standley would have been very discreet to avoid allegations of collusion between himself and those legislators in Congress who saw the bill as another means of providing strong support for the Navy. Any information of a naval nature furnished the Commerce Committee would have been passed along by "second echelon" personnel, as was customary during this period.[57] Whenever data was needed to support the Navy's position on any legislative matter, as occurred during the hearings on the Merchant Marine Act, it was almost always furnished by representatives of the various Bureaus or other personnel assigned to the Office of Naval Operations.

Standley's commitment to the establishment of a merchant vessels policy within the Navy Department has also been largely ignored.[58] Though it has only been touched upon, this policy was instrumental in establishing the criteria for high speed, which was to be of great importance in establishing the minimum characteristics accepted by the U.S. Maritime Commission for the majority of ship types constructed by the government between 1939–45.

1. For details, see Miller, Edward S., *War Plan Orange* (Naval Institute Press, Annapolis, 1991), Table 13.1, 146.

2. Statement made by Standley in October 1933 in a radio address sponsored by the Navy League to elicit support in Congress for the Vinson–Trammell Act. John C. Walter, "William Harrison Standley 1 July 1933–1 January 1937." In Robert W. Love, Jr., ed., *The Chiefs of Naval Operations* (Naval Institute Press, Annapolis, 1980), 93.

3. Miller, *War Plan Orange*, passim.

4. Chief of Naval Operations to Commander-in-Chief, U.S. Fleet, 13 July 1933. Washington, D.C.: National Archives, Record Group 80, (hereafter RG80, NA), Secretary of the Navy—Secret Correspondence 1927–39 (hereafter SC), File A16-3/FF1. Note: Standley served as Director of War Plans in 1924–25.

5. David F. Sellers, Commander-in-Chief, U.S. Fleet, to Chief of Naval Operations, 26 August 1933, Memo concerning "Tentative Draft of Contributory Plan 0-1 (Orange)." Washington: Naval Historical Center, Operational Archives Branch, World War II War Plans Collection, CominCh-CNO (1932–39), Folder: CinCUS prior 3 1939.

6. Secretary of the Navy to General Board, AA/S1 serial (330227), 21 September 1933. Note: though this document has not be located, it is referenced in subsequent documents relating to the subject of auxiliaries and most certainly initiated the General Board study which resulted in the extensive series of "Characteristics" for auxiliaries issued in December of that year. (See General Board File 420–5 for 1933, passim, RG80, NA.)

7. Navy Day Speech of October 27, 1933. U.S. Naval Institute Proceedings, October 1934, 60:10, 1498.

8. Thomas C. Hart, Chairman, General Board, to Secretary of the Navy, "Policy in Regard To Merchant Vessels," date stamped 27 February 1937, 5–8, File 442, Records of the General Board, RG80, NA.

9. J.W. Barnett, Acting Chief, Division of Finance to Director, U.S. Shipping Board Bureau, "Standardization of Merchant Vessels and Coordination thereof with War Plans," 28 February 1934, 1. Washington: U.S. Maritime Administration Record Group 178, Records of the U.S. Maritime Commission, File 505–1 (hereafter MC File 505–1, RG178, MARAD). Note: although Standley is not mentioned by name, all evidence [e.g. see note 13] points to his involvement as the originator.

10. Barnett, "Standardization of Merchant Vessels and Coordination thereof with War Plans," 1–5.

11. Letter from Secretary of the Navy to Director, U.S. Shipping Board Bureau dated March 12, 1934 as referenced by Henry H. Heiman, Director, U.S. Shipping Board Bureau to Secretary of the Navy, March 26, 1934, File A16/QS1, SC, RG80, NA. Note: Secretary of the Navy Swanson was hospitalized on 15 December 1933 and remained indisposed throughout the first half of 1934. During his absence, many of the policy making decisions were made by Standley as Acting Secretary. This frequently placed him in the unique position of being able to endorse his own recommendations as CNO. Thus it appears extremely likely that the Navy's letter was issued under Standley's signature as "Acting Secretary," a contention supported by other documents issued during the same time period and subsequently reviewed by the author.

12. Hart, "Policy In Regard To Merchant Vessels," 3.

13. U.S. Shipping Board Bureau—Division of Loans and Sales, Committee on Standard Merchant Vessels, memoranda of first and fifth meetings, MC File 505–1, RG178, MARAD. For additional information surrounding the design activities of the "Committee," see Thomas Wildenberg, "The Origins and Development of the T2 Tanker," *The American Neptune*, Summer 1992, 155–66.

14. Michael Allen West, "Laying the Legislative Foundation: The House Naval Affairs Committee and the Construction of the Treaty Navy, 1926–1934", PhD Dissertation, Ohio State University, 1980. This excellent study discusses the importance of the Vison-Trammell Act and provides a comprehensive history of the legislative actions leading to its passage.

15. Chairman General Board to Secretary of the Navy, memo: "Auxiliary and minor combatant vessels for Treaty Navy–Program of," 16 June 1934, File A1-3/AG, SC, RG80, NA.

16. Ibid.

17. "Theoretical study of an orderly schedule of building auxiliaries and minor combatant vessels," Enclosure A attached to "Auxiliary and minor combatant vessels for Treaty Navy—Program of."

18. Robert G. Albion, *Makers of Naval Policy 1798–1947*, (Annapolis, Md.: Naval Institute Press, 1980), 91.

19. Robert Levine, "The Politics of American Naval Rearmament, 1932–1938," PhD Dissertation, Harvard University, 1972 (hereafter Levine, "Politics"), 292.

20. A somewhat jumbled version of events surrounding the budget can be found in Levine, "Politics," 301–308.

21. Claude A. Swanson to President, 25 November 1934, copy attached to "Memorandum for Admiral" [drafts of Auxiliary Bill], File S1–S68, SC, RG80, NA.

22. Ibid. To avoid Congressional obstacles to the construction program wanted by the Navy, Swanson suggested that ALL naval construction for FY1936 be financed via the PWA.

23. Levine, "Politics," 175–181.

24. "Memorandum for Admiral" [drafts of Auxiliary Bill and various memorandums], 8 March 1935, File S1–S68, SC, RG80, NA.

25. Bell to FDR, 27 April 1935, folder: "Increase of the Navy," No. 1, 1927–1937, Central File 1921–1938, RG51, NA, as cited in Levine, "Politics," 381.

26. Levine, "Politics," 384.

27. Commander-in-Chief, U.S. Fleet to Chief of Naval Operations, 6 July 1935, Confidential File A4-1, RG80, NA.

28. Joseph M. Reeves, "Annual Report of the Commander-In-Chief, United States Fleet For the Fiscal Year 1935," 11 October 1935, 9. Washington: National Archives, Record Group 313, Annual Reports of the U.S. Fleet and Task Forces of the U.S. Navy 1920–1941, Microfilm series M971, Roll #10.

29. Levine, "Politics," 387.

30. Walter, "William Harrison Standley," 95. George T. Davis, *A Navy Second To None*, 370. (Harcourt, Brace and Company, New York, 1940.)

31. Walter, "William Harrison Standley," 96.

32. Hart, "Policy In Regard To Merchant Vessels," 9. The General Board divided merchant ships "acceptable" to the Navy into two classes: auxiliaries to accompany the Fleet in time of war, and auxiliaries acceptable to the Navy. The former had to conform to the military characteristics of the naval auxiliaries into which they would be converted and generally required greater speed capabilities then the latter.

33. West, "Laying the Legislative Foundation," 188. U.S. Senate Commerce Committee, Hearings on S.258; A Bill to Develop a Strong American Merchant Marine, 1–2 May 1935, 113–114. Note: Royal S. Copeland, Chairman of the Senate Commerce Committee, made sure to include several pointed questions during hearings on the proposed act which were sure to reveal the importance of tankers as naval auxiliaries and the need to subsidize their speed.

34. Emory S. Land, Memorandum for Files, 9 August 1937. Washington: National Archives, Record Group 178, E.S. Land folder.

35. Levine, "Politics," 430.

36. R. E. McShane [Bureau of C&R] to Rear Admiral E. S. Land (CC), USN (Ret.), 23 July 1937. Washington: Library of Congress, Emory S. Land Manuscript (hereafter Land Manuscript), Box 7, Folder: Shipbuilding Data, 1937 (Note: ship names and hull numbers provided by author).

37. Levine, "Politics," 476.

38. Judge Advocate General of the Navy to Secretary of the Navy, 29 July 1983, File A1–3(1939), SC, RG80, NA.

39. Director, War Plans Division to Chief of Naval Operations, 24 August 1937, File AA/A1–3, RG80, NA.

40. Ibid.

41. Ibid.

42. Emory Land to Chairman, Maritime Commission, memo: "Tankers," 26 July 1937, Folder: Shipbuilding Data, 1937, Land Manuscript. Note: During his tenure as CNO, Standley, convinced of the need to include speed as a national defense feature in any construction program authorized by the Maritime Commission, had worked closely with Admiral Land (while still Chief of the Bureau of C&R) in assuring that this policy was adopted. See Wildenberg, "Origins and Development of the T2 Tanker."

43. Albion, Makers of Naval Policy, 170. West, "Laying the Legislative Foundation," passim.

44. Land, "Tankers."

45. W. Elliot, Acting Comptroller General of the United States to Chairman, U.S. Maritime Commission, Document #A-89721, 30 September 1938, 10. Washington: U.S. Maritime Administration, Records of the U.S. Maritime Commission, Accession # 178-55-9, File 502-23-14 (Navy Department—Acquisition of Tankers).

46. Ibid., 19.

47. George T. Davis, *A Navy Second to None*, 373.

48. "The *Cimarron*," Marine Age, March 1939, 9–10. Note: Contracts for 11 more "National Defense Tankers" would later be signed with Standard Oil Company of New York (SOCONY), and the Keystone Shipping Company.

49. *Marine Engineering and Shipping Review*, May 1938, 204.

50. Albion, Makers of Naval Policy 1798–1947, 253.

51. Davis, *A Navy Second to None*, 379.

52. "Memorandum for Admiral" lists 79 vessels (excluding gunboats) in service as of March 1935.

53. The Navy purchased or chartered a total of 35 ships. Two were transferred to Britain under Lend/lease, the others were converted into 12 AO, 8 AKA, 2 AKS, 2 AE, 2 AF, 2 APA, 2 AS, 1 AVG (later CVE), 1 AD, and 1 AH. See "Completed Contracts," Records of the U.S. Maritime Commission, MARAD.

54. Wildenberg, "Origins and Development of the T2 Tanker," 159–60.

55. It is doubtful whether the Navy could have conducted its early carrier raids without the timely completion of the Cimarron Class oilers. See Thomas Wildenberg, "Chester Nimitz and the Development of Fueling At Sea," *Naval War College Review*, Autumn, 1993, XLVI:4, 52–62.

56. Director of War Plans to Chief of Naval Operations, "Estimate of the Situation for Fiscal 1936," 31 March 1934, File (SC)L1-1 (1936), RG80, NA.

57. West, "Laying the Legislative Foundation," 189.

58. Though the CNO was the highest ranking officer of the Navy, he had no authority to direct operational forces of the fleet, whose commander (CinCUS) reported directly to the Secretary of the Navy.

The Struggle for Control of Air Power in the North Pacific, 1942

William S. Hanable

⚓

During World War II the Pacific Ocean Areas command, headed by Admiral Chester W. Nimitz, included the North Pacific. In May of 1942, Nimitz sent Rear Admiral Robert A. Theobald to Alaska to assume command of the North Pacific Force. This was a joint command that included Army Air Force and Navy air, surface, and submarine units.

Theobald went north with instructions to place the air component of his joint service force under the command of Brigadier General William O. Butler, commander of the Army's Eleventh Air Force. He chose not to do so until Admiral Ernest J. King, the Commander in Chief of the U. S. Fleet and Chief of Naval Operations, and Nimitz reminded him of his (King's) instructions.

This paper examines Theobald's recalcitrance, his rationale for his actions, and the results of them. It also looks at the Army side of the ledger, where Butler and some of his subordinates were no more cooperative than Theobald. It is important to point out that these difficulties in cooperation occurred in offices and conference rooms. The men who flew and sometimes died together in the North Pacific cooperated whether they flew in Army or Navy aircraft.

A complex history resulted in the command arrangements in the north. Before World War II, there had been little need for interservice coordination in Alaska. The Navy, in 1869, bombarded the Native village of Kake at the request of the Army and occasionally transported Army personnel to coastal points. The two services, for the most part, operated independently of each other in Alaska. Naval forces that did operate in Alaska were usually dispatched from the Navy's Pacific Squadron.

The World War II requirement to conduct combat operations against a well-armed and determined enemy defined the need in

Alaska, as it had elsewhere, for interservice cooperation. For the larger Pacific theater, the Joint Chiefs of Staff, which had replaced the Joint Army-Navy Board, tasked the Navy to be their Executive Agent in the South, Central, and North Pacific areas and the Army to be their Executive Agent in the Southwest Pacific.[1]

The Army established an Alaska Defense Command for the defense of mainland Alaska and the Naval bases at Dutch Harbor, Kodiak and Sitka. Its commander, Major General Simon Bolivar Buckner, reported to Lieutenant General John L. DeWitt, head of the Army's Western Defense Command located at San Francisco. The Navy, in May 1942, established the North Pacific Force or Task Force 8 as its operational command in Alaskan waters.

If a "State of Fleet Opposed Invasion" existed in Alaska, the Navy would direct the territory's defense. Fleet Opposed Invasion was to be invoked if the Japanese attacked the Aleutian Islands. If a "State of Army Opposed Invasion" existed in Alaska, the Army would direct the territory's defense. Army Opposed Invasion was to be invoked if the Japanese attacked Kodiak Island or mainland Alaska.

If a "State of Fleet Opposed Invasion" was declared, Army Air Forces Brigadier General William O. Butler would command the air task group in Task Force 8. For this purpose Butler reported to Theobald while continuing in his capacity as commander of Alaska Defense Command. Air elements were to report to Buckner. Navy directives setting up the task force said that, under Butler, Captain Lewis E. Gehres would command Patrol Wing 4, the Navy air element of Task Force 8. Colonel William O. Eareckson, also under Butler, would command the Army air element of Task Force 8.[2] The framework was in place for what, in current jargon, is called a "single air manager."

The command relationship between other Army forces in Alaska not under Theobald's command and Task Force 8 was to be by "mutual cooperation" rather than by unified command. Admiral King directed this cooperation, and Brigadier General Dwight D. Eisenhower of the Army's War Plans Division concurred on behalf of General George C. Marshall, the Chief of Staff.[3]

Meanwhile, Navy communications intelligence revealed Japanese plans to attack Midway Island and the Aleutian Islands in May or June of 1942. Admiral King declared a "State of Fleet Opposed Invasion" to exist in the North Pacific Ocean on May 21,

1942. This meant that Theobald had responsibility for directing the defense of Alaska and that Buckner was to play a supporting role.[4]

Prewar struggles over the control of airpower, service traditions, and personalities created a web, in 1942, that hindered U.S. air operations in the North Pacific and destroyed at least one career, Theobald's. His orders were to, in coordination with the Army, oppose the advance of the enemy in the Aleutian-Alaska area, taking advantage of every favorable opportunity to inflict strong attrition.[5] Theobald headed for Alaska in the *Reid*, DD-369, on May 22, 1942. He had been at sea only two days when he radioed Nimitz that airpower was the key to the defense of Alaska. Theobald called for "maximum concentration of available mainland based Navy planes and large concentration of similar Army planes."[6]

Immediately after arriving at the newly-established Kodiak Naval Base on May 27, Theobald conferred with Buckner, Butler, and Gehres. The four officers discussed Theobald's "estimate of the situation, functions of command, and material matters." Theobald later recorded that during the meeting Buckner and Butler thought the main Japanese attack would be on Anchorage. Because of this, and because Butler did not want to concentrate his aircraft at Cold Bay and Umnak where there were no revetments, the Army commanders resisted Theobald's wish to locate his air striking force as far to the west as possible. The admiral agreed with them about the inadequacy of the westward airfields, but still considered it preferable that the Army aircraft be sent to Cold Bay and Umnak.[7]

Although it was clear in the State of Fleet Opposed Invasion that Theobald could order disposition of the Army aircraft, he was reluctant to do so. Assertion of his authority at this point, he believed, might prejudice Butler's cooperation in the future. At the end of hours of discussion, Butler finally agreed to position the Army aircraft at Cold Bay and at Umnak.[8]

This meeting was Theobald's first with the Army commander with whom he was to cooperate and with the air officers who were to command Task Force 8's air components. After the meeting, he again advised Nimitz (and also Admiral King) that airpower was the key to the defense of Alaska and the Aleutians. "In absence of a naval force," Theobald radioed, "adequate in all types the answer to Alaska defense is adequate land based air."[9]

Theobald chose not to follow the instructions given to him by King and Nimitz regarding consolidation of the Army and Navy air elements of his task force. Only on June 15, when queried by King and Nimitz, did he do so. Admiral Theobald justified his failure to follow instructions with several reasons: (1) that a single air manager would have served no useful purpose; (2) that the Army Air Forces pushed for a single air manager only so that it could claim credit for actions attributable to naval aviation; (3) that Butler and Gehres would not have been able to work together.

Writing to Nimitz shortly after the Japanese attack on Dutch Harbor and occupation of Attu and Kiska, Theobald claimed that:

> To have interjected General Butler as an echelon between me and my Air Search Group would have served no useful purpose. All that General Butler could have done would have been to repeat my orders to Captain Gehres and to pass on to me all Captain Gehres' reports. . . . The whole matter appears to be a tempest in a teapot. It appears to be an Army Air Corps political move. It looks to me as though they feel that the only chance of avoiding undesirable comparisons as far as they are concerned is to be linked together with successful naval aviation so that the word "we" can really be given more significance from the air standpoint. Had I retained a single air force command I would have had to do General Butler's work for him by creating under his command an air search group under Captain Gehres and General Butler's own striking group. . . . There would have been a distinct clash of personality. I saw this from the first day. Butler and Gehres will not come to an open break under the present setup but they would never work in harmony in close official relationship to each other.[10]

Nearly six months later, in a memo retained for his personal files, Theobald again addressed command arrangements for the air elements of his force. He asserted that criticism that he had divided his air force lacked substance. He then drew an analogy between separate commands for surface ships performing different functions (escorting cruisers and covering force cruisers) and separate commands for aircraft performing different functions (PBYs engaged in air search and fighters, medium and heavy bombers engaged in air strikes).[11]

Believing that "The requirement that the air forces may not be divided into essential components is based solely on a pandering to popular opinion," Theobald concluded that "The attitude of the High Naval Command in this matter was completely dominated by the politics of the situation."[12]

Commenting, in 1946, on a draft history of the North Pacific Command, Theobald had still not changed his mind about the appropriateness of dividing his air command. Patrol Wing Four was, he said, "the principal scouting force of the Northern Pacific Force. Every commander desires that his scouts shall be subject to his immediate orders and shall report directly to him." To do otherwise, Theobald wrote, was to cause delay in the flow of orders and information. Theobald characterized the unified air command directed by King and Nimitz as "unnatural and undesirable arrangements."

He went on to say that he had overcome the arrangements by requiring the commander of Patrol Wing Four to maintain his headquarters at Kodiak, while the Army Air Forces command headquarters was on Adak. Theobald concluded his comments on this aspect of the draft history by noting that when Butler asked that the Naval Air headquarters join him on Adak, Theobald had denied the request in a four-page memorandum.[13]

This sequence of events raises several questions. Who was Robert A. Theobald? Who were his Army peers and subordinates? What were the consequences of bad relations between Theobald and his Army subordinates? Reportedly known as "one of the best minds and worst dispositions in the Navy," Theobald has also been described by naval historian Samuel Eliot Morison as "one of the most able and energetic flag officers in the Navy."[14] Theobald, born in 1884, began his naval career with academy graduation in 1907. By 1941 he was a rear admiral serving as type commander for destroyers in the Pacific. In the intervening years, he had been a destroyer captain and battleship gunnery officer, executive officer, and captain. His shore tours had included both student and faculty appointments at the Naval War College.

Almost half a century later, a naval officer who served under Theobald as a junior officer when Theobald was executive officer of the battleship *West Virginia* and later as commander of a PBY squadron operating in the Aleutians when Theobald was Commander, North Pacific Force, would characterize the admiral as "a dour New Englander, stern and unbending." Theobald's sometime subordinate pointed out that he and his contemporaries admired Buckner for his aggressive fighting spirit. Theobald, he commented, "was just the other way."[15]

General Buckner, Theobald's Army counterpart in Alaska, was an infantry officer who had learned to fly while serving with the Army Air Service in the United States in World War I. After the war he returned to the infantry and held a number of important staff appointments, including service at West Point (where he had graduated in 1909) as an instructor and as Commandant of Cadets. Known for his aggressive and physically active leadership, Buckner was Theobald's opposite.

Butler, theoretical commander of Theobald's air forces and the Army subordinate about whom Theobald complained most bitterly, was a West Point graduate who had seen World War I combat service as an artillery officer. After the war he had transferred to the Army Air Service and held a number of important command, staff, and school assignments prior to being designated as Commander, 11th Air Force. Described as "thoughtful," Butler was, ironically, more like Theobald than like Buckner. Despite Theobald's assumptions about the relationship between Butler and his Navy counterpart, Butler held Gehres in high regard. On the other hand, Butler is said to have had little use for Theobald.[16]

The consequences of this relationship were ominous. Indeed, affairs between Army Air Forces commanders and naval commanders in Alaska in 1942 clearly were not ideal even before Theobald's arrival. Navy officers in Alaska protested their lack of control over Army aircraft designated to protect naval installations. Navy officials as far away as Washington, D.C., protested Army flights over water, traditionally a Navy prerogative.

Army aircraft were moved onto the naval air station at Kodiak as part of the program to defend the station. They flew patrols from the Kodiak station over the Gulf of Alaska. Control of the aircraft remained with Headquarters Eleventh Air Force at Elmendorf Field outside Anchorage. While this was in accordance with Army Air Forces doctrine, it created the potential for delay in responding to enemy contacts.[17] According to one wartime report:

> If Navy patrol planes made contact with enemy forces suitable for bomber attack, the latter could not leave the ground until a contact report had been sent to Elmendorf and the necessary orders sent back to Kodiak. A practice operation on one occasion required forty five minutes from the time of contact until the necessary orders for bomber attack came through.[18]

Conferences between General Buckner, Captain Parker (Commander of the Alaskan Sea Frontier), and Commander J. Perry (naval air base commander at Kodiak) resulted in the Navy being given operational control of Army bombers for sea rescue, search, and as a striking force.[19]

At the operational level, Army-Navy cooperation worked better. As early as February 26, 1942, Lieutenant Commander (later Admiral) James S. Russell, commanding officer of Patrol Squadron 42, Captain Russell A. Cone, commanding officer of the 36th Bomb Squadron, and First Lieutenant J.C. Bowen, commanding officer of the 18th Pursuit Squadron, worked out a detailed agreement for joint operations. Commander Perry approved the agreement.[20]

The agreement stated that when one or more enemy ships were sighted, all available aircraft would take off for attack. It specified separate directions of attack, altitude separations, communications channels, and called for concentrated attack. In the event of attack by carrier aircraft, the agreement said that interceptor aircraft would concentrate on destroying enemy aircraft while Army and Navy bombers would concentrate on destruction of the enemy carriers.[21]

The first critical test of Army and Navy air elements in Alaska came on June 3, 1942. Although expected and searched for, the attacking Japanese force was able to approach Dutch Harbor without detection due to weather and garbled transmission from the one Navy patrol aircraft that did sight them. On the morning of that day, Japanese aircraft from the carrier *Junyo* and *Ryujo* bombed Dutch Harbor and Unalaska. When Dutch Harbor reported the bombing, Army fighters to the east at Cold Bay scrambled. Army fighters to the west of Dutch Harbor and Unalaska at Umnak did not receive word of the attack in progress due to poor communications.[22]

The Japanese renewed their attack on Dutch Harbor on June 4. As the carrier aircraft returned to their ships, Army P-40s based at Umnak rose to attack them and destroyed several. At the same time, Navy PBYs from Cold Bay and Dutch Harbor and Army bombers from Cold Bay and Umnak attempted to attack the Japanese carriers. Hampered by weather, opposed by Japanese fighters, and hindered by improvised weaponry (Navy torpedoes slung under Army aircraft), the bombers did little damage to the Japanese task force despite their aggressive and brave aircrews.

The senior Air Corps officer at Umnak refused to allow the Army and Navy strike aircraft there to take off to attack the Japanese without orders from Headquarters 11th Air Force at Anchorage. According to Lieutenant Junior Grade J.E. Breeding of Patrol Squadron 41, Colonel Thad V. Foster told Breeding "to stay where he was." Breeding then radioed Lieutenant Commander Paul J. Foley, skipper of VP-41 that "Six B-26s loaded with torpedoes here awaiting your orders for take off. PBYs are now loading torpedoes." Foley immediately ordered the B-26s to take off. The PBYs then followed. According to Breeding, Foster repeatedly said that he was taking orders from the Navy from a person fourteen years his junior.[23]

Within three days of the Japanese attack, the War Department was querying Buckner. Messages from Washington stated that the Navy had complained of slow action by Army units in obeying orders to attack the enemy carriers. The Navy, in this case, was either Theobald, or his subordinate, Captain Parker. Parker had radioed Nimitz on June 7 that Navy PBYs were patrolling continuously with heavy losses "without being followed by successful attacks [by the Army's strike aircraft] and compensating damage to the enemy."[24]

The months after the Japanese bombing of Dutch Harbor and occupation of Attu and Kiska islands to the west of Dutch Harbor continued to be filled with dissension. In August Butler complained to a friend on the Army Air Forces headquarters staff that "bombing operations against Kiska are becoming less profitable all the time. Under my orders (Navy) I must continue them."[25]

Asked in September about the operations summaries usually sent by Army air commanders to Headquarters Army Air Forces, Butler replied that directives required that his summaries go to Theobald. Theobald, although requested to do so, was not sending a copy on to the Commanding General, Army Air Forces.[26]

Butler got small comfort from General H. H. Arnold, Commanding General, Army Air Forces. Arnold advised him at the end of October that:

> When the final analysis is made of operations of the air units in Alaska, it won't be the Admiral of the Navy or the General of the Ground Forces who are held responsible for air shortcomings—it is bound to be the air commander.[27]

With this guidance from above, Butler seems to have had no hesitation in thwarting what he considered ill-advised orders from a battleship admiral.

As late as December of 1942, Theobald and Butler continued to squabble over command of Task Force 8's air component. By this time Theobald was retaining copies of or summarizing messages exchanged with Butler and giving them labels such as "Second Incident." Alerting Butler to a possible Japanese carrier raiding force expected to attack U.S. bases in the western Aleutians on December 3, Theobald directed that "all planes at Adak should be in the air before dawn, and the Umnak bombers should be at stations." The "fighters at Umnak, Dutch, Cold Bay and Kodiak should be on air alert [in the air], equipped with belly tanks, by daylight, unless radar coverage will permit partial alert or 'stations' for part of fighter force."[28]

Butler replied that getting all of the planes at Adak into the air before dawn was impractical due to limited facilities. He suggested an alternative plan that would get all aircraft into the air shortly after daylight. This would, he said, provide a full air alert for the first two hours after daylight and one half air alert and the remainder on ground alert for the rest of the day. Resisted by Butler, Theobald responded that he had never meant that a full fighter alert be maintained for more than two hours after daylight, "nor that bombers should be kept up continuously if attack or contact did not develop."[29]

Later in December, Theobald ordered Butler to send bombers to attack two Japanese freighters reported to be at Attu. When Butler responded that weather conditions made it impossible to attack on December 7 as ordered, Theobald ordered a second attack to take off at 1000 on December 8. Butler answered this by advising that an 1100 take off would permit reports from a weather reconnaissance aircraft that would be in the Attu area at 1000. A 1000 departure time, he added, would be too dark for a large formation of aircraft to take off and assemble.[30]

What ensued was a series of messages in which Butler indicated he had scheduled an attack mission as ordered, but pointed out difficulties related to weather forecasts, icing conditions, and so forth. Theobald consolidated the various exchanges, added comments, and preserved the correspondence in his personal files.[31] Theobald's comments justified his insistence on a 1000 departure (to fool the Japanese who were accustomed to bombers arriving from Adak after an 1100 departure) and dismissed Butler's advice regarding weather (because Theobald had an air staff officer knowledgeable about Aleutian weather). In the comments, Theobald elaborated on theories of unity of command and concluded that Butler's recommendations for changes in his orders were due to the general's desire to "conduct his operation and not that of the Task Force Commander."[32]

The December attack was the last ordered by Theobald. On the 8th of that month, he was relieved by CINCPAC. From Alaska

Theobald went to the Boston Navy Yard, where he served as Commandant, First Naval District. Two years later the Chief of Naval Personnel advised him that a Naval Retiring Board had determined "that you are incapacitated for active duty by reason of physical disability incurred in line of duty. Retirement will be effective 1 February 1945."[33] Theobald died in 1953.

Theobald's Army counterpart, Buckner, left Alaska as a lieutenant general in 1944 and went on to command the Tenth Army during the invasion of Okinawa. Japanese artillery fire killed him there on June 18, 1945. Butler, Theobald's air component commander, left Alaska on September 11, 1943, to command an Air Depot in the European Theater of Operations and retired shortly after the war.

Theobald's failure to place the entire air component of Task Force 8 under Butler must certainly have antagonized the Army Air Forces general. Butler had official orders, concurred by the Army's Chief of Staff, that placed him under Theobald's command. At the same time, Butler had guidance from the Commanding General, Army Air Forces, telling him that no matter what the organization chart said, he would be held responsible for shortcomings in air operations. Theobald's insistence on giving detailed, sometimes inappropriate, instructions for air operations must also have been irritating to an experienced flier. Since Butler left few papers, there is little evidence of his feelings toward Theobald. It is clear from surviving correspondence that he disagreed with some of Theobald's decisions. Incidents such as the one on Umnak on June 4 indicate that whatever his feelings were, Butler did not give his subordinates the impression that they were to whole-heartedly cooperate in Navy direction of Army Air Forces resources.

Ironically, the struggle for control of airpower in the North Pacific from May to December 1942 was soon glossed over by all contemporaries except Theobald. According to Dewitt:

> There was a personality clash between Admiral Theobald and General Buckner, but it was superficial and had no lasting effect on the mutual cooperation that followed. It was forgotten after Admiral Theobald was relieved and General Buckner promoted.[34]

Admiral Theobald, in his 1946 comments on the draft North Pacific Force command history, noted that he believed he had not received full cooperation from Army Air Forces under his command.

The admiral's belief derived, first, from General Butler's reluctance to base his aircraft in the Aleutians prior to the June 1942 Japanese attack on Dutch Harbor and occupation of Kiska and Attu; second, from the Umnak-based Army Air Forces commander's refusal to launch attacks against the Japanese without a direct order from Butler; and, third, from placement of the Naval Air Search Unit under Butler's command. Finally, Admiral Theobald attributed to Butler an "ever increasing reluctance to accept orders [from Admiral Theobald]."[35]

Appearing to support Theobald's beliefs, Admiral Freeman (Captain Parker's successor) and DeWitt indicated that Butler had not fully cooperated with the admiral and other naval officers. They said he had failed to establish an appropriate relationship with Gehres and failed, in at least one instance, to pass vital information gained in air reconnaissance at Kiska on to Theobald. While Marshall, DeWitt, and King agreed on the necessity of relieving Buckner as a result of his relationship with Theobald, they agreed even more strongly on the necessity of relieving Butler.[36]

Admiral King would write (after Theobald's relief by Vice Admiral Thomas C. Kincaid, USN):

> In the North Pacific Area no complete unified command has been established. Naval Forces, amphibious operations, and a portion of the Army Air Forces have been placed under the Commander North Pacific Force, to operate under the principle of mutual cooperation with the ground forces and other Air Forces.... This arrangement, made last year, has ... worked extremely well in practice, largely due to excellent cooperation between the responsible commanders concerned.[37]

The scenario that played out in the North Pacific presents a classic lesson in the value of unity of command, of some of the reasons why that principle has so often been resisted by military leaders, and of the consequences of such resistance.

In May 1943, Vice Admiral Thomas C. Kincaid, who had relieved Theobald in January 1943, commanded the North Pacific Force as it supported an amphibious operation to retake Attu. An assault force under Rear Admiral F.W. Rockwell, USN, delivered a landing force under Major General Albert Brown, USA, and later Major General Eugene M. Landrum, USA, to Attu beaches that recaptured the island.[38]

Once Attu was in American hands again, Fleet Air Wing Four PBYs cooperated with Army Air Forces squadrons in bombing attacks on Kiska and on Japan's bases in the northern Kuriles.[39] As the air attacks continued and were supplemented by naval gunfire bombardments, a Kiska invasion force assembled. Comprised of over 100 warships and nearly 35,000 ground troops, the force assaulted Kiska on 15 August 1943 only to find that the Japanese had evacuated the island.[40]

As 1943 came to a close, PV-1 Venturas of Fleet Air Wing Four and Army Air Force units began regular operations against Japan's northern Kurile Islands from Aleutian bases. Photographic reconnaissance missions were followed by bombing, rocket, and strafing attacks on Japanese bases and shipping. In early 1945, PV-2 Harpoons joined the Venturas. The attacks continued until the end of the war. Post-war analysts credited them with causing diversion of sizeable Japanese forces for defense of the northern islands.[41]

1. Cline, Roy S., *Washington Command Post: The Operations Division, Vol. II, in United States Army in World War II, The War Department* (Washington, D.C.: Office of the Chief of Military History, Department of the Army, 1951), p. 101.

2. Msg, COMINCH (Commander-in-Chief United States Fleet), to Commander-in-Chief Pacific, no subject, 21 May 1942, copy in files of the Office of History, Alaskan Command.

3. Msg, COMINCH, 21 May 1942.

4. Msg, COMINCH, 21 May 1942.

5. CINCPACFLT Operation Order 28–42, May 11, 1942, p. 2, in the Theobald Papers, Hoover Institution on War, Revolution and Peace (hereafter Theobald Papers).

6. War Diary, Commander North Pacific Force, Task Force Eight, United States Pacific Fleet (hereafter War Diary), May 22–May 31, 1942, in Box 7, Theobald Papers.

7. War Diary, May 27, 1942; Letter, June 16, 1942, Theobald to Nimitz, in Theobald Papers.

8. Theobald to Nimitz, June 16, 1942.

9. Radio to CINCUSPACFLT, information copy to CINCUSFLT, quoted in War Diary, May 30, 1942.

10. Theobald to Nimitz, June 16, 1942.

11. Theobald, Rear Adm Robert A., "Written But Never Sent," memo dated November 6, 1942, in Box 10, Theobald Papers.

12. Theobald, November 6, 1942.

13. Theobald, Rear Adm Robert A., USN-Ret., to Director of Naval History, "Command History of the North Pacific, Comments on," January 19, 1946, memo to "Alaskan Commands—North Pacific Force and Area, Alaskan Sea Frontier, Seventeenth Naval District," November 27, 1945.

14. Morison, Samuel Eliot, *History of United States Naval Operations in World War II, Volume IV, Coral Sea, Midway and Submarine Actions, May 1942–August 1942* (Boston: Little, Brown and Company, 1951), p. 166, p. 177.

15. Russell, Adm. James S., USN-Ret., January 2, 1993, letter to author, and quoted in Cloe, *The Aleutian Warriors*, 1990, p. 91.

16. Butler, Major William O., Jr., USA-Ret., February 24, 1993, letter to the author. Major Butler flew in the Aleutians as a second lieutenant when his father was Commander, 11th Air Force.

17. Commander, North Pacific Force and Area, Administrative History of the North Pacific Area, 1 August 1940–14 August 1945 (available on microfiche from the Naval Historical Center as Guide No. 156, U.S. Naval Administation in World War II: CINCPAC North Pacific Force and Area, Alaskan Sea Frontier, Seventeenth ND), (hereafter cited as Administrative History, Vol. 156), p. 61.

18. Administrative History, Vol. 156, p. 62, citing a report from Lt Col Robert O. Cork to Commanding General, Fort Greely, Kodiak, Alaska, "Employment of Air Forces Based at Kodiak," May 11, 1942.

19. Cork, May 11, 1942.

20. "Notes for Joint Employment of Army and Navy Aviation at Naval Air Station, Kodiak," February 26, 1942.

21. "Notes for Joint Employment of Army and Navy Aviation at Naval Air Station, Kodiak," February 26, 1942.

22. See Cloe, *The Aleutian Warriors*, 1990, pp. 118–134, for a detailed account of the Japanese attack and the American response to it.

23. "Report from HQ 11th Air Force Striking Group File," in Box 10, Theobald Papers. Reported to be highly eccentric, Foster carried an infantry field pack, canteen, .45 caliber pistol, Thompson submachine gun, and live grenades as he went about his garrison duties first at Anchorage and then at Umnak. (Butler, Major William O., Jr., USAF-Ret., letter to author, February 24, 1993).

24. Morison, *Coral Sea, Midway and Submarine Actions*, 1951, p. 179; Administrative History, Vol. 156, p. 107.

25. Letter, August 2, 1942, to Brigadier General L.S. Kuter, Deputy Chief of Staff, Office of the Commanding General, Army Air Forces, in Alaskan Air Command Collection, Series IV, Folder 31, Correspondence - Major General Bruce [sic] Butler, University of Alaska Anchorage Archives.

26. Letter, October 1, 1942, to General H.H. Arnold, Commanding General, Army Air Forces, in Alaskan Air Command Collection, Series IV, Folder 31, Correspondence - Major General Bruce [sic] Butler, University of Alaska Anchorage Archives.

27. Letter, October 30, 1942, to Brigadier General William O. Butler, in Alaskan Air Command Collection, Series IV, Folder 31, University of Alaska Anchorage Archives.

28. Theobald to Butler, radio, 300157 November 1942, in Box 10, Theobald Papers.

29. Butler to Theobald, radio, 300803 and 301946 November 1942; Theobald to Butler, radio, 010140 December 1942, in Box 10, Theobald Papers.

30. Theobald to Butler, radio, 080100 December 1942; Butler to Theobald, radio, 080215 December 1942; Theobald to Butler, radio, 071825 December 1942, in Box 9, Theobald Papers.

31. Radios are quoted from, summarized, and commented on in a December 14, 1942, memo signed by Theobald and found in Box 9, Theobald Papers.

32. Theobald, December 14, 1942, comments on radios between himself and Butler, in Box 10, Theobald Papers.

33. Chief of Naval Personnel, letter to Rear Admiral Robert A. Theobald, October 11, 1945, in Box 10, Theobald Papers.

34. Quoted in Morton, 1962, p. 424.

35. Letter, Rear Admiral R.A. Theobald, USN (Ret), to Director of Naval History, "Command History of North Pacific Force, Comments On," January 19, 1946, included with microfiche of Administrative History.

36. Letter, Lieutenant General J.L. DeWitt, USA, to General George C. Marshall, USA, September 5, 1942, copy in files of the Office of History, Alaskan Command.

37. Quoted in Morton, 1962, p. 424.

38. See Cloe, 1990, pp. 276–293.

39. See Cloe, 1990, pp. 298–321.

40. Cloe, 1990, p. 296, p. 320.

41. See Scrivner, Charles L., *The Empire Express* (Temple City, CA: Historical Aviation Album, 1976).

Strange Parallels in Stalin's and Hitler's Naval Programs

Jürgen Rohwer and Igor Amosov

⚓

Looking at the development of the strategic thinking and of the planning processes for shipbuilding in the Soviet Union and Germany during the years from 1922 to 1941, we can observe differences, but also some strange parallels in the threat perceptions, the ways selected to overcome the perceived dangers, and the roles Stalin and Hitler had on the development of their navies. We can analyze the development in Germany since the return of the German Naval Archives from Great Britain in the mid-sixties, and we now have several excellent studies, especially the books of Michael Salewski, Werner Rahn, and Jost Dülffer.[1] The situation with the Soviet Union was different. The many publications up to the period of perestroika gave away only very selective parts about the strategic discussions inside the Soviet Navy and the Soviet defense establishment. This has changed only in the last five years when the Soviet historians were allowed to use the archives more freely and Western experts got some access to documentary materials. So we now can count on the new publications of Mikhail Monakov, Sergei Berezhnoi, Aleksandr Basov, Vladimir Dmitriev and others.[2] Very important are also the many articles in the journals *Morskoj sbornik* and *Sudostroenie*.[3]

After the First World War and the Russian Civil War, both navies could no longer count on modern battleships, cruisers, destroyers and submarines. The Treaty of Versailles prohibited the possession of such ships by Germany and reduced the fleet to six old and pre-*Dreadnought* battleships, six old cruisers and twelve small destroyers, to be replaced only after twenty years in service. U-boats and aircraft were not allowed.[4]

Soviet Russia possessed no Navy as a real force. Only in the Baltic were there remnants of the fleet which had managed to get out of Helsinki in the legendary "ice breakthrough." The ships of the Black Sea fleet were taken by the White General Vrangel to Turkey and then to Bizerte. There were no ships in the North or in the Far East. The state of the remaining ships was terrible: without attendance, without fuel, and practically without crews, after the bloody suppression of the uprising of the Kronstadt sailors of 1921. But in the same year, the 10th Congress of the Communist Party adopted a decision "to revive and strengthen the naval power of the country with consideration of the general situation and the material resources of the Soviet Republic."[5] Many young Komsomol members were sent to training establishments of the Navy.

The rise of the Soviet Navy and the development of the naval programs can be divided into three periods. The years of restoration lasted from 1922 to 1927; capital repairs were made and some ships, laid down before the revolution, were completed. From 1927 to 1937, there was extensive building of submarines and small surface ships. Finally, the Soviets began to build a large high seas, oceangoing fleet between 1937 and 1942.

In the first period, most of the old ships were sold for scrap. Up to 1927, there were, in the Baltic, reconstituted for service or completed, three *Dreadnought*-type battleships, one old cruiser, ten destroyers, and nine submarines; in the Black Sea there were two cruisers, four destroyers, and five submarines.[6] The displacement of the fleet increased from 82,000 tons in 1922 to 139,000 tons in 1927.

The deficiencies in experience of the first leaders of the Revolutionary Navy led even the Revolutionary War Commissar Leon Trotsky to retain a number of officers from the old Imperial Navy as specialists. This might have been one reason for a continuity of strategic thinking on the lines of the so-called "old school," led by men like B. B. Zherve and M. A. Petrov. They followed the teachings of the "Russian Mahan," N. L. Klado, who died in 1919. Approximately 30 percent of the officers of the Czarist Navy served in the Red Fleet, some of them occupying command posts, such as E. A. Berens, A. V. Nemits, V. M. Altfater, L. M. Galler, A. K. Vekman, A. P. Zelenoi and others.[7]

The "old school" adhered to the theory of "control of the seas" maintained by squadrons of battleships. They wanted to have, in the future, two brigades of battleships, one of cruisers, four of light cruisers, and eight of destroyers, each consisting of four ships. They proposed to complete two unfinished battleships, to modernize one damaged battleship, and to recover the Vrangel squadron with the addition of one more battleship. In February 1924, during the conference in Rome of the naval powers not represented at the 1921–22 Washington Conference, the Soviet delegate, E. A. Berens, demanded a battleship tonnage of 491,000, only a little less than the 525,000 tons limit fixed for Great Britain and the United States.[8]

When, in January 1925, M. V. Frunze relieved Trotsky as head of the Red Workers and Peasants Army, he tried to establish a unified military and naval doctrine called the *Proletarian Military Doctrine*. Instead of Trotsky's *Workers Militia*, Frunze wanted a standing Army to realize the ideas of the Chief of the General Staff, M. N. Tukhachevskii and his comrades such as V. K. Triandafillov, who had developed a concept of mass attacks by mobile forces to strike deep into the territory of the enemies and defeat their forces there.[9]

The new Chief of the Navy, R. A. Muklevich, who relieved V. I. Zof in August 1926, included in this concept fulfilling the mission of protecting the territory of the Soviet Union against the threat of "counterrevolutionary" or "interventionary" landings, of which the officers fighting in the Civil War had become so painfully conscious. The main enemy was then seen to be Britain's Royal Navy. Because the ideas of the "old school" were unrealistic given existing conditions, the Red Fleet had to look for an active coastal defense with simple naval weapons that could be produced without great industrial expense. Officials, such as K. I. Dushenov, I. K. Kozhanov, I. M. Ludri, and A. P. Aleksandrov, became the most prominent proponents of this "New Young School."[10]

To the West, the German Navy at the end of World War I, was forced to put its remaining manpower into the great task of sweeping the big minefields from the Baltic and the North Sea. This task, and the limitations imposed by the Versailles Treaty, prevented much thinking, at first, about the postwar problems of coastal defense because the commissioning of the old battleships and cruisers had to be deferred until the end of the minesweeping. The rightist Kapp–Lüttwitz Revolt of March 1920 created the first important postwar crisis for the Germany Navy, owing to the participation in the uprising of Freikorps Marinebrigade Ehrhardt and the offer of the Chief of the Admiralty, Admiral von Trotha, to use the fleet to support the rebel regime. When the revolt broke down following the general strike of the unions and the neutral position of the *Reichswehr* under General von Seeckt, and also the opposition of the

Navy personnel and the yard workers at the naval bases, there was a danger of a total breakdown of order and discipline in the Navy. This was overcome only with the replacement of the responsible officers and the consolidation of the new Admiralty under a new chief, Admiral Behncke.[11]

In the German Republic of Weimar, there was a broad accord from the Social Democratic Party from both the left and the right wing parties that the Versailles Treaty had to be revised. In this context, the *Reichsmarine* had no great problems of starting within the limitations of the treaty with the replacement of the oldest cruisers and destroyers by building, from 1921 to 1928, five light cruisers of up to 6,000 tons and twelve destroyers of 800 tons.[12]

When the minesweeping operations came to an end in 1922–23, ideas for the employment of the fleet concentrated, aside from the coastal defense in the Baltic and North Sea, on the protection of sea lines of communication with the separated province of East Prussia, which was in a conflict with Poland and was considered the most probable location of emergency.[13]

In addition to Admiral Behncke (now called the *Chef der Marineleitung*) and his successor from 1924 to 1928, Admiral Zenker, it was of great importance to organize visits of warships in foreign harbors to reestablish friendly relations with the countries in Northern and Southern Europe and, after 1925, in other parts of the world. When the old battleships were refitted, Zenker put special emphasis on the development of night tactics for the newly built small destroyers, which were supported by the battleships.[14] More and more, the *Marineleitung* also looked at France, who was bound by a military treaty to support Poland in case of war, as a possible enemy. Against France, it was necessary to protect the German seaborne trade in the North Sea and to harass the French trade.[15]

In the mid-1920s, discussions about a future naval strategy became heated because of the publication of a book by the retired Admiral Wegener, who proposed, counting on the experience of the World War, the establishment of bases in Scandinavia to break the blockade in the North Sea.[16] While the *Marineleitung* tried to suppress its distribution as an inopportune opinion, this book was only an expression of the feelings of many naval officers, who dreamed of a new rise of Germany to *Seegeltung* (prestige at sea).[17]

The *Marineleitung* secretly invested some financial means into efforts to circumvent the limitations of Versailles, especially in the field of U-boat building. Already in 1920, the Japanese Navy obtained plans of German U-boat-cruisers and U-boat minelayers, and prominent German engineers went to Japan to assist in the building of new U-boats according to those plans. In 1922 three German yards established a construction bureau, which was transferred in 1925 to the Netherlands. Many designs for future German U-boats and for submarines of foreign countries were developed and to some extent realized.[18] The first contacts with the Soviet Navy, in 1923, were also concerned with the procurement of U-boats.[19]

Already in 1921–22, the nascent Red Army had tried to establish contacts with the German *Reichswehr*, which was interested in gaining some experience in the weapons technology forbidden in the Versailles Treaty. Following the Soviet–German Treaty of Rapallo, on 29 July 1922, a special treaty for some cooperation in the development of armaments was concluded. In April 1925, an air training center at Lipetsk was established; in 1928 a poison-gas school at Tomka near Saratov was founded; and, in spring 1929, the tank school at Kazan followed.[20] In addition there were many exchanges of visits of high-ranking officers during maneuvers and also exchanges of training courses at the general staff academies.[21]

The German Navy was more reluctant to provide support to the Soviet Navy. After the first unsuccessful contacts in 1926, there were some exchanges of visits of German and Soviet officers, and German plans of the U-boat type UB III, built in great numbers for the Imperial Navy since 1916, were delivered.[22] In December 1926, the Chief of the Soviet Naval Forces, Muklevich, declared to the chief of the German Trade Mission that he should not be interested in the outdated plans of the First World War. He asked for new plans and proposed to establish a submarine training center analog to the Army centers. The proposal was turned down by Admiral Zenker.[23] In the German Navy, there were great reservations concerning the Soviets, because there was great fear of a 'Bolshevik' infiltration, instilled by the mutinities in the German Navy in 1918.

The second period for the Soviet Navy began in 1926. To reconcile the old and the new theories and the available capacities, from 1926 to 1928, several controversial discussions about the question, "What Fleet Do We Need?" took place. While the Old School presented, in November 1926, a program for a fleet of 4 battleships, 1 carrier, 4 cruisers, 26 destroyers, and 40 submarines, besides many other smaller vessels, the Young School preached for the massive employment of mines, small submarines, torpedo cutters, and aircraft. But, after a session of the Revolutionary War Council on 8 May 1928, in which the ideas of M. A. Petrov and M. N. Tukhachevskii clashed, the ideas of the Young School won the upper hand and led to the decision to cancel most of the plans for big ships and start a first new building program of 12 submarines, 18 patrol ships and 36 torpedo cutters.[24] Great emphasis was placed on the building of this last vessel. In 1927 a new motor-torpedo-boat, designed by the aircraft engineer Tupolev, the ANT-3 *Prevents,* was commissioned. It was the prototype for a very large series of type G torpedo cutters, of which, until the end of the war, 359 boats were built.[25]

In 1931, the reconstitution of the ships of the Imperial Russian Navy was completed. To counter the strength of the Turkish Fleet, in 1930, the Black Sea Fleet got one battleship and one cruiser from the Baltic, in addition to its three modernized cruisers, five destroyers, and five submarines.[26] The Baltic Fleet, at the end of 1931, had 2 battleships, 1 old cruiser, 12 destroyers, and 10 submarines.[27]

With the Japanese conquest of Manchuria in 1931, a new danger arose in the Far East and led to the establishment of the Naval Forces of the Far East in April 1932. Because there was no shipyard capacity available, 12 medium and 28 small submarines were ordered to be built in Leningrad and Sverdlovsk and were to be sent, dismantled, by rail to Vladivostok for completion.[28] In 1933 there followed the formation of a Northern Flotilla which got from the Baltic, at first, three destroyers, three submarines, and three patrol ships by way of the new Baltic-White Sea-Canal, opened by Stalin and his entourage in July 1933.[29]

In 1932 the plans for the 2d Five Years Plan were developed and finally decided upon on 11 July 1933. They laid the main emphasis on 69 big, 200 medium, and 100 small submarines and 53 destroyers, supported by 10 destroyer leaders and 8 cruisers. In addition to minelayers and minesweepers, the coastal forces were to receive 28 armoured cutters and 25 torpedo cutters.[30] To realize this program, up to the end of 1937, a great expansion of the ship yards and the works to supply the machineries, the equipment, and the weapons was started.[31]

Because of the gap in experience in shipbuilding, foreign aid had to be sought. The Italian yard Cantiere dell'Adriatico delivered plans for a submarine, which was used in the construction of the first new Soviet submarines of the series I/D-class. And, when in

1929, for the First Five Years Plan, three new destroyer leaders were ordered, the plans for the project *Leningrad*-class were influenced by the French contretorpilleurs. But, when the French, in summer 1933, declined to deliver plans for cruisers, destroyers, and submarines, the Soviets turned again to Italy.[32] The Ansaldo yard, already building two guard ships for the Far East NKVD, was now allowed by the Fascist government to deliver plans for modern cruisers and destroyers. They became the basis for the *Kirov* cruisers and the *Gnevnyj* destroyers. And, in 1934, the destroyer-leader *Tashkent* was ordered with the OTO-trust.[33] In the same year, the German firm IvS helped to plan the series IX/S-class submarines.[34] Very high attention was given to the construction of submarines. To get early great numbers, especially of the medium series V/X-Shch-class[35] and the small series VI/XII *M*-class, from 1933 to the end of 1936, no less than 55 and 50 submarines of these types were commissioned, in addition to 14 bigger ones.[36] The completion of bigger surface vessels had to wait for the 3rd Five Years Plan.

Meanwhile, the German *Reichsmarine* had stumbled into a new crisis when, in 1927–28, the Lohmann-affair led to an uproar in the Reichstag and in the public. Captain Lohmann was the organizer of a great number of secret enterprises to prepare a rearmament of the Navy beyond the limitations of the Versailles Treaty. The *Marineleitung* supported Lohmann with financial means,[37] and when this became known in 1927–28, the *Reichswehrminister* Gessler had to retire. His successor, Groener, also relieved in October 1928 the Chef der Marineleitung, Admiral Zenker, and replaced him with Admiral Raeder. But the Lohmann-affair also had some influence on the domestic discussion about the replacement of the first old battleship with a new type, the *Panzerschiff*. During the election campaign for the Reichstag, the Social Democratic Party used the slogan "children feeding instead of an armoured cruiser." With great emphasis, Raeder tried to reestablish the reputation of the Navy with the public, and if successful, to win over the Reichstag for granting the necessary rates for the *Panzerschiff*.[38]

This new type of ship was the result of intense discussions inside the Navy concerning the best solution for the replacement of the old battleships within the 10,000 ton limit of Versailles. One possibility was to build a heavily armed and armoured but slow monitor for coastal defense, initially favoured by some admirals and by Admiral Zenker. Others were of the opinion that only a ship with at least one superior feature over the Washington-types of battleships or heavy cruisers was useful. Finally, the arguments of the latter group won when a design of a 10,000 ton vessel with a speed faster than the battleships and an armament stronger than the 20.3 cm of the heavy cruisers seemed possible: the *Panzerschiff*. By using diesel motors to save weight, this ship maintained a range which might enable the vessel to operate not only in the Baltic or North Sea, but also, for some time, independently in the Atlantic. The arms reduction negotiations at Geneva, where the Germans tried in vain to achieve a revision of the Versailles Treaty or to be included into the Washington Naval Formula of 5:5:3:1.75:1.75 for Great Britain, the U.S.A., Japan, France, and Italy on a level of 1.0 or 1.75, brought no reduction of the armed forces. And the London Naval Treaty of 1930 decreed some similar relations for the up to now excluded cruisers and other vessels, but avoided the inclusion of Germany or the Soviet Union.[39]

When the characteristics of this Pocket-Battleship, as it was at first called in a mocking way in foreign countries, became known, the other sea-powers had to react. The French and Italian Navies could replace their outdated pre-*Dreadnought* battleships with three ships of 23,333 tons or two ships of 35,000 tons. At first, the French Navy had the intention of following the first option, but the possible speed of the ship and the armament of 8 12-inch guns was considered insufficient to counter the last Italian heavy cruisers and, especially, the German *Panzerschiffe*. Thus the *Dunkerque*, laid down in early 1933, was redesigned into a fast battleship of 27,900 tons with a speed of 30 knots and two quadruple turrets of 13-inch guns. The Italian Navy changed its plan to follow the first option, build three smaller ships, as an answer to the *Dunkerque*, by starting, in 1934, to build two fast 35,000 ton battleships with 9 15-inch guns, the *Littorio*-class. A new naval arms race was on.[40] But this accelerating naval arms race should be viewed in the context of the developments in international politics. In 1931 Japan occupied Manchuria and established there a satellite state, Manchukuo. In 1933 Hitler came to power in Germany and started an enforced revisionist policy and renewed rearmament, when the disarmament conference ended in a deadlock. In 1935 the Italian dictator Mussolini started his aggression to conquer Ethiopia. What were the consequences of such developments for the Soviet and German Navies?

From 1934 to 1936, the policy of I. V. Stalin and his advisors began to change. There were probably different reasons for this change. Developments in the Far East led to an increased perception of Japan as the most dangerous possible enemy there. And in Europe, the anti-Soviet policy of Hitler produced another probable enemy on the other side of the Soviet Union. This became evident when Hitler concluded, in January 1934, a Pact of Non-aggression and Friendship with Poland, which had been considered a common enemy during the time of the cooperation with the *Reichswehr*. The introduction of conscription in Germany and the Anglo–German Naval Treaty of June 1935 led to additional fears, as did the conclusion of the Anti-Comintern Pact between Germany and Japan in November 1936. At first Stalin tried to counter these perceptions by participating in the international policy of Collective Security, by entering the League of Nations in September 1934, and by a campaign for Soviet Patriotism, at least temporarily turning away from the idea of a Communist World Revolution. He forced the *Komintern* into a policy of People's Front Coalitions, making possible, in May 1935, treaties of military assistance with France and Czechoslovakia.[41] The Italian conquest of Ethiopia, which led to the Steel-Pact between Hitler and Mussolini in October 1936, and the Italian and German support of the Franco-Regime in the Spanish Civil War added to the fears of the Soviets, unable to defend their ships which supported the Spanish Republicans against Nationalist and Italian attacks.[42] Before this experience might have given support to the proponents of a Soviet big-ship Navy in internal discussions, Stalin must already have felt the need to build homogeneous ocean-going fleets in all four regions as an instrument of world-wide power-projection. At the end of 1936, there was a meeting of the fleet commanders convened by Stalin, in which the Commander of the Black Sea Fleet, I. K. Kozhanov, pled for a continuation of the established policy of building submarines and light craft, while the Commander of the Pacific Fleet, M. V. Viktorov, made himself a speaker of the big-ship-school.[43] Even if Stalin said, "I suppose you do not know yourself what you need,"[44] he had already made his decision at this time.

On 27 May 1936, the Council of Labor and Defense accepted the proposal to build a big fleet and to assign 450,000 tons for the Pacific Fleet, 400,000 tons for the Baltic Fleet, 300,000 tons for the Black Sea Fleet, and 150,000 tons for the Northern Fleet, 1,300,000 tons in all. In June 1936 the Council of People's Commissars confirmed the plan of the big-ship group to build, through to 1947, 24 battleships, 20 cruisers, 182 destroyers, and 344 submarines.⁴⁵ Decisions of such dimensions must have had the approval of Stalin.

Stalin's decision to build a big ocean-going Navy with heavy battleships as its backbone had, at about the same time, its strange parallel in Hitler's ambitions to get a great Navy. As in the Soviet Navy, there were different opinions inside the German Navy about the best types of ships for the envisaged strategies. Up until 1933, Poland and France were seen as possible enemies to the German Navy, while it was assumed that Great Britain would remain neutral. So, the protection of sea lines in the Baltic, the separate province of East Prussia, the Swedish iron ore sources, and the German trade in the North Sea were paramount. But most officers envisioned for the future a revival of a stronger German Fleet to underline the German *Seegeltung*, which could be realized by a revision of the Versailles Treaty. So they were happy when Hitler opened up the way to overcome restrictions and allowed, in 1934, the realization of prepared plans for new *Panzerschiffe* destroyers, and U-boats.⁴⁶ A March 1934 plan proposed to complete, up to 1950, 8 *Panzerschiffe*, 3 aircraft carriers, 18 cruisers, 48 destroyers, 24 big and 48 small U-boats.⁴⁷ Already in February 1934 the two first improved *Panzerschiffe*, of 20,000 tons with 6 11-inch guns, were laid down and orders for the first 1,625 ton destroyers and the prefabrication of the first six small 250 ton U-boats were placed.⁴⁸

In June 1935 Hitler was successful in authorizing this new building program internationally by concluding, with Great Britain, a Naval Agreement allowing the German Navy a strength of 35 percent in relation to the British surface ship categories and 45 percent for the U-boats, with the acceptance of the tonnage and armament limitations of the London Naval Treaties.⁴⁹ Now, however, the characteristics of the new *Panzerschiffe* seemed to be insufficient against the new French *Dunkerque*, and the already laid down *Scharnhorst* and *Gneisenau* were redesigned officially at 26,000 tons, but were really 32,100 tons. The Navy wanted heavier armament, but because the 11-inch turrets were already in the late stages of production and because Hitler did not want to antagonize England at this time, he ordered the ships to be armed now with 9 11-inch guns in three turrets, leaving the option to rearm the ships later with 6 15-inch guns.⁵⁰ In addition, in 1935–36, 2 35,000 ton (really 41,700 tons) battleships, 2 carriers of 23,200 tons, 5 10,000 ton cruisers, 22 destroyers of 2,171–2,411 tons, 12 torpedoboats of 840 tons, 10 big, 17 medium, and 24 small U-boats were ordered.⁵¹

In addition to building a big ship Navy in both countries, there was another parallel in Stalin's and Hitler's measures. In January 1937, Stalin started a thorough reorganization of the Navy, eliminating, step by step, supporters of the small ship Navy, such as L. M. Ludri, R. A. Muklevich, V. M. Orlov, I. K. Kozhanov, G. I. Kireev, P. I. Smirnov, I. N. Kadatski Rudnev, and K. I. Dushenov. They were all eliminated between 1938 and 1940,[52] while the big ship men, such as, I. S. Isakov, L. M. Galler and G. I. Levchenko, survived and took over the most influential posts as Chief of the Construction Department, Chief of the Main Staff, and Commander of the Baltic Fleet.

When Hitler, on 4 November 1937, first described, before the Ministers of Foreign Affairs and the *Reichskriegsminister,* as well as the commanders-in-chief of the Army, Navy and Air Force, his intentions to solve the problems of Austria and Czechoslovakia, by force if necessary, and indicated his resoluteness to win the *Lebensraum* necessary for the German people in the East,[53] there was no open opposition to such plans. However, Hitler must have felt the fears of his leading military advisors. Therefore, on February 1938, he relieved Foreign Minister von Neurath, War Minister von Blomberg, and Commander-in-Chief of the Army von Fritsch, and established an *Oberkommando der Wehrmacht* under his personal direction. Hitler got rid of his opponents in a calumnious way and now had a free hand to execute his expansionist policy. In March, Austria was annexed. When Hitler expressed his decision to destroy Czechoslovakia, Chief of the General Staff Beck retired in August 1938, but Hitler had his way. After the Munich crisis of September 1938, he occupied, with the extorted consent of Great Britain and France, the Sudetenland and liquidated, in March 1939, Czechoslovakia, which led to the decisive change in the British policy.[54]

While the German Navy leadership was not as affected by Hitler's reorganizations as the Soviet Navy had been by Stalin's purges, both navies now began a hectic period of discussions about shipbuilding schedules with strong interferences from Stalin and Hitler, both of whom demanded the biggest battleships be built and completed earlier than experts thought possible.

Changes in the international situation were worsening. Danger of war loomed in the near future. But now strengthening of the Soviet economy and industry permitted the realization of building a strong sea and ocean-going fleet with ships of all classes. Since early

1936 planning for a new long-range shipbuilding program had been underway. The idea was to create powerful fleets in the Pacific and the Baltic theatres, which could stand against the fleets of Japan and Germany, and to considerably strengthen the fleets in the North and in the Black Seas in order to make them superior to any probable enemy. In May 1937, a revised plan was presented, dividing the battleships into 8 type A units of 41,500 tons with 9 16-inch guns and 16 type B units of 26,000 tons with 9 12-inch guns. Four of each type were to be laid down in the end of 1937 or the beginning of 1938. Of the 20 cruisers, 15 had 7,500 tons and 5 were of a new type. The 17 flotilla leaders were 2,020 tons and the 182 destroyers were 1,425 tons. Of the 344 submarines, 90 belonged to big types (62 alone to the new *K*-class subcruisers), 164 were of medium size, 90 of small size.[55]

After discussions, a "reduced" plan for building a Great Fleet was presented on 15 August 1937 and was decided upon by the Commissar for Defense, Marshal K. F. Voroshilov. Indeed, the plan now contained only 20 battleships: 6 of 57,000 tons with 9 16-inch guns and 14 of 48,000 tons with 9 14-inch guns, increasing the battleship tonnage by 35 percent. In addition, there were now 10 anti-Washington-cruisers of 23,000 tons with 8 10-inch guns, 2 aircraft carriers of 10,000 tons for 40–45 planes, 22 cruisers (16 of them now of 10,000 tons), 20 destroyer leaders, and 144 destroyers. The submarines were changed to 84 big, 175 medium, and 116 small units. In addition, there were 5 new types of minelayers and sweepers.[56] The distribution foreseen for the Pacific Fleet was 4+4 battleships, 1 carrier, 4 heavy and 8 light cruisers, 8 leaders, and 48 destroyers, as well as 155 submarines; for the Baltic Fleet, the distribution was 0+6 battleships, 2 heavy and 6 light cruisers, 4 leaders, and 40 destroyers, as well as 88 U-boats; for the Black Sea Fleet, the distribution was 0+4 battleships, 1 heavy and 6 light cruisers, 4 leaders, and 28 destroyers, as well as 70 submarines; for the Northern Fleet, the distribution was 2+0 battleships, 1 carrier, 3 heavy and 4 light cruisers, 4 leaders, 28 destroyers, as well as 60 submarines.[57]

New efforts were made to enlist foreign aid for the building program. Already, on 14 July 1936, the Italian yard, Ansaldo, finished the plans U.P.41 for a 42,000 ton battleship. From 1936 to 1939, there were negotiations with the U.S. government and U.S. firms about orders for battleships, armour, and guns, and diverse plans for battleships were delivered by the firm Gibbs & Cox in 1937–38. In 1939, Flagman I. S. Isakov visited the United States. An arrangement was concluded with the Czech firm Shkoda for the construction of naval guns, and orders were placed for turbine sets with the Swiss firm BBC.[58]

Meanwhile, the purges continued and led to fast changes in top positions. M. V. Viktorov, who had relieved Commander-in-Chief V. M. Orlov in July 1937, was himself relieved in December 1937 when Stalin established a separate People's Commissariat for the Navy. He made Army Commissar P. A. Smirnov its head, only to exchange him with the terrible Deputy Head of the NKVD, M. P. Frinovskii, in September 1938. But he proved to be incapable of managing a big naval program and was shot by his predecessors. Stalin then called, in April 1939, the young Commander of the Pacific Fleet, N. G. Kuznetsov, who, in 1937, was only a captain when he came back from his post as advisor to the Spanish Republican Navy, to become People's Commissar and Commander-in-Chief. His main advisors were I. S. Isakov and L. M. Galler, who exchanged their posts as Chief of the Main Staff and as head of the Construction Department.[59]

On 10 August 1939, they presented a revised plan with the number of battleships reduced to 15, but with only one type weighing 59,150 tons. The carriers, of 10,600 tons, had a low priority. But the heavy cruisers were raised from 23,000 tons and 10-inch guns to battlecruisers of 35,240 tons and 12-inch guns, and their number was augmented to 16. This decision was said to be influenced massively by Stalin himself, who liked the battlecruisers as Hitler did. The new cruisers now had 11,300 tons, the leaders 2,600 tons, and the new destroyers 2,240 tons. A great number of additional smaller vessels was also planned, and submarine building shifted from smaller and medium boats to high seas and ocean going types. Thus, from 1937 to 1939, the tonnage of the planned Fleet was raised from 1,990,000 tons to 3,027,901 tons or by 52 percent (38 percent for the Pacific, 26 percent for the Baltic, 19 percent for the Black Sea, and 17 percent for the Arctic).[60]

The 35 percent ratio of the German-British naval agreement allowed the German Navy to plan, in addition to the three *Panzerschiffe* A-C of 10,000 tons, the two battleships D and E officially of 26,000 tons, and the two battleships F and G of 35,000 tons, one more battleship H. In addition, there were two aircraft carriers, five heavy cruisers of 10,000 tons, and, added to the six already built light cruisers, were 9 more of a new type and 39 destroyers. The 45 percent ratio for submarines allowed the building of 72 U-boats.

Following the new British battleship-plans in 1937, there appeared, for the first time, six new German battleships of a new type H. While Admiral Raeder could convince Hitler, who was now very interested in the heaviest possible battleships, that a vessel of 100,000 tons with 21-inch guns was impossible to handle in German waters, the new type was finally settled at 52,600 tons with 16-inch guns.[61]

In spring 1938, it became more and more apparent to the German Navy leadership that in a future war Great Britain might also be on the hostile side and that such a war might come earlier than anticipated. Because the heavy ships might not be ready in time, a staff officer of the *Seekriegsleitung*, Commander Heye, prepared a memorandum proposing an emphasis on U-boats and the accelerating construction of new *Panzerschiffe* to cope with the potential for merchant warfare with Britain. Raeder, in May 1938, accepted this idea. He proposed to build 12 new *Panzerschiffe* of 22,145 tons with 6 11-inch guns and an operational range of 25,000 miles and to postpone the battleships H, I, K, L, M, and N. When Hitler insisted on the early completion of the six battleships and refused Raeder's request to retire in November 1938, the Navy presented Hitler several options, of which Hitler decided upon the Z-Plan, which combined Hitler's heavy battleships with a merchant warfare fleet. Raeder accepted this plan for a "homogeneous fleet" after Hitler assured Raeder he would not need the fleet before 1946–7.[62]

The plan of January 1939 envisioned bringing the fleet up to a strength of ten battleships, including the six type H, ten new *Panzerschiffe* of 22,145 tons, four carriers, five heavy cruisers, 18 light cruisers (of which 12 were of the new type M of 7,800 tons), 20 small reconnaissance cruisers of 3,914 tons, 64 destroyers, 78 torpedoboats, and 249 U-boats (of which 60 were of small, 100 of medium, and 62 of big size, while the remaining 27 belonged to special big types for cruiser warfare overseas).[63] After smashing Czechoslovakia without a shot in March 1939, Hitler next decided to 'solve' the Polish question by forcing Poland to acquiesce in the return of Danzig to Germany. When Poland refused, he revoked, on 1 April 1939, the non-aggression treaty of 1934, and because of the rising opposition of Great Britain to his policy, he, at the same time, also revoked the German-British naval agreement.[64]

In the spring of 1939, the expansion policy of Hitler forced Stalin to choose between an alliance with the Western democracies or with Hitler if he wanted to win time for the build-up of his Army and

Navy. When the British and French declined to sign an alliance, allowing the Red Army to enter Poland, Hitler offered to divide the country and give way to Soviet ambitions in the Baltic States. Stalin decided for this option. Hitler now had a free hand to launch his attack to conquer Poland. His attempt to 'solve' this problem by a Blitzkrieg, without causing a simultaneous war with France and Great Britain, failed. They declared war without being able to assist their ally. Stalin used the situation to occupy the eastern part of Poland and to establish bases in the Baltic States, while his attempt to win over Finland was only partially successful after the Winter-War.

The treaties between Germany and the Soviet Union also had important consequences for the Soviet Navy.[65] Against economic aid and leasing of base rights in the area of Murmansk, the People's Commissar for Shipbuilding, I. T. Tevosyan, during a visit to Berlin, presented requests of assistance in Soviet naval build-up, ranging from the delivery of plans for the battleship *Bismarck* and the carrier *Graf Zeppelin* to the purchase of three heavy cruisers, of armour plates and heavy gunnery with fire control instruments, of gunnery and equipment for four light cruisers, and of mines, torpedoes, minesweeping gear, submarine periscopes, and electrical batteries.[66]

Hitler was reluctant and allowed only the delivery of the incomplete heavy cruiser *Lutzow*. He also made one other offer as a result of a curious parallel: In the Soviet Union, the battlecruisers of the *Kronshtadt* type were developed—on Stalin's personal insistence—to replace the 23,000 ton "anti-Washington" cruisers, considered insufficient against the German *Scharnhorst*. In Germany, the rearmament of the *Scharnhorst*-type with 15-inch turrets, planned for 1941–42, had to be postponed to keep the two ships available. To use the 15-inch turrets already in production, the planned *Panzerschiffe* were cancelled in July 1939 and were replaced by three battlecruisers of 28,900 tons with three 15-inch twin turrets each. This was to the great satisfaction of Hitler, who got more heavily armed ships already in 1943. But when the war started in September 1939 and these ships were cancelled—with the other big ships of the Z-Plan— to free the yards for U-boats, it was determined that the turrets could be used to fulfill Tevosyan's request for the Soviet battlecruisers. This led to the reconstruction of the two already laid down Soviet battlecruisers, *Kronshtadt* and *Sevastopol*, with three German 15-inch twin turrets, 10 m optical range finders, and 150 cm searchlights to a design approved by Admiral Kuznetsov on 18 October 1940.[67]

As in Germany, where the available yard capacities forced a reduction of the planned 12 *Panzerschiffe* to 10, then to 8, and finally to 3 battlecruisers, in the Soviet Union, in the discussions about the plan of August 1939, I. T. Tevosyan had forced the Navy to reduce some numbers to accommodate shipbuilding capacities. The revised plan, which was approved by Admiral Kuznetsov on 27 July 1940, reduced the battleships to 10 and the battlecruisers to 8. The cruisers were reduced to 14, but the smaller ships and the submarines were again augmented.[68]

Notwithstanding the fact that Stalin tried to obey the economic arrangements, Hitler had decided, at the close of his campaign in France, to prepare his attack to crush the Soviet Union in summer 1941. The Germans were concerned when the Soviets used the German engagement in the West to occupy the Baltic States, Bessarabia, and the Bukovina. These were assuaged only when V. M. Molotov presented the Soviet wishes during his visit to Berlin in November 1940. The Soviets were also concerned with the German policy of delays and their military preparations. While Hitler was forced, because of the war against Great Britain, to give up his great battleship fleet to allow U-boat building, in the Soviet Union, the Navy leaders were forced to accept cuts in their big-ship programs to get capacities free for the faster built light ships and submarines and to transfer production facilities to the Army. On 19 October 1940, the Soviet Government decided to finish, for the time being, only the three *Sovetskii*, five *Soyuz* battleships, and the two *Kronshtadt* battlecruisers already begun. They would postpone other big ships and the carriers.[69]

On the other hand, in Germany, after the conquest of Norway and the French west coast in the summer of 1940, new grandiose plans for a World Power Fleet were discussed in the *Seekriegsleitung* and approved by Hitler, who gave the naval build-up priority over the Army and Air Force. The decision to attack the Soviet Union in summer 1941, however, again forced a postponement of such plans until the successful conclusion of operation "Barbarossa."[70] And in the Soviet Union in 1944, when the victorious end of the war against Germany and Japan was no longer in doubt, Stalin renewed the plans to build a big ocean-going fleet.[71] The German and the Soviet navies could not complete their big plans before Hitler started his war, first against Poland and the West, then against the Soviet Union. But it may be of interest to compare the number of ships both navies laid down from 1921 to 1 September 1939 in Germany and from 5 March 1927 to 22 June 1941 in the Soviet Union.

Type	Germany Number/tons	Soviet Union[72] Number/tons
Battleships, Battlecruisers, and *Panzerschiffe*	9/ 296,100	5/ 347,930
Aircraft Carriers	2/ 46,400	—/ —
Heavy Cruisers, and Light Cruisers	14/ 132,800	16/ 161,558
Destroyer Leaders, and Destroyers	26/ 60,437	88/ 182,273
Torpedoboats, and Patrol vessels	40/ 33,478	39/ 26,060
High Seas Minesweepers	24/ 16,368	63/ 32,886
Submarines	69/ 38,511	297/ 180,614
Together	184/ 578,889	508/ 831,321

In summing up, we have seen that both dictators, in the mid-1930s, started to plan and to build ocean-going fleets with super battleships far beyond their need to defend the territories of the Soviet Union and Germany. This led to great reshuffling of resources from the armies and air forces to the navies, which was possible only against the resistance of politicians and soldiers who were opposed to such unrealistic dreams of world power. They had to be eliminated by liquidation or by forced retirement.

We think it the task of historians to find out more details about the motivation of the politicians and military and naval leaders in the 1930s. Did the similarities between Stalin's and Hitler's naval programs have their roots in similar ambitions to win the domination of the world? Did they feel this might be possible only in a final fight against the Anglo-American and, eventually, also the Japanese sea powers?

1. Salewski, Michael: *Die deutsche Seekriegsleitung 1935–1945*, Vol. I–III. Frankfurt/Main: Bernard & Graefe, 1970–1975. Rahn, Werner: *Reichsmarine und Landesverteidigung 1919–1928*. München: Bernard & Graefe, 1976. Dülffer, Jost: *Weimar, Hitler und die Marine. Reichspolitik und Flottenbau 1920–1939*. Düsseldorf: Droste, 1973.

2. Monakov, Mikhail: "Sud'by doktrin i teorii." 1–4. In: *Morskoi sbornik*. November 1990 ff. Bereznhoi, Sergei: *Korabli i suda VMF SSSR 1928–1945*. Moskva: Voenizdat, 1988. Basov, Aleksandr: "Der Bau der Seekriegsflotte der UdSSR vor dem Zweiten Weltkrieg." In: *Revue Internationale d'Histoire Militaire 1*, No. 73, Stuttgart, 1991, pp. 119–135. Dmitriev, V. I.: *Sovetskoe podvodnoe korable-stroenie*. Moskva: Voenizdat, 1990.

3. Morskoi Sbornik Zhurnal Voenno-morskogo flota. Moskva: Izdatel'stvo 'Krasnaya Zvezda,' monthly. Sudostroenie. Ezhemesyachnii nauchno-tekhnicheskii i proizvodostnebii Zhurnal. Sankt-Peterburg: 'Sudostroenie,' monthly.

4. Der Friedensvertrag zwischen Deutschland und den Alliierten und Assozierten Mächten. Amtlicher Text der Entente und amtliche deutsche Übertragung. Im *Auftrage des Auswärtigen Amtes*. Charlottenburg, 1919.

5. Basov, Aleksandr: op.cit., p. 119.

6. Breyer, Siegfried: *Enzyklopädie des sowjetischen Kriegsschiffbaus*. Vol. 1: *Oktoberrevolution und maritimes Erbe*. Herford: Koehler, 1987.

7. Boevoi put' Sovetskogo Voenno-morskogo flota. N. A. Piterskii, ed. Moskva: Voenizdat, 1964. 3rd edition ed by V. I. Achkasov et al. Moskva: Voenizdat, 1974. pp. 125, 137, 143–145, 521–533.

8. Zherve, B. B.: "Flot segodnisshnego dnia: Boevye sredstva." In: *Krasnyi flot*. (February 1922). Petrov, M. A.: "Zametki o taktiki malogo flota." In: *Morskoi sbornik* (September 1923), pp. 45–61. Monakov, M.: op.cit., part 2, 1923–1925. In: *Morskoi sbornik* (December 1990), pp. 17–23. League of Nations: Official Journal (February 21, 1924), pp. 708–710.

9. Erickson, John: *The Soviet High Command. A Military Political History, 1918–1941*. London: Macmillan, 1962.

10. Herrick, Robert W.: *Soviet Naval Strategy: Fifty Years of Theory and Practice*. Annapolis, Md.: U.S. Naval Institute, 1969. Gorshkov, Sergei (German translation): *Die Rolle der Flotten in Krieg und Frieden*. München: Lehmanns, 1975, pp. 77–105. Monakov, Mikhail: op.cit., part 2, pp. 22–23.

11. Rahn, Werner: op.cit., pp. 38–58. Dülffer, Jost: op.cit., pp. 51–84.

12. Gröner, Erich: Die deutschen Kriegsschiffe 1815–1945. Fortgeführt und herausgeben von Dieter Jung und *Martin Maass. Band: Panzerschiffe, Linienschiffe, Schlachtschiffe, Flugzeugträger, Kreuzer, Kanonenboote*. München: Bernard & Graefe, 1982.

13. Rahn, Werner: op.cit., pp. 114–122.

14. Rahn, Werner: op.cit., pp. 133–14.

15. Dülffer, Jost: op.cit., pp. 67–89.

16. Wegener, W.: *Die Seestrategie des Weltkrieges*. Aufl., Berlin, 1929. 2.durchgesehene und erw.Aufl., Berlin, 1941.

17. Rahn, Werner: op.cit., pp. 85–194. Dülffer, Jost: op.cit., pp. 59–66.

18. Rössler, Eberhard: *Geschichte des deutschen Ubootbaus*. Band 1: Entwicklung, Bau und Eigenschaften der deutschen Uboote von den Anfängen bis 1943. 2.Aufl., Koblenz: Bernard & Graefe, 1986. pp. 130–145.

19. Fock, Harald: *Vom Zarenadler zum Roten Stern*. Herford: Mittler, 1985. pp. 195–200.

20. Groehler, Olaf: *Selbstmörderische Allianz. Deutschrussische Militärbeziehungen 1920–1941* 1. Berlin: Vision-Verl, 1992.

21. Groehler, Olaf: op.cit.

22. Fock, Harald: op.cit., pp. 196.

23. Rahn, Werner: op.cit., pp. 176–180.

24. Stenogramma zasedaniya RVS SSSR s Komanduyushchimi voiskami MVO, UVO i BVO i Nachal'nikami morskikh sil Baltiiskogo i Chernogo morei ot 8-go Maya 1928 goda. ZGA-SA, f.4, op.1, d.752, L.213. Basov, Aleksandr: op.cit., pp. 120–121. Postanovlenie soveta truda i oborony 26.XI.1926: O programme

stroitel'stva morskikh sil RKKA. 1Pr.STO No. 295. Monakov, Mikhail: op.cit., part 4. In: Morskoi sbornik (March 1991), pp. 24–31. Breyer, Siegfried: op.cit., vol. 2: Konsolidierung und erste Neubauten. Herford: Koehler, 1989.

25. Breyer, Siegfried: op.cit., vol. 2, pp. 40–43. Berezhnoi, Sergei: op.cit., pp. 153–184.

26. Boevoi put' . . . : op.cit., pp. 137–139. Zonin, S. A.: Admiral L. M. Galler. Moskva: Voenizdat, 1991, pp. 236–250.

27. Berezhnoi, Sergei: op.cit.

28. Morskoi general'nii shtab. Sbornik materialov po poytuboevoi deyatel'nosti voenno-morskikh sil SSSR. No. 39: Opyt perevozok podvodnykh lodok i malykh korablei pozhleznym dorogam v Velikuyu otechestvennoi voinu. Moskva: Voenno-morskoe izd. 1951. Zakharov, C.E. et al.: Krasnoznamennii Tikhookeanskii flot. 2nd ed., Moskva: Voenizdat, 1973. pp. 117–125.

29. Boevoi put' . . . : op.cit., pp. 140. Kozlov, I. A., Shlomin, V. S.: Severnii flot. Moskva: Voenizdat, 1966. pp. 69–83.

30. Dmitriev, V. I.: op.cit., pp. 32–63. Afonin, N. N.: Lideri eskadrennykh minonostsev tipa "Leningrad". In: *Sudostroenie* (March 1985), pp. 66–69. Breyer, Siegfried: op.cit., vol. 2., pp. 75–81.

31. Basov, A. op.cit., 122.

32. O programme voennogo sudostroeniya na 1936 god.25.2.1936 1. TsVMA, op.0018448, d.82, l.360. Dmitriev, V. I.: op.cit. pp. 129. Greger, René: Sowjetischer Schlachtschiffbau. In: *Marine-Rundschau* (August 1974), p. 466.

33. Yarovoi, V. V.: Kreiseri tipov 'Kirov' i 'Maksim Gorkii.' In: *Sudostroenie* (July 1985), pp. 46–48. Aleksandrovskii: 'Kirov.' Pervenets sovetskogo kreiserostroeniya. In: *Sudostroenie* (November 1986), pp. 51ff. Greger, René: Anfänge des sowjetischen Kreuzerbaus. In: *Marine-Rundschau* (April 1989), pp. 228ff. Breyer, Siegfried: op.cit., vol. 3, *Flottenbau und Plansoll*. Herford: Koehler, 1991. pp. 25–31. Afonin, N. N.: *Skhodili so stalelei esmintsi*. In: *Sudostroenie* (May 1985), pp. 61–65.

34. Rössler, Eberhard: *Die deutschen U-Boote und ihre Werften Band 1: U-Bootbau bis Ende des Weltkrieges, Konstruktionen f r das Ausland und die Jahre 1935–1945 (Teil I)*. München: Bernard & Graefe, 1979. pp. 75–86. Dmitriev, V. I.: op.cit., pp. 133–149.

35. Berezhnoi, S. S.: op.cit., pp. 43–75. Dmitriev, V. I.: op.cit., pp. 240–264.

36. Dmitriev, V. I.: op.cit., pp. 133–149.

37. Rahn, Werner: op.cit., pp. 208–247. Dülffer, Jost: op.cit., pp. 90–97.

38. Sandhofer, G.: "Das *Panzerschiff* 'A' und die Vorentwürfe von 1920–1 bis 1928." In: *Militürgeschichtliche Mitteilungen* No. 1/1968, pp. 35ff. Rahn, Werner: op.cit., pp. 233–247. Dülffer, Jost: op.cit., pp. 109–129.

39. Dülffer, Jost: op.cit., pp. 98–203.

40. Garzke, William H., Dulin, Robert O.: Battleships. vol. II: *Allied Battleships in World War II*. Annapolis, Md.: U.S. Naval Institute Press, 1980. pp. 33–76. Greger, René: *Schlachtschiffe der Welt*. Stuttgart: Motorbuch-Verlag, 1993. pp. 81. Giorgerini, Giorgio, Nani, Augusto: *Le Navi di Linea Italiane 1861–1961. Roma: Ufficio Storico della Marina Militare, 1962*. pp. 241–260. Garzke, William H. and Dulin, Robert O.: Battleships. vol. 3: *Axis and Neutral Battleships in World War II*. Annapolis, Md.: U.S. Naval Institute, 1985. pp. 371–436.

41. Der Grosse Ploetz. *Auszug aus der Geschichte*. 29th ed. Würzburg: Ploetz, 1980. pp. 864–869.

42. Frank, Willard C.: "Naval Operations in the Spanish Civil War, 1936–1939." In *Naval War College Review*, No. 37, 1984.

43. Basov, Aleksandr: op.cit., pp. 125.

44. Kuznetsov, Nikolai G.: *Nakanune*. Moskva: Voenizdat, 1966. p. 257.

45. TsGA VMF, f.r-1483, op.1, d.501, 1.112–113. *Tablitsa rasiregeleniya korablei po teatrach po programme stroitel'stva Voennogo-morskogo flota*. TsGA VMF, f.1877, op.9, d.56.

46. Dülffer, Jost: op.cit., pp. 204–278.

47. *Zielplanungen im März 1934*. BA/MA II M 34/1. Nach. Dülffer, Jost: op.cit., p. 566.

48. Rohwer, Jürgen: *Baudaten der von 1921 bis zum 31.8.1939 für die deutsche Reichs und Kriegsmarine in Auftrag gegebenen Kriegsschiffe*. In: Dülffer, Jost: op.cit. pp. 570–587.

49. Dülffer, Jost: op.cit., pp. 279–353.

50. Gröner, Erich: op.cit., pp. 55–56.

51. Rohwer, Jürgen: op.cit.

52. Dates for the changes: *Boevoi put* . . . : op.cit., pp. 521, 529. Volkogonov, Dmitrii: *Triumf i Tragedia. Politicheskii portret I. V. Stalin*. Moskva: Novosti, 1989. Zosin, S. A.: op.cit. Azurmanian, A. M.: *Admirala flota Sovetskogo Soyuza I. S. Isakov (1894–1967)*. Yerevan: Izd.Ayastan, 1973. Yevgrafov, B.: *Dva ventsa admirala Levchenko*. In: *Morskoi sbornik* (November 1990), pp. 82–87.

53. Hossbach, F.: *Zwischen Wehrmacht und Hitler*. 2.Aufl. Gottingen, 1965.

54. Hillgruber, Andreas: *Deutschlands Rolle in der Vorgeschichte beider Weltkriege*. Göttingen, 1967. Hildebrand, Klaus: *Vom Reich zum Weltreich. Hitler, NSDAP und die koloniale Frage*. München, 1969. Jäckel, Eberhard: *Hitlers Weltanschauung. Entwurf einer Herrschaft*. Tü bingen, 1969. Müller: Klaus-Jürgen: *Das Heer und Hitler. Armee und nationalsozialistisches Regime 1930–1940*. Stuttgart: Deutsche Verlags Anstalt, 1969.

55. Brief, S. Berezhnoi from TsGA VMF, f r-1483, op.1, d.431, 1.9 und d.02, 1.7–8, 110, 133.

56. Tablitsa . . . : op.cit., see foonote 43. TsGA VMF f.r.1483, op.1, d.502, 1.224–232. Kuznetsov, L. A.: *Ne isklyuchalas' i postroika avianostsa* . . . : In: *Gangut Vypusk* 3. St Peterburg, 1992. pp. 63–70.

57. Op.cit.

58. Greger, René: *Sowjetischer Schlachtschiffbau*. In: *Marine Rundschau (August 1974)*, pp. 466ff. Zapis' razgovoras g-nom GIBS of firmy Gibs Kaks ot 17 Noyabrya 1937g. and other reports of the negotiations of the delegation on 22 November 1937 with General Electric, on 1 December 1937 with 'Rajt' and 'Vorgan' by D. A. Rozov. Report of the Chief of 'Amtorg,' A. Kirilyuk, to P. A. Smirnov 27.7.1938 and *Otchet o rabote morskoi komissii v SShA of 20.X.1938*. Zapis' peregovorov Zam.Narkoma VMF falgman ranga tov.Isakov s predstaziutelem amerikanskoi firmy Gibbs i Kaks g-nom Dzhois, 13 Noyabrya 1938 g.

59. *Boevoi put* . . . : op.cit., pp. 521–529. Volkogonov, Dmitrii: op.cit.

60. *Narodnii Komissar VMF SSSR*, 10.8.1939, 9911/ss/ob. TsGA VMF, f.1877, op.3, d.56, 1.140–142.o

61. Rohwer, Jürgen: op.cit. *Narodnii Komissar* . . . , (see footnote 54).

62. Salewski, Michael: op.cit., vol. I., pp. 44ff, from BA/MA K 10-2/6, Bl.6-13. Dülffer, Jost: op.cit., pp. 477ff.

63. Dülffer, Jost: op.cit., pp. 500, 569, from BA/MA Case 1504. Anl.1/Skl.IIIa 5/39 gKdos.
64. Der Groáe Ploetz: op.cit., pp. 867–870, 988–991.
65. Fock, Harald: *Vom Zarenadler zum Roten Stern. Die Geschichte der russischen/sowjetischen Marine.* Herford: Mittler, 1985. pp. 207–211.
66. Salewski, Michael: op.cit., Vol. I., pp. 156–159, 375. Breyer, Siegfried: *Die Kreuzer 'K' und 'L' der deutschen* Kriegsmarine. ('Seydlitz' und 'Lützow') In: *Marine-Rundschau* (January/February) 1963, pp. 20–28, 99–100.
67. Uzov, V. Ju.: *Tyazhelnie kreiseri tipa 'Kronshtadt.'* In: *Sudostroenie* (November 1989), pp. 57–58. Breyer, Siegfried: *Sowjetische Schlachtkreuzer mit Krupp-Kanonen.* In: *Marine-Forum* (März 1991), pp. 301–303.
68. Komiteta oborony pri SNK SSSR: *Ob utverzhenii pyatiletnego (1938–1942gg) plana sudostroeniya dlya RKVMF I pyatilatnei programme sudostroeniya na 1943–47gg.* TsVMA f.2, d.39526, 1-13-33.
69. Prikaz Narodnogo Komissara Voenno-morskogo flota SSSR. No.00263. 23 Octyabr 1940 g.
70. *Lagevorträge des Oberbefehlshabers der Kriegsmarine vor Hitler 1939–1945.* Gerhard Wagner, ed. München: Lehmanns, 1972. pp. 108, 113–120, 143–146, 252. Salewski, Michael: op.cit. vol. I: pp. 234–241, espec. 238, 399–518, 524–527; vol. III: *Denkschriften und Lagebetrachtungen 1938–1944.* Frankfurt/Main: Bernard & Graefe, 1973. pp. 168–188, 189–214. see 1/Skl.1942/41 gKdos. v.4.2.1941. For the designs of battleship H from 1941 to 1944: Gröner, Erich: op.cit., pp. 62–65.
71. Gribovskii, V. Yu.: *Lineinie korabli tipa 'Sovetskii Soyuz'*. In: *Sudostroenie* (July 1990), pp. 55–59. Platonov, A. V.: *Iz letopisi sozdaniya Sovetskikh avianostsev.* In: *Sudostroenie* (May 1992), pp. 40–46.
72. Dülffer, Jost: op.cit.: pp. 570–587. Basov, Aleksandr: op.cit., pp. 129–130.

Down but Not Out: German Attempts to Regain the Submarine Initiative, May 1943–February 1944

W. J. R. Gardener

⚓

Between May 1943 and February 1944, the Germans attempted to shake off the effects of the undoubted defeat in the Battle of the Atlantic they suffered in May 1943. In analysing the causes of the setback, they drew certain conclusions which led them towards new concepts in submarine warfare, arguably driving this warfare discipline in the direction it was to take for the next fifty years. How appropriate these measures were to the battles which Dönitz's submarines actually had to fight will be examined, as well as the progress of German efforts in the contexts of the maritime and general war. Specifically, after reviewing the general situation in May 1943 and a German shift of submarine warfare rationale, German preparations for return to the Atlantic battlefield will be described. Then, the operations of the period will be examined, noting any differences between German perceptions of them and real results. Lastly, German aspirations and preparations for the longer term will be considered together with ramifications which extended well beyond the period in question.

By May 1943, the weight of the Grand Alliance was beginning to be felt. In North Africa, American and British forces had just expelled Axis forces prior to the re-entry into Europe through Sicily in July. The Russian colossus had stemmed German advances at Stalingrad and was about to mark the reversal of the strategic direction in the gigantic Battle of Kursk. Over Europe, the bombing campaign was gaining in intensity, with large efforts by both RAF and USAAF, leading to an ever-growing proportion of German resources being devoted to defence against air attack. In the Pacific, American island hopping was proceeding on two fronts; by February 1945, Manilla was to be liberated. Elsewhere, by the end of the period, the Allied invasion of northwest Europe was imminent, and Russian armies had continued steadily westward, now stretching in a line approximately from Leningrad to the Crimea. It was not the Axis forces' finest hour, and, in this context, the submarine war in the Atlantic still seemed to hold out the prospect if not of success, at least of holding the flood of the Allied advance.

Refocusing on May 1943 and the Atlantic, the scale of the submarine defeat was clear. Certainly submarines had sunk 36 ships of some 190,000 tons in that month, but this fell far short of any realistic hope of conducting a significant tonnage reduction campaign.[1] Further, submarine losses had been high: no less than 41 boats had been lost in the same month.[2] This exchange rate of more than one submarine for each merchant vessel sunk was quite unacceptable to Dönitz, and the decision was taken to withdraw submarines from the main attack on cross-Atlantic routes.

There can be no doubt that the Allies had won an impressive and important victory. The reasons for this result are complex and wide-ranging. Although some later historians would credit single causes as responsible for this outcome, the factors originate from a broad base of force adequacy, technology and tactical proficiency rather than from any unique source. This is borne out by examining the whole campaign from the resumption of attacks on cross-Atlantic convoys in the middle of 1942 up until the climactic point of May 1943. Here, as well as the violent seesaw of March–May 1943, long-term trends in Allied favour can be identified.[3] But the importance of this lies not in analyses conducted long after the event, but on the effect it had on Dönitz and the subsequent shaping of his policies. This will be described in the next section, but the immediate actions taken by the Germans are of interest.

On 24 May 1943, decisions were taken which led to the most effective submarines being moved to areas southwest of the Azores in an attempt to target the U.S.-Gibraltar convoys. Other submarines were left around the main North Atlantic routes, not to attack shipping, but rather to attempt to conceal the withdrawal from the Allies.[4] A further factor in the decision was the inadequate number of unprotected berths available in the Biscay ports.[5] Notwithstanding a degree of overestimation of previous sinkings, Dönitz clearly noted the failure of the tonnage campaign and a mere week later was putting forward a new rationale for submarine warfare. In this the criterion was no longer the sinking of maximum tonnage, but rather the tying down of Allied naval and air forces which might otherwise be used offensively against the Reich.[6] The validity of this strategic justification will be addressed later in the paper.

Two sidelights might usefully be cast on this strategic defeat for Dönitz. First, there is no evidence to suggest that weakening crew morale was in evidence or played any part in the decision. Second, this must be a rare example of such a setback being treated by the Führer with such calm. It argues that his understanding of maritime warfare was especially poor, together with the likelihood that different rules were applied to the German Navy and Army. Nearly two years later, this latter proposition was perhaps to receive its ultimate justification with Dönitz's elevation to succeed Hitler.

Despite this radical shift in the basis of submarine warfare, the fundamental operational methods were to remain unchanged, at least initially. Thus, the *Rudeltaktik* or wolfpack method was to continue to be the bedrock of the continuing, if diminished, attacks on convoys.

But the limited return to the Atlantic was only intended to serve as an interim measure before submarines became available which were more suitable for the hard struggle that Atlantic warfare had become. The ultimate aim was a submarine with very much improved underwater performance, which could close a convoy at speed, attack it and withdraw safely, all without surfacing. Such a vessel would largely counter the potent threat of Allied air power, as well as being able to evade most escorts. But in 1943, such a vessel was some way off and, although progress towards it was being made rapidly, there was no realistic hope of it becoming ready for use in 1943, or even the first part of 1944. Again, this subject will be returned to later.

A more immediate solution was clearly perceived and the greatest bar to a renewed freedom of operations, if not success, lay in countering the Allied capabilities which had built up over the last eighteen months. Measures were needed to deal with surface escorts, but the greatest problem was perceived correctly as being the threat from aircraft, both on transit routes (especially in the Bay of Biscay) and in the vicinity of convoys. This translated into two types of equipment. One was to help win the race to initial detection, so that a submarine would know of an aircraft's presence before the latter found the submarine. The second was the ability to counter an attacking aircraft better.

The total collection of measures necessary was identified quickly and found expression at the Führer Conference of 31 May when the following were identified: a better radar intercept set, a radar jammer, submarine air warning radar, radar reflective material, four-barrelled anti-aircraft guns, anti-escort torpedoes, and land-based air support against Allied air forces over the Bay of Biscay.

Broadly speaking, these were accomplished, although some measures lagged or were of little use, or little used. Thus both the radar jammer and the air warning radar appear to have made little impact on the battles that followed; certainly there is little mention of them in accounts of subsequent operations.

An anti-escort torpedo, the *Zaunkönig*, which homed on the sound of escort's screws, was developed ahead of schedule and successfully deployed later in 1943. The Allies, however, were able to field countermeasures against this weapon very quickly. Air support in the Bay of Biscay became even more important in the months ahead, as the Allies were able to turn ever more effort into this area. Not only would Dönitz's submarines have to contend with the short and medium range aircraft, which had often operated in the Bay because they could operate no further afield, but there were two other aircraft too. The Allied success in the mid-Atlantic campaign permitted the redeployment of long-range aircraft to the Bay. A further difficulty arose with the use of fast twin-engine aircraft, such as Beaufighters and Mosquitos, with guns, cannon and later rockets, all of which were effective against submarines.

But perhaps the most fascinating aspect of the reequipment was that of radar warning receivers. This is a complex story, too long to be done full justice in this paper. It involves Allied radars operating in two different frequency bands, slow German perceptions of at least one of those, difficulties in producing effective warning receivers, and a German wild goose chase down the track in which their warning receivers' own radiations provided the means by which Allied aircraft could home on submarines from great distances. The result of all this was that even when German submarines had efficient warning receivers, they were often distrusted to the point where they were switched off, to the benefit of searching aircraft.

Even the full interim improvement program, implemented in just a few months, was no small achievement. But, with the possible exception of *Zaunkönig*, most of these were survival aids, rather than items which helped sink more merchant ships; even the torpedo was intended principally as an anti-escort weapon. Most of the items were concerned with evasion from, or the counterattack of, aircraft. Evasion in the form of submerging let the submarine fight another day, but probably at the cost of losing convoy contact; counterattack might also save the submarine, even lead to aircraft casualties, but this might again be at the expense of the main aim, that of sinking ships.

Evaluating Dönitz's operations and the impact of Allied ASW operations on the Germans provides a measured strategic assessment. Broadly, the period May 1943 to February 1944 can be split into several parts, for which the unifying theme might be seen as the demise of the *Rudeltaktik*. From about early 1941, this technique had served the Germans adequately in general terms and well in the prosecution of convoys. It was virtually the only method which stood a chance of success against mid-Atlantic convoys; and it was effective, too, in other places when Allied air effort was absent, as was often the case. But as the increasingly bitter battles of mid-1942 to mid-1943 were fought, the methods of the *Rudeltaktik* remained unchanged, but the Allied ability to prevent closure increased. At the same time, the attack and post-attack phases became more and more costly to the aggressor.

Dönitz's intention at the end of 1943 was to continue the use of the *Rudeltaktik*, but in other places less liable to receive intense Allied attention. Thus the move in late May to the area southwest of the Azores. This operation, involving the 16 submarines of *Gruppe Trutz*, which lasted into July, achieved little substantial contact, except on shore and ship-borne aircraft. As a result, 5 of the submarines were sunk, either during or shortly after the operation.[7] Here we can see, although obviously the Germans could not, the influence of Ultra. Not only did it permit the convoy evasive manoeuvres that led to *Trutz's* failure, but it also allowed the maximum efficacy of air assets.[8] A further element of Ultra's success was the denial of much useful intelligence to the German *B-Dienst* by means of making the convoy codes virtually opaque.[9] The operational—or even strategic—level switching of assets was again attributable largely to Ultra.[10] Such a failure, together with other pressures, was to result in no further concerted attempts being made against convoys until well into September 1943—in itself a useful outcome for the Allies.

Nor did much go well for Dönitz in other areas. As Hessler notes, not only did the quarter June–August result in the loss of 70 submarines, but a growing proportion of these sinkings were not in operational areas but in transit.[11] This reflected the large-scale offensive, largely conducted by aircraft, against submarines. This paper is too short and its scope too extensive to permit sufficient space to cover this phase in much detail.

It is important, however, to note several things about the Bay offensive. First, it only became possible to devote the degree of resource that was used because of the earlier German withdrawal from the mid-Atlantic. Second, it was the perception gained from Ultra that this situation was likely to continue that allowed the offensive to be continued at high intensity. For example, not only were long-range aircraft moved into the Bay,[12] but so, too, were surface warship Support Groups. Greater aircraft availability permitted multi-aircraft attacks on both the heavier-armed submarines and the tactic of keeping boats in groups to maximise anti-aircraft fire. Further, the arrival of surface ships on the scene put submarines in the dilemma of having to face concerted and heavy gunfire, or else submerge to be attacked by underwater weapons.

A complex struggle ensued with Dönitz playing the combinations of day and night, surfaced and submerged passage, together with single and group passages. On the Allied side, metric and centimetric radar, in combination with shifting German perceptions of that threat and the effectiveness of their countermeasures were factors.[13] A further factor against the surfaced submarine was the deployment of aircraft not specialised in ASW with strong gun and cannon armaments. In the end, Dönitz discovered that by largely submerging and hugging the Spanish coast with his submarines, he had a reasonably safe method of their reaching the operational areas. This was effective, but costly in passage time.[14]

But as well as the north Atlantic, there was a move to capitalise on an old Dönitz theme: the exploitation of the margins. For a while, this could even be regarded as successful in that it accounted for the bulk of the shipping sunk during the summer of 1943. From 20 June to 20 August, submarines claimed some 37 ships of 236,000 tons in the western Atlantic as far south as Rio de Janeiro and off west Africa.[15] But even this was to be bought at the price of 14 submarines lost. Dönitz also saw the Indian Ocean as an area of opportunity. In a plan known as Operation Monsun, a group of up to 11 submarines were to be underway in June so as to be in the Arabian Sea in September.

The ability to conduct this latter campaign depended on two factors: support afloat and, in the longer term, the establishment of a littoral base. Both of these bolstering measures were to fail: the former through direct Allied countermeasures, the latter because of a combination of Allied action and lack of Axis cooperation. Notwithstanding these setbacks, the Indian Ocean campaign was to prosper, at least for a while, largely because of the relative dearth of Allied assets there and the still-significant presence of independently-routed shipping. A further helpful factor was the employment of Japanese submarines in that area. By the end of the whole period under consideration, up until February 1944, the latter's operations were to dominate the sinking statistics. Other areas, such as Northern waters and the Mediterranean, were to yield little. Although as the Allied stranglehold on the north Atlantic tightened, these other areas were to experience a transient rise in relative importance. It might be argued that it is wrong to include such distant waters in what is primarily a north Atlantic view, but it should be remembered that not only did all the German submarines originate from northwestern European bases, but also that Dönitz perceived all operations as part of one grand campaign. It is therefore legitimate to consider success and failure in these theatres as part of the Atlantic battle—the North Atlantic itself nevertheless remained the crucial arena.

Although the summer of 1943 could hardly be considered successful, Dönitz was optimistic about the prospects for later in the year. In the third week of September, operations against cross-Atlantic convoys were begun by the 19 submarines of Group *Leuthen* against the outward bound convoys ON202 and ONS18 southeast of Greenland. This operation is principally distinguished for the first operational use of *Zaunkönig*, the acoustic homing torpedo. The actual results achieved by *Leuthen* were significant enough—six merchant ships of some 36,000 tons and three escorts sunk for the loss of three submarines—but a combination of Allied air activity and the *Zaunkönig* post-firing procedure made it difficult to ascertain success. As a result, 12 escorts were claimed sunk, a gross overestimation.[16] Understandably, both Dönitz and the higher command were pleased.[17] Although the OIC had attempted to divert the convoys, this was thwarted by there being errors of interpretation in the order of some 100 miles. Curiously, largely as a result of an earlier misinterpretation of an Ultra report, the Allies were well on the way to producing a counter to the acoustic torpedo.

For the next two weeks, *Leuthen* made vain attempts to gain contact on further outbound convoys in the same area. These were frustrated by poor intelligence and enemy action. By 8 October, the survivors, now known as *Rossbach*, were formed to intercept either HX259 or SC143, both eastbound. German success was to be meagre: one escort and one merchant ship sunk for the loss of three submarines. From the Allied side, this operation was particularly interesting. SC143, with a reinforced escort, was deliberately driven, guided by Ultra, at *Rossbach*, not so much to sink submarines—although that was what happened—as to allow the less strongly protected HX259 to pass unscathed.[18]

The convoy ONS20 was now to receive the attention of the group which was further reinforced to become *Schleiffen* by 16 October. This action has two features of interest: the useful German deployment in submarines of VHF DF, which was effective against convoy tactical diversions,[19] and a German decision to attempt to fight through to the convoy on the surface. The latter was responsible in part for the loss of six submarines for the scant reward of one straggler.

From there, the remaining submarines made their way to the east of Newfoundland, where a series of different search operations in single group formation was begun, then with two groups and finally five small groups. Despite these active dispositions, no convoy was found; by early November the search was abandoned and the submarines ordered back to the eastern Atlantic.

Meanwhile, American CVE successes against U-tankers caused acute difficulties for Dönitz. Operational boats, adequately fuelled, had to be diverted to supply other submarines. Most of these sinkings were Ultra-cued, and these, together with later deliberate targeting of tankers and other supply vessels, were to cause some intra-Allied debate. The British were a little reticent, with good reason, that too blatant exploitation of Ultra might lead to compromise, whereas the Americans tended to be more aggressive in its use. In a sense both were right. German suspicions were aroused, although the proper interpretation was never made: thus proper countermeasures were not taken. On the other hand, tanker attrition was an important factor in limiting submarine operations.

The Allied judgement made at the time that U-boat tankers were an important target has received some recent support in the work of Brian McCue. Using the techniques of operational research, he examines both what happened and several conjectural cases in the campaign during the period January 1942 to May 1944; eight cases are considered. His results are expressed in terms of theoretical scenarios. The most interesting cases are those where no submarine tankers are sunk and where the sinkings are doubled. These produce the largest variations in the results: minus 484 for the no-tanker case as against plus 347 for tanker doubling, both results compared to an actual base of 1650.[20]

The theme of using a number of small (three boat) patrol lines simultaneously was continued by Group *Eisenhart* in mid-November west of Ireland. Despite receiving some support from a partially resurgent *B-Dienst*, no convoy contact was made.

The previous month, after a judgement that attacks on mid-Atlantic convoys were difficult, it was decided to start short onslaughts on those between Gibraltar and the United Kingdom, now redesignated MK or KM. The first of these involved seven submarines against MKS28, northbound at the end of October. With the help of air reconnaissance and a daylight sighting of the convoy, one ship of 3,000 tons was sunk at the cost of a submarine. Such operations were to continue throughout November, and all followed a similar theme of air reconnaissance and short attacks. The established mid-Atlantic Allied ploy of using Ultra to evade submarine patrol lines was, as in 1941, not generally usable on this route. But intelligence derived from this source could be used to reinforce convoys, and this was done to some effect. Not only escorts themselves, but the use of escort carriers denied Dönitz the success he sought. As a result, four operations resulted in only a single merchant ship sunk and one damaged for the loss of six submarines.[21]

This disappointment was to lead to the virtual abandonment of the *Rudeltaktik* and, in effect, the demise of the concept of the submersible torpedo boat. From now on, submarines had to spend most of their time underwater, severely restricting both visibility and mobility. It would be going a little too far to depict the submarine at the turn of the year as a migratory mine, but neither was it a true submarine. Technical developments were to move it in the latter direction, as will be described later in this paper, but as the period under consideration drew to a close, the position in the war on shipping was a gloomy one for the Germans. Notwithstanding their claimed shift in rationale in May 1943 to a policy of tying down Allied assets, there is little doubt that genuine attempts were still being made to target shipping. That lack of success can be typified by the fact that, between November 1943 and February 1944, only one ship of less than 2000 tons was sunk whilst in a formed convoy.

Certainly, there were rather more escorts sunk, including *Woodpecker* of Captain Walker's famous Support Group, but this period marks a very low point indeed for Dönitz.

At this point, it is worth making a brief survey of other areas over the whole period of this paper. First, some exclusions. The Baltic and Black Seas, together with the Pacific Ocean, will not be considered. Their contribution to the German effort was either zero or negligible, with the qualified exception of noting the Baltic's importance for submarine training.

The Northern Theatre, despite a significant deployment of submarines, never achieved high and sustained successes. But occasionally, it would do relatively well. For example, in the last poor period in the Atlantic recently discussed, when the four months, November 1943 to February 1944, produced under 100,000 tons total sunk, this compared with the admittedly abnormal figure of over 20,000 tons in the North in January alone.

The Mediterranean could hardly be considered as highly important. Further, its sinkings were often of very small craft indeed.[22] But there were months when the Mediterranean approached the Atlantic in tonnage terms. And, in February 1944, the Mediterranean did better.[23] This serves to highlight the poor Atlantic performance, rather than elevating that of the Mediterranean. Further, the German position there deteriorated throughout the period, losing the support of their Italian ally and only being able to operate from unprotected bases.

The Indian Ocean, however, performed rather well in relative terms. It should be stressed that this is a comparative judgement; not once during the period did its monthly sinkings reach, far less exceed, 100,000 tons. But on no less than six of the nine months under consideration, the Indian Ocean did better than the Atlantic. These results were achieved by a small number of submarines, never more than ten, and more often five or six.

However, a caveat must be entered against even this relatively bright spot in submarine performance. Although the performance per boat *on station* was good, the very long passage times diminished overall efficiency greatly. Thus, the successes were expensively bought. Further, although Indian Ocean submarines tended to suffer somewhat less than their Atlantic cousins, they were still subject to attrition both en route and in area. A loss in the Indian Ocean took a long time to replace.

Allied forces were scarce in the Indian Ocean, it occupying a slightly awkward strategic position, both geographically remote and between the major theatres. As a result, the general lack of resources tended to limit the application of escorted convoys. Sometimes, these were set up in response to specific intelligence, but the general deficiency allowed the Germans some effectiveness. However, the Allies were able to use Ultra to attack German supply operations, and the support ship *Charlotte Schliemann* was attacked and sunk in February 1944.[24]

During the period from June 1943 to February 1944, the Germans sank 31 escorts and other warships as well as 181 merchant vessels of some 916,769 tons for the loss of 178 submarines; this was virtual parity for merchant shipping. In terms of exchange, this was poor. Although the upward curve of supply meant that the overall number of boats at the end of the period had gone up, the number of operationally ready—or *Frontboote*—had declined from around 200 to about 170. What had been destroyed was not only the steel and other raw materials used in making a submarine, but also the skill of their crews.

As explained earlier, Dönitz had made a very rapid turnaround of strategic rationale in May 1943, declaring that Allied tonnage loss was no longer his objective; rather the tying-down of Allied assets was to be the aim of the German Navy in general and the U-boat arm in particular. For this reason, using tonnage sunk as an indicator of German success or failure, as adopted in this paper, might be considered irrelevant. However, there are good reasons for doing so. First, some doubt can be cast on the soundness and sincerity of the May declaration. The general continuation of the same methods—albeit on a diminished scale—gives no hint of a new strategic outlook. The abandonment of the methods of the *Rudeltaktik*, in November 1943 off Newfoundland, was the counsel of desperation and the reaction to Allied strength and success, not some stroke of strategic genius.

Second, it took the Germans a very long time to articulate a numerical basis for the rationale. Indeed, this was not to be stated until after the period covered by this paper. But as it is central to understanding the basis of German aims, or more probably the lack of them, it is helpful to describe it here. As adduced earlier, the policy was first announced in May 1943. The first numerical rationale of the policy did not appear to surface, however, until over a year later in June 1944.[25] The basis of the argument was the claim that the U-boat campaign absorbed the effort of some 3,340 ASW vessels, both British and American, together with some 1,450 British aircraft. On such evidence, there is some justification for the view that the operations of some 450 submarines were worthwhile, even if few merchant ships were sunk and U-boat losses were fairly high. The question arises of whether the figures used were of the right order to justify the policy.

The figure used by Dönitz for British surface ASW ships is broadly accurate, although it could be argued that units *capable* of ASW[26] is not the same as units *employed* in ASW. In the case of Coastal Command aircraft, the German data overestimates the number by a factor of two.[27] Dönitz makes the point that if aircraft were freed from ASW duties, they would be available for the air offensive against Germany. In 1944, with the Reich under heavy air attack, this proposition was politically timely.

Dönitz's argument is fundamentally sound in its own right; it fails, however, in one further particular. It may well have cost the Allies a great deal more to defend themselves against the U-boats than it cost to deploy the submarines in strict monetary terms. But the Allies could, by and large, afford to pay their costs, perhaps rather more easily than the Germans could pay theirs. More importantly, the Allies considered that when *all* criteria of cost were weighed, they could not afford to lose. A historiographical coda can be found in the works of Admiral Gorshkov.[28] He claimed 25 Allied ships and 100 aircraft for every U-boat. This, too, was special pleading.

It is possible that the economic concept of opportunity cost, that is, what might have been done with the Allied maritime forces had the U-boat offensive been abandoned totally, could be deployed in this instance. But there are both methodological and historical difficulties with this approach. It would be difficult to actually devise an economically sound, far less rigorous, method which could evaluate the vastly different types of ASW units, from corvettes to Catalinas, in terms of alternative uses. In campaign terms, the obvious option would be the Pacific campaign in which fleet carriers and landing craft were of more significance than sloops and Sunderlands.

In historical terms, even supposing Dönitz's May 1943 withdrawal had been complete rather than partial, what would have been the likely Allied reaction? It is probably fair to suggest that there might have been a spectrum of views ranging perhaps from

Admiral King, who might have suggested the transfer of at least some assets to the Pacific, to the British, whose innate caution and concern would have put them in the position of arguing for Atlantic retention. A likely, and fairly proper, contention might have been that unless and until the campaign was not only ended, but also the capability to take it up again no longer existed, it would be foolish to consider the mass transfer of assets to another theatre. A less conjectural point is that many of the Battle of the Atlantic forces were also required for the vast amphibious enterprise of June 1944 in northwestern Europe. These were to be used not just for the direct protection of the vast and vulnerable invasion armada from submarines, but also for other general purpose tasks.

It must also be admitted that focusing on the tonnage battle, and the associated losses for the Germans, makes it easier to monitor the progress of the campaign and produce analytically based conclusions. But the other points made about the German rationale indicate, if not insincerity, then at least a marked degree of both special pleading and political opportunism. For that reason, what might be regarded as the classical analyses of effort, merchant vessel losses and submarine sinking can still be regarded as useful measures of the efficacy of submarine warfare in the period.

Using such tools, the period must be regarded as poor for the Germans. The keys to this lie in some ways in the period before that in question. There has been a tendency to see the short span from March to May 1943 as a wild fluctuation, especially in Allied fortunes. This has led to a tendency to try and seek some single cause within that period alone which initiated the turnaround. But, if a longer view is taken, the mid-Atlantic battle, which started in the middle of 1942, exhibited the characteristics of growing Allied predominance, a feature which continued until May 1943. What happened then and continued into 1944, if not the end of the war, was an Allied strategic change of gear.

Long-term factors, such as growing strength of escorts, aircraft and merchant vessels; improved equipment and techniques; greater experience of operators and their being welded into effective teams, were much in evidence. It was perhaps only because these had reached such high levels that the exploitation of Ultra could go on to the greater levels that it did. Thus, despite the technical proficiency of codebreaking by the spring of 1943, it was often not possible to achieve what it had done in the latter part of 1941. Threatened convoy reinforcement might be possible, but the density of deployed submarines in early 1943 made evasion highly improbable. For instance, the onslaught on HX229/SC122 in March 1943, the nadir of the Allied campaign, was largely triggered by a submarine not involved in the search for these convoys.

But after the success of May 1943, Ultra could not only be used for evasion and reinforcement, as it was, but also as the main factor in freeing forces for other purposes. Thus such intelligence allowed both air and surface forces to be deployed in the Bay of Biscay in the secure knowledge that the convoys these would otherwise have been protecting could continue unmolested. In turn the submarine sinkings and delays incurred in the Bay implied yet less pressure on convoys.

Had Dönitz and others in the high command had any doubts as to the suitability of third generation submarines for Atlantic warfare in 1943–44, the results of operations in that period should have swept any questions aside.[29] Particularly evident was, notwithstanding Dönitz's earlier dismissal of the aircraft as having as much chance against a submarine as "a crow against a mole,"[30] the efficacy of air attack and, more markedly, air surveillance as a potent anti-submarine measure. Any longer-term path to a return to the heady days of 1940–42 had to at least take account of, if not provide an entire solution to, the problem of aircraft.

The events of 1943–44 probably put an end to the concept of staying on the surface and out-fighting the aircraft. This had proved a costly distraction, both in terms of outfitting submarines as flak-ships and in actual submarine loss and damage. The first was basically an attempt to turn the submarine into what it was not; and whilst it had performed well in the earlier part of the war as a gun-boat, with the incidental benefit of being able to submerge, an AA cruiser it was not. The extra guns often affected stability;[31] the extra crews for them made habitability even more inadequate than before, and, in any case, Allied tactics of multiple aircraft attacks and integration with surface warships often overcame even the most spirited submarine resistance.

The solution lay in improved underwater performance. The key to Allied success in beating off submarine attacks on convoys had been making a submarine submerge, converting it from a 17 knot torpedo boat with adequate speed differential to close convoys for days, if need be, to the 8 knot blind and largely deaf submarine which could maintain even this miserable performance for a period of barely hours; even that presumed a fully charged battery.

In fairness to the Germans, such problems had been anticipated long before the setbacks of May 1943, far less than those in the months which followed. The perceived solution to the problem lay in putting to sea a submarine of radically improved underwater performance. This found first expression in the Walter boat, a submarine which combined much improved hydrodynamic performance with an ingenious high performance propulsion system. The latter was, however, risky in two senses. First, it was theoretically ahead of its supportive technology. It was intended to work by the use of hydrogen peroxide to provide the necessary oxygen for burning with fuel in a turbine. This certainly worked, but the chemicals needed were difficult to manage in a technical sense; perhaps more important, as in some of the early German rocket aircraft, the materials were extremely hazardous to the crews. It is very easy in hindsight to condemn the Germans for travelling down the Walter path for too long. But the principle was considered sufficiently promising for at least two nations to attempt to use German research after the war.[32] Neither did very well, but their persistence indicated recognition of the potential.[33]

Although the realisation of the Walter boat was to evade the Germans, at least some of its development work was not to be wasted. An alternative policy of two designs was worked out, using the technologies of improved underwater hydrodynamics and greatly increased battery capacity.[34] A further innovation was the Schnorkel, which was also developed separately.[35] Put together, these resulted in two designs, the Types XXI and XXIII. The former, an ocean-going boat of some 1,600 tons, was capable of much greater underwater endurance than earlier generation submarines: on full charge it could move 340 miles at 5 knots, as compared to only 80 miles at 4 knots of the Type VIIC. Perhaps more important, it could move at 17 knots, albeit only for one hour, whereas the earlier submarine could barely manage 7 knots.[36] The second was a small submarine of 234 tons intended for coastal operations. In July 1943, the decision was taken to give these submarines the highest production priority.

The production and operational deployment of these submarines lies well outside the scope of this paper; the first boat was not to be completed until the summer of 1944, and the first patrol did not occur for nearly another year. But the concept of these boats, and the new dimension that it was hoped they would allow, served as an inspiration to the Germans and a matter of concern for the Allies. The former hoped not just to regain the initiative at sea tactically, but also to deploy sufficient numbers to affect the whole balance of the war. This called for large-scale production, and this appeared at least possible with the placing of all naval production under Armament Minister Albert Speer, which was done in May 1943. This was important, because it put naval construction on a level playing field with other projects, rather than the bruising, often ineffective, Third Reich infighting which had preceded it.

Speer put Otto Merker in charge of construction. Previously distinguished by his efforts in mass producing fire engines, he presented an innovative plan for new boats involving prefabricated construction at inland factories, with final assembly taking place in shipyards.[37] This admittedly drew inspiration from the achievement of American industry in making large numbers of merchant ships. Again, this gave hope to Dönitz of a revival of submarine warfare.

It was appreciated that not only equipment but also tactics would have to change. Although the performance of the new submarines was impressive, it is arguable that they still were not true submarines. They were still not yet free of dependence on the surface for battery charging, although this was much reduced by comparison with their predecessors. Typically, they might have to charge their batteries, via a Schnorkel, for about three hours a day, as opposed to the Types VIIs and IXs, which spent most of their time on the surface unless forced down. Such characteristics rendered the *Rudeltaktik* virtually impossible, with its emphasis on the lavish use of radio communications. Similarly, visual reconnaissance became very difficult. These factors suggested independent operations in areas of reasonably concentrated shipping. This, in turn, led to a return to inshore waters, where the very limited German submarines had started off in the First World War. Such operations took place later than the period of this paper, but German thoughts were tending in this direction in late 1943 and early 1944.

Thus in the second half of 1943, we have the contrast of abysmal results combined with considerable—even justified—optimism for the future. It was the latter which was to sustain the *Kriegsmarine* in the last phase of the war. The foundations laid in this earlier period were also to maintain and enhance the reputation of Dönitz, maintaining Hitler's confidence to the end, and to the *Grossadmiral's* eventual nomination as Hitler's successor.

For naval warfare beyond the Second World War, there were also profound implications. The concept of the true submarine was carried forward, albeit as a reaction to Allied surface and air dominance, and its realisation was to dominate the next fifty years. Admittedly, its main further developments were neither conceived nor realised by the Germans. These were nuclear propulsion; finally severing the dependency on the surface; the development of the submarine as an antisubmarine vehicle; and, lastly, the evolution of the submarine as the strategic missile platform *par excellence*. None of these were foreseen by Dönitz's *Kriegsmarine* of 1943–44, but it is in the demands and solutions of this period that their genesis undoubtedly lies.

1. All tonnage data is abstracted from Jürgen Rohwer's *Axis Submarine Successes 1939–1945*, Cambridge, 1983. The major sources for this paper include Admiralty Staff History, *Defeat of the Enemy Attack on Shipping*, London, 1957 (often referred to as Barley and Waters); Admiralty; *The U-boat War in the Atlantic*, London, 1950, and 1977, (referred to as Hessler); W. J. R. Gardner, "Prelude to Victory: the Battle of the Atlantic 1942–1943" in *Mariner's Mirror*, August 1993; S. G. Gorshkov; *The Sea Power of the State*, Pergamon, 1980 (English ed); F. H. Hinsley, et al., *British Intelligence in the Second World War, Volume III, Part I*, London, 1984; John Jordan in *Soviet Submarines: 1945 to the Present*, London, 1989; Michael McGwire and John MacDonnell (eds); *Soviet Naval Influence: Domestic and Foreign Dimensions*, New York, 1977; Brian McCue; *U-boats in the Bay of Biscay: an Essay in Operations Analysis*; National Defence University Press, Washington, D.C., 1990; Alfred Price; *Aircraft versus Submarine*, London, 1980; Albert Speer; *Inside the Third Reich*, London, 1970; Kapitan Zur See Werner Rahn, "The Development of New Types of U-boats in Germany during World War II. Construction, Trials and First Operational Experience of the Type XXI, XXIII, and Walter's U-boats," in *Les Marines de Guerre Du Dreadnought au Nucleaire*, Paris, 23–25 November 1988; Jurgen Rohwer; *Axis Submarine Successes 1939–1945*, Cambridge, 1983; S. W. Roskill, *The War at Sea*, Volume III, part I (London, 1960); No author given; *Führer Conferences on Naval Affairs*: London, 1990.

2. Submarine loss data is drawn from the Admiralty's Staff History, *Defeat of the Enemy Attack on Shipping*, London, 1957 (subsequently referred to as Barley and Waters), Appendix 2(iii).

3. See W. J. R. Gardner "Prelude to Victory: the Battle of the Atlantic 1942–1943" in *Mariner's Mirror*, August 1993.

4. Admiralty; *The U-boat War in the Atlantic*, London, 1950–1977, subsequently referred to as Hessler; II, p. 113.

5. Hessler III, p. 8.

6. Führer Conferences on Naval Affairs—31 May 1943.

7. Hessler III, Diagram 22.

8. Although this was an excellent example of Ultra at its best, there were still interpretational difficulties. The Americans believed the positional data indicated that the submarines were where they actually were, whereas OIC thought it at least possible that the vicinity of Newfoundland was a feasible alternative, as Hinsley admits. Hinsley III, 1, p. 212.

9. S. W. Roskill; *The War at Sea*, Volume III, part 1 (London, 1960), p. 19.

10. Roskill III:1, p. 29. Despite Roskill making no overt mention of Ultra, he was aware of its existence and significance. This is a counter argument to the post-Ultra revelation argument that "now Roskill will have to be rewritten."

11. Hessler III, p. 21, covering the period May–August, notes the loss of as many in the relatively short period in the Bay of Biscay as in a much longer time in the operational areas. There are some minor discrepancies between Hessler on the one hand and Barley and Waters on the other.

12. Previously, the Bay had largely been the domain of short and medium-range aircraft, which were incapable of operating in the mid-Atlantic.

13. One of the most thorough and generally available accounts is found in Alfred Price; *Aircraft versus Submarine*, London, 1980.

14. A statement on the time it took was made later in the period by the Germans. In 1944, it is estimated that the return Bay passage took 10–12 days against the earlier 3–5. This not only had to be subtracted from operational time, but also imposed extra crew pressures. Hessler III, p. 54.

15. Hessler III, p. 18. Postwar analysis reduced the figure somewhat.

16. Hessler III, p. 26.

17. Führer Conferences, p. 369.

18. This is doubtless one of the origins of the part of the Ultra mythology; the claim that Ultra was used to risk merchant ships in order to provoke encounters with submarines.

19. Known variously as *Grenzwellenpfänger* or *Presskohle*, Hessler, p. 30. Credence was not given to the effectiveness of the equipment at the time.

20. Brian McCue; *U-boats in the Bay of Biscay: an Essay in Operations Analysis*; National Defence University Press, Washington, D.C., 1990, p. 143. As can be deduced from his work on tankers, the book covers rather more than the title suggests. Another case that he presents is that of an earlier introduction of the Type XXI submarine; interestingly, this has less influence numerically than the more modest one of doubling the tanker force.

21. Including the operation previously described starting in October.

22. In the period, 10 of these were under 100 tons, two less than 30. Rohwer, pp. 246–255.

23. Atlantic, two ships of 7048 tons; Mediterranean, 4 of 7354.

24. Her emergency replacement, *Brake*, was also sunk the following month, just outside the period of this paper.

25. Hessler III, p. 62 citing *B d U Diary* of 15 June 1944.

26. *Ibid*. A further point of possible contention is that Dönitz counts ASW ships in all theatres of war against the overwhelmingly Atlantic basis of the submarine deployment.

27. Barley and Waters; Volume 1B (Plans and Tables); 1957, Plan 9.

28. Gorshkov, S. G.; *The Sea Power of the State*; Pergamon, 1980 (English edition), p. 120.

29. The classification of submarines into generations is somewhat arbitrary, but considers the crude submarines early in the century as first generation, and those of the First World War as second. Perhaps German boats of the first two thirds of the Second World War were too derivative of the second generation to be considered truly a new generation, but for these purposes it is a useful classification. This can then be extended to consider Types XXI, XXIII, and their many post-war derivatives as fourth generation and the nuclear submarine as fifth.

30. Quoted in Price, p. 86.

31. Hessler III, p. 42 and Price, pp. 191–2, note the excessive rolling caused by limited armor protection for gun crews. The former also notes that this excessive motion was detrimental to visual search, not only limiting warning against aircraft but also vitiating visual search for shipping, an important point.

32. Russian attempts are alluded to in Michael McGwire and John MacDonnell (eds); *Soviet Naval Influence: Domestic and Foreign Dimensions*, New York, 1977, p. 152. A short reference to these attempts is also made by John Jordan in *Soviet Submarines: 1945 to the Present*, London, 1989, pp. 22–23. This also makes the point that British exploitation of the technology was lengthy and troublesome.

33. The technology was overtaken by nuclear propulsion, but this development was almost impossible to foresee in 1945, far less 1943.

34. For an account of the development and deployment of these submarines see Kapitän Zur See Werner Rahn; "The Development of New Types of U-boats in Germany during World War II: Construction, Trials and First Operational Experience of the Type XXI, XXIII and Walter U-boats," in *Les Marines de Guerre Du Dreadnought au Nucléaire*, Paris, 23–25 November 1988.

35. The first (ordinary) submarine fitted with Schnorkel was sunk on its first patrol in February 1944.

36. By 1943, this was reduced still further, largely caused by the underwater drag of extra AA guns.

37. Albert Speer; *Inside the Third Reich*, London, 1970, p. 273.

Images of Naval Aviation in the Second World War

Michael Paris

⚓

Towards the end of 1944, the Hollywood producer Walter Wanger confidently summed up the role of the film industry to the war effort: "When future historians write the story of World War Two, a bright chapter will be assigned to the contribution of America's motion picture industry in winning the war."[1] And popular cinema did indeed play a significant part in boosting morale, encouraging the population, explaining the cause of the war and reconstructing the visual image of the battlefield for Home Front America. Yet even Wanger's rather smug assessment of the industry's performance seriously undervalues the role that Hollywood played and has continued to play ever since. I would like to suggest that, quite simply, film has become, for most people, the major source of historical knowledge for the Second World War.

Films made during the war years are continually reshown on television and made available on video cassette, and new features are regularly produced which reconstruct battles, campaigns, great events and the parts played by individuals in various aspects of that conflict. For the vast majority of the population today, and especially for the young, their understanding of the cause and course of the war and its visual images come via the screen. Successive generations have "fleshed out" their schoolroom history with accounts of Pearl Harbour, the Battle of Midway, Iwo Jima or the strategic bombing of Japan from narrative and documentary films.

Here it is important to avoid academic elitism—for there is absolutely no reason why most people should delve into scholarly works when the cinematic history lesson comes in such an exciting and colourful, two-hour package. In rational moments, audiences are aware that film is, at best, an artistic reconstruction of the past—that when the great events of history are recreated for the screen, filmmakers simplify, exaggerate, and distort for dramatic purposes. Yet audiences rarely analyze what they are shown; the magic of cinema is just too powerful. Most accept the interpretation that is projected. Usually this is of little concern to the historian, although there are perhaps dangers inherent in a film such as Oliver Stone's *JFK*, a highly influential but excessively personal study which reveals more about the paranoia of the film maker than it does about the assassination. But, if as I have suggested, cinematic images of the Second World War are the main source of historical knowledge for the general public, then the historian is committed to a familiarity and understanding of those images in exactly the same way that they must familiarize themselves with the other influential secondary sources for the topic under scrutiny. The historian is not concerned with the aesthetic aspects of film, but rather with how a production reflects the period in which it was made and the messages transmitted to the audience.[2] In our context, film provides another layer of knowledge and complements the traditional sources of the historian in understanding how the contribution of naval aviation to the eventual victory was relayed to the public during the war years and how that image has been subsequently revised in the years after 1945. However, for the historian of naval aviation, it has to be noted that there is not an overwhelming amount of source material to be found in the film archives.

The subsequent rise of naval aviation was a popular one for film makers during the inter-war period; there are, for example, far more films about naval flying than there are about army aviation. Even in the last months of peace, Hollywood studios released several major naval films, including *Flight Command* and *Dive Bomber*. But that dominance did not continue after Pearl Harbour. In the period between 1941 to 1976, there were just seven films made about naval air operations and another six dealing with marginal topics: the naval contribution to the Doolittle Raid, PBY patrols, or Marine Corps aviation. (I'm sure the Marines won't like being referred to as "marginal," but I'm afraid that in this context they are.) For the same period, there are over thirty films dealing with the air force and that doesn't include films made by Hollywood studios about American pilots serving with the Royal Air Force. In reality, of course, naval air operations in the Pacific include a number of relatively clear-cut victories and are far more quantifiably successful than the air force strategic offensive, which is still a matter of some controversy. Yet it is, in large measure, air force training and operations upon which the film industry has concentrated. Why this should be so is an interesting question, but one beyond the scope of this paper. However, one would certainly have to consider production costs and the difficulties of recreating naval battles as part of the explanation.

Hollywood's involvement with wartime naval aviation began with the release of *Wake Island* in the autumn of 1942. It is the story of the heroic but doomed defence of the island by a detachment of Marines and the Grumman F4Fs of VMF 211. The film tells its story through the experiences of the marine commander, and its coverage of the air aspects of the defence is slight. We see the first Japanese air raid on the 8th of December, which destroyed eight of the squadron's twelve Wildcats, and the desperate attempts by the ground crews to keep the remaining planes airworthy. A pilot, whose wife has been killed at Pearl Harbour, goes after a Japanese cruiser bombarding the island in what is virtually a suicide mission. He gets the cruiser but is killed in the attack. On the final day of the siege, the last Wildcat pilot takes off to intercept the enemy bombers. In the ensuing dog fight, his aircraft is crippled and, in a scene which became almost "de rigueur" for wartime aviation films, he is machine-gunned by a smiling Japanese pilot as he helplessly floats down on his parachute. The final narration declared that "These marines fought a great fight. They wrote history. But this is not the end. . . . there are other leathernecks, other fighting Americans—140 million of them—whose blood and sweat and fury will exact a just and terrible vengeance."

The Halsey-Doolittle Raid on Tokyo inaugurated that revenge on 16 April 1942; an Army Air Force operation but one in which the Navy played a vitally important role. The film industry's first reference to this mission was in the 1943 Warner Brothers production, *Destination Tokyo*, the story of the submarine *Copperfin* and her mission to penetrate Tokyo Bay and land an Air Force officer to gather vital information for the bombers. The raid is reconstructed by using documentary footage of the take-off from the *Hornet* and models for the actual attack. Far-fetched? Yes, of course, but that doesn't really matter. The story line appeared credible and showed the service playing a positive role in combined operations at a time when the public was concerned at what appeared to be a lack of initiative on the part of the navy. The Doolittle Raid received detailed treatment in the documentary style feature, *Thirty Seconds Over Tokyo*, a 1944 production based on Ted Lawson's best-selling book of the same title. The film made use of scenes actually filmed aboard the *Hornet*, and MGM recreated a sixty foot replica of the flight deck for other sequences. Bosley Crowther, the influential film critic of the *New York Times*, referred to the production as a "true and tremendous story... told with magnificent integrity and dramatic eloquence... handled with restraint and in a realistic style."[3] Clearly, the major focus is on Doolittle and his Army Air Force pilots, but the film does show the contribution of the carrier in getting the Mitchell bombers to within range of the Japanese mainland.

Less than two months after that first raid on Tokyo came the remarkable Battle of Midway, a vindication for the theorists of naval air power and a battle which even the astringent commentator, Basil Ladle Hart, referred to as the "turning point that spelt the ultimate doom of Japan."[4] This was surely splendid material for a film industry which pursued patriotism with profit. And, indeed, before the end of the year, John Ford's highly-acclaimed documentary, *The Battle of Midway*, was released. This short film, which deals with what the narration calls the "greatest naval victory of the world to date," is, however, rather brief on the naval contribution. Ford, working for the Navy's Photographic Unit, was actually on the island during the attack, and this obviously coloured his perceptions of events. We see a considerable amount of footage of the bombing raids and the air battles over Midway. But when, as the commentator tells us, "the trap is sprung," it is army B17s taking off to attack the Japanese fleet that we see, an attack which most historians regard as ineffective. Ford later cut in scenes of carrier planes, and there are some interesting close-ups of naval pilots who took part in the action. "The Battle of Midway is over," the commentator tells us, "our front yard is safe." But there is precious little in the film to tell exactly how that victory was won or of the decisive part played by naval aviation.

Ford's film was given the Oscar for best documentary of 1942, and, certainly, the message of triumph and it's magnificent, if somewhat sentimental, images and commentary ensured its popularity with cinema audiences. But however well-received these films were by the public and critics, and however positive their images of the navy's contribution to combined operations, they only skirted the fringes of the central focus of naval aviation—the aircraft carrier—and it was not until mid-1944 that a film dealing specifically with carrier operations was released. *Wing and a Prayer: The Story of Carrier X*, from Twentieth-Century Fox, opens with a shot of newspaper headlines: "WHERE IS OUR NAVY?" and an editorial that reads, "Three months have passed since the tragedy at Pearl Harbor and people are at a loss to understand why our Navy does not strike back." Another headline blares, "COMMITTEE DEMANDS PROBE OF NAVY FAILURE TO FIGHT." The scene then moves to a naval board room; a senior officer addresses his fellow admirals explaining that the service must not allow itself to be drawn by accusations of a failure to fight and that the Navy, having now regrouped and developed its strategy, is going onto the offensive. The Japanese, it is explained, are supremely self-confident after their successes and will almost certainly launch an invasion of Pearl Harbor, but first they must take Midway Island. American strategy, therefore, will be to persuade the enemy to split his forces and bring them to battle when and where the United States has the advantage. This task will be carried out by Carrier X, whose mission will be to convince the enemy that American naval strength is scattered and morale destroyed.

Having set the scene, the film then shifts its focus to Carrier X. The story really centres around the men of the carrier's squadron VT-5, a fictional, newly formed unit of TBFs. The pilots are hungry for combat and are not pleased when the air officer tells them that "when enemy planes are encountered do not engage them. Return to the carrier at once." It is difficult for these young and eager pilots to run from combat and give the Japanese the impression that they lack stomach for a fight. Gradually, however, they learn discipline and the squadron becomes a cohesive fighting unit.

Finally, the time comes when the American forces are ready, and the air groups are launched into the attack on the Japanese fleet. Apart from the initial attack by VT-5 on a Japanese carrier, little is actually seen of the battle; it is presented to the audience through a series of radio transmissions relayed throughout *Carrier X*. This dramatic device is an effective solution to the film makers' problems in attempting to recreate the battle, but still allows the audience to gain an understanding of the excitement and confusion of modern battle.

Twentieth-Century Fox followed *Wing and a Prayer* with a feature length documentary about carriers, *Fighting Lady*, released in January 1945. This film recounts the story of an *Essex*-class carrier from its launching through the most dramatic episodes of the Pacific

War, including the battles of Kwejalein, Truk, Guam, Saipan, and the Philippine Sea. One of the more interesting aspects is the way that the film examines the work of the various departments and how essential it is that everyone plays their part if the ship is to fulfil her role as an effective fighting unit. Narrated by the actor Robert Taylor, then holding a Naval Reserve commission, the film took over fourteen months to complete. Documentary films were never as popular with audiences as feature films; despite this and the fact that most people were bored with war pictures by 1945, the film did remarkably well, winning the Academy Award for the best documentary of the year.

Released at the same time as *Fighting Lady*, MGM's *This Man's Navy* dealt with the lighter than air units of naval aviation—perhaps the most little known branch of the Service. The film concerns a braggart veteran airship pilot, played by Wallace Beery, and a young recruit thrown together on active service. Most of the film deals with the training program of airships at Lakehurst, but eventually the crew sees action and sinks a German U-boat off the east coast. Transferred to the China–Burma theater of operations, they heroically rescue the passengers of a naval transport aircraft which has crashed in the Burmese jungle. Aside from the Hollywood heroics, the film is an interesting look at an area of naval aviation virtually ignored by film makers. *This Man's Navy* is, however, something of a throwback to the over-the-top features of the 1930s rather than the serious and realistic mood of the other wartime features.

There is one other narrative dealing with naval aviation from the war years that needs to be mentioned—or perhaps not mentioned. A nonsensical 1943 production from Universal called *We've Never Been Licked* is the story of a young American pilot, an apparent enemy sympathizer working for the Japanese, who, during the Battle for the Solomons, takes over a Japanese dive bomber and reveals the enemy position to an American carrier group. Not content with that, he then dives his plane into the Japanese carrier, sinking her with all hands. For this, he is awarded a posthumous Congressional Medal of Honour. *We've Never Been Licked* is an example of the worst kind of Hollywood propaganda of the early war years, cheaply made with shoddy production values and minimal characterization. Americans are all wonderfully heroic, and the enemy is the "beast from the east." Bosley Crowther suggested that the plot was so ridiculous it was an embarrassment.[5]

But what of these other films? Were they too just so much Hollywood hokum with a veneer of patriotic fervour? Films have their own history, and if we follow what Thomas Cripps has called the "paper trail" of production documentation, it provides an insight into the making of these films.[6] The script for *Wake Island*, for example, was based on Marine Corps records, employed several Marine Corps officers as advisers, and the Corps provided Wildcats for use in the film. In order to achieve visual accuracy, Paramount hired the construction company that had built the original Wake Island installation to recreate it on the location in the Salton Sea area. *Midway*, the documentary, was filmed, as it happened, by John Ford, the well-known Hollywood director then serving in the Field Photographic Unit for the Department of the Navy. Although there is some evidence that Ford pressured President Roosevelt to keep the more sentimental images in the film, what appears on the screen, however, had the Navy's approval.[7] Some even thought the far-fetched *Destination Tokyo* so realistic in its scenes of the submarine service, it was, so the story goes, adopted by the Navy as an instructional film.[8]

Thirty Seconds Over Tokyo was made with the cooperation of both services and used documentary footage taken by air force and naval cameramen. In that sense, these films were what we might term "semi-official," in that the Department of the Navy had a considerable degree of control over their making and what they revealed of naval operations. That being so, it must be assumed that what they projected was what the Navy wanted shown; that they were images the Navy was happy to endorse. As for *Wing and a Prayer* and *Fighting Lady*, that control was even more obvious. Work started on the former in early 1943. The Navy agreed to assist in the production but insisted on a realistic script. To achieve an accurate portrayal, the writer, Jerome Cady, worked from the combat records of the air groups that took part in the Battle of Midway. The Department of the Navy allowed Henry Hathaway, the director, and a small crew to film on the newly commissioned carrier *Yorktown* during her shakedown cruise. "For seven weeks," the director later wrote, "we captured everything on film: take-offs, landings, crashes, pilots getting in and out of their planes, everything."[9] This film was added to the footage taken of the studio mock-up and fleshed out with combat footage supplied by the Navy. Lieutenant Robert Middleton, a Pacific veteran, acted as technical adviser to the studio and later commented on the impressive degree of realism achieved in the picture.[10] And this view was echoed in Thomas Pryor's review of the film in the *New York Times*: "Director Henry Hathaway has so skilfully woven documentary film footage into the story that it is difficult at times to spot the ending of an incident out of history and the beginning of an episode fashioned on the typewriter of scenarist Jerome Cady."[11]

The origins of *Fighting Lady* were somewhat different. Towards the end of 1943, no doubt influenced by the many films which paid tribute to the other services, Captain H. B. Miller of the Naval Bureau of Aeronautics conceived the idea of producing a documentary film which would give the public a detailed view of life aboard an aircraft carrier. The film was shot by naval cinematographers under the direction of Commander Edward Steichen and Lieutenant Commander Dwight Long. However, an arrangement was made with Twentieth-Century Fox by which the latter would produce and release the film for theatrical performance. Most filming took place aboard the *Yorktown II*, and indeed the film was intended as a cinematic biography of that ship, but some filming did take place on board the *Essex*, *Lexington*, and *Hornet*. The result was, according to one reviewer, "a picture every American should see that he may better know and appreciate what our Navy is doing in the Pacific,"[12] which was exactly what the Navy wanted. Admiral Chester Nimitz, having seen the film, reportedly proclaimed it "a real picture of real men and real fighting." Later he was quoted as suggesting that "the Japanese should see this picture some day with our bombs and our compliments."[13] The Navy, then, shared in an active partnership with commercial studios in the production of these pictures and was apparently satisfied that the "product" showed naval aviation in a realistic manner but with the proviso that feature films had to be allowed a degree of dramatic licence in terms of characterization and plot. But what overall messages do these films convey?

The overriding impression is that naval and marine fliers are tough, dedicated and professional. Younger men, the fledglings, are eager for combat. Indeed, their weakness is a tendency to attack without thought of the consequences and often against orders. If we take *Wing and a Prayer* as an example, we find that the hardest lesson young aviators have to learn is discipline—accepting that they are part of a team and that senior officers actually know what they are doing. However, once that lesson is learned, teamwork and mutual dependence becomes the hallmark of the unit.

1. Quoted in Leif Furhammer and Folke Isaksson, *Politics and Film*, (London, 1971), 66.
2. See, K.R.M. Short (ed), *Feature Films as History*, (London, 1981), Introduction, 16–36.
3. Bosley Crowther, *New York Times*, 16 November 1944.
4. Basil Ladle Hart, *History of the Second World War* (London, 1970), 353.
5. Bosley Crowther quoted in James Farmer, *Celluloid Wings* (Blu Ridge Summit, PA, 1984), 195.
6. Thomas Cripps, "The Moving Image as Social History: Stalking the Paper Trail" in J. E. O'Connor (ed), *Image as Artifact*, (Malabar, Florida, 1990), 136–155.
7. See Dan Ford, *The Uniquiet Man: The Life of John Ford*, (London, 1982), 173–174.
8. Furhammer and Isaksson, 67.
9. Quoted in Bruce Oris, *When Hollywood Ruled the Skies*, (Hawthorne, CA, 1984), 90.
10. Ibid.
11. Thomas Pryor, *New York Times*, 31 August 1944.
12. Pryor, *New Yorker Times*, 18 January 1945.
13. Nimitz was quoted in the *New York Times* on 21 January and 10 February 1945.

Intelligence and Hunter-Killer Groups, 1943–1945

David Syrett

⚓

U.S. Navy hunter-killer groups, built around escort aircraft carriers, are credited with sinking 52 German U-boats,[1] which is about seven percent of the 785 U-boats lost by the Germans in the course of World War II.[2] The U-boats sunk by American escort carrier hunter-killers are thought by Samuel Eliot Morison to be "the greatest single contribution of the United States Navy to victory over the enemy submarines."[3] It is now known that the success of the U.S. Navy hunter-killer groups depended absolutely on communications intelligence. William T. Y'Blood, the historian of American escort carrier operations, has concluded that *"Enigma intelligence"* played an important role in every one of the 52 German U-boats sunk by American escort carrier hunter-killer groups.[4]

Before 1974, it was thought that the main source of Allied communications intelligence during the Battle of the Atlantic was shore based HF/DF[5] fixes.[6] After 1974, with the revelation of the *ultra* secret,[7] it was believed that the most important source of Allied communications intelligence during the Battle of the Atlantic was decrypted German radio messages. In fact, *ultra* was thought in some quarters to be an all inclusive source of information. One historian has even gone so far as to maintain that the decryption of German radio messages gave the Allies "an unprecedented overall view of the enemy's naval operations and intentions."[8] However, in practice, the use by the Allies of communications intelligence in the Battle of the Atlantic was never as comprehensive, as straight forward, or as simple as a number of people, after the event, would have it.

There are several ways in which the Allies, during the Battle of the Atlantic, exploited German radio traffic to and from U-boats for intelligence purposes. One was to locate the source of a radio transmission by shore based HF/DF. A second was to recover the contents of a coded radio message by means of decryption. A third was to identify an individual radio transmitter by the electronic characteristics of an intercepted transmission from which information on individual U-boats could thus be obtained.[9] A fourth source of information from radio transmissions is known as radio traffic analysis. For example, from the type, "length of dispatch," and other characteristics of a radio transmission, the Allies could determine if it was a sighting, sinking, position, reconnaissance, or weather report.[10] Historians tend to overlook the importance of various types of non-decryption communications intelligence. No doubt this confusion is because of a knowledge of *ultra* and because, during the war, for reasons of secrecy, all information, especially from decryption concerning U-boats, was obtained from the interception of radio messages and was cited as coming from D/F.[11] Nevertheless, it is clear that, even without decrypting German radio messages, the Allies could obtain significant amounts of intelligence on German U-boat operations from analyzing and D/Fing the radio transmissions of the U-boats.

To intercept and D/F U-boat radio transmissions, the Allies established a string of intercept stations around the shores of the Atlantic. When the establishment reached full strength, it numbered fifty-one intercept stations manned by Americans, British, and Canadians.[12] At first the American intercept stations were equipped with commercial D/F equipment, but, as quickly as possible, they were reequipped with high speed DAJ HF/DF sets. There were, at the beginning, long delays in reporting bearings; however, these delays were reduced with the establishment of a system of high speed electronic communications, with the result that some U-boat D/F fixes arrived in Washington at the office of the Commander-in-Chief U.S. Fleet [COMINCH] within ten minutes of an enemy vessel transmitting.[13]

Determining a U-boat's position by means of D/F fixes, however, "was more an art than a science." The state of the weather and the ionosphere, human mistakes, and equipment imperfections could all produce errors.[14] The accuracy of a D/F fix depended, above all, on the skill of the HF/DF set operator. Nevertheless, with six or seven D/F bearings or "cuts," as they are called, obtained by different shore based D/F intercept stations, it was possible to plot, at long range, the location of a U-boat transmitting within twenty or thirty miles.[15] Morison gives the example of the U-58 which was fixed by four different shore based D/F bearings on 30 June 1942. Then, on the basis of this information, the U-boat was located, attacked, and sunk near Bermuda by a U.S. Navy aircraft.[16] It is clear that shore based HF/DF fixes, when combined with information about the electronic characteristics of a radio transmission, were one of the best sources of information available to the Allies for locating U-boats in the Atlantic.[17]

Of even greater importance than shore based HF/DF to the Allies for locating U-boats was the decryption of German radio messages. The British first broke the German naval codes in 1941.[18] Some information on U-boats was given to the U.S. Navy in 1941 by the British from the decryption of German radio messages.[19] But on 1 February 1942, the British could no longer read the coded radio messages to and from the U-boats, for the Germans instituted a special code for U-boats in the Atlantic which involved the use of a fourth wheel in addition to the three used in the standard *enigma* code machine.[20] It was not until 13 December 1942 that the British were able, once more, to decode German U-boat radio messages.[21]

Before American entry into World War II, the U.S. Navy directed most of its cryptographic effort to attacking Japanese codes.[22] Early in 1942, an agreement was reached between the Americans and British for the sharing and coordination of intercept services, D/F, and other information from radio traffic analysis.[23] The U.S. Army and U.S. Army Air Force, throughout the war, obtained from the British decryption intelligence from German sources.[24] The U.S. Navy, however, under the terms of an arrangement with the British known as the Wenger-Travis agreement and no doubt because of its operational commitments to the war against the U-boats and probably because of the wish to be to some degree independent of the British, began to decrypt U-boat radio messages independent of, but in cooperation with, the British in December 1942.[25] The U.S. Navy's OP-20Y-GA[26] decrypted the U-boat radio messages at the Naval Communications Annex at 3801 Nebraska Avenue in Washington, D.C. OP-20Y-G(A) worked closely with the Naval Section of the Government Code and Cypher School at Bletchley Park, exchanging cryptographic information daily by cable.[27]

Decrypts of U-boat radio messages moved from OP-20Y-G(A), by secure teletype or the hand of an officer, to F-211 or the Secret Room which was adjacent to F-21 or the Atlantic Section, Combat

Intelligence in the Office of COMINCH on the third floor of Main Navy. Only five persons were permitted to enter the Secret Room,[28] plus several high ranking officers such as Admirals King, Edwards, and Low.[29] In the Secret Room, decrypts of U-boat radio messages were married to other intelligence, such as D/F fixes, ship and aircraft sightings of U-boats, and prisoner of war interrogations, to produce a total intelligence picture. Intelligence, with its sources hidden, then moved out of the Secret Room to F-21's Submarine Tracking Room, the 10th Fleet, and to various combat commands.[30] Moreover, the Secret Room was in daily contact by cable with the British Submarine Tracking Room in London[31] and the Canadian Submarine Tracking Room in Ottawa.[32]

The great value of intelligence—obtained by decryption of German radio messages—is that it allowed the Allies to know what one German was saying to another German. As long as the Germans were unaware—as was the case throughout the war—that the Allies were reading their codes, there could be no possibility of deception. Moreover, decryption intelligence presented the Allies with none of the problems of information obtained from spies. Spies do not see everything, nor do they always understand what they see. Besides, spies do not always tell the truth and usually have difficulty in timely transmitting information to their masters.[33] For a spy to have obtained the information which the Allies got from decryption intelligence about German U-boat operations, he would have to have been a trained staff officer, directly linked by radio to COMINCH in Washington, D.C., standing twenty-four hours a day at the operational plot of the *Befehlshaber der Unterseeboote*! Furthermore, decryption intelligence went directly from the Germans to the Allies, and there was no possibility of distortion in the collection or transmission. Finally, the operational value of decryption intelligence was further increased by German standard procedures of command and control. Rarely did a U-boat go to sea with a complete set of operational orders. The standard procedure was for a U-boat to put to sea and, after transmitting a passage report, she would then be given, by radio, "a heading position." Later, detailed operational orders would be transmitted to the U-boat by radio.[34] The decryption of radio messages of this type gave the Allies a gold mine of information on U-boat operations.

The Germans were not to know, until after World War II, that the Allies had developed the technology not only to systematically intercept and D/F their radio communications, but also to read their coded command radio communications. The Germans knew that there was the logical possibility that the Allies could exploit the radio communications to and from U-boats for the purpose of obtaining intelligence. However, the Germans discounted the logical security dangers inherent in all radio communications and adopted a system of command and control for U-boats which required a great number of radio transmissions.[35] The Germans thought that the *enigma* code machine produced codes so complex that the Allies could never decode the messages in time to be of operational value.[36] It was also believed by the Germans that it was extremely difficult, to the point of being impossible, for the Allies to systematically and accurately intercept and D/F extremely short high frequency radio transmissions.[37] Nevertheless, at various times the Germans concluded that there was a leakage of information about U-boat operations to the Allies.[38] From time to time, various theories were embraced by the Germans, such as that the Allies were somehow tapping phones in order to gain information on U-boat operations.[39] However, the *Befehlshaber der Unterseeboote* and its security officers never came to terms with the possibility that radio communications to and from U-boats might be the main source of Allied intelligence.[40] This oversight on the part of the Germans is hard to understand, for communications intelligence played a significant role during World War I in the defeat of the U-boats.[41]

Communications intelligence, no matter how sophisticated, was, during the years 1943–1945, an imperfect guide, nevertheless, for the deployment of American hunter-killers in search of a U-boat to sink. Communications intelligence depended on radio transmissions being intercepted, D/Fed, and decrypted, and, with the end of wolf pack operations, the number of radio messages to and from U-boats greatly decreased. U-boats, during the last years of the war, according to American naval intelligence, maintained "a rigid condition of radio silence," going for as long as 30 or 40 days without making a single radio transmission. When the U-boats did use their radios, "90 per cent of all transmissions [were] 90 seconds or less." D/F fixes became much more difficult to obtain because the U-boats, when transmitting, employed "Norddeich off-frequencies." Further, the Germans made numerous small alterations and improvements in their codes which resulted in increased delays in the Allied decoding process. In these circumstances, the only way that American naval intelligence could "estimate U-boat locations is to project their course by dead-reckoning with, at infrequent intervals, the exact positions from which to correct dead-reckoning estimates."[42]

Sparse communications intelligence together with dead reckoning were a rough and ready method, and, at times, the only one of keeping track of and locating German U-boats for attack by hunter-killers. Calculations of U-boat positions by means of dead reckoning were subject to a number of variables, such as weather, idiosyncrasies of the vessel's machinery, and the predilection of the U-boat's commander. Nevertheless, American naval intelligence could, and did, track and predict the future positions of U-boats with enough accuracy for escort carrier hunter-killer operations.[43]

The tactic employed by the U.S. Navy hunter-killers was to use communications intelligence, assisted by dead reckoning, to figure out the approximate position of a U-boat or a group of U-boats. What communications intelligence did was to greatly reduce the area of ocean to be searched by the escort carrier hunter-killer groups when looking for a U-boat. One historian has estimated that this would be an area of about 10,000 to 15,000 square miles of ocean to be searched.[44] When a U-boat was "fingered" by communications intelligence, then the sea area in which the enemy vessel was thought to be hiding would be searched by a hunter-killer group. For example, Task Group 41.7, consisting of the escort carrier USS *Tripoli* and four destroyer escorts, on 13 September 1944, was sent "to conduct offensive operations against a homeward bound submarine estimated to be in the general area of latitude 05 00'N, longitude 19 11'W."[45] The day before these orders were issued to Task Group 41.7, American naval intelligence by means of communications intelligence, and dead reckoning, had concluded that the U-1062 was at 01 11'N, 11 30'W and proceeding roughly northwest at the rate of 150 miles per day.[46]

Task Group 41.7 was joined by Task Group 22.1, consisting of the escort carrier USS *Mission Bay* and five destroyer escorts. The search was continued in another area because of new information from communications intelligence and, then, on 30 September, a destroyer escort belonging to Task Group 22.1, the USS *Fessenden*, located, attacked, and sank the U-1062.[47] Even with timely and very accurate communications intelligence,[48] it took two escort carriers and nine destroyer escorts twelve days of searching to locate and sink the U-1062. As one authority after the war put it, communications intelligence could only bring the American hunter-killers "within their effective range" of the U-boats.[49]

Once the general location of a U-boat had been established by American naval intelligence or by means of communications intelligence assisted by dead reckoning, a hunter-killer group, built around an escort carrier, would then be dispatched to the region to attempt to hunt down and sink the suspected enemy vessel. The escort carrier in the hunter-killer group was the vital element, for that vessel's aircraft were capable of quickly searching large sea areas for U-boats. As the war went on, the ability of carrier borne aircraft to successfully search for and to locate U-boats was greatly enhanced by devices such as sonobuoys and airborne radar. But it was communications intelligence and dead reckoning by skilled naval intelligence officers which brought the American escort carrier hunter-killer groups within range of their prey and enabled them to bring the technology of carrier borne ASW to bear on the U-boats.

1. William T. Y'Blood, *Hunter-Killer: U.S. Escort Carriers and the Battle of the Atlantic* (Annapolis, Md., 1983), pp. 282–283.

2. S. W. Roskill, *The War at Sea* (London, 1961), vol. III, part II, p. 472.

3. Samuel Eliot Morison, *History of United States Naval Operations in World War II* (Boston, 1975), vol. X, pp. 362–363.

4. Y'Blood, *Hunter-Killer*, pp. 282–283. OP-20Y-G(A)'s history of communications intelligence and the Battle of the Atlantic lists 93 German U-boats sunk by the Americans with the assistance of communications intelligence. But a number of these U-boats were sunk by American forces other than escort carrier hunter-killers. See National Archives, Record Group 457, SRH-008, Battle of the Atlantic, vol. II, U-boat Operations, appendix I, p. 1. Hereafter the National Archives and Record Group 457 will be cited as NA.

5. High frequency direction finding.

6. Morison, *Naval Operations*, vol. I, p. 105.

7. F. W. Winterbotham, *The Ultra Secret* (New York, 1974).

8. John Winton, *Ultra at Sea* (London, 1988), p. 1.

9. NA, SRH-367, A Preliminary Analysis of the Role of Decryption Intelligence in the Operational Phase of the Battle of the Atlantic, U.S. Navy OEG Report # 66, p. 012.

10. NA, SRMN-032, Memoranda Concerning U-boat Tracking Room Operations, 02 Jan. 1943–06 June 1945, p. 098.

11. Kenneth Knowles, "Ultra and the Battle of the Atlantic: The American View," *Changing Interpretations and New Sources in Naval History*, Robert William Love, Jr., ed. (New York, 1980), pp. 445–446.

12. NA, SRH-277, A Lecture on Communications Intelligence: By RADM E. E. Stone, Director of the Armed Forces Security Agency, 5 June 1951, p. 21.

13. NA, SRH-197, U.S. Navy, Communications Intelligence: Organization, Liaison and Collaboration, 1941–1945.

14. NA, SRH-277, A Lecture on Communications Intelligence. . . , p. 21.
15. David Kahn, *Seizing the Enigma: The Race to Break the German U-boat Codes, 1939–1943* (Boston, 1991), p. 145.
16. Morison, *Naval Operations*, vol. I, pp. 227–228.
17. NA, SRMN-032, Memoranda Concerning U-boat Tracking Room Operations, 02 Jan. 1943–06 June 1945, p. 098.
18. F. H. Hinsley, et al., *British Intelligence in the Second World War* (London, 1981), vol. II, p. 163.
19. For example, Michael Gannon, *Operation Drumbeat* (New York, 1990), pp. 149–190.
20. Hinsley, *British Intelligence*, vol. II, p. 179.
21. Hinsley, *British Intelligence*, vol. II, p. 233.
22. Kahn, *Seizing the Enigma*, p. 237.
23. Hinsley, *British Intelligence*, vol. II, p. 56.
24. Public Record Office, PRO 31/20/1–24.
25. Bradley F. Smith, *The Ultra-Magic Deals: And the Most Secret Special Relationship, 1940–1945* (Novato, Calif., 1993), pp. 127–129.
26. OP (Office of the Chief of Naval Operations), 20 (Communications Division), G (Communications Intelligence), Y (Cryptanalysts), A (Atlantic).
27. Kahn, *Seizing the Enigma*, pp. 238–239; Hinsley, *British Intelligence*, vol. II, pp. 56–57.
28. Commander Kenneth A. Knowles, USN, Commander F-21; Lieutenant John E. Parsons, USNR, Commander Secret Room; Lieutenant(jg) John V. Boland, USNR, Ensign R. B. Chevalier, USNR, and Yeoman Samuel P. Livecchi, USN.
29. Admiral Ernest J. King, USN, Chief of Naval Operations and COMINCH; Vice Admiral Richard S. Edwards, USN, Deputy Chief of Naval Operations and Deputy COMINCH; and Rear Admiral Francis S. Low, Chief of Staff, 10th Fleet.
30. Kahn, *Seizing the Enigma*, pp. 237–244; NA, SRMN-038, Functions of the "Secret Room" (F-211) of COMINCH Combat Intelligence Atlantic Section Anti-Submarine Warfare, WWII (Undated).
31. Patrick Beesly, *Very Special Intelligence: The Story of the Admiralty's Operational Intelligence Centre, 1939–1945* (London, 1977), pp. 169–170.
32. Wesley K. Wark, "The Evolution of Military Intelligence in Canada," *Armed Forces & Society* (Fall, 1989), vol. 16, p. 85.
33. Cf., Sir David Hunt, *Don at War* (London, 1990), pp. 240–241.
34. NA, SRMN-032, Memoranda Concerning U-boat Tracking Room Operations, 02 Jan. 1943–06 June 1945, p. 099.
35. Karl Doenitz, *Memoirs: Ten Years and Twenty Days* (New York, 1959), pp. 62–63.
36. Jurgen Rohwer, "Ultra and the Battle of the Atlantic: The German View," *Changing Interpretations and New Sources in Naval History*, Robert William Love, Jr., ed. (New York, 1980), pp. 420–421.
37. Doenitz, *Memoirs*, p. 63.
38. Ministry of Defence (Navy), *The U-boat War in the Atlantic, 1939–1945* (London, 1989), vol. I, pp. 77–79.
39. Public Record Office, DEFE 3/738, intercepted 1640/9/11/44 decoded 1355/15/11/44.

40. Cf., David Kahn, *Hitler's Spies: German Military Intelligence in World War II* (New York, 1978), p. 524.

41. Cf. R. M. Grant, *U-Boat Intelligence, 1914–1918* (New York, 1969).

42. NA, SRNM-051A, OP-20-GI Memoranda to COMINCH F-2 on German U-boat Activities, October 1943–May 1945, pp. 146–149.

43. NA, SRMN-O34, COMINCH: Rough Notes on Daily U-boat Positions and Activities, 1943–1945.

44. Roger Stary, "The RCAF, 'Ultra' and the Anti-Submarine War in the Northwest Atlantic, 1943–1945," unpublished paper given at the 1992 meeting in Washington, D.C. of the North American Society of Oceanic Historians.

45. Naval Historical Center, Report of Operations, Task Group 41.7 during the period 13 September to 18 October 1944, p. 1.

46. NA, SRMN-034, COMINCH: Rough Notes on Daily U-boat Positions and Activities, 1943–1945, p. 1007.

47. Naval Historical Center, Daily Operations Narrative: Task Group 22.1, pp. 29–32; [TG 22.1] Chronology and Analysis of Events of 28 September to 6 October 1944.

48. NA, SRGN-001/49668, German Navy/U-boat Message Translations & Summaries, ff. 39576, 39760, 39789.

49. NA, SRH-277, A Lecture on Communications Intelligence . . . , p. 19.

Non-air-breathing Diesel Submarine Engines

J. G. Hawley

⚓

Since its original conception in 1901, various forms of non-air breathing diesel submarine engine systems have been proposed, designed, and developed to various degrees of technological advancement. In the majority of cases, the development emphasis has been focused towards its use onboard manned military vessels for the enhancement of underwater endurance greater than that possible with secondary batteries.

The other major non-air systems that have and are being considered include the steam and Stirling engines, closed cycle gas turbines, and fuel cells systems. Nuclear energy has provided the ultimate answer to underwater endurance from the energy storage point-of-view but, for a number of reasons, it cannot be used by all navies, and for all underwater applications.

This paper presents an account of the historical development of the non-air-breathing diesel submarine engine from its early conception to the present day.

In order for a diesel engine to be operated without access to "free" air, the surplus exhaust gas must be purged and disposed of whilst the remainder is mixed with fresh oxygen and recycled back into the engine intake.

The overall design of these individual non-air-breathing systems has been influenced by the technique employed to remove the surplus exhaust gas from the engine operating cycle and by the method by which this surplus exhaust gas is either retained onboard, or discharged from the vessel. The early systems were designed such that the excess exhaust gas was vented overboard by the use of compressor, as shown in figure 1.

Consequently, after a short running time, the recirculation medium (which would have been initially air) becomes carbon dioxide (CO_2) and oxygen, as the nitrogen, which takes no part in the combustion process, is eventually purged from the system. A

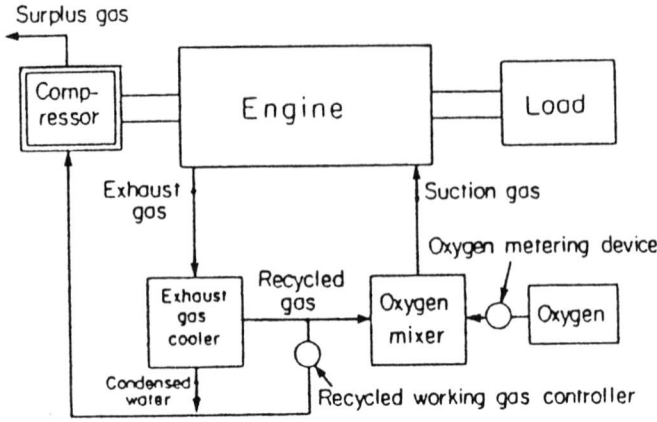

Figure 1.

CO_2/oxygen atmosphere degrades the engine's operating performance with respect to both power and fuel consumption.[1]

The designs of the more recent operating systems have usually concentrated on recreating the properties of free air such that the engine can operate closer to its performance design condition. This has necessitated the use of an absorption system which will remove the CO_2 but retain the inert nitrogen. A synthetically created air mixture then results, and such a system is generalized in figure 2.

The initial conception resulted from the work of Dr. George Francois Jaubert of Paris, in 1901, the first person to register a patent which described the operation of a diesel engine whose exhaust gases could be recirculated back into the inlet and mixed with oxygen.[2] Sabathe and Winand followed suit, in 1904 and 1906, respectively, with other patents. The impetus for the development of an underwater propulsion system at this time was the limitation imposed on underwater endurance and speed by embryonic battery technology. This limitation constrained the submarine to undertaking mainly defensive roles. Its potential offensive capabilities could only be exploited by an improved underwater propulsion system.

Practical tests were carried out in Germany during 1907 at the submarine construction yard of GW (Germaniawerft), Kiel, on a 22.4 kW (30 hp) two stroke diesel engine. The initial testbed observations were reported as promising, although no detailed results are avail-

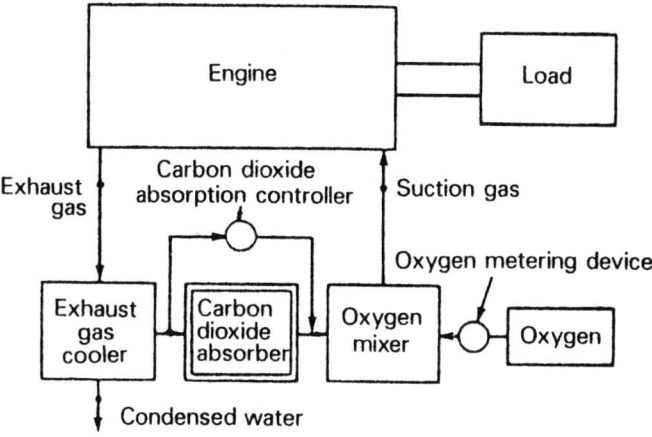

Figure 2.

able. However, immature diesel engine technology and a lack of suitably developed oxygen regulating equipment prevented further development.

During 1906, the Russian torpedo designer, S. K. Dzhevetskiy, proposed a 134 ton submarine which was to be fitted with a single diesel engine providing propulsive power through an electric generator for surface and submerged operations.[3] The *Pochtovy* was launched in 1908. No suitable diesel was available at the time, hence two gasoline engines were installed. These were supplied with oxygen from 45 compressed air cylinders, and the whole of the exhaust gas was ejected overboard by a compressor joined to a perforated pipe under the keel. The *Pochtovy* was able to travel 28 nautical miles submerged or 350 nautical miles when on the surface. This system is reported as being reliable; however, further refinement was abandoned due to steam collecting inside the hull when the boat was running submerged. She was scrapped in 1913.

Soviet interest in submarine propulsion plants that could be operated independent of atmospheric air was reviewed during the mid-1930s. The Soviet engineer, S. A. Basilevskiy, developed a non-air-breathing diesel system known as the REDO (Regenerativnyi Yedinyi Dvigatiel Osobovo Naznacheniya), which translates to "Special Purpose Regenerative Power Unit." His engine was first installed in the S-92, a unit of the M Series XII, in August 1938. The submarine's batteries were removed and replaced by a single REDO engine. The S-92 made several test runs and a single dive before the war; she was put in preservation at the Sudomekh Shipyard in Leningrad in 1941, with trials and experiments being resumed after the war. Another interesting submarine project was the M-400, also known as Project 95 in the Soviet ship designation scheme. Designed by B. L. Byezinskiy in 1939, the M-400 was a 65.5 ft (20 m) high speed submarine-submersible torpedo boat fitted with a single propulsion plant consisting of two diesel engines for both surface and submerged operation. The craft was intended to run submerged for a long period and then surface to attack its target at high speed. She was launched in July 1941, but her hull was damaged by German artillery fire during the siege of Leningrad, and construction was suspended in 1942.

In May 1941, a small coastal boat, the *M=401*, belonging to the "M" class of the Series XII-bis, was launched. She was propelled by a single non-air-breathing diesel engine designed by Kassatsir.[4] Initial sea trials were abandoned; the reason is unknown.

In the 1930s, German naval strategy necessitated the design of a high speed submarine which would be capable of increased surface and submerged speed to the point where it could work with surface fleets in all contingencies.[5]

The technical development of batteries at that time had progressed very little, and the submarine was still only capable of underwater "creep" speeds. The diesel engine, however, had progressed considerably in design and operation and had the potential to meet the requirement for increased surface speed.

The requirement for high underwater speed, at the time, could only be achieved by the use of air-independent combustion machinery. Numerous projects employing gas, steam, and diesel engines were commissioned and supported by the German Supreme Naval Command. Subsequently, the non-air-breathing diesel engine concept was resurrected, and an initial system for use in a small submersible was proposed in 1933 by Walter, figure 3. The system was designed to operate either on the surface using fresh air or subsurface using recirculated exhaust products.

It was not until 1940 that a simple recirculation system was laboratory tested at the Research Institute for Motor Vehicles and Vehicle Engines, (FKFS) Stuttgart, figure 4. A single cylinder two

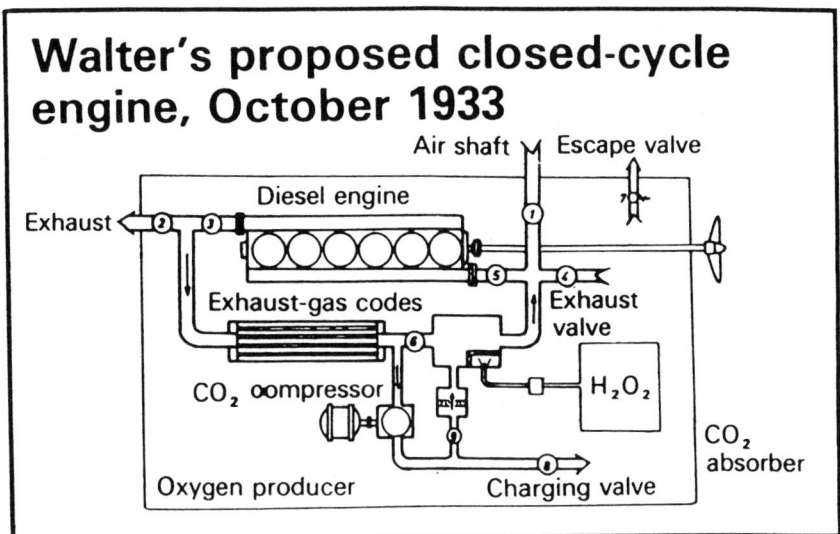

Figure 3.

stroke diesel was configured to operate such that the surplus exhaust was vented directly to the atmosphere while the remaining dried exhaust gas was fed back to the engine. After a period of running, the nitrogen was eventually replaced by CO_2.

Initial observations showed the engine to run "stiffly," and compared with air operation, a fall off in performance was observed. It was realized that improved operation could be achieved by increasing the compression ratio of the engine. However, in practice, performance recovery was achieved by increasing the temperature of the oxygen/recycle mixture by using exhaust gas pre-heat.

The Germans also investigated CO_2 adsorption and demonstrated that the unwanted exhaust gases could be completely absorbed in fresh water. The early exhaust gas management systems consisted of a gas compressor which was used to draw off the surplus gas. The gas was then either directly discharged overboard or, if it was considered undesirable to leave a gaseous discharge trace, the gas would be dissolved in seawater before being expelled.

The oxidant used in laboratory tests was initially atmospheric air, progressing to compressed oxygen for prototype systems. Investigations with hydrogen peroxide as the oxidant were consid-

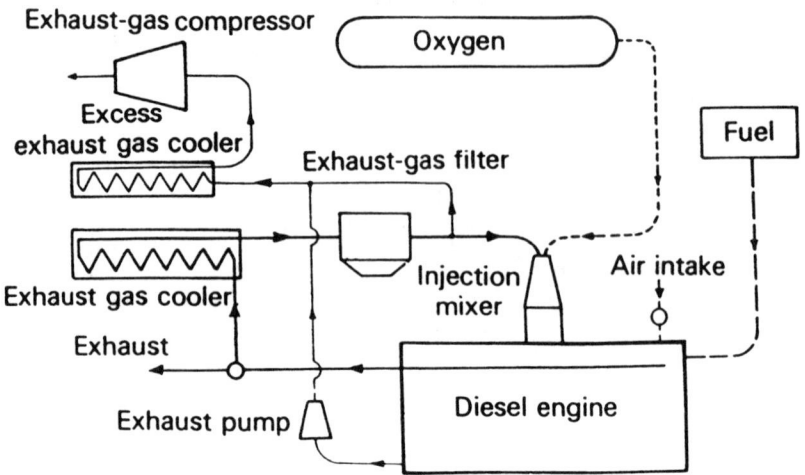

Figure 4.

ered in line with the advanced developments being made with the Walter steam turbine system.

Numerous non-air-breathing diesel projects were undertaken and prototype systems developed during this wartime period in Germany. However, due to the stop-start nature of the programs, imposed by a lack of raw materials and a shortage of skilled staff and resources being directed towards other war time priorities, none of the developed systems were ever commissioned in an operational boat.

The immediate post-war era saw the concept being developed by the British,[6] the Americans, and the Soviets. The focus of attention now was to utilize the non-air-breathing diesel as an additional onboard power source to compliment existing battery systems. The object was to increase the underwater endurance of conventional boats by the addition of an add-on or "hybrid" power system. A hybrid system consists of a low-power, high-endurance, air-independent power source for battery charging underwater; a secondary battery system for underwater quiet and sprint speed operation; and a high power open cycle diesel plant for rapid battery charging on the surface or when snorting and for surface transits.

This particular development era was primarily concerned with trying to prove the safe and efficient use of high test peroxide (HTP) as an underwater oxidant source.

The Soviets built 30 *Quebec* class submarines in the early 1950s. The *Quebec* class had a standard displacement of 540 tons when submerged, and the first of the class, the *Quebec*, was commissioned in 1954 with a non-air-breathing diesel engine system onboard (Project 615).[7] The *Quebec*'s principal designer was Kassatsir, who had worked on non-air-breathing propulsion designs in the 1930s and during the war. Serious problems were apparently experienced in trying to install and operate the non-air-breathing diesel engine. Repeated accidents resulted in numerous casualties, and the project was eventually cancelled. The early non-air-breathing diesel boats were eventually converted to operate as conventional diesel-electric craft and served into the 1970s in the Baltic and Black Sea areas. Little has been heard since that era of continuing Soviet interests in non-air-breathing diesel engine technology.

The initial British development was undertaken by Ricardo and Vickers Shipyard Engineering Limited (VSEL) until 1957. During this period, the Royal Navy also operated two experimental high-speed target submarines, HMS *Explorer* and HMS *Excalabur*, using a Walter steam turbine drive with hydrogen peroxide as the oxidant source. The state of development at that time has been summarized by MacNair.[8] First, VSEL had accumulated several thousands hours of running experience on oxygen and hydrogen peroxide recycle operation on a number of diesel engines in the 150–500 kW range. Second, a 150 kW recycle diesel prototype system was scheduled for installation in HMS *Scotsman*, which was to undertake sea trials as a proving boat for a fully recycled *Oberon*-class conversion. At this point, the whole program was cancelled in favour of the nuclear option.

During the same period, the U.S. Navy was carrying out parallel development. The Engineering Experiment Station at Annapolis ran both 4-stroke and 2-stroke Mercedes Benz engines, using liquid oxygen as the oxidant, while Becco Corporation and Fairchild Engineering Division, under Navy contracts, concentrated on HTP.[9] Fairchild eventually built and operated a small submersible with an HTP recycle engine. The U.S. work, in line with that in the U.K., was stopped in favour of the nuclear option.

In 1970 a new class of British conventional military submarine was required to fulfil future operational requirements. The risk of detection of a conventional submarine, when surfaced or snorkeling in order to recharge its batteries, had become a serious issue, particularly in light of the continuing advances being made in detection technology. Operational effectiveness necessitated increased submerged endurances beyond that capable from existing battery technology. However, the batteries were still required as they provided the sprint speed capability and silent operation when stealth was crucial. A low-power, high-endurance "hybrid" power system was again required to complement the onboard battery system, and the non-air-breathing diesel engine was considered a suitable contender.

A Ministry of Defence contract was placed with VSEL to develop a system proven by Ricardo Engineering as a suitable submarine module. The VSEL system is shown in figure 5. A test facility was constructed at VSEL and consisted of two barges, one used as the HTP store, the other as the engine test bed. The surplus exhaust gas was discharged overboard by a compressor, and, as with the early systems, the recirculated working fluid became O_2 and CO_2. The inlet temperature of the working fluid was held at approximately 120°C (by hot exhaust bypass) to ensure that the ignition temperature was reached on compression. The research contract ended in 1981, by which time VSEL had accumulated many hundreds of running hours. Little public information on the results of this detailed experimental work has been made available. The development progression of the system into an operational submarine was not undertaken, owing to financial restrictions and the emphasis on the Trident program.[10]

Since the early 1980s, considerable global research and development continues to be undertaken to exploit the potential of the non-air-breathing diesel engine for use in civil and military manned and unmanned submersibles and for static sea bed power unit applications. Developments have taken and continue to take place in the United Kingdom, Holland, Germany, Italy, Japan, Canada, and China. The rest of this paper will focus on those systems that are being developed with a seagoing application.

While the work at VSEL was being concluded, research at the University of Newcastle upon Tyne was underway to develop a system which would be completely autonomous and depth independent. The system developed is termed the Nitro-cycle, as the nitrogen is retained as the working fluid, the CO_2 being absorbed by non-regenerative potassium hydroxide (KOH) in a chemical absorption system.[11] The working fluid becomes essentially air, and, theoretically, the performance of the engine can match that during

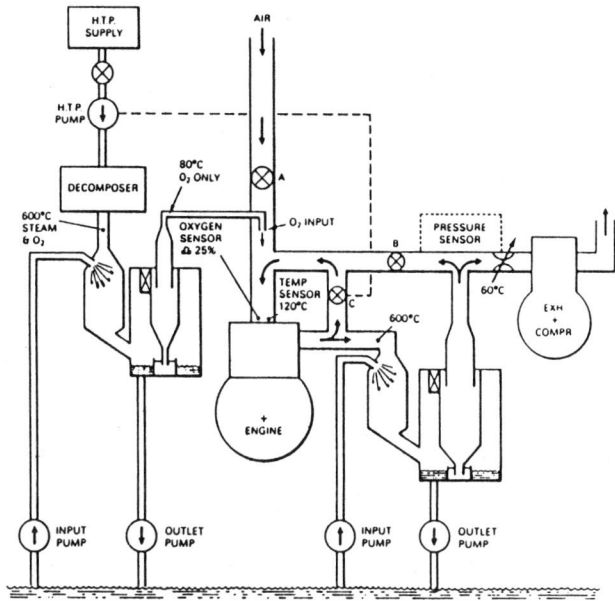

Figure 5.

naturally aspirated running conditions. However, a reduction in weight and space of the absorption unit was seen as a major area which would make the system more commercially attractive. Subsequently, the use of water as the CO_2 absorbent was adopted in view of the infinite supply within the marine environment.

Newcastle was subsequently joined by Cosworth Engineering (now Carlton Deep Sea Systems Limited) in developing the Argo-diesel system. The Argo-diesel uses sea water to absorb the mainly CO_2 surplus exhaust gas. As water is a much poorer absorber of CO_2 than KOH, a trade-off between system complexity and efficiency resulted in a water scrubber design which would not meet complete CO_2 absorption. Subsequently, rather than accept a degradation in engine performance due to recycled CO_2, argon was injected in such proportions as to maintain the ratio of specific heats for the gas mixture to a value comparable with that of air (approximately 1.4). The engine can then, theoretically, operate at its performance design condition. The operation of the Argo-diesel was highly successful, and Cosworth, subsequently, continued to develop and market the system with European partners in Holland and in Germany. The Rotterdam Boat Company in Holland developed the Argo-diesel for operational conditions. A self contained 150 kW unit has been constructed within a pressure hull section which also includes vacuum-insulated evaporators for liquid oxygen storage. The unit is able to simulate an external sea pressure of 500 meres. The application of this system was intended for use in the future class of Royal Netherlands Navy submarines, the *Moray*-class, development of which has been recently suspended.

Thyssen Nordseewerke (TNSW) of Germany has also embarked on a similar application using the Argo-diesel. The system underwent sea-trials in the early part of 1993 in a Type 205 Federal German Navy submarine, the *U.1*, which was previously used as a proving boat for the German fuel cell program. No detailed performance results have yet been released.

The Argo-diesel system is complex and bulky due to the requirement for custom designed centrifugal CO_2 water absorbers, a Water Management System, and the control and metering of argon, which is injected into the recirculated medium. Its use will be constrained to larger manned submersibles due to the weight and space limiting considerations, which are critical within smaller manned and unmanned submersibles.

The German company Bruker launched, in June 1989, an experimental 50 tonne manned submersible, the *Seahorse KD*, which is equipped with a non-air-breathing diesel engine called the Argon-diesel.[12] The CO_2 is absorbed using KOH, which, when fully saturated, is stored in tanks and discharged on return to base. Oxidant supply is LOX, and the engine can be operated in dual mode, breathing air when the vessel is surfaced or snorkeling. However, when changing from surface running to argon operation, the diesel engine must be switched off, and the entire volume of the closed system filled with argon and oxygen.

Mitsui Engineering and Shipbuilding Corporation Limited of Japan is developing the non-air-breathing diesel engine for unmanned, untethered vessels. They have undertaken the design and development of a system which uses KOH to absorb the CO_2 and is, in many ways, similar to the Nitro-cycle developed at the University of Newcastle. The project is termed *R1*, and the objective is to construct an autonomous, underwater, free-swimming vehicle which can survey a wide area of ocean ridges by measuring water

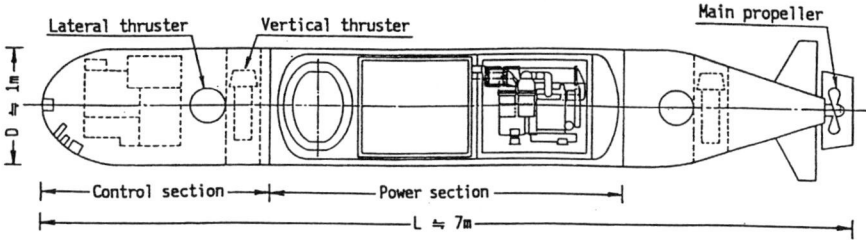

Figure 6.

temperature and other characteristics in the vicinity of the sea floor. The general arrangement of the *R1* robot is shown in figure 6. The *R1* has a target depth of 3,000 meres, and so the move to this particular type of absorption system means that the operation of the power system is depth independent. The vehicle is expected to be launched in 1994.

The non-air-breathing diesel submarine engine has gone through many development stages of a stop-start nature, and it is only now that technical maturity is beginning to be realized. The strategic development has been influenced, in many cases, by a technical void in other comparable technology. The diesel engine is a readily available, adaptable, and inexpensive prime mover. It has been developed for submarine applications, ranging from small midget craft through to blue water conventional vessels, and also for unmanned applications.

1. Hawley, J. G., "Diesel Engine Operation on Synthetic Atmospheres for Underwater Applications," PhD Thesis, Exeter University, U.K., (July 1993).
2. Rossler, E., *The U-Boat* (London: Conway Maritime Press, 1980).
3. Polmar, N., Noot, J., *Submarines of the Russian and Soviet Navies, 1718–1990* (Annapolis, Md.: Naval Institute Press, 1991).
4. Jordan, J., *Soviet Submarines—1945 to the Present* (London: Arms and Armour Press, 1989).
5. Friedman, N., *Submarine Design and Development* (London: Conway Maritime Press, 1984).
6. Puttick, J. R., "Recycle Diesel Underwater Powerplants," Society of Automotive Engineers (SAE), National Combined Fuels and Lubricants, Powerplant and Truck Meetings, Paper No. 710827, St. Louis, Mo., (26–29 October 1971).
7. Breemer, J., *Soviet Submarines: Design, Development and Tactics* (London: Jane's Information Group, 1989).

8. MacNair, E. J., "The Recycle Diesel Engine for Submarines," *Journal of Naval Engineering*, Vol. 29, No. 2, pp. 398–403, U.K., (1989).

9. MacNair, E. J., "Closed Cycle Diesel Engines for Underwater Power," 6th Intersociety Energy Conversion Engineering Conference (SAE), Paper No. 719080, pp. 577–586, Boston, Mass., (3–5 August 1971).

10. Hawley, J. G., Reader, G. T., "Closed and Recycled Diesel Engine Developments for Submersible Powerplants," 25th Intersociety Energy Conversion Engineering Conference, Paper No. 899118, Washington, D.C., (2–5 August 1989).

11. Fowler, A., "Closed Cycle Diesel Engine for Underwater Power," Trans. Institute of Marine Engineers, Vol. 96, Paper No. 47, London, (1984).

12. Bruker Meerestechnik GmbH Press Release dated October 1989.

Hostilities along the China Coast during the Korean War

Edward J. Marolda

⚓

On June 26, 1950, one day after infantry and armored forces of the North Korean People's Army smashed their way south into the Republic of Korea, President Harry S. Truman ordered the U.S. Navy into action off the Asian mainland. The military command in Washington directed the U.S. Seventh Fleet to "take station to prevent invasion of Formosa [Taiwan] and insure Formosa not to be used as a base of operations against Chinese mainland."[1]

On the 27th, President Truman publicly called upon the Chinese Nationalist government, led by Generalissimo Chiang Kai-shek and ensconced on the island of Taiwan and numerous islands along the coast of China, "to cease all air and sea operations against the mainland," then controlled by Mao Tse-tung's Communists. Truman stressed that "the Seventh Fleet will see that this is done."[2]

The *Valley Forge*, a 27,100-ton American aircraft carrier, and her escorts steamed along the west coast of Taiwan on the 29th of June. Twenty-nine fighters and attack planes from the *Valley Forge* roared northward through the strait.[3] The world was thus informed that the Truman administration intended to prevent hostilities from spreading throughout the Far East and would use the Seventh Fleet to carry out that policy. In essence, the Strait of Taiwan was to be a neutral zone in a region already at war.[4]

It has been a rather commonly held perception that the President's positioning of the fleet in the Strait of Taiwan effectively separated the Chinese combatants for the duration of the Korean conflict. That until January 1953, when Dwight D. Eisenhower took over the reins of the U.S. government, Washington not only "leashed" Chiang Kai-shek but maintained a basic neutrality vis-a-vis the Nationalist-Communist struggle. Moreover, many histories of the Korean War, even naval and military histories, leave the reader with the impression that hostilities between U.S. forces and Communist forces were confined to Northeast Asia.[5]

The purpose of this paper is to demonstrate that during the Korean War, the Chinese civil war continued unabated and that despite the Truman administration's efforts, the United States became increasingly drawn into hostilities on the side of Chiang's Nationalists. Because of this experience, and that of the brutal two and one-half year struggle on the Korean battlefield, even after the cease-fire documents were signed at Panmunjom on July 27, 1953, the United States and the People's Republic of China (PRC) remained the bitterest of enemies. This enmity brought the two nations close to nuclear conflict on two occasions during the next decade and influenced the outbreak of war in Southeast Asia in the 1960s.

Much of the blame for this animosity can be laid squarely at the feet of the Communists, whose words and deeds throughout this period revealed little but implacable hostility toward American political and economic ideals and America's Far Eastern presence. Moreover, Beijing continued to work toward the total defeat of the Nationalist forces and the occupation of all Chinese territory, even if this brought the PRC into conflict with the United States. The day after Truman's strait neutralization announcement, Foreign Minister Chou En-lai stated: "The fact that Taiwan is part of China will remain unchanged forever."[6]

Throughout the summer of 1950, the Communists concentrated 200,000 troops, over 7,000 ships and craft, and 200 aircraft on the coast for an invasion of Taiwan.[7] The U.S. National Security Council (NSC) concluded at the end of July that there were no "indications that the U.S. announcement of 27 June 1950 has caused the Chinese Communists to abandon their preparations."[8]

The evidence now shows, of course, that by mid-1950 the Communists were forced to postpone "Operation Taiwan," the long-sought final battle against the Nationalists.[9] Beijing feared U.S. air and naval power. Still, even after Chinese entry into the Korean War, the Communists continued to plan and make preparations for an invasion of Taiwan. In January 1951, the State Department learned from a Chinese informant, who apparently had access to Beijing's top leaders, that an attack might come at any time. Further, the informant reported that some of Mao's lieutenants were "determined to embroil China in war with the United States." He added that, "to this end suicide aviators and submarine crews were being trained for an attack on the 7th Fleet in the strait of Formosa."[10] To Washington, the threat was real.

Equally bent on pursuing the civil war, and enlisting the support of the United States, were the Nationalists. Chiang's forces had been ejected from the mainland of Asia in April 1949. The civil war, however, was far from over.[11] By 1950, the struggle had entered a new "maritime phase" as the Communists and Nationalists vied for control over China's coastal waters and numerous offshore islands.[12]

By July 1950, there were 500,000 men in the Nationalist armed forces grouped in 42 divisions and operating 79 warships and 540 combat aircraft. From a string of island redoubts on the approaches to the key ports of central China, Nationalist regular forces and their guerrilla allies mined coastal waters and struck at Communist-held islands and targets on the mainland. Chiang supposedly adhered to Washington's straits neutralization policy but frequently used the guerrillas against the Communists, disingenuously reporting to Washington that he had no control over the irregulars, many of whom were life-long bandits, pirates, and smugglers.

Nationalist naval vessels and armed junks also preyed heavily on their enemy's waterborne traffic along the coastlines of Fukien and Chekiang Provinces and on China's overseas commerce. For instance, on the night of September 8, 1952, an armed trawler operated by guerrillas surprised the British-registered merchantman *Admiral Hardy*, which was making way for the port of Foochow. After firing bursts of machine-gun fire, forty armed guerrillas stormed the ship, subdued the crew, and took possession of the cargo. Between 1949 and 1953, the Nationalists seized 26,120 tons of cargo and fifteen merchant vessels. There were 90 instances in which the Nationalists interfered with ships destined for Chinese Communist ports.

Other major military operations that the Nationalists carried out during the Korean War were amphibious raids, "some with and some without our prior knowledge," according to the U.S. Ambassador to Taiwan, Karl Lott Rankin.[13] Although usually described as "raids," many of these operations were large-scale efforts involving sizeable regular forces and guerrillas.

Early on October 11, 1952, the navy embarked troops and guerrillas at Quemoy and transported them to another island off Fukien. Apparently achieving surprise, and with the help of the guns of a naval task force, the ground troops stormed ashore. The Communist garrison, soldiers of the 83rd Division, put up stout resistance. Their comrades of the Third Field Army on the mainland, three times during the day, attempted to reinforce the garrison, but each time they were repulsed by the Nationalists. By mid-afternoon, when the island fell to the invaders, the Communists had lost almost 1,300 men.

Having done so throughout the years of the Truman administration, the Nationalists continued to carry out raids after Eisenhower became President. In July 1953, Chiang mobilized a large force for a "raid" against Tung Shan Island northeast of Swatow. Over 6,500 troops, 50 aircraft, and 48 warships and amphibious vessels were involved in the three-day operation, which ended in a debacle for the Nationalists, who lost 1,400 men.

The execution by U.S. forces of Truman's directive to prevent an invasion of Taiwan increasingly compromised U.S. "neutrality" in the Chinese civil war. The President's words alone would not have deterred or defeated a Communist amphibious assault on the Nationalist-held island. It was necessary to establish a semi-permanent U.S. military presence in the strait, and this presence increased the likelihood of U.S.–Communist hostilities. It also fostered a close U.S.–Nationalist relationship.

Navy planners estimated that a Communist invasion flotilla would be able to reach Taiwan in one day.[14] But, it would take the Seventh Fleet, which normally operated in Korean waters, at least two days steaming time to reach the strait. Hence, to defeat a Communist invasion attempt, it was absolutely essential that U.S. and Nationalist forces receive early warning. Accordingly, during the second week of July 1950, the patrol aircraft of Fleet Air Wing 1 began aerial reconnaissance missions in the strait.[15] Throughout the war, one seaplane and one land-based squadron (operating either P4Y or P2V patrol planes) carried out patrols of the strait from bases in Okinawa, the Philippines, and the Penghu Islands in the strait.[16] Dean Acheson, the Secretary of State and the primary architect of Truman's Far East policies, approved the inauguration of photographic reconnaissance flights over the coastal area of China. But in doing so, he was only able (because of military necessity) to "strongly urge that it be conducted to the maximum extent possible from outside Chinese territorial waters."[17] Patrol plane pilots were advised to "exercise particular caution not to violate Soviet or

Chinese territory or territorial waters."[18] Nonetheless, these military professionals wanted to obtain clear and detailed intelligence photographs. So, in the words of one squadron commander, "we got the pictures of the whole coast and forgot the twelve mile limit."[19]

In July 1950, General of the Army Douglas MacArthur, the Commander in Chief, Far East, approved the Seventh Fleet Commander's recommendation that the patrols be publicized. These officers felt that the measure was necessary for deterrence to work.[20] Of course, Beijing was not pleased when the United States announced that its warplanes were operating on China's borders.

The strait patrol also involved surface ships. In August, Commander, Seventh Fleet, Vice Admiral Arthur D. Struble, established a continuous U.S. Navy presence off China with the creation of the Formosa Patrol Force. For the rest of the war, the contingent, normally made up of three or four destroyers, steamed on patrol outside the 12-mile limit of the PRC. The Formosa Patrol Force operated from Keelung on the north tip of Taiwan. To both sides, this deployment symbolized the growing American identification with the Nationalist cause, because, for the first time since the evacuation of the mainland port of Tsingtao in May 1949, U.S. Navy forces were stationed at a Nationalist port.[21]

The military requirements for sustaining an air and sea patrol of the strait helped to erode Truman's neutralization policy. So, too, did the actions of U.S. military and civilian officials who clearly favored the Nationalists in their fight against the Communists. In this group were MacArthur, Secretary of Defense Louis Johnson, Rankin, and most Navy leaders.

In the summer of 1950, Admiral Forrest Sherman, the Chief of Naval Operations, wanted to let the Nationalists bomb concentrations of Communist amphibious forces on the coast.[22] Truman and Acheson vetoed that proposal feeling, with justification, that the action could involve the United States in war with China and motivate Chinese intervention in Korea or Indochina.[23]

When MacArthur visited Taiwan in July, he spoke of the Republic of China and the United States as "allied against a common enemy and for a common purpose." The Communist reaction to the MacArthur visit was not long in coming. On August 5, the journal *Jen Min Jih Pao* related the visit to "American aggression and invasion of Taiwan."[24] Later that summer, MacArthur, in a paper he intended to be read at a Chicago gathering of the Veterans of Foreign

Wars, spoke of U.S. air and naval power based on Taiwan and elsewhere in the Far East that could dominate "every Asiatic port from Vladivostok to Singapore."[25]

At the same time that the general's words were leaked to the Press, Secretary of the Navy Francis Matthews, who idolized MacArthur, called on the United States to become the "first aggressors for peace." The secretary suggested "instituting a war [against the Communists] to compel cooperation for peace."[26] Matthews' prescription for world disaster and MacArthur's observations were quickly and publicly disavowed by Truman. A contrite Matthews later explained to the President that he spoke as he did because he had heard so many "admirals and other high Navy people" speak of preventive war.[27]

American officials also differed on whether the Nationalists should be allowed to stop merchantmen trading with Beijing. In August, the State Department apprized Taibei that the United States did not recognize any Nationalist right to stop, search, and seize ships on the high seas. Because of the U.S. military's strongly held views on the subject, however, Acheson and his subordinates did not press the Nationalists to comply with the U.S. government's pronouncement. Thereafter, according to a contemporary Navy memo, the "United States generally overlooked the numerous deviations from [the] policy set by the State Department."[28]

Truman's strait neutralization policy was further undermined by the war in Korea. After November 1950, when Chinese Communist forces debouched from the rugged terrain of North Korea and sent allied ground forces reeling south in bloody retreat, the U.N. command was in dire straits.

MacArthur, from his headquarters in Tokyo, repeatedly advocated a naval blockade of China, air and naval attacks against China's war making industries, and the use of Nationalist Chinese troops in Korea and on the mainland.[29]

Despite the later efforts of Truman, Acheson, and even members of the Joint Chiefs to cast MacArthur as a dangerous lone wolf,[30] others in the national security establishment shared many of his views. The Commander in Chief of the Pacific Command, Admiral Arthur W. Radford, agreed with MacArthur's call for air strikes against China, as did Air Force Chief of Staff General Hoyt Vandenburg.[31] Admiral Sherman felt that "Communist China has for all intents and purposes become an enemy of the U.S." He observed that since the war was no longer limited, the United States should replace the government in Beijing and prevent Chinese Communist expansion in the Far East.[32] To achieve these objectives, Sherman suggested that the UN intensify the economic embargo of trade with China, establish a naval blockade, and provide logistic support to guerrillas in southern China.[33]

While the U.S. government never carried out the more serious measures recommended by various policymakers, Washington did turn up the heat on China. By the end of 1951, Radford reported that his command was assisting the CIA in its "Anti-Communist operations in China."[34] The CIA-run and Taiwan-based Civil Air Transport (CAT) firm supported its activities from the U.S. Air Station at Atsugi, Japan, and from a former U.S. Navy tank landing ship anchored in Kaoshiung, Taiwan.[35]

Operations by regular U.S. military forces along the China coast during 1951 and 1952 also resulted in Sino-American hostilities. The Seventh Fleet continued its air patrol, which became increasingly risky. Communist naval vessels and aircraft fired on American aircraft all along the coast. In September 1952, off Shanghai, two Communist MiG-15 jets pounced on a P4Y of Patrol Squadron 28, but despite five firing runs, failed to down the American plane.[36] The patrol force was not as lucky in January 1953, when a zealous pilot flew his P2V Neptune inland, where Chinese gunners shot it up. He was able to fly the plane out over the coast, but had to ditch it close offshore. A U.S. Coast Guard seaplane dispatched from the Philippines crashed and sank after it tried to lift off with surviving crewmen of the Neptune. U.S. and British ships and aircraft then raced to the scene. Communist coastal guns straddled one of the ships with shell fire, antiaircraft guns opened up on the aircraft, and a Communist MiG joined the fray. Despite this opposition, the allies picked up ten crewmen and flew them to safety.[37]

American leaders also called for the periodic dispatch of a Seventh Fleet carrier task force to the strait. There was general agreement among American officials that Beijing feared U.S. air and naval power, so they recommended that deterrence actions continue.[38] At the end of March 1951, Admiral C. Turner Joy, Commander Naval Forces, Far East, proposed a springtime carrier task force deployment to the China coast, when the weather would be relatively favorable for an enemy invasion attempt.[39] The State Department, General of the Army Omar Bradley, the Chairman of the JCS, and

General J. Lawton Collins, the Army Chief of Staff, feared the operation might be provocative, especially if the carrier force operated, as was proposed, near Hainan, far to the south of the strait. So, Joy was told that the naval task force would neither mount a show of force nor proceed south of Hong Kong.[40]

During the second week of April 1951, the carriers *Philippine Sea* and *Boxer*, and their escorting destroyers, under Rear Admiral W. G. Tomlinson, sortied from the Korean battle zone. For two days patrol aircraft of the two carriers flew along the mainland coast and over the cities of Amoy, Swatow, and Foochow. The sweeps were at such low levels that the pilots could observe human activity in the towns and villages below.[41] While this mission was not supposed to be a show of force, at each location the aircraft sparked considerable Communist antiaircraft fire.[42] Moreover, when the task force returned to Korean waters on the 16th of April, the Seventh Fleet commander expressed satisfaction that his "show of force" mission had gone well.[43] Radford observed that the action was a "powerful deterrent to further expansion of Communism" in Southeast Asia.[44]

The need for the Seventh Fleet was again addressed with the onset of the 1952 invasion season. The Navy was even more interested in 1952 than it had been the year before in Hainan, because Radford and others felt that the island could be "useful as a springboard for possible raids on the mainland of China by Chinese Nationalist forces."[45]

As in 1951, State Department representatives again feared that the proposed naval operation would be provocative. The new CNO, Admiral William Fechteler, this time won the day. He argued that the action would expedite the conclusion of armistice negotiations in Korea. And, this time there was no question that the mission would entail a show of force over Taiwan and in the strait and photographic reconnaissance of the China coast, including Hainan.

Special Task Group 50.8, composed of the aircraft carriers *Essex* and *Philippine Sea* and eight destroyers, all under Commander Carrier Division 3, Rear Admiral A. Soucek, put to sea from Subic Bay on July 18. The following day, aerial reconnaissance aircraft from the two carriers flew over and photographed Chinese Communist military facilities on Hainan and the nearby Chinese mainland. On the 24th, the carrier force sent aloft 53 aircraft, which carried out low-level photography of the airfields, naval bases, ports, and anchorages at three ports. The Communists directed small arms and antiaircraft fire and launched fighter aircraft against the American photo planes.[46]

Radford wanted to make sure that the world knew of the operation. After the mission, United Press International quoted a CINCPAC spokesman as saying that the task group's mission was designed to "show that the Navy could bomb the coastal cities of Amoy, Foochow, and Swatow anytime without draining its forces in Korea."[47]

This announcement was not applauded in Washington. Acheson telephoned Secretary of Defense Robert A. Lovett and observed that the press statement would mean that "we will have the British and other Allies after us, and probably receive a propaganda protest from the Chinese." Lovett responded that CINCPAC's public statement was "sophomoric—just crazy . . . a ridiculous, silly thing."[48]

The Navy was not finished, however. The following day, Acheson called Lovett for the "daily reading on the Navy." Acheson read verbatim a UPI wire quoting Fechteler, who was then visiting the Far East. The CNO observed that he was partly responsible for the fleet deployment off China. To cap his press statement, Fechteler observed that the Navy "could deliver baby atom bombs in Korea if it is ordered to do so." After listening to this, Lovett observed to Acheson that "these gratuitous interpretations were causing embarrassment to the Government."[49]

Not to be outdone, on July 24, Secretary of the Navy Dan Kimball delivered an address at the Navy League convention in Chicago and spoke of operations in which Navy flyers overflew Chinese cities "instead of keeping outside the three-mile limit."[50] Finally, on July 28, Lovett informed Acheson that he believed the Navy leaders were under control.[51]

In conclusion, the Truman administration's deployment of naval forces to the Strait of Taiwan did not prevent the spread of conflict throughout the Far East. During the Korean War, there were significant hostilities on the China coast, including large-unit conventional battles for coastal islands, naval engagements, merchant ship seizures, Communist attacks on U.S. aircraft, guerrilla raids, and clandestine operations. In addition, the pronouncements of Communist and U.S. officials revealed only mutual loathing, fear, and hostility.

Truman's attempt to neutralize the strait failed for several reasons; the PRC continued to seek the defeat of the Nationalists along

China's maritime periphery despite the presence of U.S. naval forces; the Nationalists continued their military operations against the Communists on the China coast, in the offshore islands, and at sea; to accomplish the neutralization mission, the U.S. Navy's carrier task forces and air and sea patrol units had to operate on China's borders and cooperate with Nationalist armed forces; the Korean War heightened passions and convinced both Beijing and Washington that the threat from the other side was regional and not restricted to the Korean Peninsula; and finally, there was persistent action by key American leaders, especially military leaders, to undermine the Truman-Acheson policy. Consequently, the cease-fire in Korea did not mark the end of Sino-American hostility, but only the end of a phase in the continuing Far Eastern confrontation.

1. OPORDER 5-50 in msg, COMNAVFE to COM7FLT, 270915Z Jun 1950, Post-46 Plan File, Operational Archives, Naval Historical Center (OANHC). OPORDER 5-50 First Revision, in msg COMNAVFE to COM7FLT, 301119Z Jun 1950, Post-46 Command File, OANHC, stipulated that the Penghu Islands were also to be protected from invasion.

2. Quoted in Walter S. Poole, *1950–1952*, Vol. IV in series *History of the Joint Chiefs of Staff: The Joint Chiefs of Staff and National Policy* (Washington: Historical Division, Joint Secretariat, JCS), 1979, *(hereafter History of the JCS:IV)*, p. 388. See also OPORDER 5-50 Second Revision, in msg, COMNAVFE to COM7FLT, 230334Z Jul 1950, RG 9, box 60, NAVFE ORDERS, Douglas MacArthur Archives (MACAR).

3. OPORDER 5-50 in msg, COMNAVFE to COM7FLT, 270915Z Jun 1950, Post-46 Plan File, OANHC.

4. James A. Field, Jr., *United States Naval Operations: Korea* (Washington: GPO, 1962), pp. 54–55; Clay Blair, *The Forgotten War: America in Korea* (New York: Times Books, 1988), p. 74.

5. Blair, *The Forgotten War*; Robert Leckie, *Conflict: The History of the Korean War* (New York: Putnam, 1962); Richard P. Hallion, *The Naval Air War in Korea* (Baltimore: Nautical and Aviation Pub. Co. of America, 1986); Malcolm W. Cagle and Frank A. Manson, *The Sea War in Korea* (Annapolis: Naval Institute Press, 1957); Walter Karig et al, *Battle Report* (New York: Farrar & Rinehart, 1952).

6. Quoted in *China: U.S. Policy Since 1945* (Washington: Congressional Quarterly, 1980), p. 91.

7. Office of the Chief of Naval Operations (OPNAV), Estimate of the Taiwan Situation, (10 Jul 1950), CNO File, 1950, box 2, OANHC.

8. National Security Council (NSC), Prospects for an Early Successful Chinese Communist Attack on Taiwan, Jul 26, 1950, NSC Records, box 19, Harry S. Truman Library (HSTL).

9. Allen S. Whiting, *China Crosses the Yalu: The Decision to Enter the Korean War* (New York: The Macmillan Co., 1960), p. 63. The view that the deployment of the Seventh Fleet to the Taiwan Strait deterred a Communist invasion is shared by a

number of historians. See Nancy Bernkopf Tucker, *Patterns in the Dust: Chinese-American Relations and the Recognition Controversy, 1949–1950* (New York: Columbia Univ. Press, 1983), p. 206; Edwin Martin, *Divided Counsel: The Anglo-American Response to Communist Victory in China* (Lexington, KY: Univ. of Kentucky Press), pp. 159–60.

10. Memo of Conversation, Prepared in the Department of State, various dates, Jan 1951, *Foreign Relations of the United States: 1951* (hereafter *FRUS:1951*) *Korea and China*, Vol. VII (Washington: State Department), pt. 2, pp. 1486, 1498.

11. Edgar O'Ballance, *The Red Army of China: A Short History* (New York: Praeger, 1963), in his military history of the civil war, makes scant mention of the fight for the offshore islands during 1950–1952.

12. Most of the information from the following section is found in Office of Naval Intelligence (ONI), *The ONI Review* (Dec 1952); ONI, "Southeast China Coast Today," *The ONI Review* (Feb 1953); ONI, "The Struggle for the Coastal Islands of China," *The ONI Review* (1953 Supplement); ONI, "Harassing the Red China Trade," *The ONI Review* (Jan 1954 Supplement); and ONI, "An Analysis of the Amphibious Capabilities of Nationalist China," *The ONI Review* (Spring 1954), Post-46 Command File, OANHC.

13. Msg, CINCFE to COMNAVFE, 020813Z Jun 1951, JCS Records, RG 218, Geo. File, Far East, 1951–53, box 14, CCS 381, Far East, sec. 6, National Archives, Military Branch (NARANNMP).

14. OPNAV, Estimate of the Taiwan Situation, p. 13.

15. COM7FLT, Operation Order 9-50, in msg, 140200Z Jul 1950, JCS Records, RG 218, Geo. File, Formosa, 1948–50, box 17, CCS 381 Formosa, sec. 4, NARANNMP.

16. CINCPACFLT, Interim Evaluation Report, "Korean War," Chap. 7, OANHC; *Suisun*, Operation Report, Apr 26 to Nov 27, 1950, Post-46 Report File, OANHC.

17. Memo, SECSTATE to SECDEF, Jul 31, 1950, State Dept. Records, RG 59, Office of Chinese Affairs, 1945–50, box 18, TS 2P (1950), National Archives, Diplomatic Branch (NARANNF).

18. Msg, COM7FLT to CTG70.6/CTF77, 290008Z Aug 1950, RG 9, box 57, Inc. Navy, MACAR.

19. Ltr, Weisner, Jan 29, 1951, Post-46 Report File, OANHC. See also CNO, "Interview of LT. COMDR M.F. Weisner, Commanding Officer, VP-46," Feb 21, 1951, Post-46 Command File (Chronological), OANHC.

20. CINCPACFLT, Interim Evaluation Report, "Korean War," chap 7, OANHC.

21. On June 28, U.S. destroyer *Brush* made a short-term port call to Keelung, during which the local people waved signs that read "God Bless America; Down with Mao Tze-tung [sic]; Down with Russia." Quoted in Karig et al, *Battle Report*, p. 45. See also COM7FLT, OPLAN 7-50, ser 021, Jul 20, 1950, Post-46 Plan File, OANHC; ltr, COM7FLT to CNO, "Summary of Seventh Fleet Problems and/or Recommendations," ser 00033, Jun 25, 1951, CNO File, 1950; COM7FLT, OPs Report, 1951–1952, encl. 1, p. 25, OANHC; Field, *History of United States Naval Operations: Korea*, pp. 135, 396; Reference Summary, "Taiwan Patrol Force," Oct 1966, Reference File, OANHC; James F. Schnabel and Robert J. Watson, *The Korean War*, Vol. III in series *History of the Joint Chiefs of Staff: The Joint Chiefs of Staff and National Policy* (Washington: Historical Division, Joint Secretariat, JCS, 1978), p. 509;

Juneau and *Saint Paul* Command Histories, *Dictionary of American Naval Fighting Ships* (Washington: Naval History Division), Vol. III, p. 576; Vol. VI, p. 252; Commander U.S. Taiwan Patrol Force/Fleet Air Wing 1, Command History, ser 386, Aug 10, 1959, Post-46 Command File, OANHC.

22. Memo, CNO to JCS, ser 000159P35, Jul 27, 1950, enclosed in JCS 1966/35, Jul 27, 1950, mic A-167, pt. 2, Far East, reel 2; Kenneth Roy Flint, "The Tragic Flaw: MacArthur, the Joint Chiefs, and the Korean War," (Duke Univ., PhD Dissertation, 1976), p. 188. See also Doris M. Condit, *The Test of War, 1950–1953*, Vol. II in series, *History of the Office of the Secretary of Defense* (Washington: Historical Office, Office of the Secretary of Defense, 1988), p. 176.

23. The same result attended MacArthur's intention to dispatch three U.S. fighter squadrons to Taiwan in the event of an attack. The President instructed the JCS to inform the general that U.S. air forces would not be stationed on Taiwan without JCS (read his) approval. Schnabel and Watson, *History of the JCS: III*, pp. 508–09, 511–13; Poole, *History of the JCS: IV*, pp. 391–92; msg, JCS to CINCFE, 88681, Aug 14, 1950, *FRUS,1950*, Vol. VI, p. 439; Condit, *The Test of War*, p. 177; Briefing Paper for MacArthur Hearings, n.d., Sherman Papers, box 5, OANHC; msg, Johnson to MacArthur, Def 88014, Aug 5, 1950, RG 6, box 8, Formosa, MACAR.

24. Quoted in Whiting, *China Crosses the Yalu*, p. 82. See also Dean Acheson, *Present at the Creation: My Years in the State Department* (New York: W. W. Norton and Co., 1969), p. 422.

25. Quoted in Secretary of State to Certain Diplomatic Offices, Aug 26, 1950, *FRUS, 1950*, Vol. VI, pp. 451–53.

26. *New York Times* (Aug 26, 1950), pp. 1, 6.

27. Harry S. Truman, *Memoirs: Years of Trial and Hope* (Garden City, NY: Doubleday and Co., 1956), p. 383.

28. Memo, CNO to JCS, Blockade of China Coast by Nationalist China, ser 000296P35, Aug 20, 1951, enclosed in JCS 2118/21, Aug 22, 1951, JCS Records, RG 218, Geo. File, Far East, 1951–53, box 15, CCS Far East, sec. 8, NARANNMP.

29. Schnabel and Watson, *History of the JCS: III*, pp. 366–67, 400; Blair, *The Forgotten War*, pp. 471, 523, 532–33, 566–68, 589–91.

30. Truman, *Years of Trial and Hope*, pp. 349, 355, 447–52, 520–21; Acheson, *Present at the Creation*, pp. 472–73, 477, 514–15; U.S., Congress, Senate, Committee on Armed Services and Committee on Foreign Relations, *Hearings to Conduct an Inquiry into the Military Situation in the Far East and the Facts Surrounding the Relief of General of the Army Douglas MacArthur from his Assignments in that Area* (hereafter *The Military Situation in the Far East*), 82nd Cong., 1st sess. (Wash: GPO, 1951), pp. 725–1151.

31. Arthur W. Radford, *From Pearl Harbor to Vietnam: The Memoirs of Admiral Arthur W. Radford*, Stephen Jurika, ed. (Stanford, CA: Stanford Univ. Press, 1980), pp. 247, 252; Trachtenberg, "A 'Wasting Asset.' " p. 25.

32. Memo, Sherman to Bradley/Collins/Vandenberg, Apr 20, 1951, Sherman Papers, box 4, OANHC.

33. Memo, CNO to JCS, JCS 2118/5, Jan 3, 1951, mic A-167, pt. 2, Far East, reel 2. See also Blair, *The Forgotten War*, pp. 623–25.

34. Ltr, CINCPAC to CNO, ser 00068, Dec 28, 1951, enclosed in JCS 2118/31, Feb 5, 1952, mic A-167, pt. 2, Far East, reel 2. See also CIA, memo prepared for NSC,

Jan 11, 1951, *FRUS, 1951*, Vol. VII, pt. 2, p. 1504; Vulnerabilities of Communist China, SE 5, May 22, 1951, *FRUS, 1951*, Vol. VII, pt. 2, pp. 1673–74.

35. William Leary, *Perilous Missions: Civil Air Transport and CIA Covert Operations in Asia* (Birmingham, AL: Univ. of Alabama Press, 1988), p. 126. See also pp. 108, 113–24.

36. COM7FLT, OPs Report, 1952–53, pp. 67–68; CINCPACFLT, Interim Evaluation Report, "Korean War," Chap. 4, pp. 4-8–4-9, 4-11, 4-12; Minter, Interview, pp. 279, 283–84.

37. Minter, Interview, p. 282. See also U.S. Coast Guard, Gerald W. Stuart Gold Life Saving Medal Citation, Nov 16, 1955, re sea rescue of Jan 18, 1953, Coast Guard History Ofc, Washington, D.C.

38. Clubb, memo, National Intell Estimate of Comm China, Jan 19, 1951, RG 59, Office of Chinese Affairs, Numerical File, 1951, box 30, 440.2 (1951), NARANNF; Rankin, *China Assignment*, pp. 83–85; memo of telecon prepared in State Department, Feb 5, 1951, *FRUS, 1951*, Vol. VII, pt. 2, p. 1561.

39. Msg, CINCFE to JCS, C 58575, Mar 25, 1951, *FRUS, 1951*, Vol. VII. pt. 2, pp. 1608–09.

40. Memo re Department of State–JCS Meeting, Apr 4, 1951, *FRUS, 1950*, Vol. VII, pt. 2, pp. 1617–18.

41. Report, COMCARDIV3 to COM7FLT, ser 004, Apr 17, 1951, Post-46 Report File, OANHC; Field, *History of United States Naval Operations: Korea*, p. 344.

42. Report, COMCARDIV3 to COM7FLT, ser 004, Apr 17, 1951, Post-46 Report File, OANHC.

43. COM7FLT, OPs Report, 1951–52, encl. 1, p. 18.

44. Ibid., encl. 4, p. 1.

45. OP-301F1, Agenda for Discussion with Admiral Radford during period 22–25 January 1952, Jan 18, 1952, CNO File, 1952, box 6, OANHC.

46. Report, COMCARDIV3 to CINCPACFLT, ser 0014, Jul 27, 1952, Post-46 Report File, OANHC. See also report, CTG50.8, Jul 27, 1952, Post-46 Report File, OANHC; memo, Commander Naval Forces, Far East to Admiral Fechteler, Jul 28, 1952; *Essex*, Action Report, ser 0153, Sep 4, 1952, Post-46 Report File, OANHC.

47. Related in memo of telecon between Lovett and Acheson, by Kitchen, State Department, Jul 23, 1952, *FRUS, 1952–1954*, Vol. XIV, pt. 1, p. 79.

48. Ibid., p. 80.

49. Ibid., p. 81.

50. Memo re telecon between Lovett and Acheson, Jul 25, 1952, *FRUS, 1952–1954*, Vol. XIV, pt. 1, p. 84. During a March visit to Taipei, Kimball had informed the press that the United States and the Republic of China were "allies in every sense in the great struggle to achieve freedom and democracy in the Far East and throughout the world. I am proud that the United States has such allies as I find here." Kimball, Statement by the Honorable Dan A. Kimball, United States Secretary of the Navy, Taipei, Mar 25, 1952, Kimball Papers, General File, box 6, Far Eastern Trip, HSTL.

51. Kitchen, Memo of Telephone Conversation, Lovett/Acheson, Jul 28, 1952, Acheson Papers, Memoranda of Conversation, box 66, HSTL.

The Single Air Manager Controversy of 1968

Jack Shulimson

⚓

In January 1968, operating directly under the III Marine Amphibious Force (III MAF) in South Vietnam's I Corps, the 1st Marine Aircraft Wing supported two reinforced Marine divisions and flew, when available, supplemental missions for the Seventh Air Force. The commander of the Seventh Air Force, General William W. "Spike" Momyer, made no secret about his unhappiness with the air arrangements. As the USMACV (U.S. Military Assistance Command, Vietnam) Deputy for Air, Momyer wanted operational control of Marine air.[1]

While Marine commanders held up the Korean War aviation arrangements as the precedent to avoid at all costs, Momyer frankly declared that it was his objective to get them the same way they were in Korea. The siege of Khe Sanh, the insertion of the 1st Air Cavalry into northern I Corps, and the launching of the Communist Tet offensive would bring the issue of control of Marine fixed-wing air in Vietnam to a head.

Using the enemy threat at Khe Sanh in early January, Momyer convinced Army General William C. Westmoreland, Commander USMACV, who had overall responsibility for U.S. forces in South Vietnam, to support the Seventh Air Force position. General Westmoreland, who already had doubts about Marine leadership, planned to issue a Single Manager directive placing Marine fixed-wing tactical and reconnaissance aircraft under the operational control of General Momyer.[2] This issue would dominate Air Force and Marine relations throughout the rest of the year and, in reality, throughout the remainder of the war.

Marine aviation officers influenced strongly the original MACV air directive. As Lieutenant General Victor H. Krulak, the Fleet Marine Force Pacific (FMFPac) commander, pointedly stated in mid-1967, the Marines had the air-ground team in Vietnam that they had wanted in Korea. According to Krulak, this was no accident. We have CincPac [Admiral Ulysses S. Grant Sharp, who had overall command of the Pacific Theater, including MACV] to thank for putting his foot down and saying "No.... We have to thank him, plus the stubborn persuasion on him by a few Marines." Furthermore, the FMFPac commander correctly observed that, notwithstanding all the talk about the Marine air-ground relationship, the Vietnam arrangement provided the Marine Corps, for one of the first times in combat, the air-ground team in its classic sense.[3]

On 18 January 1968, when General Westmoreland proposed altering the existing air relationships by placing Marine fixed-wing aircraft temporarily under Momyer, Admiral Sharp remained somewhat leery. He asked the MACV commander to consider all the ramifications, including the probable inter-Service wrangle that would result in a change of the existing order. Before making a final decision, the CincPac commander stated that he wanted to review the recommendations and viewpoints of both Generals Momyer and Marine Lieutenant General Robert E. Cushman, commander of III MAF, on the matter.[4]

Three days later, on 21 January, after the initial heavy enemy bombardment of Khe Sanh, Westmoreland decided against pursuing at that time the subject of control of Marine air. Having already implemented the first phase of his Khe Sanh air campaign, codenamed Niagara, with B-52 Arc Light strikes, he ordered the second phase to start. In a message to Admiral Sharp explaining his actions and future plans, he stated that it had never been his "intention to in any way interfere with the close air support so essential to the Marines." Westmoreland radioed, however, that he still required the "authority to delegate to my deputy commander for air, the control that I deem appropriate." He declared that, in Niagara II, he had charged Momyer "with the overall responsibility for air operations for the execution of the plan." While the Seventh Air Force would coordinate and direct the employment of tactical air in Niagara II, General Westmoreland carefully added that the Marine wing would make available only those sorties not required for the "direct air support" of Marine units. The MACV commander observed that the Seventh Air Force commander and the Marine command would work out the details for the coordination of their effort. Interestingly, both III MAF and the Seventh Air Force received a copy of this message, which was not the case of the earlier communications between Westmoreland and Sharp.[5]

III MAF and the Seventh Air Force quickly resolved the particulars between the two relative to Niagara II. Major General Norman Anderson, the 1st MAW commander, visited the Seventh Air Force headquarters at Tan Son Nhut in Saigon to complete the coordination between the two. For the Khe Sanh sector, the Seventh Air Force established an airborne command and control center (ABCCC), an electronically equipped Lockheed C-l30E transport. From its orbit over eastern Laos, the ABCCC controlled all aircraft in Niagara II, except Marine close air support fixed-wing planes and helicopters.[6]

Although somewhat formalized, the aviation arrangements at Khe Sanh were at best ad hoc and sometimes confusing. As General Anderson described it, at first all sorties within the range of Marine air support radar teams would be "directed by our forward air controllers" and would be a 1st Wing responsibility. With the beginning of the B-52 sorties, however, "this became a jumbled arrangement as well" and air control became a matter of "expediency" rather than "doctrine."

Air Force controllers complained that Marine aircraft over Khe Sanh too often ignored the Seventh Air Force ABCCC. From an Air Force viewpoint, this duo air control relationship "perpetuated the existence of two air forces operating in a compressed area." General Momyer believed that the Niagara compromise placed "too much emphasis on geographical considerations." He considered that Marine air was fighting its "own private war at Khe Sanh" rather than fitting into the overall air campaign. As Air Force historian Bernard C. Nalty later wrote: "Momyer thought in terms of using a limited number of aircraft to attack an increasing number of targets over a wide area; the Marines focused on providing the swiftest and deadliest support for the man with the rifle."[7]

In contrast to Momyer, Marine generals were relatively satisfied with the arrangements for Niagara II. While still uneasy about MACV and Seventh Air Force motivations, they believed that for the most part the questions about air control had been put to bed. On 23 January, in Washington, Major General Keith B. McCutcheon, Deputy Chief of Staff, Air at Headquarters, Marine Corps, informally wrote to Norman Anderson, the wing commander, that the Marine Corps was "watching with great interest the OpCon command relationship game and the flurry of message traffic between the powers-to-be." McCutcheon, who incidentally had a hand in the original air directive as a member in 1965 of the CincPac staff, acknowledged, however, that the Niagara implementing order was "simply a restatement of existing procedures." In reply, about two weeks later, the wing commander assured General McCutcheon that III MAF relations with the Seventh Air Force "have again no one realized."[8]

While apparently accepting, with relative good grace (at least outwardly), Admiral Sharp's initial denial of his effort to bring Marine fixed-wing air under the Seventh Air Force in Operation Niagara, General Westmoreland remained concerned about air support for the newly arrived 1st Air Cavalry Division in northern I Corps. With the establishment of the 1st Cavalry command post in northern I Corps by the end of the month, Westmoreland became even more agitated on the subject. According to the MACV commander, he met with Generals Cushman and Norman Anderson and told them that he wanted the Marines to provide air coverage for the Army division. Westmoreland claimed that he received assurances from both Marine commanders that the Marine wing would establish liaison and make the necessary arrangements.[9]

The three commanders had different impressions about the results of their meeting. While generals Anderson and Cushman promised that III MAF would furnish air support, their understanding about the undertaking was at great variance from that of General Westmoreland. General Cushman later recalled that the Marines flew air support for the 1st Air Cavalry, but that the Army division did not know how to employ it. The 1st MAW commander, General Anderson, related that the problem was one of communication. According to Anderson, he told General Westmoreland that the Marine wing would support the Air Cavalry, but that there would be need for the Army division to establish a communications network with the Marine air command and control system.[10]

The upshot of the situation was that the 1st Cavalry, after it deployed into its base camp, had not tied into the Marine Tactical Air Direction Center. According to General Westmoreland, about 24 hours to 48 hours after he had broached the subject to the Marine commanders, he visited Major General John J. Tolson, the 1st Air Cavalry Division commander, at his CP and discovered that there had been no liaison with the wing.

Until that juncture, Westmoreland claimed he had been content not to alter the air command system, but now "I blew my top . . [this] was absolutely the last straw. I go up there and nothing has happened and here I've got a division up there . . . and they [III MAF] just ignored me." The result, according to the MACV commander, was his decision to go ahead with the single manager directive.[11]

Much of the ensuing unhappiness between MACV and III MAF revolved around the expectations of the various commanders and their differing recollections of their various meetings. This was especially true about the debate over the communication net with the 1st Air Cavalry. While General Anderson remembered emphasizing this matter, General Westmoreland denied that the subject was ever brought up and fully anticipated that the Marines would have provided liaison parties with the 1st Air Cavalry Division. In a letter several years later, Major General Anderson recalled that General Cushman accompanied General Westmoreland during the latter's visit to General Tolson. According to Anderson, Cushman sensed the MACV commander's vexation about the situation and "directed my personal immediate attention to the issue." The wing commander then visited the 1st Air Cavalry with his communications officer. He discovered that the Army division lacked the technical ability to connect into the Marine aviation close air support radio net. Anderson remembered "that we had a problem finding within the wing assets" the necessary communication equipment to provide the link. He recalled that it took about 24 to 48 hours to make the connection and this was "unacceptable" to General Westmoreland. As far as the wing commander was concerned, however, this resolved the problem, and he also recalled that General Tolson told him a few days later that the Air Cavalry had no complaint about the quality of its air support. Apparently, however, the damage had been done. Westmoreland, obviously, had expected the Marines to take the initiative, while the wing commander believed that the Army division should have taken the first steps to ensure that it was in the Marine air radio net.[12]

Despite General Westmoreland's later contention that it was the dispute over the air support to the 1st Cavalry Division that caused him to go ahead with the single manager issue, it would appear that it was only one of many contributing factors. The discussion over air support to the 1st Cavalry occurred over a two or three week span at a series of meetings where it was only one of several topics. General Anderson believed that it became a matter of concern sometime before Tet, but was not sure exactly when. On 28 January, Marine Brigadier General John R. Chaisson, the director of the

MACV combat operations center, wrote home to his wife relating the deteriorating relations between III MAF and MACV. He mentioned that "Westy [Westmoreland] is a bit jumpy and is up to some major moves which have an adverse impact on U. S. Marines." Chaisson claimed that he "worked on him [Westmoreland] considerably and got him to give a little, but not entirely." While aviation support may have been one of the disputed areas, the Marine brigadier made no reference to the 1st Air Cavalry Division and implied that his concern was over the general tenor of the MACV and III MAF relationship. In his own general entry in his historical summaries for this period, General Westmoreland made little reference to air control, but wrote of the limitations of the III MAF staff to handle the number of divisions in I Corps and the necessity of establishing a MACV Forward Headquarters. Finally, in his book, the MACV commander implied that it was a meeting on 7 February with General Cushman that resulted in his final disillusionment with the Marine command and forced his hand on single management.[13]

While Westmoreland's accounts of the 7 February meeting deal largely with his unhappiness about the fall of Lang Vei, a Special Forces Camp south of Khe Sanh, and the slowness of III MAF, at its headquarters at the sprawling Da Nang Airbase, to react to the NVA threat there during Tet, the subject of air control must also have been a factor. Up to this point, at least at the III MAF and 1st Wing level, neither General Cushman nor General Anderson appeared to worry about the air control situation. Indeed, on 7 February, General Anderson wrote to Major General Keith B. McCutcheon in Washington that the "the heat is temporarily off in doctrinal matters . . . We both can live and perform our jobs while respecting the others doctrinal position. For the time being, it appears that Spike Momyer is willing to do this." Less than a week later, however, Anderson informed McCutcheon that he had been "too optimistic" relative to the Seventh Air Force. According to the wing commander, his liaison officer to the Seventh Air Force had told him that General Westmoreland was about to approve a proposal for General Momyer to take over all air operations in defense of Khe Sanh."[14]

Worried about the possible ramifications, on 17 February 1968, Major General Anderson met at III MAF headquarters with Major General Gordon F. Blood, the Seventh Air Force Deputy Chief of Staff for Operations. According to Anderson, the meeting resulted "in no meeting of the minds." General Anderson fully expected the

Seventh Air Force commander "to attempt to influence General Westmoreland to issue a flat order" for the 1st Wing to turn over its control and scheduling of Marine fixed-wing assets to the Air Force. While General Cushman would appeal any such order, Anderson predicted a troubled time ahead for the Marine air-ground team.[15]

The Marines did not have long to wait for the other shoe to drop. On 19 February, General Westmoreland radioed Admiral Sharp that, with the reinforcement of the Army divisions in the north, the situation required "a new and objective look at the control of tactical air." He wanted one man to bear the responsibility for this air effort and that man logically was General Momyer, who already commanded the Seventh Air Force and was his deputy for air. Westmoreland told Sharp that he had directed Momyer to develop a plan "that will give him [Momyer] control of the air assets," excluding helicopters and fixed-wing transport. Momyer was to coordinate his effort with III MAF.[16]

After a briefing by Momyer, General Cushman immediately protested to General Westmoreland. On 22 February, the MACV commander attempted to placate Cushman and told him that, as the ground field commander in I Corps, the III MAF commander would still retain the "tactical air assets available to support your forces, subject to modifications that I might invoke as the situation dictates." At the same time, Westmoreland stated that his air deputy, Momyer, "would have general direction of all routine matters relating to the procedures for requesting, fragging and controlling air support." In Saigon, a week later, Brigadier General Chaisson jotted down in his diary: "AF [Air Force] is doing real job on III MAF, Will get op con [operational control] of 10 wing. Very unprofessional work." The Marines had lost the fight in Saigon.[17]

At CincPac Headquarters in Honolulu, Admiral Sharp finally acquiesced to Westmoreland's request. On 28 February, General Westmoreland sent Major General Blood of the Seventh Air Force "to make sure Admiral Sharp understood the arrangement in detail." According to the MACV commander, he wanted to reassure Sharp that this was not an "Air Force maneuver," but rather his "initiative as a joint commander." This effort apparently counterbalanced any influence that the Marines may have had in Hawaii to reverse the decision. Lieutenant General Krulak, the FMFPac commander, whose headquarters was in the same building as that of Admiral Sharp, admitted his failure to persuade the Navy admiral.

According to Krulak, Sharp refused to listen to the Marine case, "telling me that he already knows our side, and anyhow, that Westy is a big commander, and should have what he wants." In a later interview, Admiral Sharp declared that he approved the Single Manager concept because, with the arrival of large Army forces in I Corps, he "thought it a reasonable thing to do."[18]

With only minor revisions, Westmoreland's implementing order differed very little from the proposal that he had forwarded to CincPac. Published on 7 March to be implemented three days later, in the form of a letter from General Westmoreland to General Cushman with six enclosures, the Single Manager Directive outlined the new aviation command arrangements. Westmoreland officially placed with General Momyer the "responsibility for coordinating and directing the air effort throughout Vietnam, to include I CTZ and the extended battle area." General Cushman was to make available to Momyer, as the MACV Deputy Commander for Air Operations, all strike and reconnaissance aircraft and that part of the Marine air command and control system that related to the employment of these aircraft. Marine fixed-wing transports, observation aircraft, and helicopters were exempted from the directive. According to the order, the MACV and III MAF control systems were to be joined for fixed-wing jet operations, but they were to retain the "integrity of the Marine tactical control system. . . . " Marine aviation officers were to augment the various Air Force/MACV control systems.[19]

Despite the decision and the issuance of the order on Single Manager, there were still several rough edges to its implementation. Major General Anderson observed that III MAF did not receive a copy of the directive until 9 March. Furthermore, according to the 1st MAW commander in a report on 18 March, the system was not working. Anderson believed that MACV and the Seventh Air Force, "in the haste to implement the procedure," overlooked too many details, and the necessary air control facilities were simply not prepared to take on their new tasks. Anderson admitted, however, that the Marine and Air Force agencies were identifying and sorting out many of the problems and that the wing was receiving "more cooperation than expected." He declared, however, "until such time as 7th AF/MACV can formulate, man, and put into being a modus operandi for I Corps, the wing will continue to do what is needed to operate and provide the necessary support." As he concluded, "I see no other way to go, without causing undue risk to our ground Marine currently in critical contact."[20]

Still, as General Anderson observed to General McCutcheon, the issue of Single Manager for III MAF was a "closed issue." In Washington, General Leonard F. Chapman, the Marine Corps Commandant, had already officially placed the matter before the Joint Chiefs of Staff. The Commandant stated that he could not "concur in such an arrangement" and asked that the Joint Chiefs review the entire subject. He maintained that both General Westmoreland and Admiral Sharp had exceeded their authority relative to Marine air in Vietnam.[21]

While the Single Manager controversy never formally went beyond the Department of Defense, General Westmoreland remembered that shortly after the publication of the directive, he received a telephone call from President Johnson. According to the MACV commander, the President asked him bluntly, "are you screwing the Marines?" Westmoreland claimed that he explained the reasons for his decision and that the President apparently accepted, for the time being, his rationale. In his book, the MACV commander wrote that the single manager was the one issue "to prompt me to consider resigning."[22]

On 25 March, at the weekly meeting of the Joint Chiefs, General Chapman formally brought up the subject. Major General McCutcheon accompanied the Commandant and made the presentation before the Chiefs. Generals Earle N. Wheeler, the Chairman, and Howard Johnson, the Army Chief of Staff, were both absent. Major General Haines, Army Deputy Chief of Staff, represented the Army; General John P. McConnell, the Air Force Chief of Staff, the Air Force; and Admiral Thomas H. Moorer, the Chief of Naval Operations, the Navy. According to both Generals Chapman and McCutcheon, the reception was much what they expected. Admiral Moorer openly supported the Marines. The two Marine generals believed that the Army's actual position was favorable, but that it had "probably made some sort of a deal with the Air Force and in all probability go 'agin' us." They had no doubt what General McConnell's stance would be. General McCutcheon also assumed that the chairman, General Wheeler, "was locked in concrete against us." Actually, the meeting resolved little. General McConnell suggested that no vote on the subject be made until the return of General Wheeler. General Chapman agreed and observed that he would "get McCutcheon to pitch to him [Wheeler] as soon as I can corner him." According to General McCutcheon, the "die has been cast, we are on record in the JCS and the Commandant will continue the fight."[23]

On 5 April, the full Joint Chiefs of Staff again took up the subject, this time with both the Chairman, General Wheeler, and the Army Chief of Staff, General Johnson, in attendance. At the meeting, much to the surprise and delight of the Marine Corps, General Johnson reversed the Army position and supported the Marines. In the final vote, only General Wheeler and the Air Force Chief of Staff, General McConnell, favored Single Manager. The next step was to send the matter up to the Secretary of Defense. McCutcheon wrote a few days later, "I feel better about it [Single Air Manager dispute] than I have in a long time."[24]

In Honolulu, Lieutenant General Krulak was not sanguine about the probability of the Secretary of Defense overruling Westmoreland. As he told General Cushman, he expected the Secretary to hold a hearing on the subject but, "knowing how those things operate, I do not believe that General Wheeler would have permitted the matter to [go] forward to SecDef [Secretary of Defense) without first laying the groundwork for the decision he seeks." Krulak suggested to General Cushman another alternative means of attack. He recommended that the III MAF commander should avail himself of the "complaint channel to CincPac," referring to the 30-day evaluation period called for in the initiating directive. General Krulak warned: "When we go down this track, we have to have the aces to a degree that will make it absolutely impossible for CincPac to ignore us or brush us off."[25]

Perhaps partially influenced by Krulak's message, but largely on their own initiative, III MAF and the 1st MAW had begun the process of evaluating the Single Manager process and forwarding their conclusions to higher headquarters. In early May, General Cushman forwarded to General Westmoreland both his concerns and those of General Anderson. Cushman basically stated that his analysis of the period 1–30 April drew him to the following conclusions. While air response time may have improved over the initial implementation period, it occurred only because air controllers had diverted aircraft from preplanned targets. Marines had scrambled some aircraft, in certain cases, to cover the diverted missions. He expressed dissatisfaction with the long lead time for preplanned missions. He protested the fact that, while the number of Marine aircraft "fragged" for Army units increased every day, the number of "Air Force sorties remained significantly below the program level established for Army battalions." Finally, the III MAF commander recommended "that management of Marine strike and reconnaissance aircraft . . . be returned to me."[26]

The Seventh Air Force evaluation of the system contrasted sharply with that of the Marines. General Momyer's command reported no significant problems "other than those associated with training and familiarity with a new system." While admitting that Single Manager was not perfect, the Air Force report asserted that "with better understanding by the Marine ground units and more experience on the part of all concerned . . . this system will work." The Air Force insisted that "in consideration of proposed large-scale ground offensive operations in being and planned the air effort available must be concentrated, flexible and integrated to provide the tactical air support essential to all ground units."[27]

Bombarded by conflicting points of view, General Westmoreland still held to the concept of centralized control, but began to look to the modification of some of the workings of the system. According to General Chaisson, the visit to Saigon at the end of April by the Marine Corps Assistant Commandant and former III MAF commander, Lieutenant General Lewis W. Walt, played some part in the MACV commanders changing perspective. Chaisson wrote that when Walt met with the MACV commander, "he scared the daylights out of Westy by telling him that it was the most dangerous decision he had made—and that it would backfire." The Marine general repeated what the Marines had been saying all along: too long a delay in the approval of preplanned missions; too many "diverts," which often resulted in the use of the wrong ordnance on the target; and the 3d Marine Division was not obtaining the "desired level of support."[28]

Generals Westmoreland and Momyer were under some pressure from higher headquarters relative to the single management issue. Upon receiving both the III MAF and MACV preliminary reports about the workings of the new system, Admiral Sharp decided to send his own evaluation team, headed by Marine Brigadier General Homer G. Hutchinson, Jr., the CincPac Chief of Staff for Operations, to examine the situation. According to Lieutenant General Krulak, General Westmoreland protested the move and asked the CincPac commander to defer the arrival of the team until he held his own hearings on the subject. Admiral Sharp apparently denied the request. At that point, as related by General Krulak, Westmoreland made the statement that the CincPac team would "come back and recommend to you that the system be returned to the old status quo."[29]

The Hutchinson evaluation group arrived in Vietnam on 4 May and visited both MACV in Saigon and III MAF at Da Nang. While not directly criticizing the decision for Single Management, its report discussed in detail what it considered several shortcomings in its implementation and operational procedures. Admitting that the Army units in I Corps received, in April, more air support than they had in the past, the report, nevertheless pointed out that Marine ground units did not enjoy "as much or as responsive tactical air support" as under the old system. Like all the other evaluations of Single Manager, the report remarked upon the long lead time for preplanned sorties and the resulting large number of diversions. It observed, moreover, that the Marine wing met the most urgent "unfragged" requests from Marine ground units by overflying by 22 percent its aircraft "programmed sortie rate." At the same time, Air Force aircraft flew only at a 96 percentage of their "utilization index."[30]

For his part, General Krulak, in Honolulu, continued his efforts to convince Admiral Sharp to intervene in the Single Management issue. According to the FMFPac commander, he persuaded Sharp to send a message to Westmoreland, again noting that General Cushman remained unhappy with the present working arrangements of the Single Manager system. In his reply, General Westmoreland agreed to a conference on the subject in Honolulu but observed that many of the rough spots of the system had been worked out. General Krulak warned the Marine Corps leadership, "Westy is not going to let us get away with a presentation only of our gripes, but will include his own story too."[31]

The Honolulu Conference, for the most part, proved to be a restatement of already established positions. As planned, on 10 May, the representatives from the respective Services and commands of MACV made their standard briefings before Admiral Sharp. As for General Anderson, who made the case for III MAF, he remembered that the Seventh Air Force indicated its willingness to make adjustments "in accordance with any criticism that we might have, which had the effect of taking the rug right out of us." As the wing commander recalled, "Admiral Sharp elected to not intervene." Anderson observed that Sharp was near the end of his tour and "must have felt that further protest would have to be at [a] higher level."[32]

Admiral Sharp may have been aware that the Department of Defense was about to act upon the referral of the Single Management issue to the Secretary. Secretary of Defense Clark Clifford, who replaced Robert S. McNamara in February, delegated the decision to his Deputy Secretary Paul A. Nitze. On 15 May, after listening to the formal presentations and reviewing the various position papers by the respective Services, Secretary Nitze generally supported the position of Generals Wheeler and Westmoreland. The secretary stated that he agreed with the Chairman that "the unified combat commander on the scene should be presumed to be the best judge of how the combat forces assigned to him are to be organized." He, nevertheless, expressed concern about the apparent weakness of the present Single Manager system relative to responsiveness, but presumed that General Westmoreland was taking action to rectify the situation.[33]

By this time, all concerned with the issue were looking toward some settlement of the dispute. On 18 May, at a meeting with Admiral Sharp, General Westmoreland discussed his intention to make some changes in the working of the Single Management system at the end of the month. The MACV commander wanted a 30-day trial period until the end of June and planned to ask "III MAF to withhold comments" until that time. Admiral Sharp indicated his general approval of Westmoreland's course of action. General Westmoreland also received prodding from General Wheeler, who directed that MACV in conjunction with both III MAF and the Seventh Air Force, "continue to evaluate the effectiveness" of Single Manager.[34]

While neither General Westmoreland nor Momyer was willing to return to III MAF full authority over Marine fixed-wing sorties, they made a drastic change in the scheduling of preplanned ground support missions. On 21 May, General Westmoreland outlined the new procedures. MACV now divided preplanned strikes into two categories, one to be determined weekly and the other daily in two separate frag orders. According to the modified system, 70 percent of all preplanned sorties were to be contained in the Seventh Air

Force weekly frag order. While the frag order designated number of aircraft, time on target, and basic ordnance load, the supported ground commander could use these sorties any way he desired, "consistent with aircraft and control capabilities." In essence, as General Krulak observed, III MAF made available all its air "attack and reconnaissance capability" to the Seventh Air Force, who in turn handed about 70 percent back "to the Marine command."[35]

Admitting that the modification provided more flexibility, Marine commanders and staff officers still pointed to several continuing disadvantages. While prescribed ordnance loads and time on targets could be adjusted, III MAF still had to match the ground requirements of its subordinate Army and Marine units with the predetermined 70 percent sorties in the weekly frag order. The Marines still considered the Single Management system, even with the changes, more cumbersome than necessary. As General Cushman remarked, "until Marine air assets are returned to full opcon of CG III MAF, command relationships will remain more complex."[36]

At the same time that MACV was altering Single Manager, General Chapman and the Marine headquarters staff in Washington proposed their own modification to the air arrangements in South Vietnam. The idea was for MACV formally to return to III MAF operational control of 70 percent of Marine fixed-wing assets, while retaining sortie control of the remaining 30 percent. General Chapman planned to forward the proposal to the Secretary of the Navy, who would forward it to the Secretary of Defense.[37]

Lieutenant General Krulak agreed with the Washington approach. He believed that the Marine headquarters recommended modification to the air control system "gets the camel's nose back into the tent—most advantageous, since the tent happens to be our own." The FMFPac commander then observed that he had not mentioned any of this to Admiral Sharp as he was of the opinion that "the impetus just has to come from the top down." Krulak stated that if Chapman wanted, he (Krulak) would "take him [Sharp] on immediately. But my recommendation is to give him a few thousand volts from above first."[38]

The Commandant's efforts, once more, to have higher authorities in Washington reverse Single Manager by edict from above failed. While the Navy Secretary endorsed General Chapman's recommendations, Deputy Secretary of Defense Nitze again refused to dictate air policy to MACV. Using much the same rationale as he had on 15 May, Nitze stressed that ComUSMACV was studying the responsiveness of the new procedures established at the end of May and that the secretary was sure that the field commander would make any changes that were necessary. At the same time, while General Wheeler, the Chairman, forwarded the Commandant's memorandum to CincPac and ComUSMACV, the Joint Chiefs also declined to take any action on their own.[39]

Given Secretary Nitze's two unfavorable decisions, General Chapman believed any further exertion on his part to influence action through DOD to be self-defeating. Instead, he planned to revert to pressure from below. As he advised Lieutenant General Henry W. Buse, Jr., his former Chief of Staff at HQMC and new Commanding General, Fleet Marine Force, Pacific, who relieved General Krulak at the end of May, "move from Saigon may be our best bet at this time."[40]

The Commandant's change of course was based, in part, on the actual or scheduled reshuffling of the key personalities both at CincPac and at MACV. At CincPac headquarters in Hawaii, in addition to General Buse replacing General Krulak, Admiral John C. McCain was to take over command from Admiral Sharp at the end of July. In Saigon, on 15 June, General Creighton W. Abrams became ComUSMACV in place of General Westmoreland, who returned to Washington to become the U.S. Army Chief of Staff. Both Generals Norman Anderson, the commander of the 1st MAW, and also General Momyer, the commander of the Seventh Air Force, were scheduled for reassignment. The hope was that, with a different cast of commanders in place in strategic command billets, there would be more room for compromise. Both General Buse, the new FMFPac commander, and General George S. Brown, the new Seventh Air Force commander, had less prickly personalities than their predecessors, Lieutenant General Krulak and General Momyer.

While not too much was known about General Abrams' position, except that he wanted to ensure adequate fixed-wing air support for Army units in I Corps, Marine commanders assumed that he was more flexible about the Single Manager issue than Westmoreland. General Chaisson, who also rotated at this time, observed that Abrams, while often critical of the Marines and publicly supporting the Single Management policy that he inherited, was not as adamant as Westmoreland and "has it [single manager] up for review."[41]

In one of his first actions, Lieutenant General Buse made arrangements to visit Vietnam to discuss the situation with General Abrams. On 16 June, the new FMFPac commander met with Abrams in Saigon. Buse described Abrams as "very cordial," and the two had a very frank discussion. According to General Buse, he told the MACV commander that he "wasn't down there to critique at what he [Abrams] was doing operationally, nor was I going to tell him what to do operationally." In turn, Abrams replied that he had no particular problems in I Corps, "unless air control could be so considered." Seeing an opportunity, Buse suggested that Abrams end the emergency in I Corps and return control of Marine air to III MAF. The MACV commander, however, was not prepared to take such drastic action. Abrams countered that the "Marines use more air support more than anyone," and not only because of their lightness in artillery and helicopter support. Buse explained that "air support is part of our life and that we were structured, trained, and accustomed to use it to maximum benefit." General Buse then asked Abrams directly if he felt as strongly on the subject as General Westmoreland. The MACV commander answered "in a definite and strong negative." In assessing his meeting with Abrams, Buse considered Abrams still open on the subject and that "a tinkle has been heard from the bell of freedom."[42]

General Buse agreed with General Chapman that the best channel for reversal of the policy was through Saigon and possibly Honolulu. The FMFPac commander stated that there was possibly a means of compromise through reducing the span of control of III MAF in I Corps. He posed the possibility of dividing I Corps into two sectors, one Army and one Marine, possibly divided at the Hai Van Pass above Da Nang. If that occurred, Buse thought Abrams might be induced to "return control of Marine air."[43]

The Marine efforts with General Abrams, however, came to naught. Despite Marine arguments to the contrary, the MACV commander saw no need to alter the air arrangements. In Washington, Major General McCutcheon expressed little surprise that General Abrams was relatively satisfied with the modified Single Air Manager system. As McCutcheon wrote to Major General Charles J. Quilter, the new 1st MAW commander who had relieved General Anderson on 22 June, "It is only us Marines who have noticed the diminution in effectiveness." McCutcheon even admitted that this so-called reduction in effectiveness "isn't very much now since they [the Air Force] incorporated all our suggested changes." The nub of the matter was, according to McCutcheon, "we still don't have the OpCon [operational control]."⁴⁴

With the departure of Admiral Sharp as CincPac, Marines believed that the chances were good that his successor, Admiral McCain, would side with them. Marine Brigadier General Hutchinson, the CincPac J-3, wrote to General McCutcheon that "we had McCain as near fully locked in on a decision to return about 70 percent of our fixed-wing assets to Marine control as it was possible to be short of having the decision signed off."⁴⁵

Again the Marine aspirations were to lead to frustration. After assuming command, in August, Admiral McCain, together with Lieutenant General Buse, visited General Abrams in Saigon. Their visit also coincided with one by General Chapman to Vietnam. General Hutchinson related that McCain had "withheld his final decision for the obvious protocol reasons of being able to say he had discussed the subject directly with Abe." In the meeting over Single Management that included the two Marine generals as well as McCain and Abrams, General Abrams apparently was willing to modify Single Manager in return for an alteration of command relations in I Corps. The Marine generals, at that point, decided not to push the issue. According to Brigadier General Hutchinson, this course of action made "it impossible for McCain to do anything but go along." Hutchinson stated that the admiral was not yet "in writing, but I would guess that after he sees Chapman . . . the issue will be closed out." In General Chapman's version, Admiral McCain, a close personal friend, told him, "that he was new on the scene, that such an order was vehemently opposed by his principal commander in the field and that he just didn't feel persuaded that it was a good idea and that he ought to do it, and he never did."

Through the rest of 1968, the Marines would continue to bring up the Single Manager issue, but with diminishing expectations. The MACV commander opposed what he considered double management and hoped to end the dispute once and for all. Supported by General Wheeler, the JCS Chairman, Abrams ended the formal monthly evaluations of the system. As he stated in November 1968, "We do not wish to appear intransigent about this matter . . . but it is vital that ComUSMACV retain the centralized control and direction of TacAir (tactical air) in the hands of a single individual."⁴⁶

While General Abrams remained firm in his support of Single Manager as modified in May, the Marine Corps continued the struggle the following months and years but in different forums. While the Commandant continued to raise the issue among the Joint Chiefs, only the Navy, since General Westmoreland became the Army Chief of Staff, now supported the Marine position. As General McCutcheon observed to General Quilter, the 1st MAW commander, on November 26, 1968, "I am working . . . on the philosophy that single management is here, and the way to beat it is to join it and out manage them."[47]

Using this tactic, the Marines in a series of local arrangements and working agreements managed to obtain, in 1969 and 1970, practical control of their aviation assets. In early 1969, III MAF had succeeded in vetoing an attempt by MACV to modify its Air Directive 95.4 to include the term "operational direction" to define the relationship between the Seventh Air Force and III MAF. Finally, in August 1970, Lieutenant General McCutcheon, as CG III MAF, agreed to a new MACV air directive that gave "formal sanction" to the changes that the Marines had succeeded in obtaining from MACV and the Air Force. The Air Force accepted the Marine Corps interpretation of "mission" and "operational direction." Under the new directive, III MAF retained operational control of its aircraft and it also included a provision permitting the Marine wing to withhold "specialized Marine support sorties" from the Seventh Air Force. If the Marines obtained much of what they wanted, than as Bernard Nalty, an Air Force historian asked, "Why the fuss?" Nalty answered his own question with the conclusion: "Tactically, the single manager meant nothing. Doctrinally, however, it affirmed a principle, centralized control, that the Army Air Corps and U.S. Air Force had consistently championed, and in doing so, it established a precedent for the future."[48]

1. LtGen Keith B. McCutcheon, "Marine Aviation in Vietnam, 1962–70," *Naval Review 1971* (Annapolis: U.S. Naval Institute, 1971), pp. 122–55, hereafter McCutcheon, "Marine Aviation in Vietnam, 1962–70"; Gen William W. Momyer, *Air Power in Three Wars* (Washington: U.S. Air Force History, 1978), pp. 285–7; Gen Keith B. McCutcheon, Intvw, Apr 1971, p. 6 (Oral HistColl, MCHC); BGen John R. Chaisson Intvw, 19Mar69, pp. 235–36 (Oral HistColl, MCHC).

2. Historical Summary, General Entry, 27Dec67–31Jan68, v. 28, History File, Westmoreland Papers, CMH, hereafter Westmoreland, General Entry, 27Dec67–31Jan68; Westmoreland, *A Soldier Reports*, pp. 344; Graham A. Cosmas, "General Westmoreland and Control of the Air War," Naval Historical Division, *Command and Control of Air Operations in the Vietnam War, Colloquium on Contemporary*

History, January 23, 1991, No. 4 (Washington, D.C.: Naval Hist Center, 1991), pp. 29–38.

3. CGFMFPac, "Pacific Operations," General Officers Symposium Book, July 1967, Tab F, p. 21.

4. Westmoreland msg to Sharp, dtd 18Jan68, Doc no. 2, and Sharp msg to Westmoreland, dtd 18Jan68, Doc no. 3, HQMC, DCS Air Folder, Single Manager, Jan68–15Aug70.

5. Westmoreland msg to Sharp, dtd 21Jan68, Doc No. 4, HQMC, DCS Air Folder, Single Manager, Jan68–15Aug70; ComUSMACV msg to CGIIIMAF and CG Seventh Air Force, dtd 22Jan68 (Doc No. 58, III MAF Incoming Msgs, Dec67–1Feb68); MACV ComdHist, 1968, pp. 423–24.

6. Norman Anderson, Memo For the Record1 dtd 29Jan68 (Norman Anderson Papers, PC 1263, MCHC); John Schlight, *The United States Air Force in Southeast Asia. The War in South Vietnam, the Years: the Offensive, 1965–68* (Washington: Office of Air Force History, 1988), pp. 277–85; CGIIIMAF to Cdr, Seventh Air Force, dtd 24Jan68 (3d MarDiv, Messages, Jan68).

7. MajGen Norman Anderson, intvw, 3d Session, 17Mar81, pp. 199–201 (Oral HistColl, MCHC), hereafter N. Anderson, intvw, 17Mar81; Schlight, *Years of the Offensive, 1965–68*, pp. 277–78; Bernard C. Nalty, "Operation Niagara, Air Power, and the Siege of Khe Sanh," in Naval Historical Center, *Command and Control of Air Operations in the Vietnam War*, p. 44, hereafter Nalty, "Operation Niagara"; Bernard C. Nalty, *Air Power and the Fight for Khe Sanh* (Washington: 28 Office of Air Force History, 1969), pp. 72–74, hereafter Nalty, *Air Power and the Fight For Khe Sanh*.

8. McCutcheon ltr to Norman Anderson, dtd 23Jan68, Letter No. 45 and Anderson ltr to McCutcheon, dtd 7Feb68, Letter No. 50, File A, 1968 Correspondence, Box 20 (McCutcheon Papers, PC464), hereafter Anderson ltr to McCutcheon, 7Feb68.

9. Gen William C. Westmoreland, intvw, 4Apr83, p. 47 (Oral HistColl, MCHC), hereafter Westmoreland, intvw, 1983. Westmoreland did not recall the date of this meeting but he did meet with Cushman and Anderson about aviation arrangements on 19 January 1968. See Westmoreland entry for 19Jan68, Historical Summary1, Westmoreland Papers, CMH.

10. Gen Robert E. Cushman, intvw, Nov82, pp. 33–34 (Oral HistColl, MCHC), hereafter Cushman, intvw; Westmoreland, intvw, 1983, p. 38; N. Anderson, intvw, 17Mar81, pp. 192, 194–5; MajGen Norman J. Anderson ltr to BGen Edwin H. Simmons, dtd 8Sep83, Norman Anderson Papers, PC1263 (MCHC), hereafter N Anderson ltr, 8Sep83.

11. Westmoreland, intvw, 1983, pp. 38–50, quote is on p. 39.

12. Ibid., p. 42; N. Anderson ltr1 8Sep83; N. Anderson, intvw1 17Mar81, pp. 192, 194–95.

13. BGen John R. Chaisson ltr to wife, dtd 28Jan68, Chaisson Papers, Hoover Institute; Westmoreland, General Entry, 27Dec67–31Jan68; N. Anderson intvw, 17Mar81, pp. 194–5; Westmoreland, *A Soldier Reports*, pp. 342–3. In his interview with Marine Corps historians, General Westmoreland insisted that the difficulty with air support related to the 101st Airborne Division. This apparently was incorrect, as the headquarters of the 101st did not arrive in I Corps until the beginning of March. Major General Anderson is adamant that he had no problems with the 101st

Division and, moreover, in his book, General Westmoreland mentions only the 1st Air Cavalry relative to this matter. Westmoreland, intvw, 1983, p. 42; Westmoreland, *A Soldier Reports*, pp. 342–43; N. Anderson ltr, 8Sep83; N. Anderson, intvw, 17Mar81, pp. 192, 194–95.

14. Gen William C. Westmoreland, Historical Summary, 1–29Feb68, pp. 4–5, Fldr 29, Westmoreland Papers (CMH); Westmoreland, *A Soldier Reports*, pp. 342–43; N. Anderson ltrs to MajGen Keith B. McCutcheon, dtd 7 and 13Feb68, Letters Nos. 50 and 58, File A, 1968 Correspondence, Box 20 (McCutcheon Papers, PC464).

15. MajGen Norman Anderson, Memorandum for the Record, dtd 17Feb68, Subj: Control of Air in the Defense of Khe Sanh (Norman Anderson Papers, PC1263), 29.

16. Westmoreland msg to Sharp, dtd 19Feb68, Doc 7, HQMC, DCS Air Folder, Single Manager, Jan68–15Aug70.

17. MACV ComdHist, 1968, I; COMUSMACV ltr to CG III MAF, dtd 7Mar68, Subj: Single Management, Doc 14, HQMC, DCS Air Folder, Single Manager, Jan68–15Aug70; COmUSMACV msg to CG III MAF, dtd 22Feb68, Doc No. 13, III MAF Incoming Msgs, 20Feb68–1Mar68; BGen John R. Chaisson, entry 29Feb68, Diary, Jan–Jun68, Chaisson Papers, Hoover Institute.

18. Westmoreland, *A Soldier Reports*, p. 344; chronology of events and Briefing for new CinCPac at HQMC. Command Relations and Air Control in CTZ, n.d. [May68] Dcc 20, HQMC DCS (Air) Single Manager, Fldr, Jan68–15Aug70, hereafter Chronology of Events, Doc 20; CGFMFPac msg to CG III MAF, dtd 6Mar68, Dcc 2, III MAF Incoming Msgs, 4–14Mar68, hereafter CGFMFPac msg to CG III MAF, dtd 6Mar68; intvw with Sharp quoted in Nalty, *Air Power and the Fight for Khe Sanh*, p. 77.

19. COMUSMACV ltr to CG III MAF, dtd 7Mar68, Subj: Single Management, Doc No. 14, HQMC DCS (Air) Single Manager Fldr, Jan68–15Aug70, hereafter COMUSMACV ltr, 7Feb68, Single Management.

20. CG 1stMAW msg to CG III MAF and CGFMFPac, dtd 18Mar68, Doc No. 8, III MAF Incoming Msgs, 15–27Mar68.

21. MajGen Norman Anderson ltr to McCutcheon, dtd 19Mar68, Ltr No. 67, File A, McCutcheon Papers, PC464; CMC memo to Joint Chiefs, Subj: Single Management, dtd 4Mar68, Doc No. 13, and Chronology of Events, Dcc 20, HQMC DCS (Air) Single Manager Fldr, Jan68–15Aug70.

22. Westmoreland, intvw, May 1983; Westmoreland, *A Soldier Reports*, pp. 344–5. There is some contradiction between the interview and the book. In his book, he makes no mention of a telephone conversation with the President, but does mention discussing the subject with the President in April when on a visit to Washington.

23. CMC msg to CGFMFPac, dtd 26Mar68, in Folder, Memos for the Record, 1966–68, hereafter CMC msg 26Mar68, and McCutcheon ltr to MajGen Norman and BGen E. E. Anderson, dtd 26Mar68, Ltr No. 64, File A, 1968 Correspondence, (McCutcheon Papers, PC464), hereafter McCutcheon ltr, 26Mar68. While not a formal member of the Joint Chiefs at that time, the Marine Corps Commandant had a vote on all matters relating to the Marine Corps, which was usually interpreted in the broadest terms. For all practical purposes, the Commandant was a sitting member of the Joint Chiefs.

24. McCutcheon ltr to BGen E. E. Anderson and MajGen Norman Anderson, dtd 9Apr68, Ltr No. 68, File A, 1968 Cor, McCutcheon Papers, PC464. See also Gen Leonard F. Chapman, intvw, 28 Mar 1979, pp. 70–76 (Oral HistColl, MCHC), 30.

25. CG FMFPac msg to CG III MAF, dtd 14Apr68, Doc No. 19, III MAF Incoming Msgs, 7Mar–13Aug68.

26. CG III MAF msg to CMC, dtd 4May68, HQMC Msgs Mar–Jun68.

27. MACV ComdHist, 1968, I, pp. 437–39.

28. BGen John R. Chaisson ltr to wife, dtd 2May68, Chaisson Papers, Hoover Institute; MajGen Norman Anderson, draft of Memo for the Record, n.d. [2 or 4May68], Subj: Single Management, Norman Anderson Papers, PC1263, hereafter Anderson draft memo, Single Management; CG III MAF msg to CMC, dtd 4May68, HQMC Msgs, Mar–Jun68.

29. CGFMFPac msg to CMC, dtd 3May68, HQMC Msgs, Mar–Jun68.

30. BGen Homer E. Hutchinson ltr to McCutcheon, n.d. (May68), Doc No. 21, HQMC DCS (Air) Single Manager Fldr, Jan68–15Aug70 and attached CinCPac Evaluation Team, draft rpt, n.d. [May 1968], Subject: Single Management of Air Support.

31. CGFMFPac msg to CMC, dtd 7May68, HQMC Msgs, Mar–Jun68.

32. FMFPac, MaropsV, Apr68, p. 60, May68, p. 68; N. Anderson, intvw, 17Mar81, pp. 194–5.

33. Depsec of Def, Paul H. Nitze memo to Chairman, JCS, dtd 15May68, Subject: OpCon of III MAF Aviation, Assets, Doc No. 17, HQMC DCS (Air) Single Manager Fldr Jan68–15Aug70. Relative to HQMC presentations to DepSec Nitze, see HQMC, Briefing, Apr68, Doc No. 31, HQMC DCS (Air) Single Manager Fldr, Jan68–15Aug70 and McCutcheon ltr to MajGen Frank C. Tharin, dtd 24Apr68, Ltr No 37, File T, 1968 Correspondence, McCutcheon Papers, MCHC.

34. CGFMFPac msg to CMC, dtd 25May68, HQMC Msgs, Mar–Jun68; BGen John R. Chaisson, diary entry, 20May68, Chaisson Papers, Hoover Institute; JCS msg to CinCPac and COMUSMACV, dtd 20May68, Doc No. 19, HQMC DCS (Air) Single Manager Fldr Jan68–15Aug70.

35. CGFMFPac msgs to CMC, dtd 21 and 26May68, and HQMC, ATA21 Point Paper, dtd 28May68, Subj: Change to the Single Management HQMC Msgs, Mar–Jun68 and MaropsV, May68, pp. 68–69.

36. CG III MAF msgs to CMC, dtd 26May68 and 30May68, HQMC Msgs, Mar–Jun68.

37. ATA21, Point Paper, dtd 28May68, Subj: Change to the Single Management . . . ; CGFMFPac msgs to CMC, dtd 26May68 and 30May68; CG III MAF msgs to CMC, dtd 26May68 and 30May68. All in HQMC Msgs, Mar–Jun68.

38. CGFMFPac msgs to CMC, dtd 26May68, HQMC Msgs, Mar–Jun68.

39. HQMC Talking Paper, Air Control in Vietnam; CMC to CGFMFPac, dtd 19Jun68, HQMC Msgs, Mar–Jun68, hereafter CMC to CGFMFPac, 19Jun68.

40. CMC to CGFMFPac1, 19Jun68.

41. BGen John R. Chaisson, debriefing at FMFPac, May68, Chaisson Transcripts, pp. 147–73, p. 164.

42. CGFMFPac to CMC, dtd 16Jun68, HQMC Msgs, Mar–Jun68; Buse, intvw, p. 191.

43. CGFMFPac msg to CMC, dtd 22Jun68, HQMC Msgs, Mar–Jun68.

44. FMFPAC, MaropsV, Jun68, p. 62; HQMC Talking Paper, Air Control in Vietnam; McCutcheon to MajGen C. J. Quilter, dtd 15Jul68, Ltr No. 35, File Q, 1968 Cor, McCutcheon Papers, hereafter McCutcheon to Quilter, 15Jul68. While as Deputy Chief of Staff for Air at Headquarters Marine Corps, General McCutcheon was not in any chain of command relative to the administration or operations of Marine aviation in Vietnam. While fully aware of this, General McCutcheon kept himself fully informed about Marine aviation matters in the country through an informal correspondence. As he wrote earlier to General Quilter, he would write from time to time as I did Norm [General Anderson] and Ben [Major General Louis B. Robertshaw, an earlier commander of the 1st MAW] and occasionally get on the phone. "I think we both understand that FMFPac is sensitive to being passed over so in most cases the kind of information that will be passed personally will be of such a nature that it will not compromise FMFPac's command prerogatives." McCutcheon ltr to MajGen Charles J. Quilter, dtd 5Jul68, Ltr No. 34, File Q, 1968 Correspondence, McCutcheon Papers.

45. The sources for this and the following paragraph are: Hutch [BGen Homer G. Hutchinson] to McCutcheon, nd. [Aug68], Ltr No. 48, File H, 1968 Cor, McCutcheon Papers. See also Chapman, intvw, p. 76.

46. For the wing's initial optimism, see A/CS, G-3, 1st MAW memo to CG 1st MAW, dtd 10Sep68 (Rpts and Letters, Jun–Dec68, Quilter Papers). For General Wheeler's support, see CMC msg to CGFMFPac, dtd 26Sep68 (HQMC Msgs, Jul–15Oct68). General Abrams is quoted in CG III MAF msg to CMC and CGFMFPac and CGFMFPac msg to CMC, dtd 8Nov66 (HQMC Msgs, Jul–Dec68).

47. McCutcheon to Quilter, dtd 19Nov68, Ltr No. 39, File Q, 1968 Cor, McCutcheon Papers.

48. Charles R. Smith, *U.S. Marines in Vietnam 1969 High Mobility and Standdown* (Washington: Hist&MusDiv, HQMC, 1988), p. 225–26; Graham A. Cosmas and LtCol Terrence P. Murray, *U.S. Marines in Vietnam, 1970–71* (Washington: Hist&Mus Div, HQMC, 1986), 273–77; Bernard Ce Nalty, "Operation Niagara, Air Power, and the Siege of Khe Sanh," in Naval Historical Center, *Command and Control of Air Operations in the Vietnam War* (Washington: NHC, 1991), p. 46. The new directive defined Mission/Operational Direction as the authority delegated to DepComUSMACV for Air Operations (Cdr, 7th AF) to assign specific fixed-wing air tasks to the CG, III MAF, on a periodic basis as implementation of a basic mission assigned by ComUSMACV." (MACV Directive 95.4, dtd 15Aug70, as quoted in Cosmas and Murray, *U.S. Marines in Vietnam, 1970–71*, p. 277).

The Design and Construction of Soviet Navy Submarines in the Cold War

Igor Spassky

⚓

This paper summarizes the history of submarine construction in the U.S.S.R. from the end of World War II to the early 1990s.

At the beginning of World War II, the submarine force of the U.S.S.R. Navy numbered 206 boats, and, during the war, another 54 vessels were completed. At the same time, 103 submarines were lost in combat operations.

At the beginning of the postwar period, the 10 year program of naval shipbuilding, approved in 1937, stipulating the construction of 386 submarines, was still in effect. That is why the construction of submarines was continued using the most successful designs devised during the prewar years: type C (IX series), eight boats; type III (X series), two boats; type M (X) series, one boat; and type M (XV series), fifty-three boats. A total of 64 submarines were built.

During this period, the views of the role of submarines in the Navy had not changed significantly. Submarines were still considered as an important but not a major component of the Navy, and they were to engage in the following combat operations: actions on ocean lines and in the vicinity of far-off naval bases against naval ships, convoys, and individual transports; reconnaissance in far-off regions; screening of friendly convoys on ocean lines; and minelaying on sea-lanes.

For efficient performance of these combat missions, high submerged speed was considered to be the decisive factor, and, for this reason, all the efforts of designers and research workers during this period were concentrated on increasing speed. In order to achieve the high speeds necessary over long durations, the following goals were sought: increasing propulsion motor power rating and storage battery capacity; providing for diesel operation in submerged running; and using turbine and boiler-turbine plants for submarine cruising while submerged, or the so-called Walter cycle. While these concepts were used to guide the design of new submarines, war experience was also taken into account. These submarines started to join the Navy between 1951 and 1953.

The changing political situation—the transition from Allied relations during World War II to the Cold War—gave a strong impulse to submarine construction in the U.S.S.R. The attitude toward the submarine force also changed, and, eventually, submarines were acknowledged to have priority in the Navy. Two factors influenced the final definition of the status of submarines: owing to the difficult economic situation in the country, the construction of a well-balanced, large Navy, equivalent to the U.S. Navy, was impossible; and the unfounded views of national leaders, particularly Party Secretary N. S. Khrushchev and Marshall G. K. Zhukov, the Defense Minister until 1957, on the role of surface ships in naval general purpose combat forces. Some leaders of the Navy defended a policy of building a large, multipurpose fleet capable of opposing the naval forces of the probable enemy, but these contradictions were resolved in a purely administrative manner: longtime Fleet Admiral of the Soviet Union N. Kuznetsov was dismissed from his position.

Thus, the first submarines of postwar production are listed below. (U.S.S.R. Navy submarine projects were numbered, but this article uses the Western codenames for convenience.)

1. Diesel-electric submarines: *Whiskey*-class submarines of medium displacement (1,500 tons); 215 of such submarines were constructed between 1951 and 1958.

2. Diesel-electric submarines: *Zulu*-class of greater displacement (1,831 tons); 26 boats.

3. Diesel-electric submarines: *Quebec*-class of small displacement (406 tons), equipped with diesel engines capable of operations in submerged running; 31 boats from 1953 to 1958.

4. Steam-gas turbine experimental: Project 617 of 950 tons displacement; launched in 1956.

Building these submarines should be considered the first stage of submarine fleet development in the postwar U.S.S.R. During these years, the paramount importance was to build a new generation of submarines to replace the veterans of the war and also to improve the skills of submarine designers and, more importantly, to expand and improve the submarine production facilities so that industry might solve even more complicated problems in the near future. The tactical and technical parameters of these submarines, in comparison with the prewar submarines of the IX series, are shown (see Table 1).

Judging by the figures in this table, one can conclude that, regardless of the improvement of certain submarine parameters, the cardinal change of combat capabilities did not take place. During this time, the greatest contribution to the construction of submarines was made by the chief designers, A. Antipin, S. Egorov, and A. Kassatsier.

The further improvement of Soviet submarines was connected to a number of radical changes of major combat and technical facilities, which defined not only the improvement of quality but also the transformation of submarine architecture as well. The creation of new weapons—ballistic and cruise missiles with special charges—and successful developments in nuclear energetics, a program headed by academicians A. Alexandrov and N. Dolezhai, determined the possibility of building completely new types of submarines capable of remaining underwater for their total period of endurance.

Activities aimed at creating nuclear reactor propelled submarines were undertaken in the U.S.S.R. at the very beginning of the 1950s; the following three projects were launched:

1. The nuclear multipurpose torpedo submarine *November*. This submarine was the first to make a breakthrough, thanks to its chief design engineer, Naval Architect V. Peregudov.

2. The nuclear submarine *Hotel*, which carried ballistic missiles.

3. The nuclear submarine *Echo-1*, which was armed with cruise missiles.

All these submarines were equipped with a nuclear power plant of the same type that used water as a coolant. Later, one multipurpose nuclear submarine, named Project 645, was propelled by a reactor that used liquid metal (lead and bismuth alloy) as a coolant. In a long-term competition between submarine nuclear reactors with water and those with liquid metal coolants, nuclear power plants with water coolant were the winners, mainly because the thermal technical advantages of liquid metal coolant could not compensate for the technological difficulties occasioned in operating those plants, inasmuch as they demanded very sophisticated base facilities.

TABLE 1.

Tactical &
Technical Parameters IX Series

	Type S	Whiskey	Zulu	Quebec	617 Project
Disp. tons	840	1050	1831	406	950
Weapons					
torp tube, pcs	4 forward	4 forward	6 forward	4 forward	6 forward
	2 aft	2 aft	2 aft	2 aft	2 aft
Spare torp	6	6	6	6	6
Guns x Cal in mm	1 x 100 and 1 x 45	1 x 57	1 x 57	1 x 25	NA
Surf speed max knots	19.5	18.25	17.0	16.1	11.0
Submergd speed max	9.1 w/in 1 hr	13.1 w/in 1 hr	15.0 w/in 1 hr	15.0 w/in 3 hrs	20.0 w/in 6 hrs
Diving dpt	100	200	200	120	200
Endurance	30 dys	30 dys	75 dys	10 dys	45 dys

In any event, during the years when the Soviet Navy built only diesel-electric submarines, only one design agency existed in the U.S.S.R. In 1948, with the special purpose of developing submarines with high submerged speed (including the submarine with steam-gas turbine plant using the Walter cycle), a second design agency was established; this agency was reoriented toward the design of nuclear reactor driven submarines in early 1953. The strict distribution of activities between these two agencies, dictated by the type of submarines they designed—the older one specializing in diesel driven vessels, the newer, in reactor driven boats—did not last for a long time. Design of the first types of nuclear propelled submarines was the result of the work of designers from both agencies. Some time later, a third design agency was established which specialized in the design of nuclear submarines of limited displacement. The Central Scientific Research Shipbuilding Institute of the Navy and Krylov Shipbuilding Research Institute held first place among the many research and industrial organizations which created the submarines of all types during this formative period.

Enormous difficulties accompanied the procedure of design and construction of the first nuclear reactor submarines. Neither the designers of the submarines, as well as the equipment, nor the naval operators realized in full measure all of the specialized aspects of these totally new power systems. Many things had to be learned and many arrangements, traditional for submariners, and methods of damage control had to be reconsidered. It was very difficult to realize the radiation danger. Unfortunately, heavy accidents, resulting in the loss of human lives, took place. The greatest difficulties were experienced in the production and operation of the steam generators, the first specimens of which did not survive the total period of service life. To the credit of the specialists participating in these activities, it is necessary to mention that, by means of joint efforts, these problems of growth and associated errors were overcome within a period of several years and that the creation of the next generation of nuclear submarines, which was commenced by the designers and specialists of industry in the beginning of the 1950s, was supported by the accumulated knowledge and experience.

As noted above, the totally new type of weapons—ballistic and cruise missiles, in particular—was introduced on submarines. The fact that missiles and submarines were developed in parallel resulted in certain difficulties, especially in the process of design, inasmuch as 100 percent coincidence of the initial parameters planned by the weapon designers with the final results of development was not achieved in all cases. One must do justice to the diesel-electric submarines of the *Whiskey* and *Zulu* types; due to good design and excellent shipbuilding of these submarines, the wide range of experimental research activities for the development of missiles was carried out on them.

For instance, from 1957 to 1958, the first experimental marine cruise missiles were tested on the *P-Whiskey* and *P-Zulu* submarines. Out of two totally different types of missiles, the system developed under the leadership of academician V. Chelomey was selected. The cruise missiles were stored in containers with collapsed wings that were to be opened automatically at the moment when the missile left the container. This missile served as the prototype of all subsequent types of marine cruise missiles. From 1960 to 1963, eleven *Whiskey* submarines were refitted to carry cruise missiles. On the first modification of these submarines, two cruise missiles were installed and four on the second one. The development of these diesel-electric submarines was completed by building sixteen *Juliet*-type submarines. With the commissioning of nuclear submarines of the *Echo-I*-type, bearing 6 missiles, starting in 1961, and their further modification in 1963, with the *Echo-II* bearing 8 missiles, no more cruise missiles were installed on diesel-electric submarines. Naval Architect P. Pustyntsev served as the chief designer of all of these submarines.

The *Zulu* and *Whiskey* types also served to introduce ballistic missiles into the marine environment. In 1955, two vertical containers for launching surface ballistic missiles were installed on *W-Zulu* submarines. The containers were located inside the pressure hull of the submarine and their upper portion in the extended conning tower. By means of a lifting device, the missiles were hoisted from containers and, naturally, were launched only when the submarine was surfaced. After successful test firing of missiles with a range of 120km to 150km, five more submarines were refitted under the AW-*Zulu* Project.

In 1957, on both sides of the *W-Whiskey* submarines, two vertical containers were installed to test the underwater launching of experimental ballistic missiles; one was for launching the missiles and the other, on the opposing side, was a counterweight. Academicians N. Isanin and S. Korolev directed the initial tests of this system, and academician V. Makeev succeeded Isanin soon afterward.

The successful tests of the installation on submarines of ballistic and cruiser missiles bearing nuclear warheads strengthened the opinion of the highest political authorities of the U.S.S.R. that submarines should become the major striking forces of the Navy. From that time forward, the design and construction of a powerful underwater fleet, equipped with nuclear power plants and bearing mighty missile weapons with intercontinental firing range, became one of the tasks of national importance. Strains in the international political situation initiated the rapid increase in the nuclear potential of the Soviet Navy. The appearance of Soviet submarines in the Atlantic Ocean and the Pacific Ocean, heretofore controlled exclusively by the U.S. Navy and NATO navies, enabled the Soviet Navy to decrease, if not eliminate, to a considerable extent the maritime advantages of the Western nations and, in any case, provided the possibility of striking back with nuclear weapons.

Considering this, from the start of the 1960s, when the first experience of outfitting submarines with these new weapons was accumulating, the following main types of U.S.S.R. submarines were defined. First, the TYPE I submarines were underwater missile carriers bearing strategic ballistic missiles intended to destroy important opposing land-based objects. The development of the underwater strategic missile carriers, in the first half of the 1960s, headed in two directions: the construction of diesel-electric submarines of the *Golf*-type, bearing three ballistic missiles, and the construction of nuclear reactor driven submarines of the *Hotel*-type, carrying three missiles of the same kind. Before 1963, these missiles could be launched only from the surface, but, starting in that year, these submarines were modified to conduct underwater launchings. A small ammunition establishment and a short firing range resulted in the restriction of the number of *Hotel*-type nuclear submarines to 8 vessels. Later, some of these vessels were used as experimental boats. The final phase of the *Hotel*-type submarines was completed under the leadership of academician S. Kovatev, who also directed the work on the design and construction of the *Yankee*, *Delta*, and *Typhoon* types years later. N. Isanin served as the chief designer of the *Golf*-type diesel-electric submarine.

Beginning in 1967, much more efficient *Yankee*-type submarines, armed with 16 ballistic missiles, joined the fleet. These vessels founded the family of nuclear missile bearing submarines which are known in the West as *Delta-I*, *Delta-II*, *Delta-III*, and *Delta-IV* boats. The main difference between these submarine classes was in the arrangement of the missile systems, with the result that the firing range increased over the course of development. At the same time, improvements in warheads and increasing charge capacities were carried out.

The variety of underwater missile carrier types was the result of constant improvement of missiles and was accompanied by their increasing dimensions. Simultaneously, new radio electronic equipment was introduced, and the parameters of power plants and ship systems were improved.

The further realistic assessment of the U.S.S.R. and U.S.A. armament levels enabled our two countries to adopt a set of reasonable strategic arms limitations based on the ideas of containment and defense adequacy.

The *Typhoon*-class submarine, commissioned in 1981, embodied the greatest achievements of Russian science and technology and sounded the final chord in the history of U.S.S.R. ballistic missile bearing, nuclear reactor driven submarines. The totally new architecture of the *Typhoon* provided the solution for the problems of the "boat-missile weapons" system interface in the best way and provided the maximum survivability and reliability of this system.

TYPE II submarines were underwater carriers of torpedoes or tactical cruise missiles intended for the destruction of large opposing ships and ship units, especially for the destruction of aircraft carriers, which presented a threat to vitally important centers of our country. During the first years of operation, the submarines of the *Echo-I*-class were armed with cruise missiles intended for hitting surface targets; however, this was not highly advisable owing to the short firing range of the missiles. In 1967, this class of submarines was completed and a new class, the *Charlie*-class, was launched; in 1969, the *Papa*, the fastest Soviet submarine and the first submarine with a titanium hull, joined the fleet. These submarines were armed with underwater launched cruise missiles.

The new stage in the development of submarines armed with cruise missiles was marked by the construction of the *Oscar*-class submarines. The ammunition establishment of these submarines—24 missiles—enabled her to fight opposing surface ships and forces in the most efficient way. Navy Architect V. Vorobiev was the chief designer of the *Charlie*-class, and Doctor I. Baronov designed the *Oscars*.

TYPE III submarines were multipurpose nuclear reactor driven vessels armed with missile-torpedoes and torpedoes intended to fight against submarines and also to destroy opposing surface ships and transports. The development of these classes of submarines (the *Victor*, the *Alfa*, and with the highest level of automation and centralized control, the *Sierra* and the *Akula*) was undertaken in an evolutionary manner. The quality and quantity of the ammunition establishment increased. The underwater speed of these submarines was increased because their mission was to track and oppose aircraft carriers. Doctor G. Chernyshev and Naval Architects M. Rusanov and N. Kvasha led in the design of these submarines.

TYPE IV vessels were diesel-electric submarines, whose production was never halted in the U.S.S.R. The *Zulu* and *Whiskey* classes laid the basis for a number of subsequent designs. The diesel-electric submarine of the *Kilo* class and a number of its modifications are the latest achievements in this field. The construction of this submarine is carried out for the Russian Navy, and for foreign customers as well. The development of diesel-electric submarine designs is directed by Doctor Yu. Kormilitsin.

In its own category was the *Komsomolets*, the first submarine in the world with a diving depth of 1,000 meters. The idea behind these submarines was to illustrate the utility of cruising at such great depths and to encourage the further development of underwater shipbuilding. Unfortunately, the tragic loss of this submarine left a number of problems unsolved.

During the last decade of the U.S.S.R. Navy, a large scope of works aimed at increasing combat efficiency and stability of all classes of submarines was carried out. It included the improvement of discretion of submarine magnetic signatures and the improvement of their sonar systems. The problems of decreasing noise and interference levels affecting the sonar operation were solved, in the first instance, by means of decreasing equipment vibration activity in the source. Greater progress in this direction would be desirable by improving ship facilities by means of shock mounts and damping of structures.

Increasing the duration of cruises meant the U.S.S.R. submarines appeared in areas of the world oceans far from their bases, and this required considerable improvement of habilitability; this was achieved by enhancing the living and sanitary quarters, introducing rehabilitation complexes, and new air conditioning, cleaning, and refrigeration systems.

With the end of the Soviet Union, the Russian Navy faced difficult times. The general economic recession and significant changes in the nation's international policy directly affected the fleet and all of the structures participating in the construction and operation of the Navy. Also, the influence of conversion procedures is of the greatest importance. In the highest levels of leadership and military science, all efforts were made in order to define the optimum and minimum composition of the Russian fleet on the basis of the defense adequacy principle.

Even now, the submarine designers are developing new submarines which can be commissioned only in the twenty-first century. The outlook for these submarines is not quite clear for us at present. We are convinced that in the visible future the submarines of all types, considerably less in number, will comprise the important part of navies in many countries.

The Naval Institute Press is the book-publishing arm of the U.S. Naval Institute, a private, nonprofit, membership society for sea service professionals and others who share an interest in naval and maritime affairs. Established in 1873 at the U.S. Naval Academy in Annapolis, Maryland, where its offices remain today, the Naval Institute has members worldwide.

Members of the Naval Institute support the education programs of the society and receive the influential monthly magazine *Proceedings* and discounts on fine nautical prints and on ship and aircraft photos. They also have access to the transcripts of the Institute's Oral History Program and get discounted admission to any of the Institute-sponsored seminars offered around the country.

The Naval Institute also publishes *Naval History* magazine. This colorful bimonthly is filled with entertaining and thought-provoking articles, first-person reminiscences, and dramatic art and photography. Members receive a discount on *Naval History* subscriptions.

The Naval Institute's book-publishing program, begun in 1898 with basic guides to naval practices, has broadened its scope in recent years to include books of more general interest. Now the Naval Institute Press publishes about one hundred titles each year, ranging from how-to books on boating and navigation to battle histories, biographies, ship and aircraft guides, and novels. Institute members receive discounts of 20 to 50 percent on the Press's more than eight hundred books in print.

Full-time students are eligible for special half-price membership rates. Life memberships are also available.

For a free catalog describing Naval Institute Press books currently available, and for further information about subscribing to *Naval History* magazine or about joining the U.S. Naval Institute, please write to:

Membership Department
U.S. Naval Institute
291 Wood Road
Annapolis, MD 21402-5034
Telephone: (800) 233-8764
Fax: (410) 269-7940
Web address: www.usni.org